RENEWING ETERNITY

INDICA

RENEWING ETERNITY

TRADITIONAL PERSPECTIVES FOR THE MODERN HINDU

TWENTY ONE WIDE-RANGING ESSAYS

MARAGATHAM

IA

Copyright © Maragatham 2025
Published by Indica
All Rights Reserved.

ISBN 979-8-98783-417-6

This book has been published with all efforts taken to make the material error-free after the consent of the author. However, the author and the publisher do not assume and hereby disclaim any liability to any party for any loss, damage, or disruption caused by errors or omissions, whether such errors or omissions result from negligence, accident, or any other cause.

While every effort has been made to avoid any mistake or omission, this publication is being sold on the condition and understanding that neither the author nor the publishers or printers would be liable in any manner to any person by reason of any mistake or omission in this publication or for any action taken or omitted to be taken or advice rendered or accepted on the basis of this work. For any defect in printing or binding the publishers will be liable only to replace the defective copy by another copy of this work then available.

Disclaimer

Many of the ideas presented in the essays in this book are at the level of hypothesis. I have attempted to connect historical dots as logically as I could and I have marshalled evidence to support those connections in the form of data from the past and by quoting the opinions of scholars. Nevertheless, I am aware that the evidence is circumstantial and coloured by my intentions. The aim of these essays is not to create a watertight factual case for any point of view but to help imagine an intellectual perch from which we can see beyond our current dilemmas. I leave it up to real scholars and students in the social sciences to either prove or refute these hypotheses. My intent is integrative and compassionate in essence. These essays are aimed at urging Hindus to re-evaluate their relationship with the past, to be more mindful of their unconscious embrace of a Western future, and to see clearly the true nature of the internal and external forces ranged against us—all of which are needed to gain a clear-eyed, positive, authentic view of self.

For my fellow deracinated Hindu...
regardless of what flavour you are,
whether you stand against me or with me,
whether you agree with me partially or wholly...
this book is for you.

Praise for the Author's Essays from Online Readers

"*Extraordinary writing and dazzling clarity of thought.*" – Ashish Dhar

"*Among the most remarkable writing I've ever read. Thank you.*" – Raj Singh

"*Naman. Your every essay is a gem. I have made a file of them. Those are only things I read nowadays. I discuss them in my friends' group and they are overwhelmed. Thank you.*" – Sandeep Bose

"*This is seminal thought and work. I'll never forget these words by you. Liberated me.*" – Amritanshu Pandey

"*Profound essays! This is the kind of Pūrva Paksha that needs to be presented before the world. Thank you Maragatham for this brilliant writing.*" – Hiren Shah

"*Exquisite. Succinct. Deeply motivating. Touched the concern of civilisational consciousness in the most beautiful way. Please read. It is high time we realise this. Half of the battle is fought in the mind.*" – Sayantan Chatterjee

"*Profound. Thank you for publishing this masterpiece. It is a new foundational reset framework for Sananthan and its place in the present-day world. Incisive insights. Outstanding writing. Brilliant.*" – Vichitra

"*I really admire your work. It's like slaking a thirst, especially for an erstwhile deracinated existentialist (nihilist) atheist like myself.*" – K. Yogi

"*Another piece of brilliance. You write like a dream. kudos. A big fan. This should be read by every Indian & westerner trying to understand India.*" – Dr. Pingali Gopal

"*As if you have articulated my own thoughts. Thank you, thank you very much.*" – Saurav Ghosh

PRAISE FOR THE AUTHOR'S ESSAYS FROM ONLINE READERS

"So much to learn from this! How beautifully and lucidly explained the world around us. Answered so many unspoken questions in the obscurities of our mind while we try to tread a path to be more Dharmic." – Bhaskar Tripathi

"जी आपके दोनों लेख पढ़े। कई महत्वपूर्ण विषय आपने प्रस्तुत किये जैसे सार रूप मे पर और अपर

दोनों का हित साधक सनातन संस्कृति (Trad Culture) और भौतिक एवं स्वेच्छाचार (Techno & Whatever Culture) का आंतरिक संघर्ष।+शशांक पोद्दार – Agastya M

विदेशी दृष्टि के स्थान पर धर्मानुकूल दृष्टि के आधार पर विषयों का मत और मूल्यांकन करना।

शैली मेरे अभ्यास से भिन्न होने के बाद भी असहजता नहीं हुई। बधाई सहित धन्यवाद।
– Anuj Mishra

"Read, reread, reread again. Digest and internalize." – Pramod

"Sir, All I have is humble appreciation and gratitude. This is probably the most concise yet still extensive article I have ever read. Huge respect for this masterpiece." – Arjun Bharadwaj

"Through Maragatham's words, I see my innermost thoughts reflected in crystal-clear fashion." – Abhishek Kumar Panda

"This...is really REALLY well-written. It's truly beautiful and I can't help but feel disappointment that that world of yore is no longer within reach. This really rang true for me." – A. Jayasimha

"Wonderful! So many of these currents have been floating in my mind for a long time but I wasn't able to stitch them together in spite of trying a lot. Thank you for putting them together so succinctly!" – Karthik Mishra

"Connecting dispersed dots and making sense in their entirety is truly your most valuable contribution. I keep sharing these essays with my close friends."
– Rupam Raj

PRAISE FOR THE AUTHOR'S ESSAYS FROM ONLINE READERS

"Your articles contain some of the finest thoughts on our culture and customs!"
– Vivek Seshadri

"A very necessary read." – Viva Kermani

"These are topics that anyone with any kind of allegiance towards Sanatana Dharma cannot, or rather should not, avoid." – Halley Kalyan

Praise for the Author's Published Books

Highly recommend this useful & amazing book.

1) Helps kids understand 'caste' without the guilt-tripping
2) Many stories here serve as a framework to start discussions on Hindu concepts
3) Lists terms every Hindu kid should be familiar with

Buy it, read it, re-reread it, gift it!
– Rekha Achyutuni

What an amazing short book - "It's Not for Nothing that we Stand for Something" by Maragatham

Must read book for all Hindus!

So many of our confused thoughts are articulated in words. I found myself nodding vehemently to some lines in the book. This book is so "insight-dense", that every sentence packs a punch. The author's clarity of thoughts and his effort in making the book crisp and succinct is commendable.
– Ganapathi Subramanian

Praise for the Essays in This Book

AWAKENING

"Liberalism isn't just an ideology—it's a hidden theology. This eye-opening essay unpacks the religious structure of Modernity, revealing how Liberty, Equality, and Fraternity mirror the Christian Trinity, and how the ideal of Progress neatly replaces Heaven. It exposes how Hindus, through colonial and modern education, have unknowingly adopted this worldview, leading to a deep alienation from their own *Dharmic* roots.

A compelling call to decolonize the Hindu mind and rediscover the civilizational vision of *Sanatana Dharma*."

– **Shri Nithin Sridhar,** *Director & Chief Curator of INDICA, Center for Moksha Studies, responding to Chapter 1.1*

CLARITY

"This is not an endorsement but an expression of the boom of resonance that I felt when I read this essay by Maragatham.

Almost every sentence felt like words being snatched from my mouth if not from my heart. These ideas that I share so wholeheartedly with the author, would not have been articulated by me as read-ably and lucidly as done by him here. There is a very good flow of thought and argument and an overwhelming throw of terms and concepts in this powerful critique of the now mainstream colonial ideas that have developed around the traditional categories of *Varna* and *Jaati* and the modern category of Caste.

One of my maxims is 'tribe is a caste/*jaati* that lives in isolation and a caste/*jaati* is a tribe that lives in association (with other tribes)'. Maragatham too uses the words *jaati* and caste inter-changeably. That the word 'caste' is being used in government certificates too to refer to *jaati* and not to any hierarchical position of a community is not usually realized. Spending time and arguments on the etymological origins of the word caste, as many do today, to conclude that 'caste was introduced in India by the

PRAISE FOR THE ESSAYS IN THIS BOOK

colonizers', is neither sound nor useful as an argument. Maragatham avoids this path altogether and guides us through the perplexing maze of ideas that have developed around these crucial concepts in a way that resolves the puzzle leading the reader from the known to the knowable.

I can't wait for this essay to reach all *Bharateeyas* affected by or concerned about the false narratives around these aspects of Bharat's society and culture."

– **Dr. Nagaraj Paturi**, *Kulapati (Vice Chacellor), INDICA, responding to Chapter 2.4*

CULTURE & VALUES

"This work is an intriguing attempt to engage with crucial topics pertaining to Indians. Maragatham makes an attempt to compare Indian and European cultures correctly acknowledging that many of the stories we consider to be our own are actually a part of the Western-Christian experience. Even while one may not always agree with his viewpoints, it is impossible to deny that a comparative analysis of Indian and Western cultures is necessary for understanding Indian culture in the future. Navigating through many confusing accounts of Indian culture, he has made an attempt to resolve pivotal issues. I have to admit that he has built his argument in a very understandable and straightforward manner.

This writing will appeal to lay-readers as it connects to what they already know as part of their lived reality."

– **Prof. M. S Chaitra**, *Director & Senior Fellow, Foundation for Study of Indian Culture, responding to Chapters 3.1 & 3.2*

COMMUNITY & SOCIETY

"Maragatham focuses on what constitutes the foundations of community and what keeps societies sane and healthy. Maragatham unpacks for us how Western/modern organizing principles – individualism, autonomy, and rights - have sapped us of our moral sense and strength, made us weak, unhealthy, and susceptible to becoming wanderers in a disconnected, dystopian "free" world. The "Age of the Machine," he argues, has weakened or destroyed our communities, made us lone rangers unwilling or unable to collaborate with others, and has led our civilization to the brink of collapse right before our eyes. If we are to save ourselves from falling off the ledge, we should

PRAISE FOR THE ESSAYS IN THIS BOOK

rediscover "our" organizing principles for community, society, and civilization – our *Dharma* and our *dharmic* way of life.

The past does not merely intersect with the present but shapes it. If we try to ignore the past or even seek to discard it, as those in a rush want to do, we pave the path to anarchy. People cannot find their feet 'afresh' every generation as we are creatures of the past; we embody history. If we are willful in our disposition then we destroy, and our first victims are ourselves. But we forget. And it takes sages to help us recall and redeem ourselves.

Maragatham is our guide here, our coruscating gem energizing the fading light of the past, helping us rediscover the path to wise, intelligent living."

– **Dr.Ramesh Rao**, *Professor, Department of Communication, Columbus State University & Chief Editor, India Facts, responding to Chapters 4.0 & 4.1*

PURVA PAKSHA

"One of the best criticisms of Modernity, intelligible to the modern mind, but articulated using the fundamentals of *Bharateeya parampara*. That is the uniqueness and beauty of this very fine piece."

– **Shri Shivakumar GV**, *Director, INDICA, responding to Chapter 5.1*

"The author makes a commendable effort to decolonize the Hindu mind by engaging with contemporary societal challenges and raising thought-provoking questions about the uncritical adoption of Western ideologies—particularly those that seek to universalize values, dissolve traditional communities, and redefine concepts of gender and identity. What makes these essays especially relevant is their method: they first frame key societal issues in modern terms, then offer an alternative perspective rooted in a civilizational worldview.

A must read for those who want a good diagnosis of the disharmony in modern social life and the resulting societal sickness it brings about and to understand the importance of the preservation of civilizational *drishti* as a bulwark against societal disintegration."

– **Shrimati Vijaya Vishwanathan**, *President, Infinity Foundation, responding to Chapter 5.3, 5.4 & 5.5*

PRAISE FOR THE ESSAYS IN THIS BOOK

ENQUIRY

"*Dharma* is a compact of religion, tradition and community. The modern mind malnourished by inadequate neural and tactile feedback loops with the life processes prefers the 'end product' approach to all relationships that make up our life. We want the feel good religious and spiritual experience but not the traditions and structure of communities that gave us that - the selfie dysmorpia culture. We adopt an ala-carte mindset and then wonder why we are not having a full experience.

With searing clarity and extraordinary moral force, Maragatham straddles the entire landscape of philosophy, psychology, technology and history to hold a mirror to Hindus of all hues. To the *Sanantanis*, to the Hindu liberals, to nihilists to mercantilists. He has questions that will compel us to reflect and doesn't shy away from giving us the answers we are afraid to face."

– **Shri Raghava Krishna,** *Founder & CEO, Brhat Culture Engine, responding to Chapter 6.1, 6.2 & 6.3*

ALL PRAISE TO SARASWATI DEVI

शारदे करुणानिधे
सकलानवाम्ब सदा जनान् ।
चारणादिमगीत-वैभव-
पूरिताखिल-दिक्तते ॥

A heart-felt *Dhanyavaad*
to all my readers and supporters,
I'm glad we have resonance; and especially to
Harikiran Vadlamani ji, Nithin Sridhar ji and Ramesh Rao ji,
without whose active support, this book would not have seen the light of day.
Thanks to Nagaraj Paturi ji, MS.Chaitra Ji, Shivakumar GV ji,
Vijaya Viswanathan ji and Raghava Krishna ji for their endorsements.
Thanks also to the excellent Michael Thorn,
who made the difficult work of editing these essays appear simple.
And finally, thanks to Dimple Kaul for the final push
and to INDICA for bringing this to print.

Contents

Introduction 21

Preface 25

Section 1   Awakening

Section 1 | Chapter 1.1   Self-Sacrifice 44

Section 1 | Chapter 1.2   Our Palace of Purushaarth 55

Section 1 | Chapter 1.3   A Matter of Time 65

Section 2   Clarity

Section 2 | Chapter 2.1   Caste 101 82

Section 2 | Chapter 2.2   Caste 102 91

Section 2 | Chapter 2.3   Not Oppressed 106

Section 2 | Chapter 2.4   Drawing the Line 118

Section 3   Culture & Values

Section 3 | Chapter 3.1   The Hindu Traditionalist Part I: On Culture 142

Section 3 | Chapter 3.2   The Hindu Traditionalist Part II: On Morality 153

Section 3 | Chapter 3.3   The Hindu Traditionalist Part III: On Reform 178

CONTENTS

Section 4 Community & Society

Section 4 | Chapter 4.0   No Branches without Roots – Introduction............198

Section 4 | Chapter 4.1   No Branches without Roots – Part I...................... 200

Section 4 | Chapter 4.2   No Branches without Roots – Part II..................... 214

Section 4 | Chapter 4.3   No Branches without Roots – Part III.................... 245

Section 5 Purva Paksha

Section 5 | Chapter 5.1 274

Section 5 | Chapter 5.2   A (T)Radical Critique of Modernity......................290

Section 5 | Chapter 5.3   Man, Woman and Machine – Part I......................312

Section 5 | Chapter 5.4   Man, Woman and Machine – Part II.....................339

Section 5 | Chapter 5.5   Man, Woman and Machine – Part III....................370

Section 6 Enquiry

Section 6 | Chapter 6.1   Artha, Kama, Moksha and a Gaping Hole in the Middle – Part I...390

Section 6 | Chapter 6.2   Artha, Kama, Moksha and a Gaping Hole in the Middle – Part II..411

Section 6 | Chapter 6.3   Work. Life. Balance..423

Epilogue 435

Appendix 457

INTRODUCTION

The greatest shock that I ever faced, probably after the event of my actual birth, was my coming face-to-face with the United States of America. It was a four-year-long wrenching of my Self from everything that it knew to be true about life and living and people and relationships. Of course, I figured out how to cope, perhaps even thrive, but there's no denying that I have spent the next twenty-five years of my life trying to un-wrench myself.

It was not the good people I met that I had a reaction to, but the very fundamentals of the life they had accepted as normal and desirable even. The sheer disconnect, the subsequent absence of wholeness, the rootlessness, the rampant cynicism and the casual irreverence, all ultimately triggered something visceral in me that I, presciently, at that time, started to describe in my research as 'inauthenticity'. That entire world seemed 'made-up'. Politeness and legality were the band-aids that attempted to paper over the loss of understanding of one's place in the world. And, in that 'made-up' world, nothing organic was ever afforded the honour of being 'real'. It seemed always that the 'system' was looking for ways to 'position' every phenomenon, pin it down and then market it. Life was constantly forced to yield to Lifestyle. The deification of Choice seemed to have something to do with this. If everything *could be*, and perhaps *should be, chosen*, then the windows of reality themselves start to hinge on a very, very flimsy framework of personal (and ultimately corporate) whim.

Like many young people, dimly conscious of a sense of irreparable loss, I started to search for a sense of belonging in something whole, first in foreign cultures that seemed 'alive' and then in causes that seemed to be 'vital'. That twenty-year-long journey took me through Rock'n'Roll, Latin America, Rural India, Environmentalism, Organic Farming, Sustainability, New-Age, Intentional Communities and Un-Schooling.

Though I have put a lot of skin in this game, I finally realized, in my mid-forties, that living in a mud house among still-rooted and traditional rural folk meant nothing if all I was doing was basking in the glow of *their* authenticity. Where was *mine*? I glimpsed, through a two-decade-old haze, a kernel of truth. Unlike the hippies of the West with their burned bridges, a Hindu does not have to look for belonging *out-there*, because belonging is already *in-here*, ready-made for each one of us. It is *we* who have turned away. Our ancestral tribes still exist, as do our *Kula Devatas*, our *panpaadugal* and traditional duties.

Surprisingly, or perhaps not so surprisingly, with that recognition of my own inheritance, came the respect for everyone else's. I saw, consciously for the very first time, that it is in *this* peculiar Mutual Respect grown out of commitment to one's own inheritance, that the foundation for the building of wholeness rests. This vision is not only polytheist in essence, but also, in its ability to see both the One in the many *and* the many in the One, it is actively *Sanatani*. In that epiphany, the Marxist lens that had been foisted upon me in my unconscious youth, lay shattered. I knew then also that merely watching a drama unfold is not a sufficient show of love—it is in the playing of one's role in the drama that love manifests. Participation is essential and, though improvisation is allowed, there is also the ancestral role that has to be honoured so coherence and transmission of the divine script can be achieved.

It is in the absence of this complex understanding that the modern mind starts to see our fall from divine grace as inevitable. And because our minds constantly seek to rationalize experiential reality, that fall from grace eventually comes to be seen as desirable, and we begin to embrace our own disintegrations as our true natures. It is *this* cultural abyss that a vast majority of modern people inhabit today.

For my fellow travellers, a summing up of this insight might strike a chord. Two roads diverge in the wood… true, but counter to what the zeitgeist insinuates, there is a jolly good reason why one was less travelled. Our forebears, in their wisdom, knew that it was a path that led *away* from the recognition of Inheritance and that it is from the recognition of Inheritance that the principles of Mutual Respect and Participation emerge, from which, eventually, a re-conception of the ideal of Stewardship can manifest. This is the basis of all true culture. The ground under the Banyan tree, where our civilizational drama unfolds may be magical, but it does not exist by magic. It needs *us* to maintain and water it. We cannot

INTRODUCTION

love something, without also caring for all the other things that make that thing possible.

For my friends and family who have seen me through different segments of my journey, and who may now think that I have changed beyond recognition, I would like to say that I don't think the compassionate vision of what I/we want to see manifest in the world has changed (it was what set me on this journey in the first place), and we still share a lot of that. It's just that I no longer believe that the road I (and many like me) had taken all these decades was the right one to get to that destination. Wiser people have already laid out the road to get there, and it passes by paddy fields, coconut groves, *yeri karais*, forest glades, temple towns, village Commons, red-roofed homesteads…and everything else I hold dear.

This is my incomplete, intellectual defence of that road.

Preface

Ending Hindu Self-Hate: A Primer

In July 2021, The South Asia Scholar Activist Collective along with Audrey Truschke of Rutgers University, published online their *Hindutva* Harassment Field Manual.[1]

In September 2021, co-sponsored by departments and centres of more than 53 universities—including Harvard, Stanford, and Princeton—the Dismantling Global *Hindutva* Conference was held online.[2] No doubt it would have been held in a brick-and-mortar building on the premises of Syracuse University (the organizer), if COVID restrictions had not then been in place.

In September 2023, the Progressive Writers' Association organized the *Santana Ozhippu Maanaadu* or Eradicate *Sanatana* Conclave in Chennai.[3]

The words *Hindutva* and *Sanatana* used in the above examples are merely placeholders for the Hindu people. Pagan-haters (including brainwashed people of Hindu origin) cannot openly say anymore (due to political correctness) that they wish harm upon us simply because the Abrahamic scriptures urge them to do so, instead they resort to verbal gymnastics to hide their true long-term intentions: "Oh, Hinduism and *Hindutva* are not the same", "Oh, *Sanatana Dharma* only refers to the 'caste system'", "Oh, Hinduism is nothing but Brahmanism" etc.

As these academics and intellectuals provide cover-fire, their cauldron of pagan-hate is kept warm on the ground by their political mouthpieces throughout the length and breadth of this land:

> The roots of Brahminism are very deep and the reason for all the disparity is also Brahminism itself. There is no religion called Hindu, Hinduism is just a hoax. There is a conspiracy to trap the *Dalits*, tribals and backward people of

PREFACE

> this country by calling the same *Brahmin* religion as Hindu religion, which is actually *Brahmin* religion. If there was Hindu religion then tribals would have been respected, *dalits* would have been respected, backward people would have been respected but what an irony... [4]

> India is the reason for the global disease in the name of castes, dividing people on caste lines...Indians living in other countries also propagating castes in the name of Hindu religion, so Hindu religion is the biggest menace not only to India, now it becomes menace to the entire world.... [5]

These public statements by public institutions and figures are just the tip of the iceberg. What is being said behind closed doors by actual Abrahamic religious figures and Abrahamicized political figures to their flock is anybody's guess. All of this sounds eerily similar to anti-Jew propaganda unleashed by Christians in Germany prior to the carting off of Jews to extinction camps. An excerpt from Eitzen's 1936 essay provides just such an example:

> "Actually, the Jewish religion is nothing other than a doctrine to preserve the Jewish race." (Adolf Hitler). "In resisting all government attempts to nationalize them, the Jews build a state within the state (Count Helmuth von Moltke). "To call this state a 'religion' was one of the cleverest tricks ever invented." (Adolf Hitler). "From this first lie that Jewry is a religion, not a race, further lies inevitably follow (Adolf Hitler)".
>
> – Kurt Hilmar Eitzen, *Ten Responses to Jewish Lackeys*, 1936 [6]

But astonishingly, ordinary Hindus continue to dream of sending their children to study at Harvard, Princeton, Stanford, Rutgers or Syracuse universities. Many of our elite continue to believe that this 'progressivism' is a good thing and many Hindus continue to vote these political leaders into power.

The six questions that need to be asked at this point are:

1. Are Hindus aware of what is being said about them and the fate being prepared for them?
2. If they are not aware, why are they not aware?
3. If they are aware, then are they aware what the end goals of these institutions are?
4. If they are aware, then why do they remain mute spectators?
5. If they are aware and angry, what is it they plan to do?

PREFACE

6. Will they be allowed to do what they plan to do?

The answer (or lack thereof) to each of these questions shines a light on a particular aspect of the colonized mental state we live in. My main interest, the facets of which I explore through the essays in this book, lies in helping to tackle the problem signified by point number four.

We Hindus display *both* a lack of awareness of the outer world *and* a lack of awareness of Self (which, if present, might have led to a normal robust reaction to the above-mentioned anti-Hindu events/statement). Simultaneously, where there is awareness, we display acute paralysis of action and a propensity to submit to coercion and bullying by established institutions (both religious and secular) which maintain the omerta around rampant Hindumisia. This was not how we always were. This was *not* how our ancestors behaved in all the difficult centuries before 'independence'.

(Clarification: *Sanatana Dharma* is not a paganism but it is seen as such by our opponents because it functions as a super-set for paganisms.)

The spectrum of internal and external forces ranged against us is vast and complex.

There is out and out universalist *Abrahamism* which says stuff like:

> You shall surely destroy all the places where the nations whom you shall dispossess served their gods, upon the high mountains and upon the hills and under every green tree; you shall tear down their altars, and dash in pieces their pillars, and burn their Ashe'rim with fire; you shall hew down the graven images of their gods, and destroy their name out of that place.
>
> – Bible, *Deuteronomy 12* [7]

Then, there is the unique *Secularism* of the Indian State which has opened the doors to:

1. The *Waqf* Act 1954, which enables an independent *Waqf* Board to determine independently whether or not a piece of property is *Waqf* property and claim it for itself. This remarkable piece of appeasement legislation had

been functioning under the radar for seventy years until, in September of 2022, it claimed the entire village of Thiruchenthurai in Tamil Nadu[8], including its temple, and ordinary people like me finally woke up to this fresh virus in our midst. Today, the *Waqf* is the third largest owner of land in the country after the Defence Department and the Indian Railways.

Here is an excerpt from the *Waqf* Act:

> Decision if a property is *Waqf* property.
>
> (1) The Board may itself collect information regarding any property which it has reason to believe to be wakf property and if any question arises whether a particular property is wakf property or not or whether a wakf is a *Sunni wakf* or a *Shia wakf*, it may, after making such inquiry as it may deem fit, decide the question.
>
> (2) The decision of the Board on any question under sub-section (1) shall, unless revoked or modified by a civil court of competent jurisdiction, be final.[9]

Say what?!

(An amended version of this Act has since been introduced in parliament (as yet unratified) on 8th August 2024 to put this most egregious portion under bureaucratic oversight, but the question remains – What is such an act doing in a secular Republic?)

2. And our inability, post-independence, to properly repeal the Indian Church Act, 1927 which has ensured that the lands violently stolen by the British (from people who did not have a concept of private property) and leased by them to the Church continue to remain in the possession of the Church and its cronies long after the leases have run out. Experts are unable to determine if it is the Church or the *Waqf* board that is the third largest property owner in India.[10]

Here is an excerpt from the Church Act:

> At any time after the commencement of this Act the General Council may by resolution appoint such number of persons as they shall see fit (not being less than three) to represent the Indian Church and to hold property for any uses or purposes thereof, and when it is shown to the satisfaction of His Majesty the King that the said Council has appointed such persons His

> Majesty the King in Council may by Charter incorporate them and their successors with power to hold land without licence in mortmain under the name of the Indian Church.[11]

Majesty?! King?!

3. And more perverse still, the wilful expansion, by the Indian State, of British era laws that granted it dominion over religious institutions *only* with respect to Hindu temples. The Madras Hindu Religious and Charitable Endowment Act 1951 (now with copy-cat legislations throughout India) was established by the atheist, *secular* State, ironically to enable it to take over and manage all Hindu *religious* institutions.

Here is a relevant excerpt from the HRCE Act. Do read it carefully:

> The Deputy Commissioner in the case of any (Hindu) religious institution over which an Area Committee has jurisdiction, and the Commissioner in the case of any other religious institution, may suspend, remove or dismiss any hereditary or non-hereditary trustee or trustees thereof.
>
> The Deputy Commissioner shall have power to inquire into and decide...
>
> (a) whether an institution is a religious institution;
>
> (b) whether a trustee holds or held office as a hereditary trustee;
>
> (c) whether any property or money is a religious endowment;
>
> (d) whether any property or money is a specific endowment;
>
> (e) whether any person is entitled by custom or otherwise, to any honour, emolument or perquisite in any religious institution; and what the established usage of a religious institution is in regard to any other matter;
>
> (f) whether any institution or endowment is wholly or partly of a religious or secular character; and whether any property or money has been given wholly or partly for religious or secular uses; and
>
> The Deputy Commissioner may, on being satisfied that the purpose of a religious institution has from the beginning been, or has subsequently become impossible for realization, by order, direct that the endowments of the institution be appropriated....[12]

Jurisdiction? Dismiss? Appropriate? Wow!

PREFACE

We know now that under the HRCE, Tamil Nadu temples have *lost* 47,000 acres of land.[13]

And in Andhra, over *one lakh acres* of land are encroached upon.[14]

We also know that under the express protection of the HRCE department, Tamil Nadu, 1,100 *murthis* have been stolen from temples, something that ironically never happened in centuries past when we did not have the 'benefit' of CCTV and police *bandobast*.[15]

Our tryst with Secularism has gone badly for us. What was defined initially in Europe as the separation of State from religion, morphed in India into the Nehruvian maxim: The State must treat all religions equally. Pretty soon, the State realized that it *couldn't* treat all religions equally because, as it found to its own consternation, all religions were not equal (Duh!). The Indian State then started a long-term and probably unconscious process of secularization of religion itself. Given that the Indian State is weak-willed and prone to surrendering to external forces, it trained all its reformist guns only at those religions which had no centralized institutional set-up and no powerful external patrons—in other words, Hinduism. It is this sinister twist in the secular tale that has led to our current impasse. The Indian State enthusiastically reforms Hinduism 'for its own good', while mollycoddling Abrahamic religions. The Abrahamic religions with their deep institutional reach, and by putting actual Abrahamic law-makers into positions of power, use this systemic structural bias to ride the Indian State into doing their bidding.

In 2024 we were not even sure if the head trustee of the most powerful and richest Hindu temple at Tirupathi was actually a practising Hindu or not.[16] Such is our pathetic condition. The secular Indian State has become the greatest force for conversion of Hindus out of Hinduism since the dawn of human time. We are being converted in larger and larger numbers into outright Abrahamism, or into its stepping stones, Liberalism, Atheism and Marxism.

Marxism in India is a blanket term that describes a wide range of phenomena, ranging from outright gun-wielding *naxals*, to recognized communist parties that venerate Mao and Lenin, and the so-called urban *naxals*[17], left-leaning academic and media personalities who espouse, as an ideal, some form of take-down of Hinduism, Bharat and/or the Indian State.

This coalition of forces brainwash thousands of youths from ordinary Hindu families into swallowing the 'oppressor-oppressed' trope as a valid description of the world around them, thus creating a vast army of urban foot-soldiers in the global narrative wars ready, at the drop of a tweet, to assemble in protest at *Jantar Mantar* and *Shaheen Bagh*. The idea of revolution, of victimhood as a means to self-definition, and the iconic personality of Che Guevara are all used to turn entire generations of our children into leftist zombies taking their orders not from the people and cultures that birthed them but from the technocracies that control the airwaves.

The original Mao Zedong declared –

> Religion is poison. It has two great defects: it undermines the race...(and) retards the progress of the country.[18]

He ended up killing *sixty million* innocent people. Don't be confused by the ideals, keep your eye on the actions.

His compatriot from across the border, Josef Stalin declared via his magazine mouthpiece:

> ...not a single house of prayer shall remain in the territory of the USSR, and the very concept of God must be banished from the Soviet Union as a survival of the Middle Ages and an instrument for the oppression of the working masses.[19]

He ended up sending *thirty million* people to the gulags of Siberia to die. Watch the actions and remember those numbers. Give no quarter to people who venerate these monsters and their monstrous ideas and ideals.

In post '47 Bharat, openly communist parties with loyalty to Lenin and Mao were allowed to function by the somnolent Indian State knowing full well that they were working towards the complete overthrow of the State.

Here, we have it from the constitution of the CPI(M) [italics not in the original]:

> The Communist Party of India (Marxist) is the revolutionary vanguard of the working class of India. Its aim is socialism and communism through the establishment of the state of *dictatorship of the proletariat*. In all its activities the Party is guided by the philosophy and principles of Marxism-Leninism which shows to the toiling masses the correct way to the ending of exploitation of man by man, their complete emancipation. The Party keeps high the banner of proletarian internationalism.[20]

Not a word about the culture and traditions of the people they imagine they represent.

Here, from the document "Urban Perspective" published in 2018 by the (now banned) CPI (Maoist):

> However, we should not belittle the importance of the fact that the urban areas are the strong centers of the *enemy*. Building up of a strong urban revolutionary movement means that our Party should build a struggle network capable of waging struggle consistently, by sustaining itself until the protracted people's war reaches the stage of strategic *offensive*. With this long-term perspective, we should develop a *secret party*, an united front and people's *armed elements*; intensify the class struggle in the urban areas; and mobilize the support of millions of urban masses for the people's war.[21]

Here is JNU professor, Nivedita Menon calling India an imperialist country:

> ...If people are raising slogans for *azadi*, shouldn't this be looked at in the context of India being seen as an imperialist country internationally?[22]

In making this incredible claim, she doesn't use an indigenous value system for judgement, but the metric of international conscience. How ironic, given that there is nothing more imperialistic than the West that built that internationalism upon the bodies and beliefs of our ancestors.

Here is Booker Prize winning author Arundhati Roy speaking as she received the 45th European Essay Prize –

> ...the ruling Bhartiya Janata Party's message of Hindu supremacism has relentlessly been disseminated to a population of 1.4 billion people. Consequently, elections

are a season of murder, lynching and dog-whistling – the most dangerous time for India's minorities, Muslims and Christians in particular.

It is no longer just our leaders we must fear, but a whole section of the population. The banality of evil, the normalisation of evil is now manifest in our streets, in our classrooms, in very many public spaces.[23]

Again, a pattern is evident. Hindus are painted as evil. Abrahamics, who carried out genocides over multiple continents for over a thousand years are painted as victims, and Indian Democracy is depicted as sharing a screenplay with the latest Tarantino film.

Even if they are not outright Communists, today's Leftists and Wokes who decry Capitalism as exploitative, rightly see it as a force for the destruction of nature, community and human liberty. But, instead of turning to tradition which has for millennia stewarded nature and community, and supported a limited but reasonable liberty, they turn to more and more outlandish forms of victimhood, all of which ultimately draw their power not from the Gods but from the very centralized global systems they claim to stand against.

These misguided groups are regularly found aligned with the broad coalition of organizations and institutions that form the global coalition of Breaking India Forces.[24] They insist that India and Hinduism have nothing to do with each other and in fact *should* have nothing to do with each other. They insist upon the *Aryan Invasion Theory* as a justification for all subsequent invasions of Bharat. They insist on the *Aryan-Adivasi-Dalit-Dravidian* divides to lend moral justification to Islamic and Christian goals of a Hindu-free Bharat. They say we were never a nation but a mere collection of disparate *jaatis* until the Abrahamics welded us into one nation. They say there is no such thing as Hinduism and in the same breath accuse *Hindu supremacy* of being a threat to the *Real India*. This school of thought plays a strategic double game. On the one hand, it presents our diversity as proof of the immaturity of our national consciousness (while simultaneously pursuing diversity as one of the great moral goals of modern civilization) and, on the other hand, dismisses all signs of our cultural and political unity as bigotry, revisionism, fascism, majoritarianism etc.

PREFACE

Comments by former political director of Equality Labs, Bangladeshi Muslim, Sharmin Hossain, give us a lay of the land:

> Caste has informed every social, political and economic structure in the Diaspora. Arguing to salvage Hinduism is dominant caste rhetoric. Caste is rooted in the Hindu scriptures. It is not a theological debate.
>
> Absolutely, *Brahmins* have appropriated all their Gods from *Dalits* and *Adivasis*. *Brahmins* have stolen the *Buddha*, and the hand of Fatima & other Islamic relics. Hinduism cannot be a part of progressive discourse until we dismantle Brahmanism.[25]

Divya Dwivedi and others write in their astonishing essay "The Hindu Hoax: How upper castes invented a Hindu majority" published in *The Caravan*:

> According to this (*Hindutva*) perspective, "Hindu" is both an ancient religion and an ethnic group mythically born with it, thus making "Hindus" the eternal natives of India. This political project seeks to return India to an ahistorical past in which Hindus were supposedly free of external "*mlechcha*," or impure, mixtures—from the ancient Greeks to the European colonial powers.[26]

The authors make a cardinal error in the above opening paragraph by assuming (in their colonialized Europeanized minds) that *Sanatana Dharma* is defined as a racial category. It is not; it is a behavioural category. That this land is a mixture of all kinds of tribes from the ancient past is accepted by all Hindus. The native Hindus only ask that the tribes follow the principle of Mutual Respect and at their own convenience join the larger river of *Sanatana Consciousness*. What the modern Breaking India mindset fails to grasp is that *Sanatana* unity takes the form of a *thaali* and not that of a melting pot. It is the *thaali* that brings the myriad cultures of this land together in shared harmony. The modern idea of diversity as a melting pot is drawn from the American experience, and idealizes the inter-mingling of 'races' around a shared commonality of consumerist excess. This vision has neither culture, nor diversity nor Mutual Respect. It has as its end goal, uniformity under the flag of the dollar sign.

Another example from *The Caravan* will demonstrate more precisely the predicament that Hindus face with respect to the accusations being hurled at them by Breaking India Forces. In September 2022, *The Caravan* published an article by Sagar, a staff writer of the journal, that carries the title "Road to Nowhere: Why Dalits must abandon the *Kanwar Yatra*".[26] The author declares that the majority of participants in the *Kanwar Yatra* are "*Dalits*" and OBCs, including describing, in lyrical prose, his own personal experiences going on the *yatra*, but then inexplicably veers off track and insists that *Kanwar Yatris* must now abandon their tradition because it is Brahmanical! This is classic Caldwellian double-speak.

In his 1849 classic *The Tinneveli Shanars*, Robert Caldwell writes:

> The Hindus are not the only depraved people in the world; but it may be asserted with confidence that the extent and universal prevalence of their depravity are without a parallel.[28]

He continues with misplaced authority:

> The worship of *Subrahmaniya*, the second son of *Siva*, having been popular in Peninsular India, from an early period, the majority of the Shanars symbolize with the higher castes by attending the annual festival in his honour at *Tiruchendoor*. *Shasta* also, the *Hari-Hara putra* of the *Brahmans*, and rather a demon-king than a divinity, being guardian of boundaries and protector of paddy fields is worshipped to a considerable extent in his official missions... A streak of holy ash, the mark of *Sivism*, is the only trace of the influence of legitimate Brahmanism which one can see. Demonism in one shape or another may be said to rule over the *Shanars* with undisputed authority.[29]

Here we see the classic forked tongue of the evangelist. On the one hand, when the *Shanars* visit Thiruchendur, he accuses them of "symbolizing with the upper castes" and on the other hand when they follow their own traditions they are said to be "shaped by Demonism"!

It is this sleight of hand that is employed again and again by seasoned practitioners of the Breaking India coterie. When *Sanatana Dharma* builds the bridges that bring the Hindu communities together, it is denounced as hegemonic Brahmanism, and when *Sanatana Dharma* leaves Hindu communities alone to follow their own traditions, it is denounced as exclusionary and oppressive. This is the 'Heads I Win, Tails You Lose' rhetorical device that has been used to devastating effect against the Hindu mind. Ordinary Hindus, who cannot imagine such perfidy, and have not grasped the full import of what is being done to them, end up floundering when faced with this device.

"Oh, are we bad when we are diverse?"
"Oh, are we also bad when we are united?"
"Oh, are we bad when we leave each other alone?"
"Oh, are we also bad when we come together?"

It is much better and simpler to recognize these entities as being irrevocably adversarial to *Sanatana Dharma's* unique, forest-inspired, *Rta*-derived, ethical vision of diversity in unity or *Purusha-Consciousness*, and directly attack their genocidal past and the abysmal turpitude of their culturally perverse and ecologically unsustainable 'modern society'. Of course, it is also equally important that we start building a more overt collective consciousness of our own, and institutions that will represent that consciousness.

Right now, we have none.

For Hindus of colonial consciousness, we did not become free when we overthrew the yoke of foreign rule, but when we adopted the colonizer's values and ideals in our Republic! Among this crowd, which includes many of us modern secularized Indians, there is wide prevalence of the notion that our ancestors were immoral and it was the saviour British who civilized us, no matter that our ancestors of *every community* fought tooth and nail against them.

The Sanyasi Rebellion of 1770 led by Pandit Bhabani Charan Pathak; the Cotiote Wars between 1793 and 1805 led by Pazhassi Raja; the Polygar Wars of 1799 to 1802 led by Rani Nachiyar and the Palayathkaars; the Anglo-Maratha Wars of 1775 to 1819 led by the Maratha Confederacy; the 1825 Revolt led by Kittur Rani Chennamma; the Agrarian Revolt of 1847 led by Narasimha Reddy; the Anglo-Sikh Wars of 1845-1849 led by the Sikh Confederacy; the Santhal Rebellion of 1855 led by Sidhu and Kanhu Murmu; the Great Uprising of 1857 led by Nana Sahib, Tatya Tope and Rani Lakshmi Bai; the Munda-Oraon Rebellion of 1875 led by Birsa Munda; the Rampa Rebellion of 1924 led by Alluri Sitaram Raju; the Gond Rebellion of 1940 led by Komaram Bheem— and innumerable other examples—all show just how ferociously our ancestors resisted British Rule in every corner of Bharat. Why did they fight? What was

PREFACE

it they were protecting that was so precious that it was worth more to them than life itself?

Unless this story of valour and uncompromising cultural *maryada* is told in conjunction with the story of reconciliation enacted by the Congress and other modern political groupings, we will never have a grasp of the true nature of our Independence and the responsibility that comes with it. It is clear that the political independence achieved by the reconciliation faction must be married to the dream of cultural independence paid for in blood by the civilizational faction.

It is now one thousand three hundred and eighty-seven years since Umar Ibn al Khattab was sent packing from Thane by Pulakesin II. It is now also two hundred and eighty-two years since Maharaja Marthanda Varma's absolute naval victory over the Dutch East India Company led by Admiral Eustachius De Lannoy. Between those two victories lay one thousand one hundred and five long years of resistance. The late examples of Raja Chatrasaal, Shivaji Maharaj, Marudhu Brothers and Rajaram Jaat, all show in different ways that the twin flames of *Swayambodh* and *Shatrubodh*[30] were undimmed even after that long odyssey. But alas, after 1857 CE, the year we fought our last war for independence, Hindus inexplicably seem to have given up. Our leaders post 1857, no matter how brave, how clever, how well-meaning, all suffered from various forms of *dhimmitude*. So much so that we all now display a form of multi-modal *dhimmitude*. We owe allegiance to multiple foreign overlords all of whom have successfully convinced us that it is not *they*, but *we*, who are the problem. Today we are wracked with self-doubt and insecurities. It appears that our weakening over one thousand years of resistance and the final British victory over us have had a long-term impact on not just our nation and communities but on our self-perception as well.

Halley Kalyan has coined a particularly useful and pithy phrase—"What about *Sati*?"—to describe this phenomenon that plagues us modern Hindus: our modern tendency to constantly judge ourselves by (what we now consider to be) the worst aspects of our religion/society instead of by the best of what it enabled.

When was the last time you heard Abrahamic religionists lamenting their history of slavery or genocide? When was the last time you heard modern Liberal

PREFACE

Capitalists lamenting their lives built upon a history of theft and colonialism, or the Left lamenting the evil of Stalin's gulags or Pol Pot's killing fields? The answer is either never or seldom. Each of these groups lament the failings of other groups, never their own. It is only Hindus who reliably and unrelentingly lament themselves.

It's ok if we want to be hard on ourselves and hold ourselves up to the highest *Dharmic* standards, but do we ever stop and think why we don't apply those same standards to our rivals? Why do we give our rivals a free pass for their history of depravity while we indulge in daily self-flagellation?

The essays in this book are a squirrel's contribution towards catalyzing a reappraisal of our place in the battlefield of modern ideas. Through them, I critique our unquestioning embrace of Western Modernity, Liberalism, and Progressivism while providing compassionate anthropological frameworks in support of our indigenous values and society.

References and Links

1. https://www.hindutvaharassmentfieldmanual.org/
2. https://www.maxwell.syr.edu/research/moynihan-institute-of-global-affairs/events/2021/09/11/default-calendar/dismantling-global-hindutva
3. https://theekkathir.in/News/india/புதுதில்லி/petition-filed-against-sanatana-ozhippu-maanadu-at-supreme-court
4. "'Hinduism is not a religion but a hoax': Samajwadi Party leader Swami Prasad Maurya rants again", *OpIndia*, 2023
   https://www.opindia.com/2023/08/hinduism-is-not-a-religion-but-hoax-samajwadi-party-leader-swami-prasad-maurya-rants-again/
5. B. Sreelakshmi, "BJP leader shares A Raja's remarks on Hindu religion: 'creating hatred'", *Hindustan Times*, 2023

https://www.hindustantimes.com/india-news/bjp-leader-shares-a-rajas-remarks-on-hindu-religion-creating-hatred-101694519170119.html

6. Kurt Hilmar Eitzen, *Ten Responses to Jewish Lackeys*, 1936
https://research.calvin.edu/german-propaganda-archive/responses.htm

7. https://www.bible.com/bible/59/GEN.1.ESV

8. Kanishka Singharia, "In Tamil Nadu, Waqf board claims ownership of an entire village. There's a temple too", *Hindustan Times*, 2022
https://www.hindustantimes.com/india-news/in-tamil-nadu-waqf-board-claims-ownership-of-an-entire-village-there-s-a-temple-too-101663245541768.html

9. https://centralwaqfcouncil.gov.in/sites/default/files/The%20Waqf%20Act%201954.pdf

10. Priya Mishra, "Who Is the Biggest Landowner in India After the Indian Government?", *Business Outreach*, 2023
https://www.businessoutreach.in/biggest-landowner-in-india/

11. https://www.scribd.com/document/449835280/indian-church-act-1927-pdf

12. http://www.bareactslive.com/TN/tn953.htm

13. "Explained: The curious case of 47,000 acres of Tamil Nadu's 'missing' temple land", Financial Express, 2021
https://www.financialexpress.com/india-news/explained-the-curious-case-of-47000-acres-of-tamil-nadus-missing-temple-land/2273212/

14. "One lakh acres of temple land encroached in Andhra Pradesh", *The New Indian Express*, 2020
https://www.newindianexpress.com/states/andhra-pradesh/2020/dec/09/one-lakh-acres-of-temple-land-encroached-in-andhra-pradesh-2233779.html

15. "HR&CE admits theft of over 1,100 idols before Madras High Court", The New Indian Express, 2018
https://tinyurl.com/stolenmurthis

16. Srinivas Rao Apparasu, "Andhra Pradesh: Opposition slams Reddy's appointment as TTD chief", *Hindustan Times*, 2023
https://www.hindustantimes.com/india-news/andhra-pradesh-opposition-slams-reddy-s-appointment-as-ttd-chief-101691437603439.html

17. Vivek Agnihotri, *Urban Naxals: The Making of Buddha in a Traffic Jam*, 2017

18. Sarah Stern, *Sarah Stern on the Eradication of Religion in China*, Berkeley Center, 2009
https://berkleycenter.georgetown.edu/posts/sarah-stern-on-the-eradication-of-religion-in-china

19. Paul Dixon, *Religion in the Soviet Union*, Worker's International News, 1945
https://www.marxists.org/history/etol/newspape/win/v06n01-oct-1945-workers-intl-news.pdf

20. https://cpim.org/party-constitution

21. https://www.marxists.org/subject/india/cpi-maoist/s14-urban-perspective-7th-printing.pdf

22. Jahnavi Sen, "'Vilification' of JNU Professor Nivedita Menon as 'Anti-National' Labelling Continues", *The Wire*, 2016
https://thewire.in/politics/vilification-of-jnu-professor-nivedita-menon-as-anti-national-labelling-continues

23. Arundhati Roy, "Arundhati Roy: The dismantling of democracy in India will affect the whole world", *Scroll*, 14 Sep 2023
https://scroll.in/article/1055943/arundhati-roy-the-dismantling-of-democracy-in-india-will-affect-the-whole-world

24. Rajiv Malhotra & Aravind Neelakandan, *Breaking India: Western Interventions in Dravidian and Dalit Faultlines*, Amaryllis 2011

25. "Busting the Lies of Equality Labs", Unravelling the Truth,

https://web.archive.org/web/20240223004511/https://unravellingthetruth.org/busting-the-lies-of-equality-labs/

26. Divya Dwivedi, Shal Mohan and J. Reghu, "The Hindu Hoax", *Caravan Magazine*, 2021 https://caravanmagazine.in/religion/how-upper-castes-invented-hindu-majority

27. Sagar, "Road to Nowhere", *Caravan Magazine*, 2022 https://caravanmagazine.in/caste/kanwar-yatra-dalit-obc

28. Robert Caldwell, *The Tinneveli Shanars*, 1849 https://archive.org/stream/TheTinnevellyShanars_201809/the%20tinnevelly%20shanars_djvu.txt

29. Ibid.

30. Terms introduced by Pankaj Saxena, Co-Founder, *Brhat Culture Engine*

This book is divided into Six Sections. Each Section represents a particular stage in a growing self-awareness, and is comprised of Chapters. Each Chapter is an essay. Some essays explore multiple facets of a single theme and are grouped sequentially as part of 'essay sets.' They are labelled as such (Part I, Part II, Part III etc.)

Both the quality of the writing and the coherence of the ideas have evolved in sophistication over four years and that is visible as the essays progress. I've tried not to meddle too much with the originals while editing. The reader does not have to read sequentially. Feel free to pick up and read any Section based on your area of interest and/or level of re-engagement with our ancestral religion and society.

SECTION 1

AWAKENING

Section 1 | Chapter 1.1

SELF-SACRIFICE
Hindu Sheep in the Liberal Church

Maragatham, 2020

Symptom

> Of the 7000 languages spoken today, fully half are not being taught to children. Effectively, unless something changes, they will disappear within our lifetimes. There are those who quite innocently ask, "Wouldn't the world be a better place if we all spoke the same language?" My answer is always to say, "A wonderful idea, but let's make that universal language Haida, or Yoruba, Lakota, Inuktitut or San." Suddenly people get a sense of what it would mean to be unable to speak their mother tongue.
>
> – Wade Davis, *The Wayfinders: Why Ancient Wisdom Matters in the Modern World*, 2009[1]

Diagnosis

> The myriad cultures of the world are not failed attempts at modernity, they are unique manifestations of the human spirit. With their dreams and prayers, their myths and memories, they teach us that there are indeed other ways of being, alternative visions of life, birth, death and creation itself.
>
> – Wade Davis, *Interview with Alex Chadwick of NPR*, 2003[2]

The Nature of the Disease

> What do we call a disease that spreads by pretending it is not a disease, but is in fact a cure?

A Question

Why is it that when a Hindu youth enters the doors of a *madrasa* and stops believing in his traditional Gods, in the worldview of the *Veda*, in *Karma*, in multiple births, in the sanctity of life itself, we say that he has converted, but when the same youth enters the doors of a university and stops believing in his traditional Gods, in the worldview of the *Veda*, in *Karma*, in multiple births and the sanctity of life itself, we ignore his conversion and go on to praise his accomplishments and call him successful? Why do we fear our children entering the former door but not the latter when, in fact, their effects are exactly the same?

...and an answer

There are two reasons. One, from the time of our first mental enslavement by the British, we have been brainwashed into believing that the religion of Liberalism is 'neutral', and that therefore it is possible to adopt the culture of Liberalism without diluting our primary identities. The second reason is that the religious worldview of Liberalism is not expressed in material religious terms (worship rituals and temples) but in intellectual constructs, due to which we fail to recognize it for what it truly is—a religion like any other.

An Intuition

Yesterday, my wife asked me why I react so strongly to counter the cultural messages that our children receive at school. "Let them have a variety of opinions and form their own," she said. "If someone were to touch our children or sell them drugs, would you not respond strongly?" I asked. "Why is it any different when someone is pouring poison in our children's ears?"

This argument about differing opinions and the false belief that all opinions are equal is one of the most insidious conversion schemes of Liberalism. All opinions are *not* equal and we have to protect our children from opinions that draw them away from *Dharma* until they are strong enough in *Dharma* to resist those opinions themselves.

David Bentley Hart describes this phenomenon in the 2003 issue of *First Things* magazine:

> ...the liberties that permit one to purchase lavender bed clothes, to gaze fervently at pornography, to become a Unitarian, to market popular celebrations of brutal violence, or to destroy one's unborn child are all equally intrinsically "good" because all are expressions of an inalienable freedom of choice. But, of

course, if the will determines itself only in and through such choices, free from any prevenient natural order, then it too is in itself nothing. And so, at the end of modernity, each of us who is true to the times stands facing not God, or the gods, or the Good beyond beings, but an abyss, over which presides the empty, inviolable authority of the individual will, whose impulses and decisions are their own moral index.[3]

...and what it reveals

Make no mistake, the boundary-erasing, future-centric cult of individual autonomy that has arrived at our doorsteps is a religion in disguise. It goes by the name of Liberalism. It may have infected us and it is certainly infecting our children. In educational institutions, on TV, in the movies, its conversion efforts are everywhere. It is the dominant religion of our time and is spreading unrecognized and unheeded even in rural Bharat upon the wings of the internet and under the cloak of neutrality and 'progress' that its propaganda machinery has thrown over it.

If we believe that we can be both liberal and Hindu at the same time, or that Hinduism is essentially liberal, we would be mistaken. As soon as we consider ourselves liberal, we have converted out of our birth-religion and are now either wholly or partially in the grip of a foreign hand. As a Liberal of Hindu origin, our primary philosophical foundation will no longer be *Dharma*, but the ideals of the European Enlightenment—Liberty, Equality and Fraternity. Our Hinduism would now be reduced to a mere flavour, something we do out of habit or performance, not *essence*. The metaphysical precepts of Hinduism would no longer be seen as *truths* to be lived, but as an aesthetic to be worn and intellectually dissected.

Liberalism likes flavours—skin colours, religions, nationalities, languages, genders—anything that will help cover up its beating monotheistic, world-dominating heart with a veil of plural neutrality.

Wendell Berry lays open this sleight of hand with characteristic clarity:

> The social and cultural pluralism that some now see as a goal is a public of destroyed communities. Wherever it exists, it is the result of centuries of imperialism. The modern industrial urban centers are 'pluralistic' because they are full of refugees from destroyed communities, destroyed community

economies, disintegrated local cultures, and ruined local ecosystems. The pluralists who see this state of affairs as some sort of improvement or as the beginning of 'global culture' are being historically perverse, as well as politically naive. They wish to regard liberally and tolerantly the diverse, sometimes competing claims and complaints of a rootless society, and yet they continue to tolerate also the ideals and goals of the industrialism that caused the uprooting. They affirm the pluralism of a society formed by the uprooting of cultures at the same time that they regard the fierce self-defense of still-rooted cultures as 'fundamentalism,' for which they have no tolerance at all.[4]

The Morality of Nothing...

Take for example the exploding phenomenon of inter-community marriages, inter-national marriages, inter-race marriages, same-sex marriages etc. among liberals. These are not signs of their superior capacity for 'open-mindedness' (as we are schooled to believe), but are merely signs that both parties have shed their birth-identities to such an extent that they are able to accept their newly-adopted, commonly-held religion—Liberalism—as their primary identity marker. Nothing wrong with that, but let us be clear that they are essentially marrying within their commonly-held, newly-adopted religion. Don't let them label you 'closed-minded' based on their acts of boundary erasure. Call them out as converts, plain and simple. As faithful followers of their new religion, they have a new god and new rituals (as we will see). They are as devout in their fervour to this new god as any ordinary religious person (as we will see).

As per the ethical standards of the liberal world that we live in, there is absolutely nothing wrong with these acts of boundary erasure, but it should be unacceptable to us that the liberal aesthetic framework positions those boundary-erasing acts as morally superior to the ordinary acts performed by the rest of us. It is this moral ladder of its own making that creates the cultural potential field that drives the subtle conversion of our children via the media and liberal education.

Do not allow liberals to insist that their actions are 'moral' thereby slyly insisting that ours are not. Morality is judged relative to the founding principles of each belief system. Liberal morality too arises from Liberalism's fundamental axioms. What we need to do is to identify those axioms.

Liberal morality manifests in society with the following claims:

1. No-Thing is sacred
2. No Relationship is sacred
3. No Idea is sacred except for three: Liberty, Equality and Fraternity

The entire edifice of life, living, life-giving and death has been reduced and simplified to these three claims.

Again, I quote David Bentley Hart from the same *First Things* essay:

> As modern men and women—to the degree that we are modern—we believe in nothing. This is not to say, I hasten to add, that we do not believe in anything; I mean, rather, that we hold an unshakable, if often unconscious, faith in the nothing, or in nothingness as such. It is this in which we place our trust, upon which we venture our souls, and onto which we project the values by which we measure the meaningfulness of our lives. Or, to phrase the matter more simply and starkly, our religion is one of very comfortable nihilism.
>
> We live in an age whose chief moral value has been determined, by overwhelming consensus, to be the absolute liberty of personal volition, the power of each of us to choose what he or she believes, wants, needs, or must possess; our culturally most persuasive models of human freedom are unambiguously voluntarist and, in a rather debased and degraded way, Promethean; the will, we believe, is sovereign because unpremised, free because spontaneous, and this is the highest good. And a society that believes this must, at least implicitly, embrace and subtly advocate a very particular moral metaphysics: the unreality of any "value" higher than choice, or of any transcendent Good ordering desire towards a higher end.[5]

These memorable words from the 2016 animation movie Zootopia, come to mind –

> "And you little guy...you want to be an elephant when you grow up? You be an elephant...because this is Zootopia...anyone can be anything!"

...versus the Morality of Something

Unlike Liberal society, Hindu society deals with *real* difference and embraces complexity as the very face of creation. In daily life, business, and personal life we are constantly navigating real diversity. And unlike the liberals, our primary identity is not ideological but a whole host of other local, earthy, cultural, communal markers. As a corollary, our religion and therefore our morality is not ideological, it doesn't float over the surface of the Earth in an imaginary ether, but is rather a material, geographic and historic truth, tied down purposely and consciously by the spirit of our way-finding ancestors. In other words, our identities are Real. We cannot exchange them, transfer them, or barter them away for any mere idea, not even for the ideas of Liberty, Equality and Fraternity.

In contrast, the identity of a liberal is flimsy. It is based on mere ideas. Worse still, in the case of a liberal Hindu, his identity is based on mere ideas put in his head by his former colonial masters. Those of us who have bartered away our real identities, either consciously in our late teens or unconsciously through the absence of a strong cultural input at home and school, should know that we are no longer really Hindu, we are Hindu-flavoured Liberals. Our conversion is either in progress or complete. Within two generations, our children will no longer speak the language of our ancestors, nor follow their rituals, nor espouse, with any seriousness, any of their philosophical understandings on how to live life. If our conversion has been extreme, we may choose not have children at all (because "What's the use?").

The genius of Liberalism lies in its ability to pass itself off as neutral. Its immateriality fools us into believing that it's not a religion at all. But, let us be clear, *it is a religion,* and it manifests as a culture of cultureless-ness. And though it has replaced the materiality of older religions with intellectualisms, it cannot hide anymore. When we observe the followers of a faith long enough, the contours of even a hidden faith emerge into plain sight.

The Faithful

My friend told me yesterday that she is going to allow her son to choose his religion when he grows up, little realizing that this act of not imposing culture and *choosing Choice* is itself a liberal imposition upon her child which will shut the door of his tradition to him forever. This decision of hers falls in the same category as that of the Mumbai man who is suing his parents for having birthed him without asking his permission[6] and all those woke people who believe that their parents choosing their name is an imposition.[7] This stance... these very thoughts presuppose that the sanctity of individual autonomy must never be breached, that it stands apart from the lowly matrix of culture, geography and even time. This is also the same train of thinking that leads Elon Musk on a popular podcast to declare that "the human condition is merely a conduit for the emergence of Artificial Intelligence."[8]

Listen carefully to what the faithful are really saying... "There is nothing here in our relationships with each other, our ancestors, the Gods and *Bhu Devi* that is worthy and noble... all must be sacrificed at the altar of the new god in his new heaven."

David Bentley Hart paraphrases Heidegger:

> ...says Heidegger, the history of this nihilistic impulse to reduce being to an object of the intellect, subject to the will, that has brought us at last to the age of technology, for which reality is just so many quanta of power, the world a representation of consciousness, and the earth a mere reserve awaiting exploitation; technological mastery has become our highest ideal, and our only real model of truth.[9]

...and their Faith

Look at how the 'left-liberals' behave when any of their 'holy cows' are touched or questioned—minority rights, individual rights, human rights, choice, rebellion, the brotherhood of academia. Don't they behave like the faithful? Doesn't their vehemence carry a touch of the religious? Don't they take to the streets like religious people? Aren't their foot-soldiers ready to risk life and limb for their religious icons? Do any of them look remotely like neutral, dispassionate, rational observers that they claim they are? Don't they excommunicate apostates? Don't they refuse to talk even to their parents who hold differing political views from them?

Ana Russell in her 2024 *New Yorker* article writes:

> Those who have cut ties often gather in forums online, where they share a new vocabulary, and a new set of norms, pertaining to estrangement. Members call cutting out relatives going "no contact."[10]

Are they not the converted?

The fog lifts... and doubt fades. Liberalism *is* indeed a religion. Remember, it is a religion of ideas, not things or relationships. Now that we know their three sacred ideas, we need only to understand what these ideals mean to them.

> **Liberty** is defined as 'Individual Autonomy', which is freedom from any deep relationship: with the Earth, animals, plants, history, geography, tradition, family, our bodies...everything.
>
> **Equality** is defined as 'Power Redistribution', which involves the cultivation of the delusion that equal distribution of power among ideological groups will lead to the emergence of a higher morality among humans. Today, the Equality camp insists on power redistribution on the basis of gender, sexual preference, religion, ethnicity and anything else under the sun. Of course, in the natural flow of life, imbalances will forever manifest, and revolutions will be called for again and again.
>
> **Fraternity** is defined as 'Monoculture'. It is the military-industrial-media complex that is hell-bent on world domination and the imposition of one single set of Western social and economic ideas on every human, thereby making them 'brothers'.

And now to arrange these ideas in the proper religious framework:

Liberty is **The Father**—it represents Power/Control over relationships.

Equality is **The Son**—it represents a tragic Love that must be sacrificed for the sake of the Father's dominion because, ironically, Liberty and Equality are mutually exclusive (colonialism is a very clear example of this phenomenon—the White Man could pursue his Liberty only by making everyone else unequal).

Fraternity is **The Holy Ghost**—it represents the Monocultural spirit spreading through the world.

Additionally, Liberalism has a **Heaven**—A Perfect Future (an imaginary utopia that is ever receding)

It has **Baptism**—The Rebellion of Youth, where young adults are taught to clamour for both Liberty and Equality. The Liberty meme is used to free them from the embrace of their parents and community, and the Equality meme is fed to them as a sense of revolutionary purpose that will fill the hole in their hearts originally created by their adoption of the Liberty meme.

It has **Rituals**—The daily enactment of Individual Choice.

It has **Missionaries**—Academia, Entertainment and Technology.

We can view the ongoing clash between Classical Liberals/Capitalists who stand for Liberty and the Left-Liberals/Communists who stand for Equality as a fundamental faultline in the Liberal religion's conception of the world. Liberty tells us we must choose, but Equality tells us that we cannot choose because all choices are equal. The failure to bridge the divide between Liberty and Equality is the main reason for the weakening of the Liberal Religion that we are currently witnessing both in Europe and the USA. Liberty and Equality are mutually exclusive. One must be sacrificed for the other. Among postmodernists and the woke youth, the clamour for the Son to overthrow the Father is growing louder and louder. It is a full-blown rebellion. For Hindus there is no difference between the Father and the Son; we must encourage them to fight each other while we grow strong enough to withstand the spread of The Holy Ghost.

Recovery from Disease

If you find that you have been unknowingly converted out of the religion of your birth into Liberalism, you can remedy your situation by reverse engineering yourself out of its core concepts.

1. Get away from its Missionaries—stop watching TV, curate your movies, stop reading mainstream news, get away as often as you can from gadgets into Nature and People.
2. Revoke your Baptism (Rebellion)—stop rebelling and start building constructive long-term relationships.
3. Reject its Heaven (Utopian Future)—meditate, recover the Here and Now, do not fetishize the future as if it's a guaranteed solution for all problems.
4. Disbelieve in the Son (Equality)—stop believing that everything and every idea is equal; stop believing that the perfection of Equality can be achieved; think—act on a case-by-case basis with compassion.
5. Disbelieve in the Father (Liberty)—stop believing that individual autonomy is the end goal of societal organization. You are not an 'individual'...you are connected permanently to other people as well as to

Bhu Devi. Develop appropriate rituals to reflect this in your life or adopt traditional ones.

Let me now lay out a very basic counterpoint to the values of the European Enlightenment from which the religion of Liberalism has sprung. Let us examine the *Bharatiya* equivalents to these core European ideals and what each ideal enables for society and the individual.

POST-ENLIGHTENMENT EUROPE (Core Ideals and what they enable)	BHARAT (Core Values and what they enable)
Liberty – Individuality, Rights, Disruption, Depression, Cyborg	**Dharma** – Community, Duties, Integrity, Yoga, Moksha
Equality – Permanent Revolution	**Equivalence** – Harmony
Fraternity – Monoculture	**Mutual Respect** – Diversity

Does Modernity inevitably lead to Individualism? Does Individualism inevitably lead to Liberalism? Can the deep value systems of Bharat tame this beast?

If we are to create a new *smriti* under the shadow of Liberalism's overarching power at this point in history—a *Bharatiya* document for the *Bharatiya* people—we could start by replacing Liberty, Equality and Fraternity with *Dharma*, *Equivalence* and *Mutual Respect* and expand these concepts into organizational ideas.

The time for a conscious, Hinduized Modernity is now.

References and Links

1. Wade Davis, *The Wayfinders: Why Ancient Wisdom Matters in the Modern World*, House of Anansi Press, 2009
2. Wade Davis, We Are All Brothers And Sisters, Words by Wade Davis, Photographs by Luca De Santis, Cartography 2019
   https://bycartography.com/en/stories/we-are-all-brothers-and-sisters/

3. David Bentley Hart, "Christ and Nothing", *First Things*, October 2003
https://www.firstthings.com/article/2003/10/christ-and-nothing

4. Wendell Berry, *Sex, Economy, Freedom and Community*, Pantheon Books, 1994

5. David Bentley Hart, "Christ and Nothing", October 2003
https://www.firstthings.com/article/2003/10/christ-and-nothing

6. Geeta Pandey, "Indian man to sue parents for giving birth to him", *BBC*, 2019
https://www.bbc.com/news/world-asia-india-47154287

7. Danielle Braff, "Why not let children choose their own names?", *New York Times*, 2019
https://www.nytimes.com/2019/05/15/style/children-pick-their-own-names.html

8. Joe Rogan and Elon Musk, *Joe Rogan Show #1169*, 2017
https://www.youtube.com/watch?v=ycPr5-27vSI

9. David Bentley Hart, *Christ and Nothing*, 2003
https://www.firstthings.com/article/2003/10/christ-and-nothing

10. Ana Russell, "Why So Many People Are Going "No Contact" with Their Parents", *New Yorker*, 2024
https://www.newyorker.com/culture/annals-of-inquiry/why-so-many-people-are-going-no-contact-with-their-parents

Section 1 | Chapter 1.2

OUR PALACE OF *PURUSHAARTH*
Journey to a *Dharmic* Framework for Parents & Children

Maragatham, 2020

What the Deformed Baby tells us about Christianity, Islam and Liberalism

There are many doors into the rabbit hole of comparative religion but one stands out for its clarity.

Consider these questions:

Why are some of us born into kind families and others into cruel circumstances? Why are some people luckier than others? Why do bad things happen to good people?

These questions are all actually variations on the same theme. There is even a pure distillate available: "Why are some babies born with deformities?"

Common Muslims, Christians, Liberals of all flavours and Hindus will all agree that the baby is an innocent, suffering for no fault of theirs. But how do the world-views of each of these groups stand up to the test of the deformed baby's plight?

1. Christians claim that God is good and just, and loves us so much that he sent his only begotten son to die for us.
   I'm sorry but the deformed baby is evidence to the contrary.

2. Christians and Muslims claim that God is all-powerful and takes a special interest in human affairs, especially the affairs of the adherents of his favourite religion/s. They even say that he acts upon individual prayers.
   I'm sorry but deformed Christian and Muslim babies and the unanswered prayers of their mothers are a slap in the face of these beliefs.

So, what do we make of these contradictions?

   a. We can conclude that God is neither good nor just, nor does he love us. If he were good, just or loving then there would be no deformed babies in the world.
   b. Or we can conclude that God is not all-powerful and he sometimes makes mistakes. This is an unacceptable explanation that undermines the very definition of God.
   c. Which brings us to considering the idea that the deformed baby was not a mistake but a deliberate act of God. We now have some interesting ideas to consider: that God 'tests' us (as Christians believe) or that God is our master and we, as his slaves, must submit to his will unquestioningly (as Muslims tend to believe).
   In other words, God is fooling with us and we are pawns and/or slaves. Some find meaning in this vision but, without doubt, it is a demeaning vision of human life.

3. Liberal Atheists have grappled with this problem and these contradictions for four hundred years and have attempted to construct a meaningful worldview of their own (ironically centred around the idea of *meaninglessness*). Their philosophers and scientists have given it their best shot and, finally, this is what they've come up with: Everything is a matter of random chance dependent solely on the interplay of impersonal physical laws and chemical reactions none of which have anything to do with any transcendental entity, God, or spirit. The baby was born deformed because of pure bad luck, a faulty mutation perhaps.

So, what do we make of this position? We have to ask the liberal atheist:

   a. Why he cries when his father dies? Why he exults when he falls in love? Why he is proud of the work he does? Why he kisses his baby goodnight?
   b. And, more directly, the essential question: Who are you? Are you a chance meeting of cells, which in turn are a chance arrangement of chemicals? Is your love a chance eruption of hormones? Is your baby, the physical manifestation of that love, nothing but a play of chance? If yes, then why do you love your baby?

Liberals, like Christians before them, live a life of deep contradiction. Their worldview tells them one thing but daily life experience tells them something else.

The Christian belief that their God is good is refuted every single day when bad things happen. The Christian means of escaping this awful breakdown of their worldview is to invent a fiction called the Devil, a convenient fall guy when things don't go too well for them.

Similarly, a Liberal, if he is true to his worldview, must commit suicide immediately. Why live after all? Why expend effort on living when life is meaningless? Western intellectuals like Tolstoy have come to this very same conclusion and almost acted upon it. The fact that the Liberal doesn't kill himself tells us that, in the depths of his heart, he is unable to truly accept that everything is meaningless. To escape this inexorable conclusion, atheists such as Dawkins have gone so far as to write an entire book pushing the theory that our will to live is hard-coded into a string of sugar and phosphates called the Gene. Like the Devil of the Christians, the Gene is the liberal fall guy, an entity that has responsibility foisted upon it whenever the liberal mental model breaks down... those surprising moments when liberals realize that *meaninglessness cannot give them meaning!* It is *this* existential contradiction that has taken a huge psychological toll on liberal society—depression, bipolar, schizophrenia, sociopathy, you name it.

Is it any wonder then that liberal society is simultaneously the most policed and the most lawless society in the history of humankind? No society in the history of human affairs has broken its *own* laws with such frequency as liberal society. At the individual level, these ruptures are brushed under the carpet as 'psychological aberrations' and at the macro level under the carpet of 'homeland-defence'. This lawlessness is living proof of the inner contradictions of the liberal worldview and the sheer inability of its structures in ensuring compliance without the use of extreme physical force.

Bhakti – What Natural Religions tell us about Life

You see, Life has to go on, it has a logic and a magic of its own. By submitting to it, we submit to the *idea of Meaning*. Humans crave meaning, we need meaning, we need a worldview that is seamless with our lived experience.

All pagan cultures or natural religions know from birth the correct attitude to Life. These are the immutable axioms of pagan life:

1. Life is a magical gift from the unknown (so we have respect for Life).
2. As recipients of this gift, we are eternally grateful (so we display *Bhakti*).
3. We show our gratitude by making offerings of beauty to the unknowable (so we do *Puja*).
4. We know that the gift is not for us to use and squander, but for us to safeguard and pass on to our children (so we find purpose in Family, Tradition and *Dharma*).

Hinduism is a unique confluence of pagan well-springs from the bottom-up and civilizational meltwaters from the top-down. Our religion displays both the correct bottom-up pagan attitude to life as per the above axioms as well as the correct top-down explanation of life (*Karma* and *Purushaarth*) that offers us meaning without contradiction.

Seamlessness.

Karma and _Purushaarth_ – What Hindu Thought tells us about Life

The Hindu intellectual answer to the problem of the deformed baby is multi-birth *Karma*. This explanation offers us the most logical and watertight vision of life's events. It situates our 'bad luck' within ourselves. It does not raise unanswerable questions about the Gods. It does not attack the Gods for incompetence. It tells us to accept our own pasts and to look forward to better futures based on our actions in this present life—a superior explanation that fills the mind with positivity and provides society with individuals who have an in-built moral framework that needs minimal policing.

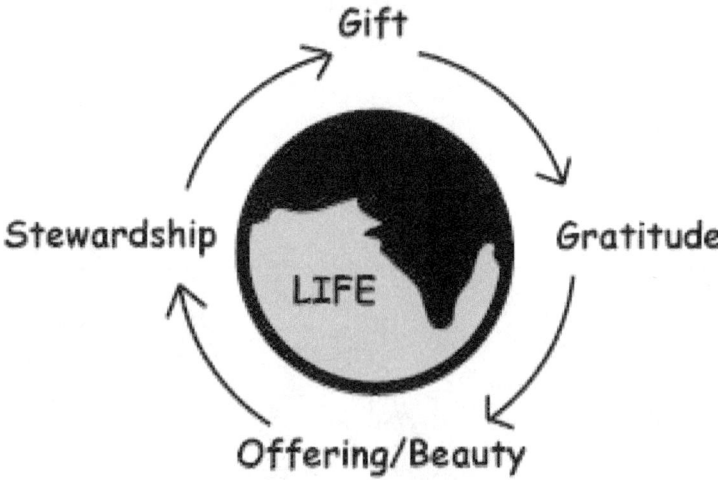

Our *rishis* didn't stop at giving us *Karma* that filled our lives with meaning and positivity—they looked further, towards purpose and divinity.

They gave us *Purushaarth*. This remarkable framework can be read at multiple fractal levels but I will look at it in its most simple form—at the level of the individual. Every individual is encouraged to engage in all four aspects of *Purushaarth—Dharma, Kama, Artha*, and *Moksha*—for a personally fulfilling life that also upholds and protects the best possible society.

The Hindu Take-Down of Liberalism

A vast number of us Hindus have lost intellectual clarity about our own religion and are floating in the liberal kool-aid of Liberty, Equality, Fraternity and their first order derivatives—Rights, Consent, and One-World/One-Love. To understand where we are going wrong, we must start by first putting Liberalism in the right Hindu perspective. For that we use the lens of *Purushaarth*.

Imagine, for a moment, the religion of Liberalism without the shine of Hollywood, without high technology, without America's armed forces. Stripped down to its essence, what is this thing, this religion that goes by the name of Liberalism? Here is it's recipe: take *Kama* and reduce it to Hedonism; then take *Artha* and reduce it to Greed; then put those two ideas together and what you get is a debased *Purushaarth*, a subset of *Kama* and *Artha* without the guiding lights of *Dharma* and *Moksha* (see diagram below).

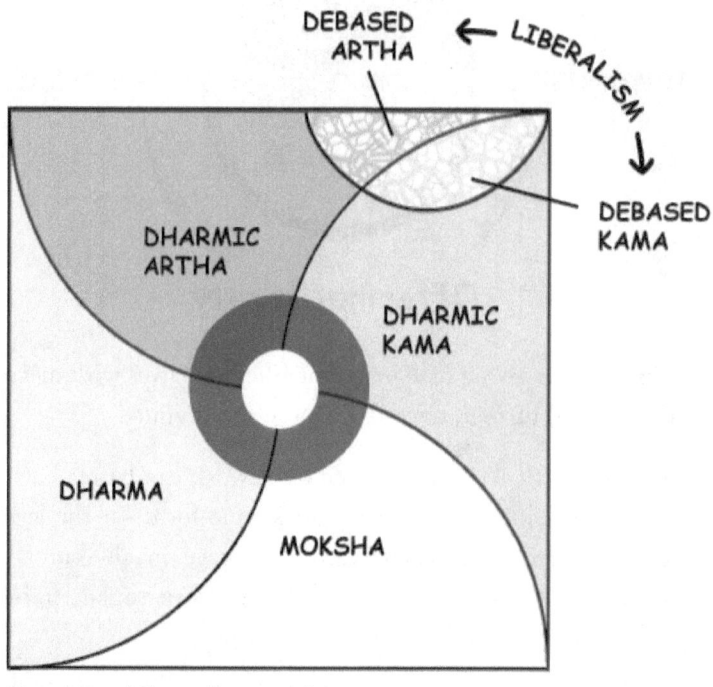

Locating Liberalism within our
PALACE OF PURUSHAARTH

Liberalism states that the aim of life is a debased *Kama* (defined as physical and sensory experience manifested as Hedonism) and to achieve this aim it argues that we need a debased *Artha* (defined as competitive economic activity manifested as greed). This debased *Artha*, the cog in the wheel, nine-to-five corporate existence is seen as a necessary evil, something we all have to get through in order to indulge in still more *Kama*, the ultimate reward.

This, from a Hindu perspective, is the sum total of all liberal life. Though they may fill their bookshelves with tomes and tomes of philosophy, ultimately the only true way to judge a set of values is by the society that those values engender. It is greed, pornography, drugs, alcohol, selfishness, casual sex, early childhood sexualization, violent games, school shootings, consumerism, the Kardashians that define the empty core, the crux, of liberal society. From this perspective, we can see now that the high-sounding ideals of Liberty and Equality are mere smokescreens to cover up the empty philosophical underpinnings of Liberalism—lonely Individualism and empty Materialism; in other words, the cold steel bars of Western scientism and determinism applied to human affairs.

The Hindu view, on the other hand, offers us *Dharmic Kama*, *Dharmic Artha* and *Dharma* itself (right action at multiple levels). It goes even further to offer us *Moksha* (self-realization leading to true freedom, the merging of the *Atman* with the *Paramatman*). *Dharmic Kama* and *Dharmic Artha* are viewed as essential pillars upon which the edifice of *Dharma* stands. And it is the performance of *Dharma* that leads one, over multiple lives, to *Moksha*.

In the Hindu context, *Kama* and *Artha* are not allowed to run amok but kept within the boundaries of *Dharma*. The '*Dharmic Kama-sphere*' refers to family life, procreation, art and music in the service of divinity, the seeking of perfection in our engagement with materiality whether it is agriculture, animal husbandry, ayurveda, sculpture or architecture.

The '*Dharmic Artha-sphere*' similarly refers to work, business and trade that allows for the maintenance of family and for support of *Dharmic* activities such as festivals, temples, education, *Anna-Daanam*, the running of a *Dharmic* state etc.

As for what constitutes *Dharma* itself, do read Nithin Sridhar's excellent book *Saamaanya Dharma* for an overview. Essential and inspirational though it is, *Dharma* gets all its substance from the fact that it is the stepping stone to something even more incredible and desirable—*Moksha*. It is this ethereal *Moksha* that lends *dharmic* acts their magic. When we act out *Dharma*, without thought of reward or personal gain but with our focus on transcendence (*Nishkaama Karma*), it is then that life and living on *Bhu Devi* matches the peerless generosity of the gift of Life itself.

Locating Liberalism within the Palace of *Purushaarth*: A Framework for Hindu Parents

The vast majority of modern people are cultural liberals, in the sense that their primary concerns are *Kama* and *Artha*. Perhaps we are liberal ourselves, perhaps we know liberals who are good people, maybe some of them describe themselves as conservative, maybe some still carry shades of their Christian or Hindu origins, maybe some like us are ordinary Hindus engaging in Hindu festivals and pujas... yes, but let us make no mistake, our conscious decision or unconscious acquiescence to exit the Palace of *Purushaarth* will, in this generation or the next or the next, manifest in our cultural bloodstream as the full force of our chosen religion, Liberalism, sets in. It is to avoid that fate that we need to locate Liberalism within the framework of *Purushaarth*.

As Hindu parents stuck in an overwhelming liberal world, how do we counter the liberal cage that is descending everyday upon our children with every cartoon they watch, every Bollywood song that they hear, every cool friend they speak to? I offer a suggestion. Look again to *Purushaarth*. Talk openly to your kids about *Purushaarth*.

Though Liberalism looms over our children's imaginations, it is but a speck, a miniscule portion of *Kama* and *Artha* that has unfortunately gone viral. We need to put this genie back in the bottle—intellectually at first, then practically. By guiding our children through the wonders of our Palace of *Purushaarth*, we can start to situate Liberalism where it belongs, in one small corner of our palace (see diagram above).

We must help our kids conceptually locate the entire edifice of liberal sensuality—TV, movies, coolness, unhinged fun, alcohol, addiction, fast food, video games, overt sexualization in media... all of that stuff—as a small segment of the *Kama*-sphere even though our media portrays it as the aim of Life itself.

Debased *Kama* is the life goal of Liberals not Hindus (see diagram below).

Help them also to conceptually locate the entire edifice of liberal greed—TV advertisements, selfishness, limitless ambition to accumulate personal wealth, consumerism, enslavement to corporations in exchange for meaningless holidays in Europe...all of that stuff—as a small segment of the *Artha*-sphere, even though our media portrays it all as the aim of Life itself.

Debased *Artha* is the life-enabler of Liberals not Hindus (see diagram below).

Also important, until we run our own *Dharmic* schools again, is for us and our kids to remember that school, college, all academia as we know it today—that beast that devours the early part of our lives—is also but a small part of the entire *Artha*-sphere (see diagram below). Deep inside, we know that twenty years of a punishing academic schedule may or may not help us get a good job, but we have to go through it nonetheless because we live in an industrial cage (whose culture is overwhelmingly liberal), and sometimes we have to work through the cage in order to step out of it. Very few of us ever will. To be able to leverage liberal knowledge to buy your family a *Dharmic* life requires a rare combination of talent, luck and years of enslavement. It is a far better option, for most of us who do not have the means or courage to simply step out of the liberal cage, to lead parallel lives at this point in history. Work within the debased 'Liberal *Artha*-sphere' to earn our livelihoods, socialize to the extent needed in the debased 'Liberal *Kama*-sphere' to maintain connections, but consciously spend the rest of our time in strengthening *Dharmic* activities within the family and in the larger Hindu community eventually aiming for the establishment of a *Dharmic* milieu.

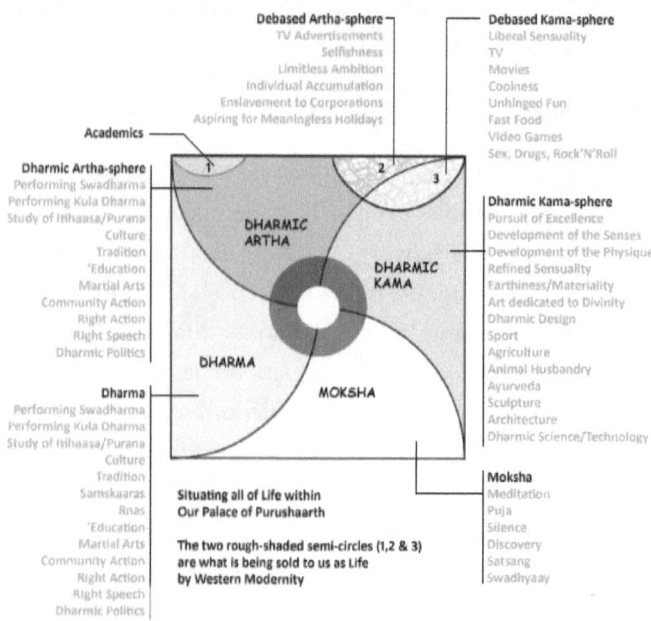

We must show our children that the sum total of what the media and their cool friends are selling them day and night are but small corners of our magnificent Palace of *Purushaarth*. Coercing them to never engage with the debased 'Liberal *Kama*-sphere' and 'Liberal *Artha*-sphere' will probably backfire, but perhaps if we do teach our kids to put all of that stuff in perspective, our perspective, then they will grow up to be *Dharmic* Hindus.

Our kids have to learn to walk in and out of the liberal world and come back to *Dharma* throughout their teens and early twenties. Ideally, from high school onwards, even as they prepare to enter the liberal world, they should be involved in *Dharmic* activity and certainly by their late-twenties, even as they keep their modern jobs, they should actively have turned their backs upon debased *Kama* and *Artha*, using their modern incomes for *Dharmic* purposes, including raising a family and passing on the *samskaaras*.

See Appendix for a *Purushaarta*-based timetable for school children based on these ideas.

Section 1 | Chapter 1.3

A MATTER OF TIME
The Ticking Clock of Hindu Conversion

Maragatham, 2020

Introduction

In an earlier essay *Self-Sacrifice : Hindu Sheep in the Liberal Church* (Section 1, Chapter 1.1 of this book), I first broached the idea that perhaps Liberalism is not the innocuous neutral formulation it posits itself to be, and that perhaps deep in its body lies a Christian heart. In this essay and the next, I explore this idea further. I attempt to reveal the deep processes by which our thoughtless embrace of Liberalism has resulted in our conversion by stealth to a form of Christianity Lite.

Western Modernity has birthed three offspring: Individualism, Materialism and Progressivism. These are the three primary values of Modernity. From these values come the three more well-known Western ideals: Liberty, Equality and Utopia (Fraternity). And, it is mostly from the quest to attain these three unattainable ideals that Western Civilization has birthed a whole host of pseudo-religious movements—Liberalism, Communism, Wokeism, Machine-*Vaad** etc.

The Mind-Map below reveals the inner workings of this beast that prowls our lands and our hearts.

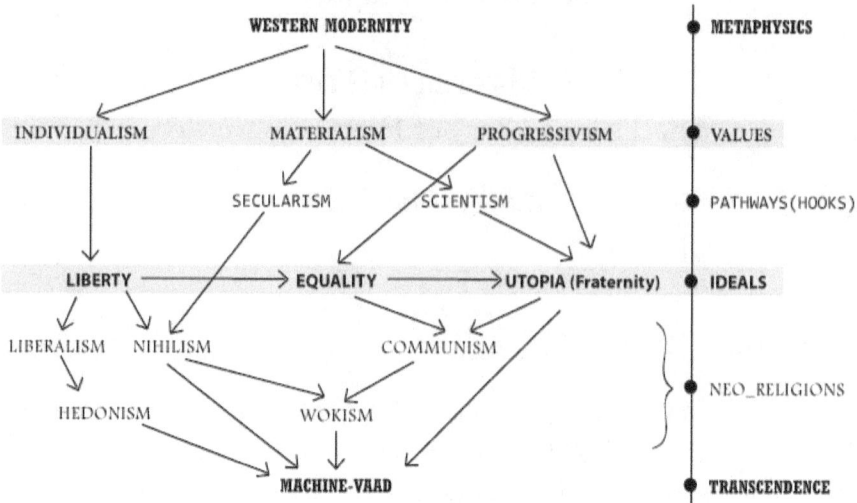

* The term Machine-*Vaad* is courtesy Halley Kalyan.

Every cultural war you see in America today will be replayed in our country on a grander scale if we don't get our act together. For decades, education was the only means they had of brainwashing us, but our notoriously high illiteracy levels delayed the coming to fruition of the Western post-colonial dream. They then turned their guns on Bollywood and our cinema-mad country lapped up their entire spectrum of communist, anti-Hindu, anti-family, consumerist claptrap. But penetration of these outlandish foreign ideas remained low. Alas, in the last twenty years, free TVs distributed by the State for political purposes and widespread internet penetration have dealt a cultural body blow to our nation. The now ubiquitous TV-inspired consumerism, cell-phone porn, fake news, and anti-Hindu narratives on social media have normalized Liberalism and Communism across all our cultures, across all ages, in the remotest parts of our land.

At the superficial level, the vast majority of the population remain Hindu, but at the deep level they have been rewired to belong in either one or more of the three modern tribes: Liberty *Wallahs*, Equality *Wallahs*, Fraternity *Wallahs*. They owe first allegiance to one or more of the ever-expanding lexicon of Western neo-religions (see diagram above), and in the process, the myriad, deep, authentic

Hindu cultures of this land find themselves slowly digested by the shallow neo-religions of Western Modernity.

Do our youth take to the street in protest against the desecration of temples, the theft of *murthis* and judicial interference in our traditions, or do they take to the streets in *Shaheen Bagh* and JNU to protest constrictions in their personal liberties and to demand recognition of their victimhoods? It's clear which way we are headed and what our real religious convictions are these days.

Today, there still exist living links to our non-modern Hindu past. Today, we can access the wisdom of the ages. Tomorrow, we are lost.

A vast number of Hindus today, both formally educated or informally educated by films, embody Western values (Individualism, Materialism, Progressivism) and espouse Western ideals (Liberty, Equality, Fraternity). These adherents of Liberty, Equality and Fraternity can be found spouting stuff that's totally antithetical to their ancestral culture. Look for example, at a popular fiction writer whose work is read by millions. The genre is mythological fiction and the stories have our Gods in human situations. Inevitably, the plots get mixed up with contemporary political messaging.

> And where did these diktats come from? They came from parents, who forced their values and ways on their children. *Brahmin* parents would encourage and push their child towards the pursuit of knowledge. The child, on the other hand, may have a passion for trade. These mismatches led to unhappiness and chaos within society.
>
> Sita proposed that all the children of a kingdom must be compulsorily adopted by the State at the time of birth. The birth-parents would have to surrender their children to the kingdom. The kingdom would raise these children, educate and hone the natural skills that they were born with. At the age of fifteen, they would appear for an examination that would test them on their physical, psychological and mental skills. Based on the result, appropriate castes would be allocated to the children.[1]

What is being proposed by way of fiction is an Orwellian nightmare,[2] many stages past the now trivial goalpost of Communism. And this radical ideology is being home delivered into the minds of impressionable youth through the vehicle of Sita Ma herself, whom they all have venerated since childhood.

I don't blame the author for this. I see this as symptomatic of a nation-wide disease which many of us have suffered from and continue to suffer from. Even you, reader, if you are reading an essay of this complexity in English, you too are probably compromised. We are all compromised in varying degrees. Our inner wiring, the fundamental philosophical foundation of our culture itself has been tinkered with by colonial and neo-colonial forces. The author, as per his own admission is a deeply devout man, but that does not stop him from perceiving the world, even the ancient world, in terms of Western neo-religions. Deep down, we have been rewired, we have all been Christianized and the sooner we realize it the faster we can step out of the long European shadow that has fallen over our civilizational heart.

What is the nature of that rewiring? How do Moksha (Freedom), Karma (Equivalence) and Dharma (Harmony) come to be replaced by Liberty, Equality and Fraternity? Is there a way to grasp the nature of this change at a deep epistemological level?

Yes, there is, and I try to prise open those connections in this essay.

David Bentley Hart, one of contemporary Christianity's most eloquent and deep thinkers, tries to make sense of what post-Christian Modernity means for Christians. With the full knowledge that the progressivism inherent in Modernity is itself a child of Christianity's original revolutionary impulse, he laments its secular shallowness and then tries to deliver some measure of hope to the still faithful (bold added for emphasis):

> So perhaps the best moral sense Christians can make of the story of Christendom now, from the special vantage of its aftermath, is to recall that the Gospel was never bound to the historical fate of any political or social order, but always claimed to enjoy a transcendence of all times and places. Perhaps its presence in human history should always be shatteringly angelic: It announces, even over against one's most cherished expectations of the present or the future, a truth that breaks in upon history, ever and again, **always changing or even destroying the former things in order to make all things new.** That being so, surely modern Christians should find some joy

in being forced to remember that they are citizens of a Kingdom **not of this world**, that here they have no enduring city, and that they are called to **live as strangers** and pilgrims on the earth.[2]

For Christians, Jesus's crucifixion and resurrection represent the original revolution, a break from the past that tore once and for all the spiritual cords that bound people all over the world with their ancestors. But the coming of Protestantism and then Modernity with its decadal revolutions (each claiming to be *the* new moral high-water mark), has made it clear, even to staunch Christians, that what was promised to be the *first and final* revolution was in fact no more than a template for today's perpetual and meaningless revolutions. Hart despondently admits as much in this excerpt above. But this does *not* lead him to question the revolutionary basis of Christianity. Instead, unable to bear the thought of abandoning the revolutionary impulse embedded in the Gospel, Hart, in a fit of intellectual dexterity, ends up embracing the problem instead of resisting it, and proclaims that the Christian response to the modern malaise of eternal revolution should be to renew their focus on otherworldliness.

As *Sanatanis*, our worldview differs in two dramatic ways from Hart's final reconstitution of Christianity. One, *Dharma* is eternal, it is not made new and ever changing as per individual will or technological progress. Even as spiritual greats and the *Avatars* of the Gods serve as fulcrums around which the wheel of *Dharma* revolves, the need to change is never our goal, it is always the re-establishment of righteousness and the eternal order. Two, our deliverance is in the here and now, not in the ever after. Realizing the eternal in the here and now is in fact our final freedom, and we approach that destination through the practice of *Dharma* which is nothing but the earthly reflection of the eternal principle. It is this understanding that protects us, *Sanatanis*, from the death kiss of irreverence and hubristic immorality, that revolution breeds.

"Elsewhere-Afterwards" versus "Here-and-Now"

Both Technological Progressivism of the Conservative type and Moral-Progressivism of the Left-Liberal type are characterized by a blind belief in 'the future'. They believe that things are always getting "better" and that one day we will solve our problems and then "everything's gonna be alright".

We Hindus must know that these are essentially superstitious beliefs. They do not stand up to scrutiny and there is absolutely no evidence that we will solve our problems and that 'everything's gonna be alright'. The only thing that can be said with certainty is that our tools have grown more sophisticated resulting in a material surplus (most probably unsustainable). It is *this* contemporary condition of ours that has been defined as 'progress' and irrationally linked to the idea of our *well-being* in order to give it a positive spin by people who make money selling this idea.

Any objective observer of modern human societies will see that the whole thing is like a water balloon. You press here and it bulges there; you press there, it bulges here. You control acute disease, you've got a chronic disease problem. You cure yourself with antibiotics, you end up killing your gut bacteria. You increase yield with fertilizer, you lay waste to the soil. You invent the automobile, you create air pollution. You fix air pollution, you have a toxic battery problem. We're never going to get it under control, ever. But if you start by defining the aim of the human life as 'progress', then obviously all forms of 'progress' are seen as a good thing, and by that circular logic we start to inhabit a self-fulfilling destiny. Instead, if we define the aim of human life as anything *real*, such as happiness or harmony or well-being, then the whole edifice of 'progress' as a means to that end collapses.

This notion of an imaginary place of perfection, Heaven, was neatly translated from Christianity into the modern notion of 'progress' with all of its epistemological implications. The fact that the end goal of 'progress', just like Heaven before it, is an imaginary construct does not seem to bother too many of us. In fact, so brainwashed by this notion was the White Man in colonial times, that he considered it his religious duty to bring this good news to every corner of the planet. Following which, unfortunately today, most of us suffer from his mental disease in varying degrees.

Hindu thought does not endorse this Elsewhere-Afterwards view of life, what I call *heaven-centricism*. The entire epistemological focus of our deep philosophies is the Here-and-Now. Enlightenment, *nirvana, moksha, samadhi,* are in the Here-and-Now. We believe that the true nature of reality already exists. We are told by our sages that we simply have to step out of our ignorance and recognize it. To enquire about the Self, to meditate upon the Breath, to Act without thought of future reward, to be in the throes of *Bhakti* or a *Dharam Yuddh*, are all means to access the radical present. You could imagine a potter's wheel turning. The centre is stationary and still, it is *presence* itself, but it is also the axle, the active principle, the animating force around which the clay of Hindu society revolves. Our cultures are organized around that central point, looking towards it, focused on it, even as we move in circles around it taking on beautiful forms.

Linear Time and the Idea of 'Progress'

For most of human history, the vast majority of cultures lived within a circular conception of time. The Earth goes around, the seasons come around, birth and death follow each other as do joy and sorrow. The Christian idea of a linear progression of time leading to an imaginary Heaven and an imaginary Second Coming, on the other hand, is a relatively recent innovation. Its modern variant is called Historical Materialism.[3] It was delineated by Marx and Engels and has permeated most of our thinking. We have bought into the idea of 'progress' and 'development' so feverishly, it is as if we are all aspiring for a Christian Heaven.

As Hindus, we are not *against* complexity in tool making and increasing material sophistication, but a true Hindu would not see these developments in religious terms. A true Hindu would not see 'progress' as a destination. At most he may see it in utilitarian terms. A true Hindu may use modern tools, may even help invent them, but most importantly would not care if they were to all disappear one day, because they do not define him nor do they impinge upon the realm of *Dharma* and *Moksha*. The minute we imbue the phenomenon of increasing material sophistication with the sentiment of 'progress' with all its positive connotations, we step out of circular time and into Christian linearity. Unfortunately, the prevailing mindset among ordinary Hindus is indeed to surrender to the neo-Christian vision of 'progress as a Holy Grail.'

Julius Evola in his 1934 classic *Revolt Against the Modern World* describes the difference between religions based on *historicism* and religions based on *eternal truths*:

> In order to understand the spiritual background typical of every non-modern civilization, it is necessary to retain the idea that the opposition between historical times and mythological times is not the relative opposition proper to two homogenous parts of the same time frame, but rather the *qualitative* and *substantial* opposition between times that are *not* of the same kind. Traditional man did not have the same experience of time as modern man, he had a super-temporal sense of time and in this sensation lived every form of his world.[4]

The Line and the Circle and their Implication for Humans

The difference between living in circular time and living in linear time is the difference between a circle and a straight line. It's as simple as that.

1. A Circle is limited (**economy**), a straight Line is unlimited (**exploitation**).
2. A Circle is connected (**relationships, culture**), a straight Line is unconnected (**loneliness, law enforcement**).
3. A Circle is stable (**marriage**), a straight Line is in constant motion (**divorce**).
4. A Circle may expand concentrically but retains its relationship with its centre (**tradition**); a straight Line expands into the unknown, there's no looking back (**revolution**).

The thing about linear time is that it imposes its value system upon us. Yes, even conceptions of time have value systems hidden deep in their very structure. Linearity has been attacking Circularity since the crucifixion of Jesus. Recent attempts in Bharat to take down the tradition of *Shri Jagganath Rath Yatra*[5] and break through the tradition of *Swami Ayyappa in Sabarimala*[6] are clear examples of vested interest groups using straight lines to puncture existing circularities. You can even imagine it clearly if you close your eyes and see a circle going round and round since forever and the attempt to push a straight line into the circle to stop it from rotating.

The Four Hidden Values of Linear Time

Every single novel, outlandish, phenomenon that you observe in Hindu society today can be explained by viewing it through the lens of one or more of these four values of linear time.

1. Change and Novelty

A line is always heading somewhere else, pointing 'forward'. A line is always leading somewhere New.

Once we absorb this value:

a. We look with disdain at the past, our parents, and traditions.
b. We salivate at the sight of a new iPhone.
c. We prefer Christ to Krishna simply because he is new and, like the English language, he represents 'progress', and 'progress', we have been told, is good. The newly 'lineating' rural Hindu cannot tell the difference between new clothing patterns, new music choices, new sexual mores, new places and new gods. Newness is all. Newness smells of progress'.
d. We obsess about the idea of growth – getting ahead at the family and national level.
e. We start to experience dis-satisfaction, restlessness, impatience.
f. Contentment, once the highest good, is now sneered upon. We look for new places, new jobs, new relationships, only the latest will do. We have to stay on top of things, to be 'in the know' otherwise we're evicted from the 'in crowd'. We fear our irrelevance most of all. The most poignant aspect of this way of being is that, as the world grows younger and newer at a faster and faster rate, each of us is inevitably growing older with each passing day. Self-hate sets in.
g. Plastic surgery, both metaphorical and literal, becomes normal.

2. Individualism

In a circle we stand shoulder to shoulder, holding hands, facing a common centre. A line breaks that formation and puts us one behind the other facing an undefined horizon. Each of us stands alone. The directionality of the line suggests to us that we should be focused on getting ahead further along the line before our compatriots do and maintaining our lead.

Once we absorb this value:

1. We look with disdain upon groups/tribes/culture.
   We start to define ourselves by the things we do, the things we own, the things we think, the things we feel. Group identities have traditions to help communally hold that identity, externalize it, celebrate it. Individual identities by definition cannot have any traditions, which leads us to the modern idea of having to 'express ourselves'. This takes on all kinds of forms—we indulge our emotions and our thoughts (both of which our seers have told us are fickle and unreal). Artists and ordinary individualists search for extreme experiences to better define themselves as separate from others. Art especially has suffered from this obsession with the egoic self and the need for uniqueness, leading to the glorification of everything disruptive, subversive, extreme[7], bizarre. It is only a small step from there to the glorification of violence[8], porn and death by sociopaths and psychopaths. Every single vision of the future[9] that has come out of the diseased Western mind has been apocalyptic. It's as if they know they are sick but an inner urge urges them onwards in the glorification of that sickness. The 2019 Todd Phillips film *Joker* is one recent example a long line of such 'Art'.

2. Psychiatric care and sociopathy become normal. A genetically modified, android future becomes normal.

Circles are wholesome and human. Art made by circular humans is beautiful, celebratory, grateful, inspirational. We can sense this impulse in our classical music and in our temple architecture, our Sanskrit plays, and our *itihaasa*.

Lines are not meant for humans. Linear humans will ultimately become non-human, moulded against their better senses by the inner form of the line itself.

3. Destination-ality

*Linear time insists that we are **going** somewhere. It points to a destination, the promised land. It will not let us be still.*

Once we absorb this value:

a. We look with disdain at people who are behind us in the race to the imaginary destination. People who wear clothes that are out of fashion are insulted. People who have old-fashioned names are laughed at. People from villages are *ganwaar* as if it was a bad thing. For millennia, a person from Manipur was a person from Manipur and person from Mumbai was a person from Mumbai; they had different customs, lives, wants. Today linear thinking forces us to think of Manipur as a wannabe Mumbai and by the same token we look at Mumbai as a wannabe New York. Everyone and every place is supposed to be getting somewhere. India has to become a first world country. It's a race to the top. But to the top of what?

b. Stillness, that most respected value, is today an unknown quality. Movement is everything, on TV, on social media, 24 hour news cycles. A sense of urgency is in the air, usually accompanied by a sense of impending doom. These poor people, these traditional people, these regressive forces may not allow us to get to our destination after all—they will snatch from us our promised land!

4. Speed

Linear time, by pointing to a destination also carries the underlying implication that the sooner we get to the destination, the better it is. We can get ahead, we can be first, we can win!

Once we absorb this value:

a. We look with disdain at everything that slows us down, that cuts our efficiency... that is inconvenient. Parents, relationships, marriages, children, tradition, all of that has to be discarded. They cramp our style, put constraints and set limits on how far ahead we can get. The more responsibility we take on, the slower we get and the more likely we are to lose the race to the promised land. Vast numbers of youth are shunning responsibility,[10] floating around, spending their fathers' money, many hoping to 'make it big' without any hard work, their fantasies amplified and preyed upon by TV shows.[11]

The Problem

Western Modernity is here to stay in the medium term. The technologies that drive individuation are ubiquitous and the break-up of our old communal selves is inevitable. The breakdown of the old circular structures is guaranteed. At this cusp of history, as *Bharatiya* people, what do we do?

The problem today is that almost all of us, even those of us who swear by *Dharma*, are actually revolutionaries. We're all some form of neo-Christian; we believe in 'progress', development, in betterment. I'm not saying these are bad, I'm just saying that these ideals will not get our society to a wholesome place. We can implement all of these without self-destruction only if we have a higher, more powerful circular cultural value that is guiding us. In the absence of that *Dharmic* force, we are just as lost as Westerners, thrashing about in the pond of life.

There has been such a large-scale movement of *Bharatiya* people away from our traditional ways of viewing life because our education is Western-Progressive. It teaches us that *Bhu Devi* herself is dead and that there is a destination elsewhere to be reached. This false view of the world leads to the building of expectations in young minds. These minds are revolutionized—they want more, they want better, and these wants become ends unto themselves. This is deeply problematic. Once you are revolutionized in your thinking, Islam and Christianity automatically become appealing to you because they are all cut from the same cloth. Hinduism on the other hand is seen as belonging to the past and a shroud of backwardness is cast over it. So vast conversions happen and even among the people who don't convert to these religions, there is a tacit conversion to American-style progressivism and globalism, accompanied by a deep shame associated with Hinduness. And, of course, there are the overt revolutionaries who discard Hinduism and take on the religion of Che and

Mao. The problem is deep, even among those of us who speak for *Dharma*, our minds are pre-programmed to think in revolutionary terms and we are essentially living a type of schizophrenia.

If we want a solution to this existential problem that faces all indigenous peoples, either we go back to being entirely traditional and risk cutting ourselves off from the engines of social life and power, or we think of some way to stand astride two disparate worlds. We may yet be capable of that; we're not infinitely inventive and flexible for nothing. Recognizing the problem with clarity is the first step.

It's not for Nothing that we Stand for Something

How to be essentially *Dharmic* in a revolutionary world? How to retain Circularity in a Linear world?

At the personal level, what rules do we set ourselves? What limits, what discipline that will remind us every day that even though we walk the roads that everyone else walks, we do so knowing all the time, that those roads are unreal and it's only our (collective) practice that is true? What vows do we take by ourselves, with friends and with family to honour circular living and the gifts our ancestors have left for us? It's not for nothing that we stand for something!

At the national level, what systemic structures will help encourage circularity? While most of governmental activity is focused on linearity for the sake of building up our economic and military strength, we could, like Israel, subsidize circular indigenous practices so that we all have the opportunity and the facility to step out of the Line and into the Circle at any time we want. One of the first steps in this direction will be the freeing of Hindu temples[12] from the linear state so they are free to function as per their circular traditions. Our temples will then become power centres of circularity influencing education, culture, art and social service. This is the first step.

The first step is just one step away. But the magic of this first step is that once it's taken, the second step is just one step away.

References and Links

1. Kulbir Kaur, "Book Review 'Sita Warrior of Mithila: In Sita we trust, in Ram we're not sure'", *Deccan Chronicle*, 2017
   https://www.deccanchronicle.com/lifestyle/books-and-art/160717/book-review-sita-warrior-of-mithila-in-sita-we-trust-in-ram-were-not-sure.html

2. David Bentley Hart, "No Enduring City", *First Things*, 2013
   https://www.firstthings.com/article/2013/08/no-enduring-city

3. https://en.wikipedia.org/wiki/Historical_materialism

4. Julius Evola, *Revolt against the Modern World*, (f.p. in Italian, 1934) Inner Traditions,1969

5. Debayan Roy, "'Lord Jagannath won't forgive us if we allow it', Supreme Court stays annual Rath Yatra in Puri due to COVID-19", *Bar and Bench*, 2020
   https://www.barandbench.com/news/breaking-lord-jagannath-wont-forgive-us-if-we-allow-it-supreme-court-stays-annual-rath-yatra-in-puri-due-to-covid-19

6. K. Bhattacharjee, "'Liberals' prove that they are willing to trample over democracy for sake of ideological supremacy", *OpIndia*, 2018
   https://www.opindia.com/2018/09/liberals-prove-that-they-are-willing-to-trample-over-democracy-for-sake-of-ideological-supremacy/

7. https://www.worldtravelguide.net/features/feature/getting-high-15-of-the-best-adrenaline-activities/

8. Lesley Anderson, "Snuff: Murder and torture on the internet, and the people who watch it", *The Verge*, 2012
   https://www.theverge.com/2012/6/13/3076557/snuff-murder-torture-internet-people-who-watch-it

9. https://en.wikipedia.org/wiki/Blade_Runner

10. Surbhi Bhatia, "Are India's Youth Giving Up On Marriage?", *Live Mint*, 2020
    https://www.livemint.com/news/india/are-india-s-youth-giving-up-on-marriage-11590763737075.html

11. Holly Peek, "The Impact Of Reality TV On Our Teens: What Can Parents Do?", *The Clay Center for Young Healthy Minds*
    https://www.mghclaycenter.org/parenting-concerns/teenagers/impact-reality-tv-teens-can-parents/

12. J Sai Deepak, *Freeing Hindu Temples from Government Control*, Sangam Talks, 2016
    https://www.youtube.com/watch?v=BA_VQdUMdeY

Section 2

CLARITY

Section 2 | Chapter 2.1

CASTE 101
The Curious Case of the Left-Liberal

Maragatham, 2019

Sample This #1

Suresh (SC) enters a work space where a number of women are working. The women are a mixture of *Paraiyars* (SCs), *Vanniyar Gounders* (OBCs) and *Agamudayars* (OBCs). Note also that all these women are sitting together and working as a team. As soon as Suresh enters the space, all the women fold their legs in respect and go through the usual Hindu womanly sequence of sitting up straight and adjusting their saris. The act of keeping one's legs outstretched is a sign or disrespect. If indeed any of the OBCs felt disrespect towards the SC man this would be the perfect opportunity to show it by refusing to fold their legs when he entered the space. None of them do that. In fact, the instinctive way in which they go through their little personal respect rituals implies that this thought has never entered their consciousness. Simultaneously, Prabhavati (OBC) makes sure that the guest is taken care of in the traditional Hindu way. She rushes to the water filter and fills up a glass then goes over to Suresh to offer him water which he accepts gratefully. He returns the glass with a "Thanks *Akka*". Elder sister! Terms of blood relations are used among people who belong. Other English terms such as Madam and Saar are used when dealing with outsiders.

Sample This #2

We're building a cowshed. Azhagu (SC) is a thatcher; he makes roofs from grass for a living. As befits the specialized work he does, his salary is Rs.600 per day. Murugan (OBC) is a 'coolie'; he works on all kinds of physically demanding jobs in exchange for a day wage of Rs.400. Note that the SC earns more than the OBC, not because of any affirmative action but because his work is more valued. It is easy to imagine a time in India not long ago when this was the case throughout the land, when artisans were respected and paid a salary commensurate with their skill.

Azhagu is on top of the thatched roof pushing the needle through the roof. Murugan is standing below to receive the needle and push it back up. As chance would have it, Murugan pushes the needle too fast or too far (I couldn't tell from where I was). Immediately, there is a volley of curses from Azhagu. *"Dai! Apidi kutthaadenu yevlavu vaati solunum da?"* (Dai, how many times do I have to tell you not to poke like that?). The shouting goes on for a minute. Murugan is silent. The tone, the use of words such as *"Dai"* and *"Da"* are all disrespectful but often used. Certainly, one can imagine people working with each other using these terms and that tone when attempting to make a forceful point. Though the tone and words are disrespectful, there is no disrespect meant—it appears to be an exchange between equals, and Murugan accepts it as such. Note that the possibility of an SC person using disrespectful words and tone when addressing an OBC person does exist. It indicates that not only is the SC person not afraid of the OBC person but also that the OBC person accepts disrespectful words from anyone when it is legitimate.

After fifteen years living in rural Madurai District, Tamil Nadu, it appears to me that the 'left-liberal' reading of history, which everybody these days is calling a Marxist reading of history, is either biased in its observations, mistaken in its conclusions, or entirely unsuitable for the Hindu context. By looking at ordinary events in an extraordinary light everything that is reflected back into the intellect is distorted.

I too grew up in a Congress-voting household, I too accepted the Western, Nehruvian narrative[1] about our society in the eighties and nineties as natural and normal and went to America for a college degree, where I quickly learned to think post-modern thoughts and where I was presented with a special pair of spectacles. These spectacles, once I put them on, showed me the world in a different light. In this light, people were either oppressors or oppressed. From a logical perspective, there is nothing inherently wrong with this point of view; it is just another way of cutting up worldly phenomena in order to examine them.

For example, we could break up the world into vegetarians and non-vegetarians, or lovers of the colour blue and haters of the colour blue. Each binary reveals the world in a different light.

Unfortunately, the chosen binary of Marx and then the Left-Libs, that of the Oppressor-Oppressed dichotomy,[2] causes deep distortions in a person's ability to both view and understand himself and the world around. The innate, connected, harmonic nature of human experience is disrupted and replaced with a harsh split personality that leaves no room for nuance or complexity. Within each one of us is seen to lie an oppressor and/or an oppressed. This causes either a guilt complex (for the oppressor) or a victim complex (for the oppressed) or a mixture of both within the person. In all cases, some level of self-hate is born and the person sets off subconsciously to cure himself of it by changing the world.

Both common sense and our culture tell us that we were born to love ourselves, so the psyche's immediate response to the phenomenon of self-hate is to see it as a cancer of the mind and respond violently. That internally felt pain leads directly to depressive thoughts. This internal struggle is often externalized in acts that cause pain outside of the person. In extreme cases, the infected person encourages the emergence of this pain in other people who, until then, may be going about their business perfectly contentedly. That is the business of revolution. "Goddammit, If people don't feel my pain, then they must be naïve, and they need to be awoken to this pain filled reality!"

What we must understand, though, is that these processes are happening deep within the psyche of the person. Most ordinary left-lib youth are unaware that they are playing out this script in a grand world-wide drama that is being fuelled by a very specific simplistic presumption about the world: that of the oppressor-oppressed dichotomy. Once this presumption is accepted as paradigmatic, everything else locks into place. The ordinary left-lib is not a mastermind consciously hatching disruptive plans, he is just being himself... totally naturally (but with the special spectacles on). I, for example, was totally immersed in left-lib ideology. I did not see it as wrong in any way. In fact, it was surprising to me that anybody would fail to see the world as I did! I was the virtuous one, the crusader in the fight to save the world. .

This desire to change the world and the unproven faith that that will heal the rift within us is so strong in the left-liberal that he is forced to demonize all other points of view. This dis-ease of righteousness is the reason that left-libs appear neurotic to everyone else.

Depending on the type of person he is dealing with, the deep questions fuelling his rage are:

1. How can you not know that you are oppressed?
2. Once you know that you are oppressed, how can you sit still and not respond violently?
3. How can you continue to participate in oppressive structures?
4. Once you know that you or your ancestors were oppressors, how can you sit idle and not atone for your/their sins?

Perhaps, for the ordinary person and also for many unconscious left-libs, this semi-psychological analysis will serve as an eye-opener. With this in mind, it becomes easier to understand a lot of the phenomena that are playing out around us in the political sphere that previously appeared nonsensical.

Now Sample This #3

My friend is out looking for farmers who grow indigo. After going round and round in circles in the villages near Villupuram, she finally finds the farmer who had been recommended. He grows indigo. They got to talking and life stories were exchanged. As she thanks him and readies to leave, he stops her and says, "You know how expensive this is, but since you are a *brahmin*, I will give you this sack-full for free." And he collects the plants into a sack and carries it over to the car.

The left-lib (many of whom are totally removed from this rural reality) will understand the farmer's actions as that of a man brainwashed by centuries of conditioning into believing that gifts given to *brahmins* will earn him spiritual merit. But wait a minute, stop that externally planted thought machine for one second and witness the act for what it is and what it represents. A farmer, in keeping with the great Hindu tradition of sharing and not letting a visitor leave empty-handed, has offered a guest something that he grows. If he grew coconuts he would certainly have offered *yelaneer* and if he grew fruits or groundnut he would certainly have offered that. Secondly, a *brahmin*, apparently in the farmer's lived experience, is a particularly respect-worthy person deserving of this special gift of expensive indigo. Why does he think that? I don't know. You would have to ask the farmer and take his words at face value. Simply witness, from a place of human emotion without your ideological bias and you will see differently. Where there is a culture of love, respect and inter-dependence, if you are a normal person, you will see it, accept it and reciprocate it.

Imagine, here in *Tamil Nadu* after sixty odd years of harsh anti-*brahmin* rhetoric by the people in power, after *brahmins* have been forced to leave the state following insults and reservations, we have this example of a still surviving sentiment that points to an ancient reality that our mainstream narrative has done its darndest to cover up. *Brahmin* communities continue to be deeply respected for their erudition and devotion, and farming communities do not see themselves as oppressed, but as the very opposite—the bestowers of gifts. Even here. Even now.

Surely our common-place understanding of "caste-relations" is deeply flawed. Surely these examples do not show us a world of oppression and oppressed. Surely, they reflect a world where differences exist but are not wished away. These differences are recognized and simultaneously respected. Internal rules of engagement that have evolved over millennia have maintained the peace between literally thousands of tribal factions* while an underlay of deep universalist philosophies has bound them together helping them to work to create the pre-eminent civilization of pre-modernity. That, in itself, is an amazing civilizational achievement that places in Western Europe, with their recent failing experiments in multi-culturalism,[3] are only now beginning to open their eyes to.

(* Tribes are simply groups of people who prioritize their group identity over their individual identities. This is not to be confused with the same term that is often used solely to describe hunter-gatherers or forest dwellers. One can be tribal even living in a city.)

I invite my left-liberal friends to take a step back and view the world around them without their special spectacles.

Finally Sample This #4

Priya (*Irular*, ST) is a doctor. She is marrying a classmate of hers, Aravind (*Mudaliar*, FC). At the wedding that takes place in Salem, the bride arrives all alone. No family, no friends, just her. At the wedding altar, the groom's father cries. He can't bear to see his daughter-in-law abandoned like this, on this, the most auspicious day of her life. Note that it is the so-called 'lowest of low', the *Irulas*, who have objected to (and boycotted) the marriage, not the *Mudaliars*. And note that it is the *Mudaliar* who has accepted the *Irula* into his family and publicly sheds tears on her plight. I don't have to dissect the irony of this situation for all of us who have been schooled in the 'high'-caste-oppressive, 'low'-caste-oppressed school of thought.

I think it's high time we dismantled altogether the remarkable framework of lies that has been injected into our cultural bloodstream by the British and their left-liberal heirs. There is no 'caste system' in this country. There are tribal communities (known as *jaatis*). Each such community is exclusive in nature, as tribal formations all over the world have been. They guard fiercely their culture, traditions and means of professional production. No doubt there have been skirmishes and jockeying for power between all of these communities. No doubt, the fortunes of communities have risen and fallen along with the ebb and tide of history. But the clear stream of *Dharma* has always flowed through our intertwined histories until the coming of the Europeans. The idea that some work is 'high' and some work is 'low' is an entirely Western idea. The Christian Europeans have always had a horror of the earth and the body which we, in Bharat, never had.

See this public statement by "Father" Ponniah, a Christian pastor in Tamil Nadu, for instance – "But we wear shoes. Why? Because the impurities of Bharat Mata should not contaminate us. The Tamil Nadu government has given us free footwear. This *bhumadevi* is dangerous, you could catch scabies from it."[4]

Our tribal frictions and their resolutions are an internal matter. As Hindus we have had the experience over millennia of settling our issues mostly non-violently. Problems have arisen, been resolved, gone away, come back in newer forms. This is the nature of the world, everywhere. Power struggles, co-operation, competition, celebration... this, the constant negotiation at multiple levels over the resolution of these problems is what creates the web of Hindu life. Unlike the West, Hindu society did not need Modernity and its nihilistic *with-us-or-against-us* choices to embark on processes of introspection and self-correction. For us this has been a continuous process. We never had to reject the past in order to modify societal customs. Wise men and women have arisen whenever the need was felt and have led our communities with the examples of their own lives on the path to mutual-respect and harmonious co-existence, and towards the other cherished values of our civilization—Shankara, Ramanuja, Basavanna, Ramananda, Ravidas, Kabir, Nanak, Sankardev, Mirabai, Narayana Guru, Vivekananda, the list goes on. What we left-libs, who ironically admire a number of these people, must realize is that the way towards change adopted by all of these greats was never the culture-levelling, Western social justice model of today but rather a model that relied heavily on Indian wisdom, compassion, self-reflection and communal sharing. Why have we abandoned this higher path in favour of the cruder, black and white, violence-ridden Western path?

Historically, our greatest social accomplishment has been our engagement in this delicate dance between the particular and the universal without succumbing to nihilistic Western final solutions, which have included the genocide of Native Americans, the slavery of West Africans, the depredations of Colonialism, the dangerous stupidity of the World Wars, the horror of the gas chambers and the *gulags*, the Cultural Revolution in China, the killing fields of Cambodia, the ridiculous Cold War, and the modern-day capitalist assault on Culture, Community and Family.

Compared to that record of 'elevated' Western thought, and despite all of our weaknesses and ugliness, India still stands as a beacon for Mutual Respect[6] in the world. It is in India that we have lived with (and at times even loved) our enemies for over a thousand years. This clichéd Christian notion—"love thy enemy"—has ironically found life only here in India and not in any of the blood-soaked Christian lands of the West.

Let us accept that problems exist between our communities, but let us also admit that the solutions to those problems lie within our own long traditions of dialogue and spiritual action,[5] and not in the pages of *Das Kapital*. Let us also admit to the possibility that the root of these problems lies not in the evilness of our ancestors as the Christians would have us believe but perhaps in the more mundane idea of economic and cultural devastation wrought by the colonial British.

Reading *The Beautiful Tree*[7] by Dharampal shows us how the traditional educational system was widespread, successful and universally available even to all those communities who today unfortunately find themselves labelled as SC. The coming of industrial technologies with the British broke the economic backs of the *jaatis* that worked with hand and land, and elevated those *jaatis* that worked with calculation and trade. The situation was made worse by the take-over of forests, lakes and village Commons by the Crown and the forcible replacement of our traditional schools with the straight-jacket of Macaulayan factory education. The debased condition that some *jaatis* (agricultural, nomadic, artisanal communities) find themselves in today is a result of that unfortunate throw of the colonial dice. But that the luckier *jaatis* did not deem it important enough to reach out to their left-behind brothers and give them a hand or leg up is entirely our failure. That, for the past century and a half, we have not lived up to the best of our own *Sanatani* traditions is a blot on our consciences. For that, and only for that, we apologize and make amends. And we forgive too, because we know that every community suffered loss and did what it had to do in order to survive. The threads that bound us together were severed and we've all had to figure out how to navigate our encounter with the paradigm shift that British industrialism brought to our world. This devastating process continues even today as more and more marginalized communities are on-boarded aboard this ship. To claim, as many revolutionaries have been taught to do, that the communities who boarded the industrial ship a mere generation or two earlier are 'privileged' is an absurd way to understand recent history.

Let the 'oppressors' among us rid ourselves of our guilt complexes and let the 'oppressed' among us rid ourselves of our victim complexes. In today's 'caste-speak', Krishnadevaraya was a *Shudra*, Gandhi was a *Vysya*, Buddha was a *Kshatriya*, Basavanna was a *Brahmana*! We built this thing *together*.

Even if our traditional community identities no longer hold in today's high-tech world, each one of us can and should be proud of where we come from and the contributions our ancestral communities have made to the building of the magnificent edifice that was Bharat.

> All Indians are free, and not one of them is a slave. The Indians do not even use aliens as slaves and much less a countryman of their own.
>
> – Megasthenes, *Indika*, 300 BCE [8]

References and Links

1. Rajiv Malhotra speaks
   https://www.youtube.com/watch?v=2aEaGdMVClE&t=0s&index=44&list=WL

2. https://en.wikipedia.org/wiki/Social_conflict_theory

3. Douglas Murray speaks
   https://www.youtube.com/watch?v=cfgcmch-1X4

4. OpIndia Staff, "Catholic priest in Tamil Nadu arrested for hate speech against Hindus: Here is what the pastor said", *OpIndia*, 2021
   https://www.opindia.com/2021/07/tamil-nadu-catholic-priest-father-george-ponnaiah-arrested-for-hate-speech-against-hindus/

5. Ashish Pandey, "Brahmin priest carries Dalit devotee on his shoulder to promote social equality", *India Today*, 2018
   https://www.indiatoday.in/india/story/brahmin-priest-carries-dalit-devotee-on-his-shoulder-to-promote-social-equality-1281134-2018-07-09

6. Rajiv Malhotra, *Being Different: An Indian Challenge to Western Universalism*, 2011

7. Dharampal, *The Beautiful Tree*, 1983

8. Megasthenes, *Indika*, 300BCE (Translated from Greek copies by W.McCrindle)

Section 2 | Chapter 2.2

CASTE 102
Our Collective Cultural Caste-ration

Maragatham, 2019

> "Caste is worse than *Jihad*!"
> – *anonymous online comment*

As the *Bharatiya* awakening continues, it's important that we at least look at ourselves with some nuance and complexity. After all, *viveka*, or the ability for discernment, has been the civilizational hallmark that has distinguished us from the Western Abrahamics and their tendency towards black and white judgementalism.

The enemies of Bharat follow a two-step process. First, they reduce all of Hinduism to 'caste' and then they reduce the complex and yet undefined entity of 'caste' to oppression. By applying these faulty axioms over two centuries they have built a hate-Bharat consensus in the wider world and simultaneously injected our colonized minds with the poison of self-hate. We are a long way down that road today. Self-hate is a widespread phenomenon in our society and many of us offer ourselves up for conversion – to Islam, Christianity, Communism, Liberalism, Globalism and all the other "isms" that have world domination as their goal.

As an indigenous civilization which does *not* believe in world domination, we must continue to fight these forces. In today's world, when their strategy has made deep inroads into our self-perception, the first step is to recover from the ill effects of self-hate by de-colonizing our minds through personal research from primary sources. The second is to speak our truth to the world unapologetically. We must stop using the language of our enemies against ourselves. Hinduism is *not* 'caste' and 'caste' is *not* oppression. Oppression is a universal phenomenon built into *all* power structures. Our fight is against oppression, not against 'caste'.

Today, every major Hindu organization wants to "strive towards a caste-less society". Implicit in this stance is the unquestioned belief that caste is a bad thing. Where does that belief come from? Why do we so easily equate caste with oppression? I know, I know, these questions must not be asked, the White Man has told us that caste is bad.

Let's wind the clock back a little and ask the primary question – "What is caste?". Only when we have a satisfactory answer to that question can we decide if it is a bad thing or not.

Tribe and Tradition

Let me start by laying out an intellectual roadmap that, if we are lucky, will lead us to, if not a definition, at least an understanding of the phenomenon that goes by the name of 'caste'.

The view that tradition is bad, that tradition has weakened us and that we have to look beyond rituals to the essence of what the rituals represent, is a common point of view of a number of people who are fighting for Hinduism's cultural renaissance. Ultimately, they think, to beat them, we have to become like them.

We can now ask, if, to beat them, we have to become like them, then why fight them in the first place?

I find myself forced to respond to a reading of our history that has led a segment of patriotic *Bharatiya* people to believe that, in order to beat the enemy, we need to abandon our traditions as weakness and each of us needs to become some version of an *Advaitin Kshatriya*. This is a reductionist view of our culture... the view of a soldier on the battlefield. But we know that not everyone is a soldier, and when the wars are won don't the soldiers all have to come home?

Visualize home, then. From every corner of *Bharatvarsh*, every village, every forest, every hill, innumerable little unique streams of ritual and tradition emerge from the earth and flow across the land. As these streams flow and water our inner gardens, they manifest our *bhakti*, simultaneously connecting us to each other and our land, thus forming the grand river of our civilization. These little streams are just as important as the more abstract *Jnana* and *Yoga*. When we disregard tradition, we are not only bringing down the specialized orthodoxy, we are also looking down upon the daily lives of hundreds of millions of common rural and urban folk for whom these traditions are the metaphorical spiritual palace that their ancestors have built and that they live in and maintain every single day of their lives. It's important that we do not reduce the awesome garden of the cultures of Bharat to simplistic labels such as 'backward', 'weakness' and 'oppression' like our enemies do. Some of our practices may or may not need reform—that is beside the point. Reform, when essential, *will* happen bottom-up only when we discard top-down narratives of negativity.

If self-hate is not a part of the Muslim and Christian self-perception, then why is it only the Hindu who carries this cross of self-hate, knowing full well that our history of oppression is minimal compared to the centuries of inter-continental Christian[1] and Islamic[2] cruelty? Is it because we have internalized the idea that we lost? And we lost because we are weak? And that we are weak because there is something wrong with us? And that thing can only be 'caste'... because the White Man told us so?

Step 1. It is essential that we stop believing this lie that the Muslim armies kicked our ass. A battle-by-battle analysis shows us that *Bharatiya* people won more battles than the Muslim armies. Start with Sitaram Goel's *Heroic Hindu Resistance to Muslim Invaders, 636AD to 1206AD*[3] and continue your research all the way to the retaking of Delhi by the Marathas[4] and the retaking of the Khyber Pass by the Sikhs.[5] We are a brave and committed people who safeguarded our culture over the longest assault in history. It doesn't get better than this. We need to celebrate this. Barring small pockets, every single other land on the planet has been conquered by Christianity, Islam or Communism. We're still standing... and growing.

It's also true that the Turks and the British ruled vast parts of this land for long periods of time and we've lost a significant chunk of our civilizational territory. We allowed this to happen to us because we made one single but fatal mistake, and we made it repeatedly. We failed to understand that people who *only* fight defensive battles are destined to lose area. For a thousand years, until Shivaji Maharaj, we didn't fight a single offensive battle. I understand... that is our ethos. It still is. *I leave you alone, you leave me alone.* I get it, that's beautiful, but unfortunately our enemies never subscribed to this worldview and we had to fight and fight and fight, all the time protecting ourselves and our ways of living. But we never took the fight to the enemy's camp with the intention to end the menace once and for all. This one thing we need to rectify.

And Step 2. We need to come to a proper understanding of 'caste' from an anthropological perspective. The *Bharatiya* people are essentially a coalition of tribes. In modern times, the word tribe has come to exclusively mean hunter-gatherer forest dwellers, but in fact it refers to any group of people who follow the same rules and taboos and define their identity via these rules and taboos. Generally speaking, tribal people are those whose communal identity is stronger than their individual identity. Every *jaati*, sect and sub-sect in India functions as a tribe. If the Yanomami and Guarani in Brazil and Paraguay, the Navajo and Sioux in the USA, the Masai and Zulu in Kenya and South Africa, the Jarawa and Sentinelese in India do not inter-dine or inter-marry that is considered normal, but if the *Bharatiya jaatis* do the same, they are deemed as evil. Why? This international take-down of Bharat needs to be addressed honestly both externally and internally within our minds. Our *jaatis* are just as old as these tribes and deserve to be looked at using the correct anthropological lens. Unlike these other tribes though, our civilizational wisdom developed philosophies and stories to bridge our divides, communicate across differences and build socio-cultural mechanisms to help us work together and live as good neighbours. This is what makes us a coalition of tribes and not just a set of isolated groups. This is also what helped us, the world's largest civilizational group of people, make the smooth transition from the Neolithic to the Agricultural Age as one people.

The words tribe and tribal are not bad words. The words community and communal are also not bad words. These words have been given a bad name by Western modernists who are adherents of the cult of individualism. This cult of individualism is a brand-new mutation in human history and is made possible by the invention of extreme technologies that feed people the illusion that they can survive all by themselves. Such individuals tend to believe that relationships are *choices* to be made individually and that one should control how much influence family and friends have on our lives. *If we have our microwave, our fridge, our shopping malls, ATM cards and internet, we don't need anybody else!* is the thinking of the individualists. Take a breath and look at where this way of being has led America, the foremost practitioner of this lifestyle: depression,[6] school shootings,[7] the world's highest rates of incarceration,[8] spring-break culture,[9] pornography,[10] drug abuse,[11] broken families,[12] loneliness,[13] and wars without end,[14] all pointing to a society, all of three hundred years young, on its last legs. Runaway individualism and the wealth and technology to make it happen are not the right answers to life's questions. With all of its technological enlightenment, the USA needs a virtual army of doctors[15] and policemen[16] to simply manage the emotional ill effects of its chosen mode of being!

Humans are a communal species. For four million years, it is *tribalism* that has protected hominids and enabled us to thrive in virtually every ecological niche on the planet. We *need* community and strong wholesome relationships with other people—ideally family and extended family. This has been and continues to be the quintessential human experience. It is this and only this that allows us to feel connected in a horizontal and a vertical matrix that lends us our place in the world. Horizontally, we are connected to our brothers and sisters via commonly-held traditions. Vertically, we are connected with our parents and our children via traditions that we receive and pass on.

Tribalism and tradition are intimately linked. Without tribalism there would be no tradition, and without tradition we would not know who our brothers and sisters are and we would not know what to say to our children about who we are and where we come from (a deeply unsettling condition that many of us in the modern world are facing today).

'Caste' and Context

> Traditionalists weakened Hinduism by putting obstacles in the way of Buddha, Shankara, Shivaji, Baji Rao
>
> – *anonymous online comment*

It is important to note that if, after fighting for 1300 years, we are still *Bharatiya*, it is because there were traditionalists who did not compromise. If we had compromised with our traditions just in order to win or escape, then who would we be when we did win? Meenakshi Jain recounts in her 2019 book, *Flight of Deities and Rebirth of Temples*:

> (Aurangzeb's) decree (in Mathura, 1669) led to a mass migration of deities. Govindadeva's long journey from Vrindavan has been reconstructed by historians. Altogether eight temples were built as temporary abodes for the deity in flight, till it finally reached Jaipur and was instated in the ninth temple, where it remains under worship today.[7]

Imagine that.

Our traditions, and the rituals that manifest those traditions, are an essential part of redefining who we are with every generation. Without these, we do not know who we are as a people; we do not have anything valuable to pass on to our children. Above and beyond this, our traditions are the continuation of our people's commitment to all that is beautiful in life—that celebration of life, living, fertility and the cycles in nature that we are all part of. All *Bharatiya* traditions celebrate the cyclical nature of life. Some communities have exuberant celebrations, some are understated, and some are philosophical, but we, along with all the ancient cultures on the planet, are a cyclic and life-affirming culture, unlike the linear, death-centric Abrahamic religions or the linear, future-centric, technology-driven Western culture.

In Bharat, since ancient times, it has been the tribal system of *jaatis* that has been that vehicle for the protection and propagation of our traditions. By calling for a destruction of this vehicle (by wrongly defining it an undefined 'caste'), we are also calling for the destruction of all that it carries. Are we thinking deeply enough about this problem?

Even assuming that it is ok 'in this day and age', as the West has constantly been telling us, to discard 'caste', we would be doing ourselves a great disservice if we do not in all honesty recognize the *jaati* system for what it was and what it enabled for our civilization. I am looking objectively at the great system of organizing labour/culture developed by our ancestors.

Here is the Rev. Joseph Roberts speaking in 1844CE, in Madras. In an address to thirty-three missionary groups, he said:

> Caste is the great barrier in India betwixt the pagans and Christ... We think however that this wonderful institution of India, maybe traced to a more probable source...we are not convinced that all the tyrannical notions ascribed to this classification of men can be received as correct...and the constant provision for all kinds of artisans and labourers so that in every emergency there might be a supply of the required workmen to meet the various wants and needs of the realm. By fixing each person in a profession, there would be a greater perfection secured in the several works of art. The children not being allowed to adopt any other calling would naturally from the first dawning of thought associate themselves with their father's pursuit and try to emulate each other in gaining the greatest reward.[18]

Let that sink in. Let us acknowledge then that it was our system of *jaatis* that stood between us and conversion to alien death-centric faiths. We are all still *Bharatiya* today *because* of the *jaati* system. If, paradoxically, this system today is seen as the root cause for conversion that is because we have been schooled to see ourselves through the images painted by atrocity literature. We fail to see that our impoverishment, loss of pride, and the collapse of the delicate web of our community relations followed directly from the after-effects of the thousand-year war, the 60 percent tax, the coming of the Industrial Age, the enforced shutting down of our traditional schools and the take-over of the Commons by the British and then the Indian government over the past one hundred and seventy-five years. Additionally, the constant demonization of our civilization by the West that we have internalized has installed permanently in us the feeling that we need to be 'reformed'. We have been told to hate this thing called 'caste'. We do not know what the definition of that word is but all of us who have had a modern education automatically hate it, whatever it is.

Here is the British Superintendent, L. Middleton, in the 1921 Census:

> We pigeon-holed everyone by caste and if we had no true caste for them, labelled them with the hereditary occupation. We deplore the caste system and its effect on social and economic problems but we are largely responsible for the system we deplore... Government's passion for labels and pigeon-holes has led to a crystallization of the caste system, which except among the aristocratic castes was really very fluid under indigenous rule.[19]

Here is Swami Vivekananda speaking in Sri Lanka in 1897. He says:

> The older I grow, the better I seem to think of these castes and other such institutions. There was a time when I used to think that many of them were useless and worthless. But the older I grow the more I seem to feel a diffidence in cursing them because many of them are embodiments of experience over centuries and they facilitate in terms of development of these communities.[20]

The tribal *jaati* system was *not* a system designed for oppression but rather an *organic* system of economic and cultural arrangement that evolved to bind a multitude of tribal groupings together who would otherwise have remained isolated and materially weak like other tribes all over the world have been. Instead, from Neolithic times till the 18th century, our socio-economic coming together made us the richest and longest-lived civilization in human history. It is quite possible that in today's high-tech industrial world our tribal system of *jaatis* will automatically become obsolete. High technology allows us to multi-task in ways that were not possible in the earlier low-tech agricultural world, thereby rendering obsolete the need for strict divisions of labour. But we need to stop telling ourselves that the ancient system that kept our ancestors alive in agricultural and pre-agricultural times was evil. Petty politics and jockeying for power between groups are human traits. At times our inter-tribal skirmishes were ugly and groups could behave obnoxiously… but evil? I mean, let's at least use the right adjective.

In Bharat, our quarrels never led to genocide, slavery, ethnic cleansing, mass rapes and wars without end, all of that *really evil* stuff that Abrahamic religions and Western ideology suffer from and perpetrate upon the rest of us. Of all the civilizations that have existed, and despite its ugly warts, Bharat alone stands tall for its commitment to humanity and its recurrent acceptance of rectification from wise men and women within.

We are a shining light.

We need to remind ourselves that organization of labour has been a fact of anthropological evolution in *every single* agricultural civilization in the world—in Europe,[21] in China,[22] in Japan,[23] in Egypt,[24] everywhere. To simply keep referring to this as a *Bharatiya* phenomenon is dubious. Anyone who has ever lived in a low-tech agricultural world will instinctively understand the nature and need for organization of labour. A lot of time-consuming physical work has to be done *each day* in order to ensure the very survival of everyone in the community!

We can loosely assume that such an order existed in Bharat too, with a culturally organized labour force and birth-based allotment of responsibility that resulted in a lean and efficient transmission of skills and trade connections—but, unlike the terrible conditions that hierarchical Pyramid Consciousness created in Europe, we have known since the time of the composition of the *Purusha Sukta* that we are all ultimately one *Purusha*. And that *Purusha*-Consciousness imbued each and every one of us with the knowledge that it takes all parts for the whole to function and that the manifestation of that whole is our divine goal. I am not denying the presence of perversions but, by and large, the *Bharatiya* view has always been more unifying and subtle than the European view. This led to a very different kind of society. Here in Bharat, power was always recognized as being in the service of a greater end. The people held in highest regard (in a ritual sense) were people whose temporal freedoms were severely curtailed and led the most austere lives. On the other hand, the people who faced ritual limitations were the people who were allowed the most temporal freedoms and temporal wealth and power. It is important to recognize that *hierarchy* in a ritual sense did *not* correspond with *power* in the temporal sense, thereby turning today's social justice arguments on their head. Over vast periods of our history, from the time of the Nandas, kings have risen up from the so-called 'lower castes'. Because renunciation was held in high regard, our morality has always tended towards honesty and sharing, not deceit and accumulation. It was in Bharat that the great monarch Chandragupta gave up his kingdom and died as a wandering Jain monk in the jungles 2000 km away from his capital city. It was also in Bharat that Marco Polo observed:

> These are the best and most honourable merchants that can be found. No consideration whatsoever can induce them to speak an untruth, even though their lives should depend on it... this Brahmin undertakes the management of it (the foreigner's goods), disposes of the goods and renders a faithful account of the proceeds, attending scrupulously to the affairs of the stranger, and not demanding any recompense for his trouble.[25]

(Nicholas Dirks[26] contends that all *Bharatiya jaatis* were called *Brahmin* at one time because it represented their highest aspiration)

It is also in Bharat, till today (especially among the remarkably generous 'lower castes'), that no stranger is left standing at the door who is not offered water and who is not invited in for a meal regardless of what time of day it is.

Unfortunately, the psychology of victimhood that the social justice machinery has injected like a virus into our minds hides from us the entirety of our complex intertwined histories, our high ideals, our proud communities, and our long history of collaborative effort. In fact, it can be argued that the secular, Western rights-based discourse is directly opposed to our native duty-based discourse, and has prepared the ground for conversion to Abrahamic religions. This is more obvious if we look at the numbers of people converting to Christianity in modern India as opposed to earlier, when non-modern ideas held sway over our minds. The more modern we get, the less *Bharatiya* we become and the more likely we are to become some form of Muslim, Christian, Communist or Western lackey. We have to ask ourselves the question why, if they were so oppressed, the so-called 'lower castes' didn't convert in the 1700 years they were in touch with Christianity and the 1300 years they were in touch with Islam? There can only be one reason–pride. Pride in who they were, pride in how they contributed and pride in their culture and their imagination of the world. They were not a broken people. Aravindan Neelakandan's article in Swarajya[27] lays it all out while looking at one particular example—that of the *Devendra Kula Vellalars*.

A community becomes broken when its traditional role becomes obsolete. A traditional people who have lost their purpose and whose members are yet to modernize themselves as individuals are a lost people open to all sorts of predatory advances. The British did a great job destroying traditional community roles by taking over the Commons and shutting down our native schools (see Dharampal's *The Beautiful Tree*).[28] The secular Indian State does an even better job.

A hundred years before 1857, before the Criminal Tribes Act and before Sir Herbert Risley and his race-based caste census, here is Edmund Burke in the mid-1700s with a deep insight into our societal organization:

> For sometimes our (English) laws of religion differ from our laws of land, sometimes our laws of land differ from our laws of honour; but in that country (Bharat) the laws of religion, laws of land and laws of honour are all united and consolidated into one, and bind a man eternally to what is called his "caste".[29]

Though he uses the wrong word—'caste'—and does not define what he means by it, and though he exaggerates with the use of the word eternal with respect to 'caste', his intellect still locks into the real key to our society—the consolidation of religion, law and honour. That's not 'caste', but that does sound a lot like *Dharma*.

Beauty and Strength

> Israel, not India, is the most *Dharmic* nation because it emphasizes courage.
>
> – *anonymous online comment*

If tradition is connected to identity and our rituals are a celebration of life via the offering of beauty, then there is also a counterpoint needed to protect it all —*Strength*. To all reformists who fight orthodoxy and believe tradition to be a weakness, I have to point out that, while I agree that context is important and victory is important, *Beauty* too is important. To all orthodox people who fight change, I have to point out that, though I admire your commitment to keeping the fire burning, context is important and especially in Bharat, evolution in tradition via expert consensus is accepted and is sometimes essential. There can be no doubt that without Strength, Beauty will die. But there is also no doubt that without Beauty, Strength loses its purpose for being, thereby dying a metaphorical death. Both Beauty and Strength are symbiotic and essential for our continued survival as ourselves.

Israel, which our modern-day *kshatriyas* say is more *Dharmic* than Bharat, actually exhibits this split personality very well. Do our e-warriors know that there is a substantial chunk of Israel's population that is considered Orthodox[30] and is free to pursue tradition? They are not required to join the army or pay taxes. In fact, they are funded by all other parts of Israel's society in their traditional religious pursuits. Sounds familiar?

Here is Al-Biruni in 1030CE:

> There is always a *Brahman* in the houses of people who administers the affairs of religion and the works of piety... he lives from what he gathers on the earth or from the trees... it is preferable that he does not trade himself. The *Brahmans*

are not, like the other castes, bound to pay taxes and perform services to the king... He must always beat the drum before the fire and recite for it the prescribed holy texts.[31]

Why did Bharat survive when all the other pagan cultures slid into extinction? Bharat was unique among all the ancient pagan cultures in that we had perfected that delicate dance between the particular and the universal. Our traditions are particular—limited to each *jaati* and geography but our philosophies are universal, limited not by geography or *jaati*. To solve ticklish tribal problems, we count on our universalizing philosophies to unite us and to solve totalitarian problems; we count on our innumerable tribal groups to raise the flag of freedom. We have avoided both genocide (extreme particularism) and dictatorships (extreme universalism), for God knows how many millennia. We are not this *or* that. We are this *and* that.

Our particularism (the tribalism inherent in our system of *jaatis*) was the unconquerable bulwark against the Abrahamic armies. Put down one rebellion and another one starts; there was no end to the constant centripetal force among the infinite unique groups. There was never one power centre that could be crushed ensuring a final victory over Bharat. The Abrahamics could never get their heads around that. Paradoxically, it is today, when we are a 'free' country that the Abrahamics sense the possibility of victory more than at any other time in history. We have created a single monolithic political structure that has a clear path for control. Simultaneously, Western technologies (the internet, telephone, highways, railways etc.) are all universalizing technologies—they aid in bringing people closer and making the world smaller. The fewer the political centres, the more universalizing the technologies, the easier it is for the Abrahamics to take control. That's their speciality. From this point of view, it can be argued that *liberal* democracy is suicidal for *Bharatiya* civilization as we know it.

To counter the rising tide of Abrahamism in Bharat, we have two options before us:

Option 1

Assert our tribalness in a massive defensive manoeuvre. I don't think this option will have any takers at this point in history. But this is something we need to keep in mind. R.Jagganathan at Swarajya has alluded to something akin to this in his 2017 article – *Will Breaking Up Hinduism Into Its Parts Preserve It Better Than Trying To Keep It As One*,[32] but he was immediately silenced by the comments section.

OR

Option 2

Assert our civilizational unity in a massive offensive manoeuvre. This is something that our activists working on the ground sense instinctively. We need to push back against our rivals using their cultural weapons. Do what no *Bharatiya* had done for thousand years until Raghunathrao stood on the walls of Attock on 28th April 1758 and contemplated taking back Kabul—take the political fight to the enemy.

We will win, even our rivals know that.

It's only we who don't.

References and Links

1. https://en.wikipedia.org/wiki/Genocide_of_indigenous_peoples#Native_American_Genocide

2. https://en.wikipedia.org/wiki/Persecution_of_Hindus#Medieval_persecution_by_Muslim_rulers

3. https://www.amazon.in/Heroic-Hindu-Resistance-Muslim-Invaders/dp/8185990182

4. https://en.wikipedia.org/wiki/Battle_of_Delhi_(1737)

5. https://en.wikipedia.org/wiki/Battle_of_Nowshera

6. Lea Winerman, "By the numbers: Antidepressant use on the rise", *American Psychological Association*, 2017
https://www.apa.org/monitor/2017/11/numbers

7. https://en.wikipedia.org/wiki/List_of_school_shootings_in_the_United_States

8. https://en.wikipedia.org/wiki/Incarceration_in_the_United_States

9. https://www.imdb.com/title/tt6710214/reviews

10. Andrew Dugan, "More Americans Say Pornography Is Morally Acceptable", Gallup, 2018
https://news.gallup.com/poll/235280/americans-say-pornography-morally-acceptable.aspx

11. https://www.cdc.gov/nchs/fastats/drug-use-illegal.htm

12. https://www.cdc.gov/nchs/fastats/marriage-divorce.htm

13. Bradley J Fikes, "3 out of 4 Americans are lonely, UCSD study says", *The San Diego Union-Tribune*, 2018
https://www.sandiegouniontribune.com/business/biotech/sd-me-wisdom-reduces-loneliness-20181218-story.html

14. https://en.wikipedia.org/wiki/List_of_wars_involving_the_United_States

15. Wullianallur Raghupathi & Viju Raghupathi, "An Empirical Study of Chronic Diseases in the United States: A Visual Analytics Approach to Public Health", *National Library of Medicine*, 2018
https://www.ncbi.nlm.nih.gov/pmc/articles/PMC5876976/

16. German Lopez, "American police shoot and kill far more people than their peers in other countries", *Vox*, 2018
https://www.vox.com/identities/2016/8/13/17938170/us-police-shootings-gun-violence-homicides

17. Meenakshi Jain, *Flight of Deities and Rebirth of Temples*, Aryan Books, 2019

18. Rev. Joseph Roberts, *Caste, In Its Religious And Civil Character, Opposed To Christianity (f.p. 1847)*, Kessinger Publishing, 2010

19. L. Middleton, *Census of India*, 1921
https://archive.org/details/in.ernet.dli.2015.55999/page/n369?q=pigeon

20. Swami Vivekananda, *Lectures from Colombo to Almora* (f.p. 1897), Advaita Ashrama, 2010

21. https://en.wikipedia.org/wiki/Feudalism_in_England#Classic_English_feudalism

22. https://en.wikipedia.org/wiki/Fengjian

23. https://en.wikipedia.org/wiki/History_of_Japan#Social_conditions

24. http://www.ushistory.org/civ/3b.asp

25. Marco Polo, *The Travels of Marco Polo*, 13th Century CE (Translated by Komroff Manuel, 1928)

26. Nicholas Dirks, *Castes of Mind*, Princeton University Press, 2001

27. Aravindan Neelakandan, "The Importance of Being Dr. Krishnasamy", *Swarajya Mag*, 2019 https://swarajyamag.com/politics/the-importance-of-being-dr-krishnasamy-in-the-quest-for-a-puthiya-thamizhagam

28. Dharampal, *The Beautiful Tree*, 1983

29. Edmund Burke, *The Works of Edmund Burke – Volume 3*

30. https://en.wikipedia.org/wiki/Haredi_Judaism

31. Al Biruni, *Al-Biruni's INDIA*, 11th Century CE

32. R Jagannathan, "Will Breaking Up Hinduism Into Its Parts Preserve It Better Than Trying To Keep It As One", *Swarajya*, 2017 https://swarajyamag.com/culture/will-breaking-up-hinduism-into-its-parts-preserve-it-better-than-trying-to-keep-it-as-one

Section 2 | Chapter 2.3

NOT OPPRESSED
A Statement of *Shudra* Pride

Maragatham, 2020

There is hardly a village, great or small, throughout our territories, in which there is not at least one school, and in larger villages more.

– Dharampal, *The Beautiful Tree* (Quoting G.L. Prendergast, 1820)[1]

It has generally been assumed that the education of any kind in India…was mainly concerned with the higher and middle strata of society (the *Brahmins*, *Kshatriyas* and *Vaishyas*). However, as will be seen, the data of 1822-25 indicates more or less an opposite position… in the Tamil-speaking areas the twice-born (in schools) ranged between 13% in South Arcot to 23% in Madras… while the *Soodras* and the other castes (later to be labeled as SC) ranged from about 70% in Salem and Tinnevelly to over 84% in South Arcot.

– Dharampal, *The Beautiful Tree* (via British Collectors reports from the 1820s)[2]

It is true that the greater proportion of the teachers came from the *Kayasthas*, *Brahmins*, *Sadgop* and *Aguri* castes. Yet, quite a number came from 30 other caste groups also, and even the *Chandals* had 6 teachers. The elementary school students present an even greater variety, and it seems as if every caste group is represented in the student population, the *Brahmins* and the *Kayasthas* nowhere forming more than 40% of the total. In the two Bihar districts, together they formed no more than 15 to 16%. The more surprising figure is of 61 *Dom*, and 61 *Chandal* school students in the district of Burdwan, nearly equal to the number of *Vaidya* students, 126, in that district. (As per Adam) only 86 of the 'scholars belonging to 16 of the lowest castes' were in the (British) missionary schools, while 674 scholars from them were in the 'native schools'.

– Dharampal, *The Beautiful Tree* (via William Adams' Reports on Education in the 1830s)[3]

In most areas, the *Brahmin* scholars formed a very small proportion of those studying in schools. (In higher learning, especially the disciplines of

Theology, Metaphysics, Ethics, and Law, *Brahmins* formed the majority) But the disciplines of Astronomy and Medical Science seem to have been studied by scholars from a variety of backgrounds and castes. This is very evident from the Malabar data: out of 808 studying Astronomy, only 78 were *Brahmins*; and of the 194 studying Medicine, only 31 were *Brahmins*. Incidentally, in Rajahmundry, five of the scholars in the institution of higher learning were *Soodras*. According to other Madras Presidency surveys, of those practising Medicine and Surgery, it was found that such persons belonged to a variety of castes. Amongst them, the barbers, according to British medical men, were the best in Surgery.

– Dharampal, *The Beautiful Tree* (via Collectors reports, 1812 onwards & Madras Board of Revenue Proceedings, 1821-37) [4]

The greatest trick the devil ever pulled was convincing the world he didn't exist.

– Keyser Soze, *The Usual Suspects*, 1995 [5]

With their 'Aryan Invasion Theory' and their 'Caste System', the greatest trick the White Man ever pulled on us was convincing us that they knew more about us than we did ourselves.

Do not believe them and their agents when they say that our ancestors were oppressed. Do not believe them when they say that we are victims. Do not believe them when they say our ancestors were uneducated and that our culture was imposed upon us by supremacist "Aryan" outsiders.

Do not believe any of that.

We are the inheritors of the greatest civilizational heritage on the planet. Period.

Our ancestors exhibited a commitment to excellence that has not been surpassed by anyone anywhere in the world. Their chisel work continues to shape light and shadow at the magnificent *Brihadeeshvara* Temple a thousand years after they lived, loved and worked. I put my heart and soul into the buildings that I build, but nothing I do today can match the magnificence of the work of our ancestors.

Question #1 – Who told us that we were incapable?

Our ancestors were stewards of our natural resources—land, water and forests. Take great pride in the knowledge that they developed, in the over fifty thousand genetic variations of rice they helped evolve, in the ten thousand medicinal plant varieties and their healing properties that they recognized and utilized, in the incredible water harvesting systems that they developed, the most sophisticated in the world:

> The extent to which it (irrigation works) has been carried throughout all the irrigated region of the Madras Presidency is truly extraordinary. An imperfect record of the number of tanks in 14 districts (of the Madras Presidency) shows them to amount to no less than 43,000 in repair and 10,000 out of repair or 53,000 in all... These data, only assumed to give some definite idea of the extent of the system, would give close upon 30,000 miles of embankment (sufficient to put a girdle around the globe not less than 6 feet thick) and 300,000 separate masonry works. The whole of this gigantic machinery of irrigation is of purely native origin, as it is a fact that not one new tank has even been made by us.
>
> – Richard Baird Smith (British Engineer Officer), *The Cauvery, Kistnah and Godavery : being a report on the works constructed of these rivers for the irrigation of the provinces of Tanjore, Guntoor, Masulipatam and Rajahmundry in the presidency of Madras, 1856* [6]

Question #2 – Who told us that we were poor and incapable of excellence?

Know that it was our ancestors who were the world's best metallurgists, making the world's best steel, and exporting it throughout the ancient world. And we must not forget our foremost contribution to wealth creation in ancient Bharat: our weaving skills. Our ancestors wove the world's best cloth, made the finest muslin, and created the world's most diverse range of patterns and colour—all part of our incredible knowledge base:

> Something has to be said about the chemical excellence of cast iron in ancient India, and about the high industrial development of the *Gupta* times, when India was looked to, even by Imperial Rome, as the most skilled of the nations in such chemical industries as dyeing, tanning, soap-making, glass and cement...By the sixth century the Hindus were far ahead of Europe

in industrial chemistry; they were masters of calcinations, distillation, sublimation, steaming, fixation, the production of light without heat, the mixing of anaesthetic and soporific powders, and the preparation of metallic salts, compounds and alloys. The tempering of steel was brought in ancient India to a perfection unknown in Europe till our own times... the secret of manufacturing "Damascus" blades, for example, was taken by the Arabs from the Persians, and by the Persians from India..

– Will Durant, *The Story of Civilization*, 1954 [7]

...that there is not a year but it costs our State to furnish into India, 50,000,000 sesterces, (fifty millions of sesterces.) For which the Indians send back Merchandise (luxury goods including cloth, spices and jewellery), which at Rome is sold for a hundred times as much as it cost.

– Pliny the Elder, *Natural History*, 77CE [8]

Every nation that ever traded to the Indies has constantly carried bullion (gold and silver) and brought merchandise in return... Their climate demands and permits hardly anything that comes from ours. They go in a great measure naked; such clothes as they have the country itself furnishes; and their religion, which is deeply rooted, gives them an aversion for those things that serve for our nourishment. They want, therefore, nothing but our bullion to serve as a medium of value; and for this they give us merchandise in return, with which their frugality and the nature of the country furnish them in great abundance... and in every period of time those who traded with that country carried specie (gold and silver coins) thither and brought none in return.

– Baron de Montesquieu, *The Spirit of Laws*, 1748 [9]

Question #3 – What is there to be ashamed of? Who told us that our work was menial? At what point in history did this thought enter our minds?

...for whereas among other nations it is usual, in the contests of war, to ravage the soil and thus to reduce it to an uncultivated waste, among the Indians on the contrary, by whom husbandmen are regarded as a class that is sacred and inviolable, the tillers of the soil, even when battle is raging in their neighbourhood, are undisturbed by any sense of danger, for the combatants on either side in waging the conflict make carnage of each other but allow those engaged in husbandry to remain quite unmolested.

– Megasthenes, *Indika*, 3rd Century BCE [10]

> The fourth (out of seven) caste consists of the Artizans. Of these some are armourers, while others make implements which husbandsmen and others find useful in their different callings. This class is not only exempt from paying taxes but even receives maintenance from the royal exchequer.
>
> – Megasthenes, *Indika*, 3rd Century BCE [11]

The liberals and evangelists who suggest that we were oppressed for millennia are actually suggesting that our ancestors were either stupid or weak. It is clear that our ancestors were neither. They were capable, strong, productive, creative and respected the world over for their excellence.

Inequality was never an issue in ancient Bharat simply because it was excellence and austerity that were the highest aims. He who did the best and he who coveted the least were the most respected. It was to their support and to the support of the divine deities that watched over us for millennia, that our kings and petty chiefs were devoted and to whom their wealth was dedicated. Our temples, our festivals, our artisans, our *brahmanas*, our *sanyasis*, our poets, our philosophers, and the well-being of our agriculturalists, these were the objects of charity for the rulers and petty chiefs of yore. So many kings consciously humbled themselves and ruled on behalf of the primary deity of the kingdom, giving away their wealth to the temples which were the great centres for education, culture and social welfare.

Inequality becomes a problem, and conversely equality a virtue, only in societies where accumulation is the highest aim. This perverse way of being did eventually come to Bharat—and our ancient, indigenous world of ethics and honour was pulled from under our feet—bringing with it our current poverty, dependence, fallen pride, and the possibility of our mental colonization by forces inimical to us. You know what I'm talking about.

A hundred and twenty years from the murder of Kattabomman is all it took. Look at the five-step process chronologically:

1. The taking of our wealth (note the tax rates, comparable to current day Scandinavian rates):

    > Principle of Assessment (circa 1798). As to the method employed in assessing the lands when surveyed, it was assumed that the Government share was about half (50%) the produce for dry lands and three-fifth (60%) for wet land...

Making the necessary allowances, however... the actual shares were one-third (33%) for dry land and two-fifth(40%) for wet land.

– Baden Powell, *The Land Systems of British India Vol:3*, 1892 [12]

2. The closing down of our indigenous system of education:
    First, His Lordship in Council is of opinion that the great object of the British Government ought to be the promotion of European literature and science among the natives of India; and that all the funds appropriated for the purpose of education would be best employed on English education alone.

    – *English Education Act*, 1835 [13]

    An admirable survey of the indigenous system of education, carried out in 1835 and the following years by Mr. W. Adam, showed that a network of primitive vernacular schools existed throughout Bengal. But no attempt was made to develop these schools. Government preferred to devote its energies to secondary and higher schools, on the theory that if Western education were introduced to the upper classes it would "filter down" ... to the lower classes.

    – Michael E. Sandler, *Calcutta University Commission*, 1919 [14]

3. The taking of our land and the forced criminalization of our ancestors (for failing to pay taxes):
    An arrear of land revenue (inability to pay taxes) may be recovered by the following processes—

    ......

    (c) by distraint and sale of the defaulter's movable property under section 154;

    (d) by sale of the defaulter's immovable property under section 155;

    (e) by arrest and imprisonment of the defaulter under sections 157 and 158;

    (f) in the case of alienated holding consisting of entire villages, or shares of villages, by attachment of the said villages or shares of villages under sections 159 to 163. 150.

    – *Gujarat Land Revenue Code*, 1879 [15]

    Thus, the old class of occupancy ryots (farmers by custom who held proprietorship over land through customary usage), who were independent of the zemindar, must become extinct...Thus, the tendency of the legislation of 1859 is to reduce, in time, all ryots to the position of tenants-at-will, or tenants by permission of the zemindars; in other words... the entire population of Bengal, a country almost entirely agricultural, will in time consist of servants of government or become servants or dependents of zemindars

From the ryot's point of view the retrospect is still, more disheartening... Besides four millions sterling (nearly) of land revenue to the Government, the ryots pay above thirteen millions sterling, net income, to zemindars and middlemen; over and above that they pay all the expenses of management and of collection, and formidable amounts of law expenses for both sides, of arbitrary cesses and exactions and of interest to money-lenders. In exchange for these enormous payments they have a state of things in which the condition of their class, in at least one entire province is wretched, and over a large portion of the remainder of the Lower Provinces is bad. And who can estimate the further immense loss to ryots from the moral degradation which is an incident of their material condition?

– R.H. Hollingbery, *The Zemindary Settlement of Bengal*, 1879 [16]

4. The take-over of our Commons:

Extinction of Rights. Rights in respect of which no claim has been preferred under section 6, and of the existence of which no knowledge has been acquired by inquiry under section 7, shall be extinguished, unless before the notification under section 20 is published, the person claiming them satisfies the Forest Settlement Officer that he had sufficient cause for not preferring such claim within the period fixed under section 6.

– *The Indian Forest Act*, 1878 and 1927 [17]

Whenever water from any such river, stream, channel, tank or work, by direct flow or percolation, or by indirect flow, percolation or drainage from or through adjoining land, irrigates any land under cultivation... irrigates any land under cultivation, and in the opinion of the Revenue Officer empowered to charge water-cess, subject to the control of the Collector and the Board of Revenue...it shall be lawful for the [State] Government before the end of the revenue year...to levy on the land so irrigated a separate cess by way of land tax for such water] (hereinafter referred to as the water-cess)

– *Tamil Nadu Irrigation Cess Act*, 1865 [18]

5. Divide and Rule:
> I had intended pointing out that there is a very wide revolt against the classification of occupational castes; that these castes have been largely manufactured and almost entirely preserved as separate castes by the British Government...We deplore the caste system and its effect on social and economic problems, but we are largely responsible for the system we deplore.
>
> – L. Middleton, *Census Of India*, 1921 [19]

The culprits are clear, and yet today so many of us believe that our ancestors were oppressed and impoverished by our own brothers, that we were victims, that we have never done anything worthwhile and can only survive with governmental support. So many of us believe that the religion and beliefs of our ancestors are to be blamed for our current fate. Some have even bought the lie that our ancestors were defeated by invaders four thousand years ago, who impoverished us and forced their Gods upon us.

This hoax—the *Aryan* Invasion and the *Aryan-Dravidian* divide—is widely accepted by our people. Who are the people who first sold us these lies? Who told us that our history is not ours, that our heritage is someone else's? That even our Gods are someone else's! That the deeds, choices and faith of our ancestors are illegitimate? That they had been duped and an alien faith imposed upon them by people cleverer than them? That they performed all those heroic deeds under a false faith to false Gods? What an outrageous concept! If you don't know who you are, go ask your grandmother, don't consult an economic theory manufactured by a German taught to you in the language of our enslavers!! What madness to believe the words of the snake-oil salesmen of foreign origin over the experiences, deeds and faith of our own ancestors.

Let us unmask the original salesman then. Read his words carefully.

> The worship of *Subrahmaniya*, the second son of *Siva*, having been popular in Peninsular India, from an early period, the majority of the *Shanars* symbolize with the higher castes by attending the annual festival in his honour at Tiruchendoor, *Shasta* also, the *Hari-Hara putra* of the *Brahmans*, and rather a demon-king than a divinity, being guardian of boundaries and protector of paddy fields is worshipped to a considerable extent in his official missions...

> A streak of holy ash, the mark of *Sivism*, is the only trace of the influence of legitimate *Brahmanism* which one can see. Demonism in one shape or another may be said to rule over the *Shanars* with undisputed authority.[20]

So, here's his game. We all worship *Muruga*, we all worship *Aiyyapa*, but when we also worship our *kula devatas*, Bam! what's 'legitimate' in our religion is termed as *Brahmanism* while the rest of our religion is "Demonism"? What kind of mind would function this way? What kind of person?

Behold!

> The Hindus are not the only depraved people in the world; but it may be asserted with confidence that the extent and universal prevalence of their depravity are without a parallel. Where else shall we find such indelicacy of feeling, and systematic licentiousness? – the habitual use of such vile, obscene expressions? – such deliberate, placid, cruelty in the treatment of inferiors and brute animals? – the commission of such flagrant acts of oppression and wrong, as matters of course, where it is supposed the injured party is too weak to resist? – such intense, all-pervading, over-mastering covetousness? – such ingratitude, selfishness and perfidy? – such a preference of under-hand trickery to open opposition? – such cheating and pilfering in all mercantile dealings? Such bribery in all legal proceedings? – such fawning obsequiousness to the great, and such haughtiness to the little? But especially where shall we find such lying – such habitual lying – such audacious lying – such multiform life-long, universal lying, as we meet with in India?[21]

Now we're awake! This remarkable string of vomit from the pen of "Reverend" Robert Caldwell, foremost British 'expert' on Tamil culture, missionary and inventor of the *Aryan-Dravidian* divide, reveals more about the mind of the writer than the society he claims to describe. Every single accusation of his is obviously false to any *Bharatiya* person and any open-minded person who has travelled and lived in Bharat. This is one of the foremost colonial minds from which came the ideas of *Brahmanism* and *Dravidianism*. Now that we have seen his truth, can there be any more doubt about the unscrupulousness of his intentions and about the falsity of his theories?

Our Gods are our own, since the dawn of time, risen from the mud like ourselves— our *Vediappan*, our *Murugan*, our *Shivan*, our *Munishwaran*, our *Aiyannar*, our *Mariamman*, our *Perumal*, our *Aiyappan*, our *Kaliamman*, our *Puthuamman*, our

Nagathamman. You cannot tell me that my ancestor's chisel marks are not laid upon the magnificent rock sculptures at Mahabalipuram. You cannot tell me that his sweat and blood have not mingled with the granite at Palani. You cannot tell me that the bronze *Natarajas* of Thanjavur were cast under oppression, you cannot tell me that their other-worldly beauty is not a reflection of our ancestor's love, his faith and yes, his *gethu*.

Close your ears to the lies, the false history and fairy tale about millennia of oppression. Turn instead to catch the sounds wafting in the breeze... of chisel upon rock, of the bells on our bulls as they draw furrows upon the land, the rhythm of the handloom, the beat of our festival drums and of bicycle bells in the morning when our children ride out to school and the modern age. They speak the truth about who we are and our incomparable contribution to all life and living in this land.

There is only one question to ask ourselves: "Are we involved, in whatever small way, in the pursuit of excellence like our ancestors were?"

References and Links

1. Dharampal, *The Beautiful Tree*, 1983
   https://archive.org/details/TheBeautifulTree-Dharampal/page/n33/mode/2up
2. Ibid.
3. Ibid.
4. Ibid.
5. Keyser Soze, character in the 1995 film *Usual Suspects*
6. Richard Braid Smith, *The Cauvery, Kistnah, and Godavery, being a Report on the Works constructed on these Rivers for the Irrigation of the Provinces of Tanjore, Guntoor, Masulipatam, and Rajahmundry, in the Presidency of Madras*, 1856,
7. Will Durant, *The Story of Civilization*, 1935

https://archive.org/stream/TheStoryOfCivilizationcomplete/Durant_Will_-_The_story_of_civilization_1#page/n627/mode/2up/search/chemical+excellence+of+cast+iron+in+ancient+India

8. Pliny the Elder, *Natural History*, 77 CE
   https://archive.org/stream/plinysnaturalhiso2pliniala/plinysnaturalhiso2pliniala_djvu.txt

9. Montesquieu, *The Spirit of Laws*, 1689-1755
   https://archive.org/details/spiritoflaws01montuoft/page/n1

10. Megasthenes, *Indika*, 3rd Century BCE

11. Ibid.

12. Baden Powell, *The Land Systems of British India Vol:3*, 1892
    https://archive.org/details/in.ernet.dli.2015.180578/page/n51

13. English Education Act, 1835
    https://en.wikipedia.org/wiki/English_Education_Act_1835#The_Act

14. Michael E. Sandler, *Calcutta University Commission*, 1919
    https://archive.org/details/in.ernet.dli.2015.281301/page/n65

15. Gujarat Land Revenue Code, 1879
    https://revenuedepartment.gujarat.gov.in/downloads/act_BLRC_1879_n.pdf

16. R.H. Hollingbery, *The Zemindary Settlement of Bengal*, 1879
    https://archive.org/details/zemindarysettleoohollgoog/page/n3/mode/2up

17. The Indian Forest Act, 1878 and 1927
    http://nbaindia.org/uploaded/Biodiversityindia/Legal/3.%20Indian%20forest%20act.pdf

18. Tamil Nadu Irrigation Cess Act, 1865
    http://www.lawsofindia.org/pdf/tamil_nadu/1865/1865TN7.pdf (irrigation Cess Act)

19. L. Middleton, *Census of India*, 1921
    https://archive.org/details/in.ernet.dli.2015.55999/page/n369?q=pigeon

20. Robert Caldwell, *The Tinnevelly Shanars*, 1849
    https://archive.org/stream/TheTinnevellyShanars_201809/the%20tinnevelly%20shanars_djvu.txt

21. Ibid.

Section 2 | Chapter 2.4

DRAWING THE LINE
A Comprehensive Rehabilitation of "Caste" in *Bharatiya* Imagination

Maragatham 2021

Exhibit 1:

To this day they remain true to their ancient laws – the moral, ecological and spiritual dictates of the *Serankua* and the Great Mother – and are still led and inspired by a ritual priesthood of *mamos*. They believe and acknowledge explicitly that they are the guardians of the world... their religious training is intense. The young acolytes are taken from their families at a young age, and sequestered in a shadowy world... inside the men's temple for eighteen years... They are enculturated into the realm of the sacred as they learn that their rituals and prayers alone maintain the cosmic and ecological balance of the world...The message is clear: It (the world) is theirs to protect.

– Wade Davis, *Sacred Geography*, 2009 [1]

Exhibit 2:

There is no notion of linear progression, no goal of improvement, no idealization of the possibility of change. To the contrary, the entire logos of the *Dreamtime* is stasis, constancy, balance and consistency. The entire purpose of humanity is not to improve anything. It is to engage in the ritual and ceremonial activities deemed essential for the maintenance of the world precisely as it was at the moment of creation...To violate a law of the Dreaming is a transgression not limited to the moment, but rather one that reverberates through all dimensions, through the eternal past and the limitless future.

– Wade Davis, *Sacred Geography*, 2009 [2]

Exhibit 3:

They have a complex understanding of astronomy, solar calendars, intense notions of hierarchy and specialization. Their wealth is vested in ritual regalia as elegant as that of a medieval court. Their systems of exchange, infinitely more complex, facilitate peace and not war. Their struggle to bring order to the Universe, to maintain the energetic flows of life, and the specificity of their beliefs and adaptations, leaves open the very remarkable possibility that the *Barasana* are the survivors of a world that once existed...

– Wade Davis, *People of the Anaconda*, 2009 [3]

Two things jump out at me. One, the remarkable similarities between aspects of Hinduism and these cultures that Wade is describing; and two, the loving respect with which this Western anthropologist treats these cultures in direct opposition to the intellectual and aesthetic crusade that the West has launched upon Hinduism for the past three hundred years.

It's time to state openly what many of us suspect privately—the compassion of the West is only reserved for those natural religions and cultures that are dead or dying, and they will continue to train all the guns at their disposal at us in order to bring our religion and civilization to the same pitiable state. To help them accomplish this, they have enlisted the support of liberal education, law, and media. In our nation, every year, more of us are taught to hate our ancestors, either for their supposed cruelty or for their supposed weakness and, above all, for their 'backwardness'.

This essay aims to shine a light on this ancient place where only darkness currently reigns.

The word 'tribe' refers to a group of people who prioritize their group identity over their individual identities. This is not to be confused with the same term that is often used solely to describe hunter-gatherers or forest dwellers (who are also tribal). One can be tribal even living in a city.

I've used the words 'tribe', *'jaati'* and 'community' interchangeably. This is as it should be. Sometimes one of these words may appear as a sub-set of another, but that is just splitting hairs. For our purposes and for a true and empathetic understanding of Hindu society, these words are indeed interchangeable. Let no Western anthropologist tell us otherwise.

In the common but undefined daily usage, I am assuming, for the purposes of this essay, that the word 'caste' is equal to *jaati* and the term caste system is the *varna vyavastha* as applied to communities (and not individuals).

Part I
The Intellectual Landscape

Words

'Caste' is the flaming tyre they have thrown around our necks, and under its weight our heads have hung in shame for two hundred years. No matter that the worst case of caste-based ugliness was nothing compared to the life-long ugliness of their religions—supremacy, slavery, genocide, Holocaust, and world domination through ethnocide.

The World is Not Enough

All four ideological religions—Christianity, Islam, Liberalism and Communism—are, at their root, supremacist and violently expansionist. They insist that they will force their vision upon every human on the planet by all means at their disposal. This agenda of world domination was pursued openly by Abrahamic supremacists when they perpetrated the genocide and slavery of the indigenous peoples of Europe, Arabia, North Africa, Persia, America, Australia, Siberia, Sub-Saharan Africa and Bharat, until sometime, perhaps three centuries ago, Christians were moved to cover up their utter depravity with phrases such as "the White Man's burden" and "bringing civilization to the world". This enduring cruelty, that brought death and impoverishment to hundreds of millions, finally came to an end on the wings of the global cataclysm that was Nazi-ism, imposed upon literally the entire human race, under the Christian banner of the *hakenkreuz*.[4] Simultaneously, an even more perverse off-shoot of Protestant thought,[5] Communism, had infected large parts of the globe and, by the end of the 20th Century, had become the single largest killer of ordinary people in human history—one hundred million by some estimates. Cortes and Hitler were chicken-feed.

Most important for the brainwashed Hindu to note is that all of this killing was done in the name of God, Liberty, Enlightenment and Equality and it's time we looked beyond these feel-good words into the heart of the cultures that use them so cynically. These depravities have been normalized by Western academics and their lackeys as an inevitable part of 'progress'. So much so that most of us look upon this history of violence and see nothing unusual in it at all! We just ignore it. The similar scale of violence perpetrated upon Hindu Bharat by political Islam from the 8th Century all the way till Aurangzeb and Tipu Sultan is invisible-ized by the self-same intellectuals. May curses rain down upon their heads.

Awaken

If we are true to the Hindu spirit, complaining about injustice is not in our cultural DNA. We move on. But this time we don't simply move on... we do so with our eyes wide open.

1. We recognize the true natures of the four major *adharmic* world-dominating ideologies. They want us dead, defeated or converted.
2. We build physical and intellectual strength to adequately defend ourselves against them and expand *Dharma* into their lands.
3. We banish shame from our minds.
4. We strengthen the bridges of mutual respect and understanding between our communities.

Internalize this: nothing ugly that happened in Bharat can compare to the ugliness, demonic cruelty and depravity of what the forces of *adharma* have perpetrated upon the world. Allow no Abrahamist, Liberal or Communist to point fingers at us. Period. Simply cancel whatever they say about us. We will no longer allow ourselves to be accused of crimes by the foremost criminals of the world. Read *Bharatiya* history, critique Western anthropology, media, economics and psychology. For many of us who have been brainwashed at school and by their media into accepting a Christian framework of good and evil, we start our debriefing now.

As an important first step, start using the words *Dharmic* and *Adharmic* instead of the Christian good and evil, and observe as entire moralities shift. Start today. Change your *darshana*.

It's a hard pill to swallow but, as I've tried to demonstrate in Chapters 1.1 and 1.3 of this book, it's time we accept that Liberty, Equality and Fraternity are not the great ideals we have been taught to believe they are. They are tools for control over ordinary humans by the Western global structure and by morally bankrupt corporations.

In lived reality, the 'Follow Your Dream' school of Liberty is nothing but the stepping stone to moral bankruptcy, pornography, broken families, drug abuse, laziness, selfishness, self-indulgence and narcissism of all kinds.

In lived reality, the "I'm Special, I Deserve whatever the Hell I Want" school of Equality is nothing but the stepping stone to disorder, familial discord, depression, revolution, violence, anti-civilizational weakness, and just plain stupidity.

Every person and community that has stood for something—anything ancestral, anything free, anything self-sufficient, ancient, real and beautiful—has been seen as an obstacle to their goal of world political domination. Take the Native Americans, the Aborigines of Australia, the Hindus of Bharat, the tribes of Africa and South-East Asia, the Pagans of Europe—most have been wiped off the face of the Earth, either physically or spiritually. We, the oldest and noblest, still stand.

Make it count. We owe it to every one of our ancestors who kept the flame burning, who spilt blood... whose sweat inspired.

Part II
A Road Runs Through It

Ideas

I've said this before and I'll say it again. People don't actually seek Liberty, they seek Purpose; People don't actually seek Equality, they seek Respect.

If the Hindu nation has failed in giving its people purpose and respect over the past two centuries, then we are at fault. We have no one to blame but ourselves. If we have bought, lock, stock and barrel, the stories that white people have told us about ourselves, we are at fault. Our public intellectuals have betrayed us and our religious leaders have turned inward.

Purpose and Respect

It was *this* that the so-called 'caste system' established in Bharat over millennia on a grand and spiritual plane. It led to Bharat's wealth, its excellence, its beauty, its diversity and its unity. It may be hard to imagine today with so many 'casteless society' narratives being spun from the silken webs of intellectual spiders, but it is true.

The ancient world was, and much of the contemporary world continues to be, Nature-centric (whether agricultural, nomadic or forest-dwelling). The limits of geography and the sheer hard physicality of a Nature-centric life leads automatically to the idea of limits—geographic particularity, tribalness, local cuisines, language diversity, economics of sustainability, Nature-connected spirituality and localized cultural practices. These are all the hallmarks of indigeneity—the idea that 'we *belong* here'. The very same limits also lead indigenous societies to be entropic in nature; they tend to fall apart into small sustainable groups that draw cultural lines around themselves. For example, the Sentinelese and the Jarawa have lived next door to each other for millennia but they do not cohabit/copulate/eat together, neither do the Zulu, the Xhosa and the Sotho. The question to ask is, are these tribes being casteist? Obviously not. But then why not? Aren't these the very traits that have been labelled as 'casteist' and strung like a garland of thorns around the memories of our ancestors?

We can see now that these basic facets of all tribal life *everywhere* on the planet are not special to Bharat. Our ancestors were not specially depraved and inhumane when they were being 'casteist'; they were merely being naturally tribal and their tribalness was a natural function of their indigeneity.[6] It was only after the invention of the first geography-erasing technologies, the telegraph and the radio, that the global consensus on morality started shifting from the legitimacy of cultural diversity informed by indigeneity towards the Western template for '*universal*' ideals with 'rights' based on those ideals. The more universal our technologies grew, the more the expectations around universal ideals spread. As Hindus, we should know then that there is nothing *innately* morally superior about these Western ideals.

Let us also be aware that our ancestral tribes were no ordinary tribes. Our *jaatis*, over millennia, learned to collaborate and come together to build the wonder that was ancient Bharat. A coalition of tribes such as this land produced has not been seen anywhere else in the world. It is the sole reason why we are still here while the pagans of Europe are in *Valhalla* and it is the sole reason why our rivals still hate us. That we could come together in diversity while they could only do so through erasure irks them no end. Hindu society is a daily reminder of their moral failure. The deep compassion of Hindu civilization recognizes the human yearning for tribalness as a natural fact of life, something that may need stewarding and direction but not erasure. It is this 'caste system' that has been our socioeconomic skeleton since time immemorial. They have been hacking and hacking away at it for the past two centuries and still it stands, fractured but proud.

The necessary condition for bringing tribes together is economic, but the sufficient condition needed to *keep* them together is philosophical/spiritual. This miracle was achieved only in Bharat. It was this 'caste system' that brought the tribes of Bharat together for millennia in shared economic and spiritual harmony. This in fact is the true nature and purpose of the inspired idea of *varna*. It is the mechanism by which the innumerable *jaatis* were organized into the manifest *Purusha*. That we are all part of one divine body is an amazing metaphor for existence. For people to think that the feet of the cosmic *Purusha* are in any way inferior to the arms or head or torso is pettiness. It is in fact an honour to live and work knowing that the entire structure of *Dharma* rests upon one's strength. Without *Shudra* ingenuity, there would be no *Vysya* wealth. Without *Vysya* wealth, there would be no *Kshatriya* strength. Without *Kshatriya* strength, there would be no *Brahmin* dispassion. Without *Brahmin* dispassion, there would be no Hinduism at all today for all of us to claim. This idea or *Purusha-Consciousness*, when fully internalized in society, results in the flowering of the values of mutual respect and gratitude. We had this in our society for a very long time until our current fall.

Yes, when we have failed in maintaining this basic etiquette we have been at fault. But disrespect and ungratefulness are not genocide. They are not slave-driving. They are not ethnocide. These *are not* and *should not* be cause for shame; these are mere blips that need correction in the ocean of amazement that is our civilization. Do the Christians and Muslims constantly apologize for slavery, genocide, aboriginal poisonings, re-education camps, rapes and ethnocide? Do they feel shame, the shame that we are taught to feel about 'caste'? Why not? Do you oppress anyone? Have you seen your parents oppress someone? No?...How about your grandparents then? No?? Then where does the oppression narrative come from? Newspaper clippings? Where does the oppressed narrative come from? Textbooks? Who writes newspaper articles and textbooks in India?

The ongoing discussions in 'conservative' circles around whether or not *varna* needs to be birth-based or *guna*-based is a coping mechanism, an attempt to force fit Hindu history into what would be acceptable to our colonized liberal minds. Much better to look at things through an anthropological lens—Varna was and will be birth-based as long as communities exist that feel their tribalism is useful to them (mostly rural Somewhere-People[7]) and it will be *guna*-based for all people who have shed their tribal identities in favour of individualism (mostly urban Anywhere-People[8]). Neither is right or wrong, each is just a state of being. But it is important for youth of today who extol the virtues of individualism over tribalism to know that our *varna* identities are not a marker of our privileges but of our responsibilities. And that changes, entirely, the way in which we examine the question of *varna* in the modern world. Before coming to any conclusions though, we need to contemplate upon the true nature of human society, our innate need for community, and what the consequences are for societies that adopt wholesale the failing Western cultural trope of individualism. Here in Bharat, we must figure out how to come to a reasonable balance between these two pulls. It is important that our individualisms do not destroy our tribalisms as has happened in the atomized West, just as it is important that our tribalisms do not suffocate our individualisms as has happened in many parts of violence-ridden Africa. These two opposing pulls have to continue to work in tandem, informing each other, as they always have. There will be a natural ebb and a flow between them. Balance. How each of us performs our *kula*-based cultural and/or occupational duties and balances that with our need for a separate self-expression is up to each one of us. In addition, a greater pan-Hindu tribalism (called *Hindutva*) is being constructed at the political level and that too will occupy some part of our identities. Keeping all these parts alive within oneself is not hard, it just requires discipline and open-heartedness.

Free-for-all, one-size-fits-all, Western-style liberalism... these are not the solutions to our identity-crises; these attitudes will not lead to our preservation.

Part III
Road Bumps and Potholes

The systematic attempts to erase 'caste' being made at all levels of Indian society today will go down as one of the most egregious acts of state-supported ethnocide in human history on a par with the Cultural Revolution of Mao. Along with cultural extinction, many communities will likely also face physical extinction as history has shown. The fomenting of nation-wide self-hate is the hallmark of a still deeply colonized slave State.

By all means let us address in all honesty the problems associated with 'caste' and our ancient tribal taboos, but let us do it our way. If our genius solution to these problems is Western-style total erasure then please note that, when we take down this skeleton of caste, the entire Hindu edifice will fall. The Christians and Liberals see this and know this, and that is why they have been targeting 'caste' since the day they set foot on this land. They know much better than us that once 'caste' is gone, once a majority of Hindus themselves believe that 'caste' is bad, Hinduism would be finished. We, on the inside, who hate 'caste' are merely hastening our own demise, much to the glee of our rivals. Here is the Rev. Joseph Roberts speaking in 1844 CE, Madras. In an address to thirty-three missionary groups, he says, "Caste is the great barrier in India betwixt the pagans and Christ..."⁹

Christianity had 1650 years and Islam 1300 years to touch the hearts of the so-called oppressed populations of Bharat. Ask why our ancestors did not join these cults all these long and difficult centuries, many even welcoming death and impoverishment in place of conversion. This is no joke. All of Persia, the twin civilization of Bharat, five thousand years old, nemesis of the Greeks, epitome of culture, converted to Islam in all of thirty years. Thirty.

For those of us who still cling to the twin DNA strands of "I hate myself because I am an oppressor" and "I hate myself because I have been oppressed" it's time we shed the oppressor-oppressed binary that has taken a hold of our minds. There is no such thing, it is a fiction, an intellectual Trojan horse. Know this now—'caste' is not the problem. If at all there is a problem between 'castes', it lies in the fact that we have internalized a foreign point of view. The true *Bharatiya* solution to any *Bharatiya* issue is the building of bridges between communities using the bricks and mortar of *Bhakti* and *Vedanta*[10] under the guidance of religious leaders and realized souls. We in modern India are yet to design the necessary institutions that would carry out this all-important civilizational task.

Walking Out of the Shadow of Ancient Taboos.

Every tribal society has had taboos, from the South-Sea islanders where the word originated to the tribes of the Brazilian rainforests. Our *jaatis* were no exception. Many taboos had ritualistic consequences and some had social consequences. Specifically, taboos around cows, death and dirt led to some *Bharatiya* communities having to live and eat separately. This is a fact. It is also a fact that these communities have their own temples, deities, traditions and family lives. They were never denied access to education or work.[11] They were landowners, their families were never broken apart, their spirituality was never stamped on. Even today, in the spiritual wasteland of Pakistan, these communities continue to light the lamp of *Dharma* long after the lamps of other communities have run out of oil. Why? Because *our religion is ours to claim* regardless of our *jaati*. I would much rather have Hindus fight over who is *more* Hindu rather than the self-hate fuelled fights of who is *not* Hindu that currently light up our streets.

The phenomenon of endogamous tribes living and eating separately was so widespread in the ancient world that not one observer of *Bharatiya* society from Megasthenes to Domingo Paes thought it fit to judge. It was not until the violence-ridden Equality principle became so widespread in global moral consciousness that common facts of tribal life began to be seen as 'social evils'. The equation of 'caste' with 'oppression' over the past two hundred years is a direct result of the application of Liberal Individualist morality (liberty, equality and fraternity) in the service of the demonization and subsequent destruction of ancient tribal arrangements, a worthy successor to the pagan-annihilation of yester-year. The question that *Bharatiyas* have to ask is this: "If individualists would not like to be held to tribal moral standards, then how is it fair that our *jaatis* are held to the moral standards of individualists?"

Unfortunately, today, for whatever reason, we are all under the influence of these foreign memes in varying degrees. It becomes imperative, for the sake of its children, that Hindu society builds the right narrative around its social history and provides the right framework for its evolution. For the sake of *Dharmic* communities who have lived under the shadow of taboos it becomes important to answer three questions:

1. Did this discrimination historically amount to oppression? No (though there were cases of oppression as are to be found in every power structure).
2. Did attitudes of inferiority and superiority coalesce around these taboos in the last two centuries? Yes.
3. Do these taboos continue to be relevant in the modern world? No.

The failure of ancient *Bharatiya* society to build a rehabilitation mechanism for people who no longer wanted to do taboo work is (in my opinion) understandable from a tribal perspective, but simultaneously represents a failure to live up to our highest ideals. Modern India has an opportunity to build those mechanisms now but our continued falling back upon the White Man's oppression template in our attempts at rehabilitation have not led to reconciliation but rather to nation-wide self-hate.

The path to mutual respect has been lit from time immemorial for us by our kings and saints, from Raja Ranti Deva to Ramnujacharya. It's time Hindu society, both rural and urban, took their messages consciously to heart. With the growing availability of modern medicine, septic tanks, electric crematoriums and mechanical waste disposal systems, along with waste treatment and recycling consciousness spreading among the entire population, the reasons for, and the foundations of, these taboos have fallen away. These three ancient taboos must go. The economics of cow protection and stewarding have to be permanently solved by the Indian State and all other taboo work needs to be re-imagined and traditional practitioners celebrated like other communities are. Ancestors from these communities have helped grow our food, build our temples, fight our wars, maintain our crafts, take care of our animals, steward our natural resources, and build our houses, apart from performing their *jaati* duties in everyday village life. *Dharmic* communities living under the shadow of these taboos must be culturally rehabilitated and this started with the temple entry movement. It is clear and moral, from a modern perspective, that work that nobody wants to do should be done by everyone or by machines. Having said this, it is also important to say that it is not clear, from historical readings, that communities who did taboo work were actually unhappy doing taboo work or if they merely saw it as having chosen an economic niche with which came certain material privileges and certain ritual restrictions (see the Epilogue of this book for some relevant references).

Sanatana Dharma is *not* a system of coercion, but it does have, as part of its ethos, a code of assuming responsibility. The problem with present-day reform is that it has bypassed, and continues to bypass, the idea of responsibility altogether.

Conservatism

Traditions are practices passed on from parent to child over multiple generations, ideally all the way back from where memory disappears into the mists of time. Individuals don't have traditions, they have habits. Only tribes have traditions. Traditions connect people backwards in time with their ancestors, forward in time with their descendants, and sideways across geography with their community. In other words, traditions hold us in place. Culture can loosely be described as a collection of traditions over multiple verticals. People who are anti-tradition are necessarily anti-culture. 'Conservatives' who bat for individualism over tribalism and 'progress' over culture are by definition anti-tradition and anti-culture. They can be described as individualists or progressives but certainly not as 'conservatives'. Which leads us to conclude that the majority of people who are anti-tradition/tribe/culture in India today but ironically self-identify as 'conservatives' are hypocrites. This is definitional; even Jordan Peterson cannot bullshit his way out of this.

The exceptional have always charted their own paths (Shivaji Maharaj, Mira Bai, Nandanaar, Sant Ravidas, Rani Lakshmi Bai all broke with established norms) but the *system* is meant to take care of the rest of us ordinary folk. What was different about ancient Bharat was that our ancestral system *itself* was exceptional. It called upon each one of our ancestors to do their duty, to sacrifice their *vaasanas* and step up towards nobility; whether we are talking of Maharana Pratap, Adi Shankara, or the un-named *Vishwakarma, Vanniyar* and *Paraiyar* builders of the *Chidambaram* temple, these are all people who stayed within the system and rose to excellence. One does not have to be exceptional if one can be excellent. The *varna vyavastha* laid the foundations for population-wide excellence knowing full well that exceptionalism would take care of itself.

I am not arguing for a return to what was—that would be impossible given the forces of global culture and military dangers that we face—but I *am* arguing for a pride-filled understanding of our ancestors' lives and a conscious evolution into a society that would better represent them and, thereby, us. A people denied access to their past will not be able to define a future for themselves.

Our traditional *jaatis* were part of an agricultural world. As more Indians move from that world to the industrial world, their occupations will change. They will lose their connections to their ancestral work and their ancestral rituals will become meaningless to them. This much is true. How each of us chooses to deal with this loss is up to each one of us. Ideally, we should engage in community-wide discussions with our elders and community leaders to determine which parts of our ancestral heritage we would like to consider core and carry on unchanged, which parts we would like to re-imagine, and which parts we would like to discard. Each community can then move on, fully cognizant and respectful of the past while holding close a conscious set of cultural standards for the industrial age.

Unfortunately, the vast majority of people will go through the liberal education factory and end up deracinated and unconnected to their ancestral ways. No *kula devata* for them, no moon-cycle world view, no *upaasana*, just some odds and ends stuck together performing the role of an anchoring system—isolated islands of Hindu ritual unconnected to either space or time, free-floating in the ocean of Liberalism. It is this societal vacuum that new-age *gurus* fill.

Sure, let us acknowledge the inevitability of the emergence of the 'caste'-free modern Indian. But why are we cheering it on as if it is a moral good? Why does it receive State support? Why do those who leave their tribes and become individualists or liberals hate where they've come from? Why do they behave like fresh converts? Why is erasure considered a better solution than pride-building?

It is apparent that the daily acceleration of assaults on ancient practices, consists of mere virtue signalling by people who do not really care about the practices themselves. These assaults are a résumé that they use to get ahead in the non-Hindu Liberal world. Why not instead work towards pride-building of all communities? How many people are working to build pride-filled narratives for the blacksmith communities, the carpenter communities, the stone sculptor communities, the agricultural communities, the weaving communities, the spirit of *kshatra*? None. While Europe and Japan maintain their ancient practices[12] and craft guilds, we are busy disembowelling every single tradition that embodied beauty and brought fame and wealth to our land. The whole 'right-wing', 'conservative' movement in India is a hoax that a colonized people have pulled on themselves. The only difference between the 'right-wing' and the 'left-wing' in India is that the 'right-wing' is nationalistic while the "left-wing" is openly disintegrative. *Culturally*, though, there is very difference.

Why must we succumb to these Western 'wings'? Can our evolution into modernity not be consciously curated? All it requires is:

a. the development of the *Bharatiya* Grand Narrative
b. the building of modern institutions that are dedicated to the conservation and propagation of traditional knowledge
c. the adoption of laws that will protect the rights of truly traditional people and institutions to go on doing what they do best

The rest of us have the rest of the world anyway... don't we?

Answer this one question – "What do *Bharatiya* Conservatives want to *conserve*?"

Do 'conservative' anti-caste warriors know that the Hindu traditions they sometimes extol have been kept alive for millennia by our *jaatis*? Do our *jaatis* not deserve our praise and recognition for this heroic act instead of the censure we heap upon them? It is the tribalism of our *jaatis* that is strong on conservatism, identity and pride and therefore continuity and tradition. When the pride of *jaatis* has been killed, when the idea of *jaati* itself is derided and outlawed by the liberal law-making machine,[13] when 'inter-caste' marriage is subsidized by the State[14] with an eye on 'caste erasure', then true conservatives have to ask "what is the vehicle that will keep Hindu traditions alive in the modern world?" Are the anti-caste 'conservatives' spending any brain-time on trying to design a new tribalism or even new laws that will protect ritualism, knowledge transfer and encourage cultural continuity, or are they happy cheering for high technology and individualism like their American counterparts?

What will we teach our children about ourselves?

Who are we?

Part IV
A Map

Caste in a New Light

In an older essay, I ruminated, "Why did *Bharatiya* cultures survive when all the other pagan cultures slid into extinction? *Bharatiya* civilization was unique among all the ancient cultures in that it had worked out the terms for a coalition—a delicate dance between the particular and the universal. Our traditions are particular, limited to each *jaati* and geography, but our philosophies are universal, limited not by geography or *jaati*. To solve ticklish tribal problems, we count on our universalizing philosophies to unite us and to solve totalitarian problems, we count on our innumerable tribal groups to raise the flag of freedom. We have avoided both genocide (extreme particularism) and dictatorships (extreme universalism), for Gods know how many millennia that we've been around. We are not this **or** that. We are this **and** that."

Unlike other civilizations, Hindu civilization did not aim to erase the past. It did not erase old Gods, it did not erase ancient loyalties, it did not erase ancient tribalisms; it instead created a series of meta ideas that built bridges of understanding—*Varna, Karma, Purusha, Guna, Dharma, Purana*...

The coming, or should I say the coalescing, of Hinduism in Bharat or anywhere else in the world does not come with violence and uprooting and destruction. It comes as a flowering. It does not erase, it embellishes. It does not degrade, it ennobles. Look at the way Sanskrit and Tamil came together as two sides of *Ishvara's damaroo*, coexisting and embellishing each other for millennia until Caldwell. If we do not have a deep sense of this, we will not be able to see our civilization for all its subtlety, complexity and beauty. Apply the crude yardsticks of Western dichotomy and all you will get is a crude reflection of those yardsticks. This applies to all of us schooled in the English medium when we introspect about our religion as well as to the openly antagonistic academicians of the Wendy Doniger school.[15]

So, who are we Hindus?

Here is a working *anthropological* description of Hindu civilization as I know it in all its diversity.

(Knowledgeable readers feel free to add to this. Note that this is *not* a *Dharmic* definition.)

> We are a **coalition** of ancient **tribes** woven together by the strands of **mutual respect** spun from the spindle of a **philosophical religion** over a period of ten millennia or more in this, our *Dev Bhumi*, Bharat.

While we as individuals may identify with only one or a few aspects of this description, it is important for a true Hindu nation to recognize all these four pillars and work respectfully towards their strengthening:

> **Pillar #1: Tribe** (*Jaati-Vyavastha, Kula Devatas*, Occupational Guilds, Ancestral Knowledge).
>
> **Pillar #2: Coalition and Mutual Respect** (*Varna Vyavastha, Sampradayas, Mathas, Gurus*, Institutions that would work towards building mutual respect, conflict resolution, the national grand narrative and *Dharma* expansion).
>
> **Pillar #3: Religion** (*Dharmic* Law, Civilizational Hinduism, Temples, Rituals, Nation-wide Festivals, *Bhakti*).
>
> **Pillar #4: Metaphysics** (*Mimamsa, Tantra, Yoga, Vedanta*, Enquiry, all other philosophical schools).

Hinduism extends from the Earth to the Sky, from the earthy to the lofty, from the so-called animism to the most sophisticated philosophical understandings of the human place on *Bhu Devi*—from Life to Meaning. All of it is us. Allow no Westernized 'anthropologist' to draw non-existent lines separating these four aspects of us and call each as either 'non-Hindu' or 'oppression'.

I pray to *Ishvara* in the big temple at Thanjavur just as easily as I pray to *Vediappan* under the neem tree in my rice fields. I am involved in *civilizational homas* designed by the *rishis* of the Bharata tribe of modern-day Haryana just as easily as I participate in *local* spirit possessions by the female energy, *Puttruamman*, residing in the termite hill down the road from my house in rural Tamil Nadu. The Western-minded will never understand that we are not this *or* that, we are this *and* that.

Unlike every other civilization, Hinduism is both bottom-up and top-down. The place where the bottom-up meets the top-down is the bridge between our local tribalisms (our falling apart) and our national civilization (our coming together). This bridge that our ancestors forged is the most definitive feature of Hinduism. It is represented by our *jaatis* willingly coming together under the banner of *varna* in the hoary past; it is represented by our *rishis* willingly retreating from the sphere of pure thought and engaging in a down-to-earth manner with the creation of the necessary conditions for human contentment (*Karma, Dharma and Purushaarth*); it is represented by the stitching together of divine alliances between our civilizational Gods and our local *Devatas* forming a rich tapestry of *puranic* truths that involve every community in a grand metaphorical national project no matter how isolated they are. Every *jaati-purana* and every *sthala-purana* tells the stories of how every one of our ancestral communities chose to hitch their particular cultural wagons on to the grand civilizational caravan. Every single Hindu in Bharat feels connected to the national project not because of crude Abrahamic-style dogma but because we are connected by metaphorical truths... a higher plane of existence that has been projected upon our sacred geography granting to our very existence a touch of divinity. These truths inform our national character—patience, understanding, hospitality, generosity, trustworthiness, innocence, wonder, spirituality, a lack of angst, a lack of a sense of victimhood, eternal positivity, belief in human goodness and an easy willingness to self-sacrifice. *This* is worth protecting. *This* is worth building a real, non-metaphorical Hindu State for.

It can be argued that some of that has led to our current weakness, but it doesn't have to be that way if we are a conscious people. Our problem today is unconsciousness—the unconsciousness that has led to our widespread absorption of Western Liberalism and its tropes of Liberty and Equality, and the manner in which we turn back and use these Western tropes to reject, disgrace and dissect our own civilization.

1. **Metaphysics** is used to undermine **Religion**:
   The "God is within you, why do you need a temple?" school of thought.

2. **Religion** is used to undermine the **Coalition**:
   The "Hindu unity can only be built when we uproot the caste system" school of thought.

3. Our **Coalition** is used to undermine our **Tribalism**:
   The "Birth-based *varna* is a sin" school of thought.

4. Our **Tribalism** is used to undermine our **Civilization** itself:
   The "We are not Hindu, we are *Dravidians, Dalits* and *Animists*" schools of thought.

Each of these is a very specific problem arising from our unconsciousness as to the true breadth, depth and greatness of our civilization... those metaphorical strands that are simply to be understood from birth and never spoken about. Simply put, we have forgotten who we are. We would rather learn about ourselves from books written in a foreign language by foreign authors than from our own grandmothers.

I give us two visions that I hope will help arrange the magnetic field of our heart's compass. These are not ideas, these are visions that we need to feel into.

So

    slow

        down

            now...

Part V
Home is our Destination

Bharatiya **Visions**

The River of Life

> High upon the icy slopes of the Himalaya, a glacier melts, drop by drop, into a pool of clear blue water. From this pristine rock-pool a stream flows...

sometimes silent, sometimes gushing... always growing. She leaps over boulders, tumbles over rock edges, smoothening all that is uneven, turning lush all that is thirsty.

As she descends into the plains, she grows wide and generous. Where previously only the most austere of *sadhus* could bear to touch her, now ordinary people approach her, fill their earthen pots with her life-giving liquid, take a piece of her back home to their children.

Through forest and field, her waters maintain their relentless onward flow. All along the way she is met by other streams, some large, some small, some tiny... each one carrying a precious cargo of life-giving water from the hills, underground springs, rocky crags and village pools where they arose. The waters mingle in the big river, their differences surrendered to a higher common purpose. The river grows as wide as the world, the gentle sway of paddy fields her constant companion. Entire cities emerge on her banks. She inspires sublime art and everyday harvest songs with the same felicity. *Bharatavarsha* is drenched in the sheer beauty of her inexhaustible capacity to gather all and give back more.

From the Himalaya to the Southern Ocean, our waters have come together, each little stream made sacred by association with the big perennial glacial river, adding to her, taking from her, *becoming* her, giving both Life and Meaning to the communities that depend on them. Together they enter the ocean blue, the ocean deep, where all our questions are answered, or perhaps where none exist.

Veda and *Vedanta*, *Itihaasa* and *Purana*, *Jaati* and *Varna*, Religion and Philosophy. – *Sanatana*.

Now go back and read again.

The Tree of Life

Raja Ikshvaku's father, *Shraddhadeva Manu Maharaj*, has crossed over to this *yuga* on a boat led by a divine fish. It's been raining here since before the beginning of time. Water from *Indraloka* pours down, blessing this land, soaking into her. *Bharatavarsha* is wet, fertile, green. *Bhu Devi* stirs. This invitation from the heavens must be met by an equal and opposite yearning, a reaching up for the skies.

A long-buried seed feels the pull. Roots emerge... reaching down into the soil, an intricate web of fingers becoming one with *Bhu Devi*, drawing life-giving sustenance from deep in her heart. The roots are innumerable, strong, stable, deep, connected; in places they break through the soil like muscles on a lion's back.

From this twisted mass of life, a perfect cylindrical trunk arises, growing, straight, tall...disappearing into the clouds...reaching for the stars...

Out of human sight, in the half-light of the mists that float above the *Bhu Devi*, the trunk branches out, an aerial mirror of the earthy web that it arose from. Some branches are dry, austere; some are leafy; some bent under the weight of flowers. Fragrance is everywhere... bees, monkeys, parrots, vine snakes, tree frogs, the swoop of a bird of paradise...

The branches sway in the breeze. Bits of colour are shaken free. They swirl their way down to the ground far below forming a perfect circle, a carpet of leaves and flowers, fallen again like the rain that started it all.

Our *Veda*, Our *Kulas*, Our *Dharma*, Our Religion. Sheer Beauty.

Diversity in the service of strength, strength in the service of beauty, beauty in the service of the life-giving pair – the Earth and the Rain, Life and Meaning.

Now go back and read again.

Let us not deride that which our ancestors built. Let us not despise that which we no longer understand. Every part of the *Varna*-Tree had its own beauty and spirituality. To think that flowers are better than roots or vice versa betrays a lack of understanding. The *Varna*-Tree represented both Life and Meaning... and everything in between.

It is obvious that the old *Varna*-Tree is dying, but those of us who have experienced traditional, compassionate, Bharat know its value. We must help plant a new one for the modern world. The soil it stands on is Reverence and the air it breathes is (divine) Purpose. We need compassionate leaders and more people willing to take on this responsibility.

In the *Varna*-Tree, the further from the ground one was, the greater the self-sacrifice that was demanded. But excellence was demanded of all. That was a society based on the idea that respect accrues to those who give (*dana*) and, indeed, those who give up (*vairagya*). Constant giving of Self is an idea that needs to fire us up again.

Sacrifice.

...that ancient aspiration

> I shall not abandon this dog today from desire of my happiness. Even this is my vow steadily pursued, that I never give up a person that is terrified, nor one that is devoted to me, nor one that seeks my protection, saying that he is destitute, nor one that is afflicted, nor one that has come to me, nor one that is weak in protecting oneself, nor one that is solicitous of life. I shall never give up such a one till my own life is at an end.[16]
>
> – Yudishtra, at the gates of *Swarga*, circa 3100 BCE

Reference and Links

1. Wade Davis, *Sacred Geography*, 2009

2. Ibid.

3. Ibid.

4. Trueindology, "Hitler Never Used Swastika: Evangelical Defamation Of Hindu Symbol", *Swarajya*, 2018
   https://swarajyamag.com/ideas/swastika-is-hindu-and-the-hooked-cross-is-nazi-the-rest-is-conspiracy

5. Eugene McCarraher, "The People's Republic of Heaven: From the Protestant Reformation to the Russian Revolution, 1517–1917", *The Hedgehog Review*, 2017
   https://hedgehogreview.com/issues/the-end-of-the-end-of-history/articles/the-peoples-republic-of-heaven-from-the-protestant-reformation-to-the-russian-revolution-15171917

6. Subhashree Desikan, "Tribes tell their own stories of celestial bodies", *The Hindu*, 2017
   https://www.thehindu.com/news/national/tribes-tell-their-own-stories-of-celestial-bodies/article19699686.ece

7. David Goodhart, *The Road to Somewhere*, C Hurst & Co., 2017
   https://mikefrost.net/people-somewhere-vs-people-anywhere/

8. Ibid.

9. Rev. Joseph Roberts, *Caste, In Its Religious And Civil Character, Opposed To Christianity*, 1847

10. Sashidhar Adivi, "Chilkur Balaji temple priest re-enacts 2,700-year-old ritual", *Deccan Chronicle*, 2017
    https://www.deccanchronicle.com/nation/current-affairs/170418/chilkur-balaji-temple-priest-re-enacts-2700-year-old-ritual.html

11. Dharampal, *The Beautiful Tree*, 1983
    https://archive.org/details/TheBeautifulTree-Dharampal/page/n33/mode/2up

12. Yabuuchi Satoshi, "Thirteen Centuries of Gratitude: Japanese, Chinese, and Taiwanese Team Recreates a Buddhist Statue from Nara's Tōdaiji", *Nippon*, 2020
    https://www.nippon.com/en/in-depth/d00643/

13. "Remove caste names from sign boards: Madras High Court directs Tiruvannamalai district administration", *The New Indian Express*, 2018
    https://www.newindianexpress.com/states/tamil-nadu/2018/oct/02/remove-caste-names-from-sign-boards-madras-high-court-directs-tiruvannamalai-district-administratio-1879921.html

14. "Centre offers Rs. 2.5 lakh incentive to every Dalit-including couple: All you should know about the inter-caste marriage scheme", India Today, 2018
    https://www.indiatoday.in/education-today/gk-current-affairs/story/inter-caste-marriage-scheme-1101331-2017-12-06

15. Koenraad Elst, "Defense against "Hinduphobia"", *Pragyata*, 2016
    https://pragyata.com/defence-against-hinduphobia/

16. Veda Vyas, *Mahabharata* (translated by Kisari Mohan Ganguli), Antiquity

SECTION 3

CULTURE & VALUES

Section 3 | Chapter 3.1

THE HINDU TRADITIONALIST PART I: *ON CULTURE*
Culture, Morality and Reform

Maragatham, 2021

"We are not here for fun, we are here to do our duty in honour of our Gods and ancestors who gave us Life. Some of that may indeed be fun and some of that may well be difficult, but what's important is that we are 'us' and not 'someone else'."

So, Who Are We?

Do we have fitting responses to the claims and questions of Secular Atheists?

"You worship elephants and monkeys, your religion is primitive."

"If God is everywhere then your temples are meaningless."

"Your 33 crore Gods could not prevent your defeat to foreign armies."

"There is no rebirth, your life is meaningless."

"There is no God."

"Your traditions are a waste of money."

"Nothing is sacred bro, it's just chemistry."

Do we need to respond? Do we respond on their terms using a framework *they* understand or do we answer them on *our* terms using our own frameworks?

I'm not one for proper definitions, but do we at least have a fuzzy understanding of how we *approach* these issues? Are we conscious of *our way*?

The thing is, there are already multiple extremely sophisticated *Bharatiya* ways of looking at the world that are millennia old. These *darshanas* were and are always intellectually available to scholars. But, for the rest of us common folk, our *rishis* left something special—an inherited system of organizing life and mind via the medium of **practice** (ritual) and **poetry** (a metaphoric understanding of history—*itihaasa*). You and I were not expected to spend fourteen years mastering philosophical verses but we were, from birth, expected to follow the ways of our ancestors and in doing so we *embodied* the *Bharatiya* vision. Not only is the *Bharatiya* vision (*Brahman*, *Rta*, Multi-Birth *Karma* and *Purushaarth*) a superior vision, but this remarkably long-lived means of transmission is also a superior, non-violent, non-didactic, and attractive way of creating civilization. Today Hollywood does the same for America in places where it doesn't go to war. We did it in Central Asia, South East Asia, in Tibet and in Japan and Korea.

So, when then did we lose the plot?

Europe stole and innovated its way to technological supremacy while we were tied down in a death match with Islam. By the 17th Century, they were already so strong, and we so weakened that they were able to walk into our country and toy with us.

What happened with the coming of the British was that we were faced with a very powerful adversary who scoffed at our practices and asked a lot of questions. We, the common people, came face-to-face with the White Man and for the first time in our long history we were shamed. Shamed because we did not *know* why we did what we did. Shamed because we didn't *know* what we stood for. Shamed because we couldn't *articulate* our view of the world in terms that were understandable to the monster at our door.

Pretty soon, we assumed that our vision was inferior; after all, we were physically inferior, so it must follow that the vision that led to this physical weakness too was inferior.

So started the great chain of reform. From Ram Mohan Roy to D.Y. Chandrachud, the only deep tradition that most educated Hindus follow today is the tradition of reform. Generation after generation, like clockwork mice, we pass on the idea to our children that we need to be reformed.

Reform started with the internalization of the idea that our ancestors were backward and superstitious... and that is why they were weak. We discarded our rituals in favour of Science (with a capital "S") and our *Itihaasa* in favour of History. In the absence of our practice (rituals) and our poetry (*itihaasa*), our *Bharatiya darshanas* became disembodied (they no longer had a vehicle that carried them) and we, the modern-day *Bharatiya* people, became culturally orphaned. Our links to the *darshanas*, so carefully maintained over hundreds of generations by our ancestors, through practice and poetry, were severed, and within a generation, our children were cut loose from even a simple intellectual appreciation of the *Bharatiya* vision.

"We're so backward dude..."

This has left us in a strange post-colonial reality today that *we* are no longer *ourselves*. With every passing year, more kids attend secular school and are kidnapped from the Hindu-sphere. They either become Hindu-flavoured Liberals, Atheists, or out and out Abrahamic. On the surface, our festivals may be louder today with laser shows and pop music but by any *deep* measure our Hindu world is going silent.

We see this in our lack of emotional response when the secular government bans our festivals[1] or dictates to us how to celebrate our Gods.[2]

One may ask why Christians and Muslims appear to survive the secular onslaught? There are deep philosophical commonalities between Secularism, Islam and Christianity which help, but for the common Christian or Muslim what really helps is that their ideological religions provide them answers. Irrational answers, but at least some answers, to the questions posed by atheistic Secularism—about the origin of things, about good and bad, about us and them. These ideological religions are simplistic worldviews with clear blueprints and instructions. They insist that the flock meets once a week to generate community, brainwash children and seek political power. Their answers may be irrational, but they provide form, shape and identity to their flock... an armour to ward off the piercing gaze of Western reductionist logic.

We Hindus on the other hand, stand here naked, without the armour of ideology. Our traditional armour, 'caste'-based tradition, has been stripped off our bodies and ridiculed until even *we*, now hate that very thing that protected us and gave us shape, form and identity all these long, difficult centuries.

Poignant.

Pathetic.

Hindus today are left with four options—to become Christian, to become Muslim, to become Liberal, or to seethe.

We seethe.

We know not why we seethe, but we seethe. And that's good because it shows that deep down we are still *aesthetically* so acculturated to the Hindu *darshanas* that we cannot abandon them. We hate our pathetic impotence, but we can't let go. And *that* is a kind of love. It is that love that I want to give contours to. In the rest of this essay (and the two subsequent essays), I offer to ordinary Hindus a set of ideas that try to explain why we are the way we are, at a deep anthropological level. Those of us who cannot afford to join a *gurukulam*, need a foundation from which to pick our way through the minefield of atheist questions and Liberal accusations.

So then, "What is Culture?"

Culture is communal habit. Plain and simple. But the important question that arises after this is where do these habits come from? What is their nature?

There are essentially three views (I will be using these three terms going forward):

"Trad-Culture"
Culture comes from Tradition which in turn comes from a particular Metaphysical Worldview. This is the Traditional view.

"Techno-Culture"
Culture is created when Humans react to the possibilities offered by Technology. This is the Modern view.

"Whatever-Culture"
Culture is *Whateverthehell* we want it to be. This is the Post-Modern view.

All of these are factual understandings of different facets of the amorphous thing that we call culture. But what is *true* for us?

I am going to consciously differentiate between the words *Factual* and *True*, so please follow my train of thought. Facts refer to happenings, occurrences in this physical world, empirical cause and effect, that sort of thing. *Truth, on the other hand,* refers to that which lends meaning to our existence.

When we say *Ram Naam Satya Hai*, what does the word *Satya* here mean? How can a name be *true*, what does it really *mean*? I would like you to take thirty seconds to think of this. Really try to define for yourself what the word *Satya* could actually mean in the context of Shri Rama's name. It's not so easy for an English thinker to get their head around this one.

That thing, that untranslatable word *Satya*, is Truth. It is not to be confused with mere Fact.

So back to culture...

Let's say that communal habits arose as a means to negotiate three existential spheres:

1. **The Gods** (out there in the great Unknown)
2. **The Gods-Made World** (the Earth and Life on Earth)
3. **The Man-Made World** (Human Community)

The ancients approached the Gods through **Metaphor**—sacrifice, poetry, art and beauty.

They approached the Gods-Made World of animals, earth, plants, and rain through **Technology**—their tools, the plough, the bow, the spear, fire, houses, boats.

And they approached the Man-Made World of communities through **Ritual**—marriage, naming ceremonies, festivals, rules around sharing, rules around war.

The ancients realized that Ritual and Metaphor were praise-giving and respectful acts but Technology was extractive. Tools are the necessary evil. They help us live, to build, to grow, to thrive but they are always taking and never giving back. To redeem our tools from their pure extractive functionality, the ancients understood that tools too needed to be brought under a metaphoric umbrella. This is why we have rituals associated with our tools in this nation and in every other traditional nation. Thanks are given (e.g. *Ayudha Puja*) and permission taken (e.g. *Bhoomi Puja*) before any extractive activity. These rituals make us conscious that our being here is a miracle and is not something to be taken for granted.

Anthropologist Wade Davis talks about this phenomenon in his 2009 book *The Wayfinders*, in the chapter 'People of the Anaconda':

> When men go into the forest to hunt or fish, it is never a trivial passage. First the shaman must travel in trance to negotiate with the masters of the animals, forging a mystical contract with the spirit guardians, an exchange based always on reciprocity. The Barasana compare it to marriage, for hunting too is a form of courtship, in which one seeks the blessings of a higher authority for the honour of taking into one's family a precious being. Meat is not the right of a hunter but a gift from the spirit world. To kill without permission is to risk death by a spirit guardian... All of these ideas and restrictions create, as anthropologist Kaj Arhem has written, (in typically reductivist Western fashion) what is essentially a land management plan inspired by myth.[3]

A delicate balance between these three existential spheres has existed since the dawn of human-ness. But slowly and inevitably, human technology grew in complexity.

It began to 'erase' the Gods-Made World. Our dependence and enslavement to geography was ended by dams, roads, ships, planes, cars, the telegraph, the telephone, the internet, hybrid seeds... This was a process whose effects became very prominent during the rise of modern Europe... the "Rise of Man" and the "Conquest of Nature". In our minds, we were no longer one of God's creations *linked* in a series of complex relationships with other creatures and processes, but we were now *separate*, alone.

With the conquest of the Gods-Made World it became clear that the Gods themselves were next. Atheism gained traction (starting with Western Europe and spreading through the world). We could take care of ourselves! We didn't need a Father! Concrete, nuclear power, modern medicine, JCBs, and now genetic modification all enable humans to perform acts that were previously in the realm of godliness. In our minds we were no longer *grateful* for the miracle of Life, but we were now *free* to do as we wished to fulfil our desires.

The last erasure has been that of the Man-Made World, that of Community. Technology and technology-generated-surplus has allowed us to literally replace other humans in our lives. We have no need for them anymore... family, community, tribe, all of this is passé. Each of us can help ourselves or pay a stranger to help us. Home appliances, entertainment, psychiatry, money, online banking, computers, social media, cloning... all of these tools lead only one way: to the end of the rituals that have defined us for centuries and millennia—marriage, child-birth, festivals, generosity, kindness, good manners, hospitability, all of these are in a state of dilution. Especially in urban areas, the Man-Made World is today replaced by a Machine-Made World and we humans limit ourselves to the internal logic of these machines in the name of convenience.

What this brief history of the world shows us is that the precepts of Techno-Culture are factual. Technology *does* change us. It changes our culture. It changes everything. If this reductionist, crude, materialist vision of history is right, then that leads us directly to conclude that the claims of Trad-Culture are *not* a given and so the claims of Whatever-Culture could possibly be right. That is to say, *if the stories and traditions of the ancients are merely artifacts of the technologies of their time then they no longer hold the sanctity that they once did.* It also follows that the term "culture" is just a word. Nothing more, nothing less. We can do with it what we will. If I get enough people to mimic *"Gangnam Style"* then that becomes our culture. If I get enough people to chant my chorus, then I've created a culture. This particular post-modernist, anything goes, aspect of Whatever-Culture is now in full flow in society, aided by all types of social media apps. Culture is being atomized, democratized, trivialized, individualized and de-temporalized (cut off from the idea of continuity). Culture today, gone tomorrow. Culture has become fashion. And as technological change intensifies, so too will the fashion of culture riding on its back.

So then, who are we?

And herein lies the crux of the matter. We, as Hindus have very deep answers to this question. Our ancients realized the perils of relativist thinking a long, long time ago. They fashioned an incredible metaphysics to deal with it. *Brahman, Moksha, Rta, Punarjanma, Karma, Dharma, Guna, Varna, Purushaarth* together created a frame of reference for ordinary humans that maximized meaning, identity (belonging), order, peace, prosperity and well-being for all.

But today, that framework has been burned to the ground by Christians, Atheists and reformist Hindus. They've done a damned good job of it. Even our very minds are no longer our own.

But... there is a small awakening happening. In a few short decades, many of us have come to realize that modern Techno-Culture and post-modern Whatever-Culture may be *factual* but they are not *true*. At least deep in our Hindu hearts we know that these ways of thinking about our place in the Universe do not lend our lives meaning.

And if you are still in doubt, ask yourself this: "Are we simply carbon-based, gadget consuming individuals whose sole raison-d'être is the maximization of pleasure?" Does this self-definition do us justice? Do we *truly feel* that we *belong* to this definition of self? Can we *truly* surrender to its implications? There are indeed some people out there who can—the druggies and sociopaths of the West, hooked on TV and chips, if not violence and porn. But is that us? The children of the noble Arya? The men who were made with Sacrifice as their middle name? The women who held fast to their Faith? Those whose blood Sanctified this land? Whose Gods walked this land? Whose Deeds are etched in stone in our temples for all time to come?

It's clear now who we are. The fog is lifted. And Arjuna speaks through us when we realize as he did that: "By thy grace I remember my Light, and now gone is my delusion. My doubts are no more, my faith is firm; and now I can say 'Thy will be done.'"[4]

The *adharmic* technologies of the West, the *adharmic* ideals of the West, the temptations of the *mayic* social structures of the West—none of these matter. We know where they all lead. Their words, their data, their facts, their lofty ideals all collapse under the weight of the crassness of their outcomes. Porn, drugs, divorce, depression, school shootings, supremacy, cruelty, loneliness, narcissism, inhospitality, selfishness and, above all, ugliness! *What*, in the end, is the *use* of their worldviews? Techno-Culture and Whatever-Culture may be factual but they are not *true*. They are certainly not true for us. Truth... that which leads us higher, that which lends Meaning, that which fills our hearts with love, pride, and joy, that which leads us away from addictions, that which sets us free from desire, *that*, and everything that points in that direction, is true for us.

We have known that this relativist physical reality is *maya* since forever. The Western man is only just discovering this. Covid-19 (a product of Techno-Culture) and Cancel-Culture (a product of Whatever-Culture) show us practically in this day and age that everything is relative, that change is the only constant. Our inability to control the outcomes of both Techno-Culture and Whatever-Culture is bringing into sharp focus the limits of the Western worldview's ability to manage reality itself. If the human relationship to reality itself becomes unhinged, then social collapse is guaranteed. The confused Western man has embraced post-modern relativism as *truth* itself. He has embraced this relativist *maya* as reality itself. This is leading to his fall. Even before our eyes, in a mere one generation, the monster grown fat on the blood of the ancients will implode. Have no doubt.

Our ancients, foreseeing all of this madness, never embraced the *maya* of relativism. Instead, they put their minds and hearts into designing a metaphysics that would help us navigate this *maya* but simultaneously lead towards the Real. If we Hindus of today choose to continue to follow their example, if we continue to plant our eyes on that which is truly Real, the eternal and the unchangeable, the formless, unknowable One—who the ancients have called *Brahman, Ishvara, Narayana, Nirguna Bhagawan*—then from that fountain will continue to flow our culture. If we opt for the relativist *maya*, we are lost.

That which helps us organize society in a way that leads to the Real is *true*. *That* is our culture and it is a culture of the True. It is ok for our rituals and art and technology to evolve as long as they continue to point towards that which is True. And the best clues we have to determine what is true are provided by our traditions. And that is why we, as Hindus, must choose Trad-Culture. Our view of culture *is* traditional, and we have to find a way in this modern world to carry forward the traditions, to consciously mediate their evolution, and not just simply dump them by the roadside. The traditions work, the traditions create Meaning, the traditions lend Identity, the traditions create Community, the traditions help us, if we are conscious, to maintain balance, harmony and well-being of all creatures in both this Gods-Made World as well as the Man-Made World.

In the medium term, we have to figure out how to accumulate the power needed to outlast our *adharmic* rivals while we continue to protect our traditions from erosion (a hard outer shell and soft inner core model). In the long term, anyway, it is guaranteed that *Dharma* will prevail. The unsustainable Techno-Culture and the relativist Whatever-Culture will implode within our children's lifetimes. If the Indian State links its fate to the West, we will all go down with it. It is important that our communities fiercely protect their autonomy while we ride the coming storm.

To recover the True from the mess we have around us requires two things:

1. To reaffirm our commitment to that which is True. We do this by re-familiarizing ourselves with our traditions and *darshanas* (knowing who we are) and re-connecting to our brothers and sisters (coming together). It is only after doing so that we can talk about the future... *an authentic Hindu* Future.
2. To interrogate our relationship with our tools. To set limits that will guarantee that never again will technology be allowed to take-over and dominate our conscious relationships with the Gods-Made World-of-Nature and the Man-Made World of Community. To make sure that it is *we* who use our tools and not our tools that use us for the fulfilment of their own internal logic.

Once we do these two things, Hindu cultural evolution will occur on our terms.

Shri Aurobindo put it succinctly:

> The whole root of difference between Indian and European culture springs from the spiritual aim of Indian civilization. It is the turn which this aim imposes on all the rich and luxuriant variety of its forms and rhythms that gives to it its unique character.
>
> For even what it has in common with other cultures gets from that turn a stamp of striking originality and solitary greatness. A spiritual aspiration was the governing force of this culture, its core of thought, it's ruling passion. Not only did it make spirituality the highest aim of life, but it even tried, as far as that could be done in the past conditions of the human race, to turn the whole of life towards spirituality.[5]

We aim to bring everything—music, dance, sex, money, alcohol, *ganja*, work, family, violence, everything—under the rubric of reverence; to give every human activity a context where it is legitimized but controlled and directed towards a higher goal. Nothing is simply for its own sake. The quelling of the impulse to irreverence is one of our shining achievements. This merely requires the discipline of our ancestors. It is *that* which we have lost and it is *that* and *only that* which will ensure our survival and eventual success.

Liberal Atheist civilization has irreverence as one of its cornerstones. This feature itself is sufficient to qualify Western civilization as *adharmic*. It will cannibalize itself within one generation if we stop supplying it with our best, brightest and youngest.

References and Links

1. "Jagannath Puri Rath Yatra: Devotees entry banned, fully vaccinated servitors allowed", *Live Mint*, 2021
https://www.livemint.com/news/india/jagannath-puri-rath-yatra-devotees-entry-banned-fully-vaccinated-servitors-allowed-11623315721604.html

2. "NGT imposes total ban on crackers in NCR, other places with 'poor' or worse air quality", The Print, 2020
https://theprint.in/india/ngt-imposes-total-ban-on-crackers-in-ncr-other-places-with-poor-or-worse-air-quality/556206/

3. Wade Davis, *The Wayfinders: Why Ancient Wisdom Matters In The Modern World*, House of Anansi Press, 2009

4. Veda Vyas, *Mahabharata* (translated by Kisari Mohan Ganguli), Antiquity

5. Shri Aurobindo, *The Foundations of Indian Culture*, 1923

Section 3 | Chapter 3.2

THE HINDU TRADITIONALIST PART II: *ON MORALITY*
Culture, Morality and Reform

Maragatham, 2021

> "Their words, their data, their facts, their lofty ideals all collapse under the weight of the crassness of their outcomes."

Counter-Culture

The idea that both the saint and the sinner are equal before God set in motion the Christian revolution two thousand years ago. It took almost one thousand six hundred years before the full impact of this radical individualism began to be felt within Christian society. It led eventually to the Protestant Reformation, which, in a few short centuries, led Christian Europe to the doors of Humanism, Secularism and personal Atheism. From then on, it was a short step to the adoption of Liberty (the idea that life is a playground for self-gratification) as one of the founding ideals of modern Western civilization. Since that moment, some two hundred and fifty years ago, Western civilization has been falling apart, slowly but surely, accelerating every day. Against all available material evidence, I stick my neck out and say that the West has been falling apart because the culture engendered by the embrace of Liberty was not really a culture at all, but an anti-culture.

In the West, the Beatles, Jimi Hendrix, Led Zeppelin, Woodstock etc. are all dubbed the counter-culture, but in reality they were the perfect manifestations of Western Liberal societal values (materialism, individualism and progressivism). What was 'counter' about them? Nothing at all. So, what goes by the name of Western culture is, clearly then, a counter-culture in essence (the Cancel-Culture of today is another symptom of the very same malaise). Culture, traditionally, has always been a sense of shared values which has tacitly enforced behavioural rules in society. When people follow these rules, stability ensues and, in the Hindu understanding, stability is the founding principle from which spring order, peace, prosperity and well-being. With the anointing of Liberty as the king of ideals, and materialism, individualism and progressivism as core values, what the West embraced was not a new culture but in fact an anti-culture that actively pursued the breaking of rules in the service of self-gratification. This type of societal carte blanche given to the breaking of cultural rules inevitably leads to the falling apart of that very same society. Western liberal anti-culture is entropic in its essence, if not outright cannibalistic.

We must acknowledge that all libertarian freedoms are subsidized, either by other people's efforts or by *Bhu Devi's* abundance. There are ancient cultures that recognized this dependency, and attempted to payback their debt (most famously encoded as the *Pancha Rna* in the Hindu context) and there are cultures that want freedoms with no thought of repayment. The latter can only thrive in the short term by borrowing from the future or from other people and places. In the case of the West, the initial subsidy came from slavery and colonial depredations. The twin engines of this parasitic system of subsidy—extreme inequality and extreme exploitation of *Bhu Devi*—have carried on to this day in less overt forms.

The immoral wealth that this exploitation produced, aided by the industrial methods and machines perfected in the West, created an economic surplus of gargantuan proportions. It was this surplus that helped feed, and indeed continues to feed, the delusion that Liberty is achievable for all individuals, for all time to come! Today, we are well past a civilizational tipping point. Many of us who have an ecological conscience can see with clarity that, with the slow disappearance of the natural resources that keep the Western industrial model afloat, the surplus that feeds the delusion of 'Liberty for all' too will dry up. And with that Liberty itself will vanish. In its place, a culture of stability must re-emerge in the West. In other words, the West will be forced, in a few short generations, to revert to a real, rules-based culture, one that harbours sustainability of natural resources and human relations at its core. Because there is no other way. I'm sorry, but humans are not going to live on Mars.

Question: So, what happens when a Liberty-fuelled anti-culture is set in motion in a Materialist society?

Answer: We get runaway Machine-Worship.

Human beings infected by this potent mix of Liberty, Materialism and Techno-Culture, start to subconsciously recognize machines (global infrastructure, aeroplanes, bikes, cars, TVs, washing machines, cell phones, internet) as the entities that bring them Liberty. And since anything that brings Liberty is sacred in their liberal universe, the Machine becomes sacred. When the Machine becomes sacred, humans start to see themselves as beholden to the Machine. If you observe the statements of an intelligent man like Elon Musk, you will see what's coming our way. Musk believes, in all sincerity, and with guarded enthusiasm, that humans were put on Earth in order to facilitate the emergence of Machine Intelligence. He sees us as the evolutionary link between apes and self-aware machines. When self-aware machines reach their full potential and begin to use us for their own benefit, eventually erasing us from the planet (while, perhaps, maintaining a store of our DNA for future reference) Elon Musk believes that human purpose would be fulfilled! This is the end-game[1] (watch 16.30 secs onwards).

This is not a Hindu vision.

Future Perfect
The Great Inversion

The materialist Western idea that all culture is determined by technology has led to a very specific vision of the human journey. This vision is one that prioritizes material sophistication as the primary benchmark of worth. This has led to the common trope that we have 'advanced' from being Hunter-Gatherers to Agriculturalists to Modern Industrial people and our cultures, during each of those phases, were merely the result of parsing the physical world through our tools.

So, if today, America has a 'hook-up culture' a Western commentator would be tempted to say that this culture has its roots in the invention of birth control, the internet, and social media apps. This is on one level factual and sometimes a useful way to look at the world, but it hides a deeper truth and that is the answer to the question "Why". Why have birth control and the internet resulted in this hook-up culture? Was it inevitable as many believe? Or did these technologies evolve this way because the White Man allowed them to evolve that way? In other words, did these technologies flow through the deep beliefs of the White Man and emerge in this shape or did the White Man flow through the deep internal logic of these technologies and emerge this way?

We have seen (in Part 1 of this essay series) that Technology impacts culture in dramatic ways. Westerners who adhere strongly to Techno-Culture are happy to go wherever their tools lead them because it is their tools that have brought them the power that they have wielded over the past three centuries. They will go live on Mars, they will implant chips in their brains, they will freeze their bodies, they will do gain of function research on deadly viruses, they will literally do anything if it smells of technology. But... if we are a conscious people, we can see that this way of being is madness and will hopefully reach its unsustainable end very soon so we can all get back to normal life.

Normal life—where culture is the stabilizing force that grants communities and individuals familiarity, predictability, shelter, identity, pride, love, ALL of that once-familiar stuff—is in short supply today. In such a society, change, when it happens, is consciously curated by citizens. In such a society, people are not forced into obsolescence every five years; parents and children have a commonality of values that they share and which make them recognizable to each other; people who master a trade can hope to contribute to society for the entire length of their lifetimes; grandparents can imagine dying at home, surrounded by their grandkids; and people can hope to eat food that is not poison. These are not unreasonable asks. These are, in fact, the qualities of life that our parents and grandparents enjoyed until a mere three decades ago. Today, a person demanding these ordinary things is seen as either a communist or a fool. By submitting to Techno-Culture and its ideological child, Whatever-Culture, we have entered a world where the rate of change in society is so great, that a great inversion is in progress. Where yesterday, parents used to represent the wisdom of the ages and the experiences of a lifetime, we now have children representing the techno-knowledge of the present and the cultural-cool of the future. Within this new paradigm, it is no longer the tribal knowledge from the past that helps humans survive, it is the ability to withstand the stress of predicting and adjusting to the constantly mutating machine-made future that helps humans survive. Parents are having to submit before the ideological and lifestyle demands of their children. Parents are having to evolve in order to appear cool to their children. Parents are having to abandon the inherited wisdom of the past and instead rely on their children to initiate them into the techno-tools and the culture-cool that serve as gateways to the future.

The values of such a world will inevitably be teenage in their essence. Over the past three decades in Bharat, there has been a huge move towards glorification of these values: impatience, change-centric economic structures, fashion culture, techno fascination, sex obsession, emotionalism, short term goals, distraction and superficiality—in other words, the MTV-ication of life itself. We see this all around us today. The fundamental idea of stability as a foundation for human well-being itself has vanished. If *Dharma* is defined as "that which lends stability" then we are free to draw our conclusions on what this new type of world should be labelled. The middle-aged and the old have no place in this world. This inversion leads only one way when we follow it to its logical conclusion—the elimination of everything that is 'backward and/or inefficient' and the dissolution of marriage, family, tribe and ultimately heterosexual reproduction itself. A Matrix-like future is predicted.

This post-Christian, Western surrender to Techno-Culture is the single reason why every Hollywood science fiction movie is set in an apocalyptic Machine-verse where the hero, always a person who is subject to human flaws, fights the Machine-ness of his surroundings and re-establishes the sanctity of the human condition. This theme pervades every movie from Star Wars to The Matrix to Gattaca to Minority Report. At a deep psychological level, each of these movies is exactly the same movie. The White Man is playing out a terrible dilemma in these movies—he knows he is sick, he wants to turn to God, to cure himself, to believe that there is some shred of sanctity left in his humanity but finds that he cannot. He has surrendered to the Machine instead. There is not a single science fiction movie that shows a future where man and beast live happily under the Gods-given sky. Instead, what we have is the repeated replay of the fall from Eden into deeper and deeper Hells. Founding myths are powerful indeed.

Let me spell it out clearly then. This stuff is no good!. This stuff is not Hindu. It has NOTHING whatsoever to do with the Hindu mythic mind. It is imperative that our technologies submit to the logic of our metaphysics and *not* the other way around. It is our traditions and not our technologies that represent us.

This brings us back to Trad-Culture and the idea that culture is a collection of traditions along multiple verticals—food, art, worship, life processes, work, war etc. These traditions flow from a worldview, a metaphysics of how the world came to be and what its true nature is. Core Hindu culture flows from a very specific set of metaphysical ideas—*Brahman, Rta,* Multi-Birth *Karma, Dharma, Purushaarth* and *Moksha*.

Similarly, Techno-Culture and Whatever-Culture flow from a higher-order metaphysics, though we have been schooled to think of them as neutral and universal. They are not neutral, and they do not have to be universal. At their heart lie the beliefs that there is nothing sacred about being human, that the Gods don't exist, that there is no good or bad, that power and pleasure can be pursued for their own sake, that Life, all-encompassing Life itself, is ultimately meaningless.

These are not Hindu values.

If you are a birth Hindu who is unconsciously veering towards these values of Techno-Culture or Whatever-Culture you are taking very significant steps away from the cultural heritage of your ancestors. Core rewiring is happening in your brain; the aesthetics of your morality itself is being tinkered with by mass media and the education system. A new metaphysical operating system is being booted into your hardware. You are the converted.

A Peek into our Hard Drives
The Idealist West and Visionary Bharat

So, let us start our *purva paksha* by defining a few terms:
1. Morality refers to a system of Values.
2. Ethics refer to a Moral code—this includes an analysis of Morality and an attempted rational justification for choosing one morality over another.
3. Law refers to the institutionalization of Ethics.

We can see now that all morality therefore comes from an a priori understanding of the world. This understanding goes by the name 'values'. Values are the direct offspring of metaphysics and are usually hidden from our minds. People living *within* a value system are usually unaware of their values; they live in the second-order framework of morals. In normal conversation people make moral judgements without specifying their value system.

The communal habits (culture) of a people are held by that society to be *moral*.

For example, when Westerners say something is bad or good in Hinduism, they are judging us as per *their* morality which in turn is based on the values of *their* metaphysics. There is nothing *inherently true* about their judgements of us.

I am told that Christian scholars accuse us of being inferior because we do not have a code of ethics. I don't know if this is a legitimate critique or not and perhaps we haven't written down a code of ethics like Thomas Aquinas and Emmanuel Kant did in the West, but does that really matter? Does that make us immoral? Does it make us incapable of framing laws?...Of writing such a thing as a constitution?

From a simple study of Hindu community behaviour it is obvious that we are a moral people. We also know that we had law established across this land via the *dharma-shastras*. So, what was different in the way our ethics were encoded in society if not in the form of rationally argued texts? I think *this* is the key question. The accusation that we don't have an understanding of ethics is patently false and has been made by people who are inordinately tied to the idea of a 'book' as being the sole dispenser of legitimacy. It only remains to ask how Hindu ethics were articulated if not in books.

I propose that our ethics were encoded in ritual. And their primary purpose was **not the upholding of ideals** (as it is in the West) but the attempt to **embody a set of divine archetypal visions** for the establishment of human welfare and individual emancipation.

The West is idealistic; Liberty, Equality and Fraternity—these are all ideals. These ideals *do not* exist in reality, but they have a certain mathematical symmetry about them which is what gives them their beauty and their attractiveness. Seemingly mesmerized by their beauty, Western society pursues these ideals like a moth to a flame, far beyond the point where they result in human welfare. Let's call this type of morality **Idealist-Morality**.

Hindu society is far more pragmatic. Our societal structures are a vast set of interlocking, moving parts that are constantly self-reflecting on the complex nature of Truth, *Satya*. Life is seen as a series of compromises that is slowly working its way towards a divine perfection. We know, deep down, that anything we do can possibly be both right and wrong at the same time, so our concern in organizing human society has been 'how do we make things a little bit right for everyone concerned?' We've focused on compassion, on sharing, on balance, on order, on peace, on sustainability, on the paths that lead to a resentment-free existence. To this end, we accept as our inner compasses the lives of our *devatas*, *pauranic heroes* and our *avataras* as archetypes. Ram Rajya, Krishna's *Vrindavan*, Shree and Vishnu in *Vaikunta*, Parvati and Shiva in *Kailasa*, *Samudra Manthan* of the *Ksheera Sagara*, the battle between Ma Durga and Mahishasura, Muruga standing on *Palanimalai*, Ganesha as his mother's gatekeeper, Hanuman leaping across the ocean, Draupadi in Duryodhana's court, Bheeshma on a bed of arrows, Arjuna at *Kurukshetra*, Yudishtra at the gates of *Swarga*, Gautama under the *Bodhi Tree*... all this imagery, all these visions are the repositories of our morality. In our insignificant personal lives, we touch the divine, every day, when we see our lives reflect these visions. From birth, we are taught to orient our lives to their aesthetic. Let's call this type of morality **Visionary-Morality**. Hindu Visionary-Morality is outcome-centric and has as its goals communal well-being and individual emancipation.

So, let us compare the two types of morality.

> **Idealist-Morality** is sharp, hard, angular and efficient. It aims to create a perfect system by the application of ideals (a type of Heaven). It is not interested in the true nature of reality. It wants, instead, to shape reality itself as a reflection of its ideals. This kind of system serves as a filter. People are drawn through this filter of ideals. On one side of the filter great and driven (and stressed) achievers are generated. On the other side of the filter collects the detritus of society growing day by day in ugliness. Being an un-natural system imposed on humans, this morality needs draconian regulation and punishment to make it work.[2]
>
> **Visionary-Morality** is blunt, soft and rounded. It is relatively inefficient but feels like home. It aims to create a pragmatic human system based on an understanding of reality. The system nudges people towards

the re-enactment of archetypal visions in its bid to create order. This re-enactment of archetypal visions lends society a great beauty, sustainability, vitality and regenerative ability. When cut off from our visions, as many of us are today, we descend into what is commonly called 'corruption'. Getting Hindu society out of corruption is hard because we have no ideals to take the place of our abandoned visions. The only way forward is to reconnect our society with our visions and that requires the long-term exposure to these archetypal visions at a young age. In other words, schooling in the Hindu *Itihaasa* and *Purana*. This is *not* teaching mythology, this is literally reconstructing our morality. This is what will lead to a corruption-free society and the foundation of a new and *desi* set of laws and systems of governance.

We are *not* an arrow released from a bow, we are the ripples on the surface of water. Our growth is not linear, it is concentric. Our destination is not an imaginary target far away but the divine centre that caused us to ripple forth. That centre is both our origin and our destination. No matter how large our circle grows, we remain defined by and focused on our centre. *That* is the very nature of a circle. There is no circle without a centre. There is also no centre without a circle and it is for *this* reason that our ancients understood that, although it is through the Gods that our traditions arose, it is also through our traditions that our Gods live on.

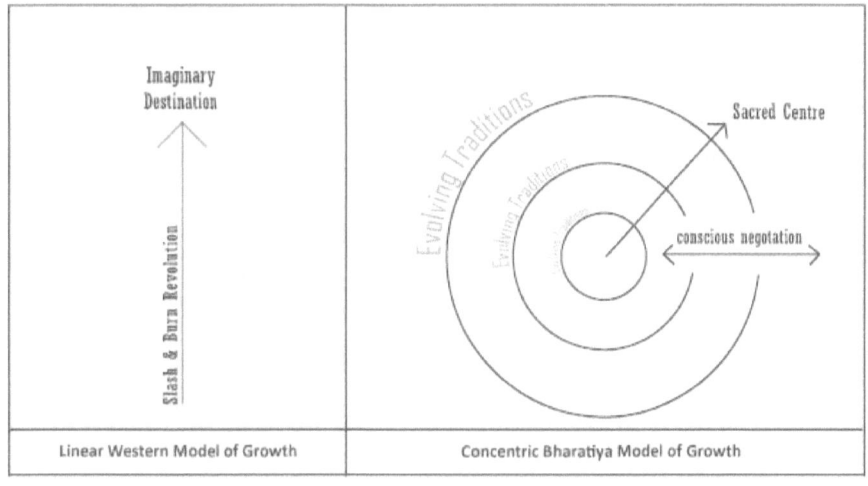

When we walk the circular patterns of our traditions, we literally call the centre into being. This is the great secret of all natural religions and traditional cultures. **We call our Gods to life in our midst when we walk in the footsteps of our ancestors.** This amazing metaphor for life is also physically enacted in many of our festivals. For example, in rural Tamil Nadu, youth from the village take a vow of abstinence leading up to the annual *Koozhu Oothara Vizha*. On festival day, as a culmination of their sacrifices, they carry the heavy *garagams* on their shoulders and assume the form of walking Gods. They walk from house to house accompanied by musicians, drummers and the local keeper of the village shrines. As the young people slowly traverse the length of the village, members of each household emerge from their homes with offerings of fruit and seek blessings for their children. They worship these now transformed youth who till yesterday were merely their neighbours. The youth, then carrying their literal burden of the *garagam* and the figurative burden of the entire village's prayers, make the final trek to the *Graama Devata* and offer their efforts to the deity, prostrating before Her.

We live in this metaphoric balance and it is this that has lent us our immense longevity and creativity. When we abandon our older traditions without creating anything of equal worth and beauty for the present (a larger concentric circle), we break our circularity, we erase our centre... we abandon our Gods.

Judgement

So, how do we compare Hindu society and Western society?

A comparison of **Western *Ideals*** with **Hindu Archetypal *Visions*** would be like comparing apples and oranges. Similarly, comparing Western *Book-based* Ethics with Hindu *Ritual-encoded* Ethics would be equally meaningless. Just can't be done. These are two totally different cognitive categories.

So, what is it that Westerners did when they encountered Bharat? How is it that they have been passing judgement on us for the last three hundred years?

All these centuries, Westerners have looked at ***our* societal outcomes** and judged them by ***their* ideals**. In doing so, they found (obviously) that we were deficient.

Squeeze Varna through the Equality filter –> FAIL
Squeeze Jaati through the Individualism filter –> FAIL
Squeeze Bharatiya Nari through the Liberty filter –> FAIL
Squeeze Traditional Communities through the Universalism filter –> FAIL

They have spent the last three hundred years judging *our societal outcomes* on the basis of *their idealist moral standards* and ridiculing us. It is time we returned the gaze. Let us judge, today, **their societal outcomes** against **our visionary moral standards** and see where they stand. We will see that by *our* visionary moral standards, Western society is sick indeed. We will also see that we do *not* have to accept judgment of *our* outcomes by *their* ideals. We will see also that Western morality is not 'natural justice', it is just as arbitrary as any other value system.

And I'm going to do this with images rather than words so we can break through the supremacy of the written word. These images will not just describe but actually show us why our values are better—because our outcomes are better. There will be no room left for doubt.

Western Social Outcome	Hindu Visionary Benchmark	Hindu Judgement of Western Outcome
1. **Older people are more likely to live alone in the U.S. than elsewhere in the world** *"...just 6% of people aged 60 and older in the U.S. live with their children"* 3 An outcome of the ideal of Individualism	**Shravana Kumar** – A Vision of Respect, Repayment and Responsibility	FAIL

2. Loneliness in America "*A startling 61% of young people aged 18-25 and 51% of mothers with young children reported miserable degrees of loneliness.*"[4] An outcome of the Western value of Individualism	**Govardhana** – A Vision of Community in the protection of its *Kula Devata* 	FAIL
3. America's Real Porn Problem "*Thus, sex is rendered purely transactional, completely separated from the God-ordained purpose not just of reproduction but of cementing a lifelong bond between a man and a woman.*"[5] An outcome of the ideals of Liberty and Equality	**Ardhanaareeshwara** – A Vision of Respect and Equivalence between Man and Woman 	FAIL

4. The trafficking and abuse of drugs in the United States affect nearly all aspects of our lives. "In 2022, 48.7 million people aged 12 or older (or 17.3%) had a substance use disorder (SUD) in the past year, including 29.5 million who had an alcohol use disorder (AUD), 27.2 million who had a drug use disorder (DUD), and 8.0 million people who had both an AUD and a DUD."[6] An outcome of the ideal of Liberty	**Vrindavan** – A Vision of Communal Work and Contentment 	FAIL
5. Astounding increase in antidepressant use by Americans "The rate of antidepressant use in this country among teens and adults (people ages 12 and older) increased by almost 400% between 1988–1994 and 2005–2008."[7] An outcome of the Western value of Individualism	**Hanuman Ji** – A Vision of Faith and Resolve 	FAIL

6. Use It and Lose It: The Outsize Effect of U.S. Consumption on the Environment *"The average American will drain as many resources as 35 natives of India and consume 53 times more goods and services than someone from China."*⁸ A combined outcome of the ideals of Liberty and the Western value of Individualism	**Panchavati** – A Vision of Sacred Perfection in Nature 	FAIL
7. ETHNOCIDE: When systematic terror is normalized, institutionalized, and legalized *"Cultural erasure became the foundation of the chattel slavery system that white colonizers forged in America. African tribal and familial bonds were shattered. African people could no longer speak their languages or practice their religions."*⁹ An outcome of the ideal of Fraternity (Universalism)	**Vishwaroopam** – A Vision of Diversity in Universal Divinity 	FAIL

8. Marriage as a Wretched Institution *"The end of most of these sentimental marriages is quite predictable. They progress, in most cases, to varying stages of marital ennui, depending on the ability of the couple to adjust to reality; most common are (1) a lackluster standoff, (2) a bitter business carried on for the children, church, or neighbors, or (3) separation and divorce, followed by another search to find the right person."*[10] An outcome of the ideals of Equality and Individualism	**Kailasa** – A Vision of *Dharmic Vivaaha* and the Promise of a Wholesome Future 	FAIL
9. 10 years. 180 school shootings. 356 victims. *"Over the past decade, there were at least 180 shootings at K-12 schools across the US. They happened in big cities and in small towns, at homecoming games and during art classes, as students are leaving campus in the afternoon and during late-night arguments in school parking lots."*[11] An outcome of the Western value of Individualism	**Gokul** – A Vision of Innocence and Childhood 	FAIL

10. Me! Me! Me! Are we living through a narcissism epidemic? "Much of our distress," MacDonald notes, "comes from a sense of disconnection. We have a narcissistic society where self-promotion and individuality seem to be essential, yet in our hearts that's not what we want. We want to be part of a community, we want to be supported when we're struggling, we want a sense of belonging."[12] An outcome of the Western value of Individualism	**Satsang** – A Vision of Sharing and Harmony 	FAIL
11. Monsanto's Harvest of Fear "Monsanto already dominates America's food chain with its genetically modified seeds. Now it has targeted milk production. Just as frightening as the corporation's tactics—ruthless legal battles against small farmers—is its decades-long history of toxic contamination."[13] An outcome of the value of Western Exceptionalism	Annapurneshwari Devi – A Vision of the Sacred Origins of Food and Interconnectedness 	FAIL

12. 'They Die Piece by Piece' "They blink. They make noises," he said softly. "The head moves, the eyes are wide and looking around."[14] An outcome of the ideal of Western Exceptionalism	Kamadhenu Ma – A Vision of the Divine in the Cow (and in all Life) 	FAIL
13. Irreverence Is the New Reverent "Irreverence permeates pop culture. From HBO shows filled with crude nudity and violence, to musicals such as The Book of Mormon where explicit ratings are applied to almost every song, to late-night comedies featuring popular show hosts"[15] An outcome of the ideals of Liberty and the value of Western Exceptionalism	Ma Saraswati – A Vision of Tradition, Beauty, Continuity and the Flow of Wisdom 	FAIL

14. Elon Musk wants SpaceX to reach Mars so humanity is not a 'single-planet species' *"SpaceX founder and CEO Elon Musk remains focused on his vision for the company: Establishing a permanent human presence on Mars, with its Starship rockets carrying people to and from the red planet."* [16] An outcome of the value of Western Exceptionalism	**Shri Varaha Avatara** – A Vision of Caring for and Protection of Bhu Devi 	FAIL
15. **American excess: A Wall Street trader tells all** *"The financial markets operate on the principle that, at our core, we're all basically shit: selfish, self-interested creatures."* [17] An outcome of the ideal of Liberty	**Sanyasa** – A Vision of Frugality and Enlightenment about the Essence of Life 	FAIL

16. 'We Will Continue to Rage': SWAT Breaks Up Massive Crowds Defying Curfew in Miami Beach "*Different groups of young women had been dancing and twerking in front of giant bluetooth speaker boxes playing rap music. In front of the shuttered News Cafe on 9th and Ocean Drive, a very large crowd had gathered around four young men having a dance off, with the unmistakable odour of marijuana hanging in the air.*" [18] An outcome of the ideal of Liberty	**Kurukshetra** – A Vision of Clarity of Purpose, Order, Purushaarth 	FAIL

Hindus need to keep in mind, when talking to Christians/Liberals about ethics and morality, that we follow a Visionary-Morality that is expressed in a Ritual-Language that they simply cannot understand unless they become practitioners. We must drag every such discussion away from their *ideals* to the level of *outcomes* and always judge *their* outcomes by *our* values... our values that are manifest in our archetypal visions. Does this look like *Ram Rajya*? Would *Ma* Parvati act this way? What punishment would Shri Krishna prescribe? What would Hanuman Ji do?

Shredding Society with the Cutting Edge of Liberty

Liberal Individualists demand the freedom to indulge in the gratification of their senses and emotions. No matter the long-term terrible outcomes for society, they deem it *immoral* if this Liberty is constrained. Note, it is not their depraved acts that are immoral but the constraining of the freedom to perform those acts that is considered immoral! This is the great and deep unseen change that Liberalism has brought into our moral landscape. The individualist believes that it is in the exploration of one's *deviance* that one 'discovers' oneself. This is an amazing idea. Believe me, even though this may appear 'normal' to some of us today, this idea is so far-fetched and crazy that the West has spent three hundred years pillaging the earth in order to post-rationalize it to themselves and to convert every other human into their fold so that the idea of deviance can be normalized. This remarkable exercise in cultural entropy and normative inversion continues today via the movies, music, social media and higher education. Our kids are not immune.

There was a time when Christian society had values. These values were not Visionary, as in the Hindu case, but were in the form of commandments. These values lent Christian society an internal moral logic (no matter how immoral they seemed to indigenous peoples all over the world). But with the Protestant and Liberal turn that it has taken, all Christian values have been discarded in favour of Secular Ideals. This Idealist-Morality, as we have seen, engenders an anti-culture that results in the falling apart of society (cultural entropy). Curiously, people who subscribe to an Idealist-Morality are prepared to follow these ideals to hell if need be and abandon all values that come in their way. For example, the ideal of Liberty is placed on such a pedestal that today there are fathers who support their daughters' OnlyFans page.[19] Similarly, the ideal of Individualism has been raised up to such an extent that a man would rather let his parents live and die alone[20] than sacrifice what it takes to have them die among family in his house. Equality has been raised up to such an extent that that progressive parents rally in support of more and more explicit sex education curricula in school for younger and younger children, in order to virtue signal that they are non-discriminatory towards the LGBTQA+ community.[21] Universalism has been raised up to such an exalted height that Americans actually believe that they will bring freedom to Afghanistan by waging war upon it.[22]

The age of consent and a quantitative definition of adulthood are both sub-routines that run within the larger Liberty routine. There is nothing automatically sacrosanct about them. Unlike Liberals, Hindus do not consider Consent and Liberty to be Gods whose very spelling is sacred. These ideals will always be held up to our visionary moral standards. We will ask the questions: "Does this consensual or liberal act fall within the broad range of acts performed by our *devatas, pauranic* heroes and *avataras*?" and "Is this act in any way *opposed* to acts that would normally fall under our Visionary-Morality?" Acts that pass this test are ok but acts that fail this test are not ok. Hindu society has every right to brand them as *Adharmic*.

The latest rage in Liberal circles, BDSM, is a case in point. From the point of view of the proponents of BDSM, it is *the only* moral relationship between man and woman because it has consent as its centre-piece. The partners consent to be physically violated thereby making an exhibition of their reverence for consent. By thus virtue signalling and putting skin in the game quite literally, they declare themselves as moral people. It's clear to some us of course, that it is only people who have lost their moral compass who feel the psychological need to thus explicitly prove their morality to themselves. Traditionally married people on the other hand, are seen as immoral because they fail the Individualism test, the Liberty test, and the Equality test.

If *Bharatiya* culture is to survive, Indian law must respond to this challenge thrown by Ideal moralists by simply ignoring their ideals and choosing instead to follow an outcome-based legal framework. And, of course, the best outcomes are those that reflect our archetypal visions. We know this in our hearts. Which laws and societal regulations will help us establish *Ram Rajya* and *Vrindavan* again in Bharat is the question that legal luminaries should be asking. If law does not follow culture willingly, then culture will be forced to follow law unwillingly, with all the associated societal stress and violence. It's a simple choice really—Western *ideals* that bring pain and deracination, or Hindu *visions* that bring joy and identity.

It helps to notice how our moralities are epistemologically structured. Equality, Liberty, Fraternity are all *Ideals* because they *do not* exist in reality. They are descriptors of an unreal space that Western people believe they need to get to, a lot like Heaven. *Dharma* and *Karma* on the other hand are seen by Hindus as *Laws* of Nature. The Gods themselves are subject to these laws and our societal structures have evolved with this understanding at their core. We do not buy into the metaphor that we are all aboard a spaceship going to la-la land because elsewhere is better than here. In perfect opposition to that escapist point of view, we Hindus live in the here and now, revelling in the full warm glow of the divine *Dharmic* law. We do not rebel against reality, we do the best we can within its constraints, all the while holding the archetypal visions of our *devatas*, *pauranic* heroes and *avataras* as our compass.

References and Links

1. Elon Musk, *The Joe Rogan Show*
   https://www.youtube.com/watch?v=ycPr5-27vSI

2. German Lopez, "Mass incarceration in America, explained in 22 maps and charts", *Vox*, 2016
   https://www.vox.com/2015/7/13/8913297/mass-incarceration-maps-charts

3. Jacob Ausubel, "Older people are more likely to live alone in the U.S. than elsewhere in the world", *Pew Research Centre*, 2020
   https://www.pewresearch.org/fact-tank/2020/03/10/older-people-are-more-likely-to-live-alone-in-the-u-s-than-elsewhere-in-the-world/

4. Richard Weissbourd, Milena Batanova, Virginia Lovison, and Eric Torres, "Loneliness in America", *Making Caring Common Project*, 2021
   https://static1.squarespace.com/static/5b7c56e255b02c683659fe43/t/6021776bdd04957c4557c212/1612805995893/Loneliness+in+America+2021_02_08_FINAL.pdf

5. David French, "America's Real Porn Problem", *National Review*, 2016
   https://www.nationalreview.com/2016/04/pornography-destroys-american-morals-culture/

6. U.S Department of Health & Human Services
   https://www.hhs.gov/about/news/2023/11/13/hhs-samhsa-release-2022-national-survey-drug-use-health-data.html

7. Antidepressant Dispensing to US Adolescents and Young Adults 2016-2022
   https://publications.aap.org/pediatrics/article/153/3/e2023064245/196655/Antidepressant-Dispensing-to-US-Adolescents-and

8. Roddy Scheer and Doug Moss, "Use It and Lose It: The Outsize Effect of U.S. Consumption on the Environment", *Scientific American*, 2012 https://www.scientificamerican.com/article/american-consumption-habits/

9. https://www.thedailybeast.com/i-cant-breathe-is-the-new-american-anthem-heres-how-we-change-that

10. Barrett Holmes Pitner, "'I can't Breathe is America's New Anthem' Here's How We Change That", *Daily Beast*, 2021 https://www.theatlantic.com/magazine/archive/1966/11/marriage-as-a-wretched-institution/306668/

11. Christina Walker, "10 years. 180 school shootings. 356 victims", *CNN*, 2018 https://edition.cnn.com/interactive/2019/07/us/ten-years-of-school-shootings-trnd/

12. Zoe Williams, "Me! Me! Me! Are we living through a narcissism epidemic", *The Guardian*, 2016 https://www.theguardian.com/lifeandstyle/2016/mar/02/narcissism-epidemic-self-obsession-attention-seeking-oversharing

13. Donald L. Barlett and James B. Steele, "Monsanto's Harvest of *Fear*", *Vanity Fair*, 2008 https://www.vanityfair.com/news/2008/05/monsanto200805

14. Jo Warrick, "'They Die Piece by Piece'", *The Washington Post*, 2001 https://www.washingtonpost.com/archive/politics/2001/04/10/they-die-piece-by-piece/f172dd3c-0383-49f8-b6d8-347e04b68da1/

15. Cindy Brandt, "Irreverence Is the New Reverent", *HuffPost*, 2014 https://www.huffpost.com/entry/irreverence-is-the-new-reverent_b_5608381

16. Michael Sheetz, "Elon Musk wants SpaceX to reach Mars so humanity is not a 'single-planet species'", CNBC 2021 https://www.cnbc.com/2021/04/23/elon-musk-aiming-for-mars-so-humanity-is-not-a-single-planet-species.html

17. Philipp Meyer, "American excess: A Wall Street trader tells all", *Independent*, 2009
    https://www.independent.co.uk/news/world/americas/american-excess-a-wall-street-trader-tells-all-1674614.html

18. Francisco Alvarado, Blake Montgomery, Pilar Melendez, "'We Will Continue to Rage': SWAT Breaks Up Massive Crowds Defying Curfew in Miami Beach", *Daily Beast*, 2021
    https://www.thedailybeast.com/miami-beach-freaks-out-over-massive-spring-break-crowds-declares-state-of-emergency

19. https://twitter.com/tumtonks/status/1339033973192798212

20. "Aging In America", *Institute On Aging*
    https://www.ioaging.org/aging-in-america

21. https://www.njspotlightnews.org/2023/04/in-nj-progressives-mobilize-against-right-wing-extremism-on-sex-ed-lgbtq-school-policies/

22. US Department of State
    https://2001-2009.state.gov/s/ct/rls/rm/9505.htm

Images

(The images, when not created by the author on ChatGPT, have been sourced from the Wikimedia Commons and are linked to below)

1. Shravan Kumar – Created by author on ChatGPT
2. Govardhan – Created by author on ChatGPT
3. Ardhanaareeshwara – Traditional Devotional Poster
4. Vrindavan – https://commons.wikimedia.org/wiki/File:Krishna_with_flute.jpg
5. Hanuman Ji – https://commons.wikimedia.org/wiki/File:Ravivarmapress.jpg
6. Panchavati – Created by author on ChatGPT
7. Vishwaroopam – https://commons.wikimedia.org/wiki/File:Vishwaroopa_darshanam.png
8. Kailasa – https://commons.wikimedia.org/wiki/File:Shiva,_Parvati_and_Ganesha_enthroned_on_Mount_Kailas_with_Na_Wellcome_V0045136.jpg

9. Gokul – https://commons.wikimedia.org/wiki/File:Baby_thief_Krishna_(bazaar_art,_c.1950%27s).jpg
10. Satsang – https://commons.wikimedia.org/w/index.php?curid=66760043
11. Annapurneshwari Ma – https://commons.wikimedia.org/wiki/File:Annapurnashiva.jpg
12. Kamadhenu Ma – Created by the author on ChatGPT
13. Saraswati Ma – https://commons.wikimedia.org/wiki/File:Raja_Ravi_Varma,_Goddess_Saraswati.jpg
14. Varaha Avatara – https://commons.wikimedia.org/wiki/File:Varaha_Raja_Ravi_Varma.jpg
15. Acharya Adi Shankara – https://commons.wikimedia.org/wiki/File:Raja_Ravi_Varma_-_Sankaracharya.jpg
16. Kurukshetra – https://commons.wikimedia.org/wiki/File:Bazaar_art_print_1940s.jpg

Section 3 | Chapter 3.3

THE HINDU TRADITIONALIST PART III: *ON REFORM*
Culture, Morality and Reform

Maragatham, 2021

PART III

On Reform

From a historiographical perspective, the *Puranic* lore and our Gods and Goddesses did not disappear with the arrival of *Veda*. *Veda* did not disappear with the arrival of *Vedanta*. *Vedanta* did not disappear with the arrival of the *Nastika* schools. The *Astika* schools and the two *Nastika* schools did not disappear with the arrival of *Bhakti*. *Bhakti* did not disappear with the arrival of Western Modernity. Still today *Indra Deva* is called forth. Still today *Agni Deva* is called forth. Still today *Varuna Deva* is called forth... as they were over five millennia ago.

This is not a small matter. This is a matter of profound importance and wonderment. In this sequence lies the clue to our future. We are Hindus, we do not erase the past, we carry it along with the present into the future... as a memory, as a ritual, as a story, as an allegory, as something.

For too long, our reformists have poured all their energies into dismantling the structures of the past, like some revolutionary Abrahamic cult. That these misguided elites have been allowed to irrevocably damage our relationship to the past is a shame from whose face we are only now beginning to withdraw the veil.

We are not ashamed anymore.

Why Re-Form?

Ok, so parts of Bharat have had a difficult last one thousand years and all of Bharat has had a very difficult last three hundred years. Does that mean we take the offer of 'convert or die' that our rivals make to us? Does that mean we start to believe that we don't deserve to live anymore as ourselves? The answers to those questions are really a measure of our vitality. "How alive are we?"—and couched within that question is a deeper question, "Who are 'we'?" I have attempted, in some way, to answer the second question in Parts I and II of this essay series but the answer to the first question is not to be found in any essay but in our hearts, and only time will tell if our answer is factual or imaginary.

So, why is it that we Hindus need to reform ourselves?

There is only one reasonable answer to this question. "Because we are now weak and we want to be strong like we were before. We want to find and uproot the cause of that weakness."

From this answer flows all the self-flagellation that we still submit ourselves to.

A Diagnosis

Our ancestors never lacked courage but they did make mistakes that are visible in hindsight.

Failure No.1: We failed to go on the offensive when our rivals were down.
Failure No.2: We failed to properly define in-group and out-group at the political level.
Failure No.3: We failed to understand the true nature of the existential threat we faced.

The first two failures are political in nature. The third failure is cultural in origin, but not, as many imagine, at the level of our social organization. It is a failure of imagination. We literally cannot imagine that people can be so bad.

Unfortunately, our reformists, ignoring this diagnosis, have insisted on locating the root of our failures in our social organization. "We are too diverse", "We are not united", "Our community tribalism is our Achilles heel", "If only we were culturally homogeneous" they lament. They insist that we cannot organize ourselves politically until these cultural weaknesses are uprooted. But the fact is, we were capable of political organization during the Battle of Rajasthan (738 CE) when, I would assume, the very same cultural weaknesses were just as entrenched, if not more entrenched, than now. Did our diversity lead to debilitating disunity then, or were our ancestors fully capable of coming together to point the Arabs back in the direction of Mecca? We were capable of political organization when Maharana Pratap came together with the Bhils (1580 CE). We were capable of political organization when Peshwa Baji Rao I came to the aid of Raja Chattrasal (1729 CE). We were also capable of political organization under Mohandas Gandhi (1915 CE) (though by that time we had been deprived of nutrition and weapons for far too long). Isn't it also true, that from the moment of birth of the idea of *Hindavi Swaraj*, it took a mere hundred years for it to manifest? All we needed then was a goal and intent—and, of course, a leader.

Disunity is a strawman. Locating the root of our weakness in disunity, and further locating the root of disunity in our social organization, are both steps in the wrong direction. For example, the Muslims of West Asia and the Christians of Europe fought amongst themselves *all* the time just like us, but that didn't prevent them from thriving. Our solution lies in using *this* observation to locate, accurately, the root of our weakness.

At the political level, the clear difference between our rivals and us is that:

a. They have a clear appreciation of 'in-group and out-group'.
b. They have a (divine) mandate to expand.

We have neither.

It appears now that if there is a cultural failure at all, it lies in our inability to understand the true nature of the existential threat that we face from our rivals. Our ancestors believed that all our rivals wanted was land and money when, in fact, what they really wanted was to eat our hearts. Once this is understood and internalized, it becomes much easier to define in-group and out-group, and politically organize ourselves accordingly. Unfortunately, even today, Hindus find it extremely difficult to believe that our rivals actually want to eat our hearts and, as a consequence, all our politics is centred around convincing ourselves that:

a. they do *not* actually want our hearts,
b. that we can *win* their hearts,
c. that we are all actually divided, and
d. that we can *only* unite under the banner of foreign memes.

All of these understandings are bogus.

Eyes Wide Shut

We have lost territory, both physical (land) and mental (culture). The physical loss continues to haunt and is the primary impulse for reform. It is a valid impulse because this *is* our *punyabhoomi* and we do not like to see it defiled. But reformists, ever since the 18th Century, had the idea that, if we were to give up mental space and adopt the ideas and cultural traits of our rivals, we could stop the loss of physical space. To be completely fair, it was a strategy that was partially successful. It lost us 30% of our landmass but bought us some time with political independence in 1947. Unfortunately, by then, our elites had given up so much of their mental space that 'they' were not 'us' anymore. With our elites becoming so much like our rivals, authentic Hindus were left with the illusion of recovered physical space when, in reality, it was still occupied by our rivals who ruled by proxy. This remarkable situation continues till today. We see that the non-elites who took power in 2014 have also lost so much mental space that they cannot help but continue on the course that their illustrious predecessors have set.

This phenomenon is put in its correct historical context by Dharampal Ji.

> In retrospect, the period from about 1919 (or perhaps from 1916 itself when Gandhiji's speech at the inaugural of the Benares Hindu University made the great Maharajas, the ruling elite, and Mrs. Annie Besant walk out of the meeting-place as a protest against what he had said) to about 1945, or perhaps even till 1947, may possibly be treated in today's environment as a period of the great illusion. For, during this period of Indian innocence, large sections of the Indian people began to believe that they could at least build a world of their own; a world constructed according to their own concepts

> and ideas; and that perhaps they may then even be able to help the rest of the world to return to sanity. Even sceptics like Jawaharlal Nehru at certain moments seem to have fallen under such an illusion. And it is possible that many in the West, especially of the more reflective and imaginative type, also at times felt that India may have a relevant message, and may perhaps serve as a world model.
>
> A similar belief about the possibility of an altogether new beginning, in continuity with the 1919 to 1945 period, seemed to have opened up, though only during a brief few days, at the end of March 1977, after the defeat of Shrimati Indira Gandhi, and the victory of the Janata combine under the inspiration of Shri Jayaprakash Narayan. But the habits and the assumptions of the past, built over several generations (during 1800 to 1919, and again during 1947 to 1977) asserted themselves and India reverted to its unthinking imitative role. This role benefits not even half a per cent of the Indian people, in European idiom, the officer class of India. It maintains their privileges, but is certainly ruinous to the social as well as private lives of at least 80% of India's people. The initiative which seems to have reverted to the majority of India's people, during 1919 to 1945 when as early as 1928, 1929, 1930 the people of India are said to have become virtually free, was again largely snatched away from them after 1947, and what remained was allowed to erode in the flow of time.
>
> – Dharampal, *The Self-Awakening of India, 1987* [1]

It is obvious now that the 'giving up mental space model' reached its logical conclusion in 1947 and ever since then it has been working against us.

Sociologist A.K. Saran calls it the Nilakantha Syndrome:

> The synthesis ideology, or the *Nilkantha* Syndrome which has continued to possess the Hindu consciousness from the days of Muslim and British domination down to the present time, is the Hindu way not only of paying the fatal price for some kind of survival, but also of masking the fact that such a tremendous price is being paid.[2]

We Arrive at a Crossroad

This really brings us to the crux of the matter.

1. What reforms will help reclaim our physical territory, because all that we've been trying so far has failed?

2. How much mental space are we willing to go on giving up in the belief that one day the tide will turn? Already many, many of us are no longer ourselves. With every passing year, secular school takes in millions of Hindu first generation learners and churns out deracinated non-Hindus at the other end of the pipeline. Of what use is the Hindu *punyabhoomi* if there are no authentic Hindus left?
3. The question that we are left with now is one of an *authentic* Hindu evolution that will lead to *both* our survival *and* our renaissance. What course will lead to wealth? What course will lead to strength? How do we walk these roads and continue to be ourselves (conservation)? How do we fashion a new self that carries all our old selves with us (the essence of *Dharmic* evolution)?

Unfortunately, with every reform that was informed by the loss of mental space, we lost still more mental space and gained absolutely no physical space. Many reformists, even today, proclaim that if we give up even more mental space, we will eventually win. There is no evidence whatsoever for this claim. If the history of the past two hundred years has taught us one thing, it is that giving up mental space and acquiring foreign memes has not helped us regain physical space. In fact, we continue to bleed physical space. The growth of the Abrahamic cults post-independence, when the giving up of mental space became our national credo, is a case in point.

When new external forces are applied on an internally balanced system, the system has to find a new point of balance. This much is a given. What that new point of balance is, depends a lot on the nature of the external forces. We have a number of options in front of us; each requires from us a different combination of strength, will, intelligence and love for our ancestors and Gods. We've tried many of them at different times, to different extents, with varying degrees of failure:

1. **The Multan Solution** — We submit to the new forces.
2. **The Maharana Solution** — We expend all our energies in repelling the forces.
3. **The Mother-India Solution** — We absorb the shock of the forces by allowing penetration and eventually slowing the forces down to a halt through sheer bulk.

4. **The Secular-India Solution** — We recognize that our rivals have won and give in substantially so they will leave us alone and maybe throw us a few crumbs.
5. **The Still-Wondering-How Solution** — We evolve in a totally original new direction that acts as a counterbalance to the new forces.
6. **The Never-Been-Tried Solution** — We attack the source of the external forces.
7. **The ISCKON Solution** — We transform the external forces through alchemy.
8. **The Chattrapathi Solution** — We lie low while we grow in strength and eventually reclaim our minds and our land.

1, 2, 3 and 4 have failed. We must focus on 5, 6, 7 and 8.

To Be or Not To Be

Survival is the primary imperative. Yes, but not unconditionally so. What use is survival if, in order to survive, we have to change so much, that we are no longer ourselves? How is that any different from conversion? How far is too far?

Each of us has to draw that line ourselves. Many feel that we have already crossed that line. Many feel that line is still ahead of us. Many feel we can draw a new line at our convenience. But it would do us good to remember that our heroic ancestors chose death instead of enslavement to foreign memes. They held that uncrossable line very, very close to themselves indeed. We, on the other hand, are so convinced that we need to survive at all costs that we are willing to sacrifice everything, even whatever little remains of our customs, at the altar of mere survival.

Such a strategy is not *Dharmic*, it is merely Darwinian.

Bringing Nuance to our Self-Perception

Hindu civilization extends from the earth to the sky. That is to say, it is a meeting of the bottom-up (community) and the top-down (civilization) in a fertile consummation (see Chapter 4.2 of this book). There are those among us who believe that the sky will stand without the earth, that the lofty philosophies of

Hinduism will outlive the destruction of the earthy communities that hold up those philosophies with their rituals. To them, I can only say "Time will tell, but by then, it will be too late."

Hindu philosophy without Hindu tribalism is dead on arrival. For sure, one part of our tribalism can indeed be a pan-Hindu political consciousness, as long as we understand that it is just *one* part of a very complex thing that we call Hindu identity. Trying to replace the entirety of that complex thing with a common tribalism for 1 billion people is a farce. The terms of such an endeavour cannot but fail to be so dilute that it would be meaningless as an identity marker. What we need is a pan-Hindu *political consciousness* for coalition-building between *Dharmic* communities. We do *not need* it for *deep identity building*. We already have our deep identities.

It is imperative then that this grand unity project be overtly political in nature and not cultural. Political unity will automatically have cultural implications but that is not our goal. The overt management of the cultural sphere must be left to our communities and their cultural and spiritual leaders. The grand unity project, if it is serious, should have two major aims. One, to rid us of two ancient weaknesses—our inability to define in-group and out-group, and our lack of an expansionist goal. Two, to consciously develop the terms for a long-lasting and binding coalition of all *Dharmic* peoples. In other words, developing the mechanisms for 'bridge-building'.

A true Hindu Nation needs to recognize all four pillars that hold up our superstructure and work respectfully towards their strengthening with the full participation of all stake-holders.

1. **Pillar #1: Tribe** — The Roots of the *Dharmic* Tree
   Jaati Vyavastha, *Kula Devatas*, Occupational Guilds, Ancestral Knowledge

2. **Pillar #2: Coalition** — The Trunk of the *Dharmic* Tree
   Mutual Respect, *Varna Vyavastha*, *Sampradayas*, *Mathas*, *Gurus*, Institutions that would work towards building mutual respect, conflict resolution, the national grand narrative and dharma expansion

3. **Pillar #3: Religion** — The Branches of the *Dharmic* Tree
   Veda, *Dharmic* Law, Civilizational Hinduism, Temples, Nationwide Festivals, *Bhakti*

4. **Pillar #4: Metaphysics** — The Flowers, Fruits and Seeds of the *Dharmic* Tree
   Yoga, Tantra, Vedanta, Enquiry, all other philosophical schools

With that complex image in mind, we can move ahead knowing that reform of any kind cannot be acceptable if it brings an axe to any part of this tree.

Our Form of Re-Form

Sati, Untouchability, Caste, Widow Remarriage et al. have nothing, absolutely nothing, to do with our predicament. These are all strawmen erected by the White Man to divert our attention. Whether these customs were widespread, localized, contextual, in need of abandonment etc. are all internal matters. They have *nothing* whatsoever to do with the White Man. But the White Man and his lackeys insist on using their hold over the means of broadcast to constantly erect these strawmen. Why? For the simple reason that they *need* these strawmen in order to bring their *Idealist-Morality* (see Chapter 3.2 of this book) to bear upon us. These strawmen serve as *entry points* (what are called 'fault-lines' these days). These entry points are those contours of our culture where the spike proteins of the White Man's viral ideals are able to find matching footholds. From these entry points the virus of Liberty, Equality and Fraternity enters our body-politic as a Trojan horse.

The Hindu notices that something seems not quite right with some of his customs; they seem to be attracting a ton of this unpleasant virus (along with a lot of uncomfortable accompanying noise). So, what does the Hindu do? Instead of attacking the virus or the source of the virus, he begins to get rid of these entry points. We see now that the desire to get rid of entry points is reactionary and not self-determined. He is now under the sway of the virus (that is, he is now acting under the demands of the foreign ideals that the virus represents). He starts to think that once he gets rid of all entry points (reforms himself), he will be strong and the Western virus will no longer attack him (he would have earned the respect of the source of the virus).

Alas for the naive Hindu, newer and newer entry points will be found and moral goal posts will be constantly shifted... community, family, temples, education, gender, marriage etc. etc. Until he understands and internalizes that the end goal of the viral Western ideals is not to help him become a better person but to control and eventually destroy him. The West does this in stealth by calling its ideals 'universal'. That is why I use the analogy of the Trojan horse.

By attacking the entry points of the virus rather than attempting to eradicate the virus, what we have allowed in post-independence India, is the spread of the virus through our body-politic. Today, the ideal of Equality, for instance, has such widespread acceptance in the populace that ordinary Hindus believe fervently that it is a self-evident truth. Our state and our intellectuals, instead of pushing back against this ideal and supplanting it with compassionate, reasonable *Dharmic* values, have allowed it free rein. This error of judgement has cost us dearly. Today, there is not a single *Dharmic* institution that is not subject to poisonous judgement by this ideal, causing them all to shrivel and hide upon contact.

By all means, let us reform, let us evolve, let us change, let us do whatever we want BUT *as ourselves,* and not under the flag of foreign ideals and the spell of self-hate that they have cast upon us. Is there a *Dharmic* reason to abandon *Sati?* Put it on the table. Are there *Dharmic* reasons to abandon our ancient taboos? Put them on the table. Let the *Dharmic* stake-holders thrash out a way forward. But let us not walk into battle with ourselves, waving the banners of Liberty, Equality and Fraternity, because this virus, let me tell you, is of a particularly virulent strain that has been home-cooked in a kitchen of European supremacy.

It's true nature needs to be called out.

Liberty leads inevitably, inexorably, to **irreverence**.

Equality leads, with equal bull-headedness, to **disharmony**.

And we know only too well that Fraternity leads to **ethnocide,** when it doesn't lead to genocide.

Do we want this stuff? NO. Then why do we insist on judging ourselves with these viral ideals? Abandon Western ideals, bring back *values*, *Hindu values*. Judge our community relations and our place in the world using *our* values and adapt accordingly.

The West is an idealist culture. It will sacrifice *all* in the service of ideals but for us Hindus, in a traditional culture, the acceptance of these ideals and their poisonous outcomes is nothing short of suicide.

In a traditional society, traditions are put in the service of culture. In an idealist society, it is culture itself that is put in service of ideals. We must resist walking into this trap. For example, if we are to adopt material Progress with a capital P as something absolutely vital at this point in history, let us adopt it as a value and not as an ideal. Let us roll out this value when it is needed in concert with the hundreds of other values that we hold dear, and roll it back when it is not needed. It must not stand alone like the Abrahamic God demanding submission of all our other values. It must be made to work with us and for us.

And, for the sake of all our Gods, let us disassociate the viral Western ideals of Liberty, Equality and Fraternity from our understanding of material progress. Look at Japan, look at China, look at Singapore. Let us make the political and economic changes needed to grow strong so we can better serve *Dharma*. Let us create a political climate and an incentive structure for the exaltation of Hindu values and not for our enslavement to viral Western ideals in the mistaken belief that it is they that lead to strength. They do not.

The Fog that Obscures. The Chain the Binds.

> *If you love something, you cannot also fail to support the conditions that make that thing possible.*

That Thing We Love

While threats from our older rivals still remain, a new threat in the form of a third-order religion, that goes by the name of Liberalism, has today gained widespread traction in a relatively short time (see Chapter 1.1 of this book). This new religion deals entirely in abstractions and has further deepened our inability to tell in-group from out-group. In our blindness, many of us embrace this new religion while continuing to call ourselves Hindu. It is against this backdrop that we need to examine the current trajectory of reformist thinking.

We have seen, in Parts I and II of this series, that Hindu ethics are encoded in ritual. Ritual therefore is the life-blood of Hindu morality.

It is *ritual* that takes the Hindu worldview and encodes it in the minds and hearts of real flesh and blood people.

Every neo-Hindu out there who loves *Vedanta*, *Yoga*, Rishikesh, the Thanjavur Big Temple, 'Seeking, Self-Discovery, *Ashram*-Hopping, Chanting, Meditation, that *Om* Tee-shirt, should know that none of this would exist today without the rituals that kept the Hindu *darshanas* alive for millennia encoded in the lives of communities that gave their sweat, blood, time, energy and faith to the maintenance and protection of those rituals and the honour of their ancestors.

It's time for payback.

Europeans needed **continuity in Ideas and Law** (manifest today in the curious idea of judicial precedence) to create the mental structures that defined their identity. That is why, when they created the myth of their origin in Ancient Greece, it wasn't the *culture* of Ancient Greece that interested them, but the philosophical ideas that were convenient for them to insert into their self-imagination.

Hindus, on the other hand, being an ancient people, need **continuity in Tradition** to create the mental structures that define their identity. We need to *feel* that we are still home, and home is that long line of people that stretches back in time till the very beginning. That is why Shri Aurobindo struggled; that is why Swami Vivekananda struggled; that is why we ordinary Hindus struggle. We cannot simply accept something new if it refuses to converse with the past. We need a hook, a cognitive and practical means to hitch this wagon on to all the others that came before.

Dr. S.N. Balagangadhara describes this essential (but now damaged) need and process:

> The process of transmitting our culture through these 'learnt' ways to other members in our culture also initiates a reinvention of the "Indian way". But it takes time (it has taken us centuries) to discover that, to make our past or present intelligible to us, western way(s) of transmitting traditions are not very 'effective'. Discovering that 'something' has gone wrong and is also going wrong in transmission (because our children are increasingly unable to relate to their own culture and society), we are forced to interrogate how we are accessing our traditions. Doing so does two things: (a) it forces and compels us to look critically at how we currently access our traditions; (b) the same movement also enables us to look at how we access our experiences. In some senses, that is our attempt now: by looking at how we access our experiences, we will discover

that we can regain access (in some fashion) to the accumulated "Indian ways". That is, we begin to invent ways to access our traditions differently. On the one hand, it is an invention. On the other, it is a rediscovery as well because we do not begin this process ab novo, out of nothing. Our point of departure is that we are Indians; even if damaged in transmission, we are recipients of what our parents, grandparents, families, etc. have transmitted. Thus, the process of rediscovery begins on these foundations and using the frameworks gifted to us from our past (however damaged the gift is). What we gain today through invention and discovery (both elements are present here) is our culture. Our relationship to the past is defined by how the reinvention and rediscovery is taking place today: we use the language of the present and are driven by our current exigencies to access our past and our traditions.[3]

In other words, authentic Hindus strive to make that connection between the past and the future. We do not simply rush forward in a flood of self-hate inspired by the application of foreign ideals on the lives of our ancestors.

One cannot love Hindu handloom and continue to destroy the communities that produce handloom. One cannot love Hindu temples and continue to destroy the communities that build those temples. One cannot love Hindu ceremonies and continue to destroy the very communities who keep those ceremonies alive. One cannot love having grown up in a caring Hindu family and continue to support a set of Western ideals that were born to destroy its very foundation. One *cannot*, if one has integrity, love Hindu philosophy and deride the very Hindu customs and communities that kept and continue to keep these philosophies alive. Without the support and sacrifice of living communities, Hindu philosophy too becomes just another accessory that one wears to virtue signal and hide one's inner Liberal behind a fig leaf of Hindu sounding words. If our *darshanas* are not ritualized, they are no longer *alive* within us. It is imperative, then, that the neo-Hindu understands this connection so that he can build a non-contradictory sense of self within his mind and heart.

Understand that rituals (including behavioural patterns that our grandmas beat into our heads) encode a worldview that would be lost within one generation without those rituals. *Understand* that a worldview *cannot* be passed on through the ages by philosophical discussions at meal-time with one's children. It can only be done by the enforcement of ritual from a young age. It is these rituals that ensured that the Hindu worldview remained embodied within us generation after generation.

Imagine our civilization as a giant *sari* woven over millennia. Every individual in every community adding a thread to the civilizational weave, every community adding a special pattern.

By the worship of the *Kula Devatas*, the re-membering of our *purana* through dance and drama in moonlit village squares, by the daily *puja* in every home, the drawing of the *kolam* on cow dung washed porches in the half-light of dawn, the *tilak* on the neem tree, the marigold on the termite hill, the *panchayat* meetings under the banyan tree, the constant and circular exchange of gifts within the community, the touching of the feet of our elders, the honouring of our ancestors, the pilgrimages to the holy sites, the daily following of the dictates of the stars and planets, the ceremonies of birth, marriage and death, the training of children in patience, hospitality, kindness and courage... by the maintenance of all of this, we live today as us and not as someone else.

By rejecting these Hindu rituals we do *not* enter a 'neutral', 'progressive' space as many of us are lulled into believing. Instead, we enter a new civilizational framework and engage in a new set of rituals. This new ritual framework goes by the name of 'Global Culture' (English-Speaking, Hollywood, Netflix, UEFA Cup, Jobs in New Zealand, Hip-Hop, Pub-Hopping, Free Love, Holidays in Italy). It is only that we are unconscious of its deep structure. This globalized world is *not* a happy family where everyone from everywhere is loved and cherished (though the brand managers want us to think that). It is in fact the fully formed structure of a civilizational metaphysics—that of Western Universalism. One cannot enter the doors of that foreign metaphysics and still continue to call oneself Hindu (though one can certainly participate in and negotiate with it as long as one is deeply rooted in one's own cultural ethos).

Wendell Berry, American conservative, nails the true nature of the "Global Culture" in this searing paragraph:

> The social and cultural pluralism that some now see as a goal is a public of destroyed communities. Wherever it exists, it is the result of centuries of imperialism. The modern industrial urban centres are pluralistic because they are full of refugees from destroyed communities, destroyed community

economies, disintegrated local cultures, and ruined local ecosystems. The pluralists who see this state of affairs as some sort of improvement or beginning of a new global culture are being historically perverse as well as politically naive. They affirm the pluralism of a society formed by the uprooting of cultures at the same time that they regard the fierce self-defense of still rooted cultures as "fundamentalism" for which they have no tolerance at all. They look with wistful indulgence and envy at our ruined and damaged traditional cultures so long as those cultures remain passively a part of our "plurality", forgetting that those cultures too were once fundamentalist in their self-defense. And when these cultures again attempt self-defense, when they assert inseparability of culture and place – they are opposed by this pluralistic society as self-righteously as ever. The tolerance of this sort of pluralism extends always to the uprooted and passive never to the rooted and active.[4]

The ideals of the Liberal religion are Liberty (sensory/emotional gratification), Equality (uniformity) and Fraternity (universalism). Common Western people who are now cut off from their traditional values have been funnelled through these idealistic filters. These broken people do their best to create a sense of home in this idealist desert. They create a new set of rituals to give shape to their new reality. No matter how crude or superficial these rituals seem to us, to the broken people these rituals are indeed home and they pass them on to their children and create art around them as if they were something precious.

Make no mistake, Western anti-culture too is given life through a set of rituals, we just need to know where to look.

Take the following: the granting of an insane range of choice to young children;[5] the fanning of desires and addictions to material things;[6] the encouragement of "I" ness in toddlers;[7] media depictions and societal expectations[8] of early sexuality;[9] the relentless pursuit of sexual gratification[10] from age 10 to old age;[11] the great departure into adulthood at age sixteen; adolescent rebellion;[12] the initiation into Liberal adulthood through raves, rock concerts, clubs, drugs and alcohol; the experience of loneliness and heartbreak; the hardening of the heart; the acceptance of social relations as utilitarian; the faith that only one person will truly understand us[13] and that the one true love will find each one of us; by divorce; by wearing the badge of honour that is depression;[14] by abandoning one's parents to loneliness;[15] by the training of children in the false knowledge that everything is possible for everyone,[16] that all problems can be solved through technology, that true difference doesn't exist and that Western ideals are universal.

These pit-stops of Western life perform the same function that rituals and *samskaaras* do in Hindu life—they just don't involve flowers and *agarbathi*.

As Hindus, when we turn our backs on Hindu rituals and encourage our kids to follow these Western rituals, we are laying the foundations for wholesale conversion. It matters not the *Ganesha murthi* in our houses or the crackers we burst on *Deepavali*—if the deep values of our morality themselves have changed, then we are the converted.

All neo-Hindu philosophy/progress lovers must note that we owe a debt of gratitude to the very rituals and communities that we believe we are today free from. And that debt will be paid for in blood one way or the other. If we fail to ritualize our modern lives, our children will grow up in the Liberal religion, no matter the depth of our love for Hinduism. Unless we embrace and enforce Hindu ritual at home, our children will not grow up Hindu. And the moment we embrace ritual we perforce have to embrace a community because traditions do not exist outside of community. And what more natural thing to do than to take on the responsibilities of our ancestral communities? (Taking *deeksha* in a *sampradaya* of one's choice is always a possibility for people particularly allergic to the idea of ancestral community.)

It is the passing on of tradition, in the form of ritual, through the generations, that comes to us as our culture. Individuals don't have tradition, they have habits. Only communities have tradition. If we understand this chain of interdependence, then we are ready to make peace with our collective past.

There would be no Hindu philosophy with us today without Hindu culture; there would be no Hindu culture without Hindu traditions; there would be no Hindu traditions without Hindu rituals; and there would be no Hindu rituals without Hindu communities. And without any of these links in the chain there would be no Hindu morality (living metaphysics).

We cannot have one without the other, we cannot pick and choose and declare one as progressive, and another one as regressive. We cannot squeeze this causal chain through the filter of Liberal Individualist-Morality and embrace only that which makes it through to the other side and continue to call ourselves Hindu.

One is a Hindu if one understands this great chain of Hindu being, given shape earlier in my description of the *Dharmic* Tree. If one can embrace some of it, that's wonderful; but it is important, as Hindus affected by Western Modernity, that we make peace with all of it. To create the foundation for an alternate Hinduized Modernity we will have to deal with every one of these inter-connected links and either maintain them as they are, absorb them into a new form or create a modern equivalent... all of this done with seriousness and respect for all that has come before us.

Anything less would be a great betrayal of our ancestors.

We are not here to taste the dessert, we are here to cook the feast, and so, my brothers and sisters, let's light a fire.

References and Links

1. Dharampal, *The Self-Awakening of India*, 1987

2. A.K. Saran, *The Crisis of Hinduism*, Studies in Comparative Religion, Vol. 5, No. 2., 1971

3. S.N. Balagangadhara, *What Does It Mean To Be Indian?*, 2021

4. Wendell Berry, *Sex, Economy, Freedom and Community*, Pantheon, 1992

5. Michal Maimaran, "Are You Offering Your Children Too Many Choices?", *KelloggInsight*, 2017
   https://insight.kellogg.northwestern.edu/article/choice-set-size-and-children

6. Becky Mansfield, "The scary truth about what's hurting our kids", *Your Modern Family*, 2021
   https://www.yourmodernfamily.com/scary-truth-whats-hurting-kids/

7. Elizabeth Daoud, "Childcare chain 'Only About Children' suggests parents should ask for permission before changing nappies", *7News*, 2021 https://7news.com.au/lifestyle/parenting/childcare-chain-only-about-children-suggests-parents-should-ask-for-permission-before-changing-nappies-c-3254089

8. Patrick Raymond Johnson, *The Impurity Truth: How Popular Media Taught Millennial Males To Get Laid And "Do It" As Early As Possible*, Marquette University Thesis, 2009 https://epublications.marquette.edu/cgi/viewcontent.cgi?article=1191&context=theses_open

9. Elizabeth Weil, "Puberty Before Age 10: A New 'Normal'?", *New York Times Magazine*, 2012 https://www.nytimes.com/2012/04/01/magazine/puberty-before-age-10-a-new-normal.html

10. Jennifer A. Smith and Mindi Wisman, *What are we doing to Girls?*, 2011 https://www.nn4youth.org/wp-content/uploads/What_Are_We_Doing_to_Girls.pdf

11. Lizzie Dearden, "Children filming themselves in graphic sexual videos for 'likes' online in growing trend", *Independent*, 2020 https://www.independent.co.uk/news/uk/home-news/paedophiles-online-child-sex-abuse-images-self-generated-streaming-iwf-a9272876.html

12. Francisco Alvarado, Blake Montgomery, Pilar Melendez, "'We Will Continue to Rage': SWAT Breaks Up Massive Crowds Defying Curfew in Miami Beach", *Daily Beast*, 2021 https://www.thedailybeast.com/miami-beach-freaks-out-over-massive-spring-break-crowds-declares-state-of-emergency

13. Mervyn Cadwallader, "Marriage as a Wretched Institution", *The Atlantic*, 1966 https://www.theatlantic.com/magazine/archive/1966/11/marriage-as-a-wretched-institution/306668/

14. Peter Wehrwein, *Astounding Increase in Anti-Depressant Use*, Harvard Health Publishing, 2011
https://www.health.harvard.edu/blog/astounding-increase-in-antidepressant-use-by-americans-201110203624

15. Joshua Coleman, "A Shift in American Family Values Is Fuelling Estrangement", *The Atlantic*, 2021
https://www.theatlantic.com/family/archive/2021/01/why-parents-and-kids-get-estranged/617612/

16. Claire Cain Miller, "The Relentlessness of Modern Parenting", *New York Times*, 2018
https://www.nytimes.com/2018/12/25/upshot/the-relentlessness-of-modern-parenting.html

SECTION 4

COMMUNITY & SOCIETY

Section 4 | Chapter 4.0

NO BRANCHES WITHOUT ROOTS – INTRODUCTION

Maragatham, 2022

Separation causes blindness. In America, the urban legend goes, when school kids are asked where milk comes from, they all answer, "From the milk bottle."

But let's go even further, as a recent Whatsapp forward reminds us—if you believe that cows *give* milk, you are wrong. Cows don't *give* milk, milk has to be earned! Earned on the back of millennia of domestication, centuries of breeding, generations of getting up at 4am, cleaning out the *goshaalas*, protecting the cows from disease and ticks, squeezing the last bit of water and green from the summer heat in order to keep the cattle alive until the next monsoon... day after day... year after year. *All* of that is what is in our ice-creams... not just milk. And certainly not just milk that the cow 'gave' us!

An understanding of inter-relationships and the terms that govern those inter-relationships is an essential component of the world of subsistence that all of our ancestors lived in, hardly two generations ago. Ironically, today, in this world of surplus, where we are more connected than ever before, we know less and less about our inter-relationships.

Both the world of subsistence and the world of surplus generate specific patterns of human behaviour. The subsistence world generates a morality of subsistence—be good, don't tell lies, help each other, have a family, respect your elders, control your anger/lust/greed. These are the values that maintain balance. Both hunter-gatherer cultures and agricultural cultures have the idea of *balance* at the heart of their social organizations. Culture is a means to maintain balance because, without it, survival itself becomes precarious.

The surplus world, on the other hand, generates a morality of surplus—greed is good, it's good to be bad, get ahead, break the rules, indulge your emotions, live young live free etc. You will see that these values are different in their intent from the values that make up the morality of subsistence. These values encourage unregulated growth and disruption. Industrial society is focused on growth without end, and *eternal imbalance* as a means to achieve that goal. If we accept that culture is a means to balance, then industrial society is essentially antithetical to that vision. It is, in fact, an anti-culture. More interestingly, in a society where morality is derived from surplus, the two sources of surplus come to be seen as Gods—Machines and the Market.

Here is a simple diagram that compares Abrahamic society, Modern Industrial Society, and Hindu society along six societal principles.

		Abrahamic Society (Christendom)	Industrial Society (The West)	Traditional Society (Bharat)
Metaphysics	Trancendental Principle	Heaven	Machine-Vaad	Moksha
	Active Principles	Jesus. Holy Ghost.	Market. Efficiency.	Karma. Dharma.
		⇩	⇩	⇩
Religion	Interactive Principle	Commandments	Ideals	Values
	Perpetuating Principle	Bible	Law	Traditions
	Living Principle	Flock	Liberty	Samskriti
The structure that ties Metaphysics to People		⇩ Church	⇩ Tech-State	⇩ Varnashrama
Sense of Self	Organizing Principle	Parish. Pyramid.	Individual. Autonomy.	Community. Collaboration.

In Bharat, our values are encoded in our traditions, and the framework of our traditions is upheld by our communities. That is how our communities are bound to the metaphysics that generated our values in the first place. Given that *Dharma* is the road to *Moksha* and *Moksha* is the metaphysical truth that generates our values in the first place, all the components come together to form an elegant circle. By rejecting any one of these principles, we break the circle.

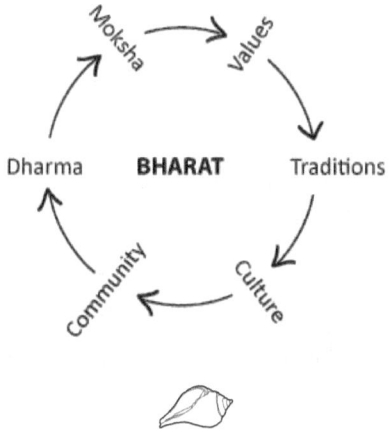

Section 4 | Chapter 4.1

NO BRANCHES WITHOUT ROOTS – PART I
Towards an Understanding of Western Organizing Principles – Individualism, Autonomy and Rights

Maragatham, 2022

The Origins and Limits of Individualist Autonomy

I too was a maverick, maybe still am. Never listened to anyone... always did my own thing.

But people like me must eventually come to realize that the high road of individualism and our yearning for liberty and autonomy have presided over the complete collapse of our inherited traditions in the few short generations since 'independence'. For anyone who has even a vague sense of the awesome civilizational heritage we are heirs to, this would be an unacceptable price to pay.

When I was in college, I made a documentary on travel, identity and culture, in which I interviewed a friend of mine. His words were prescient: "We all love to travel man" he had said. "We love going to foreign countries and eating foreign food and experiencing foreign cultures and being global human beings...I mean, it's great. But if everyone was to become like us... then who's going to be there to keep this s**t alive man?"

Forgive the language, but those were his exact words and they cut to the heart of the matter.

There is no belonging without participation... and there is no participation without the sacrifice of autonomy.

Hindu youth, as youth everywhere, must aim to channel their energies into doing more than their parents and grandparents did, but there is a qualitative difference between us and the West. The Western youth makes a point of rebelling against his father, to explicitly do what he has been told not to do, to make a religion out of his autonomy, to deliberately cut the branch of the tree he sits on, in the faith that he will plant his own tree. He doesn't realize that his son will do exactly the same to him. What that leaves us with is a bunch of stunted trees with sawn-off branches, not the magnificent banyan that civilization is meant to be.

It is for this reason that the Hindu youth must make it a point to respect ancestral boundaries, expand them if he is capable, constantly negotiate a settlement with them perhaps, but not tear them down. He is expected to take his family, his community and his ancestors along on his journey, not exist alone on his island. *"I never did what my father told me to do,"* is not a badge of honour for a Hindu youth to wear, because if we are Hindu, we realize that we are only one link in a chain that stretches back to the beginning of time. To use a chemical metaphor, Western Liberals are free radicals, we are long-chain molecules. Our family, *jaati*, *kula*, *sampradaya*, ethnicity, religion, *Dharma* all come together in an expanding, concentric and fractal identity that we wear. We are free to expand the circles, to extend the chains, to join chains together, but not to break them... that is, if we want to continue calling ourselves Hindu in essence.

One of the foundational principles of Western, post-Enlightenment morality is the idea of Individualist Autonomy. As the technologies and economic systems of the West have captured the world, so too has its morality and this principle in particular. So much so, that today, many of us Hindus too take Individualist Autonomy for granted, as an unquestionable moral good. But, do we know where this principle comes from and where it is leading us?

Where Individualist Autonomy Comes From

To use a Jared Diamond phrase, the 'world until yesterday'[1] was explicitly community-centred. Why? Because in the World-of-Nature (earlier referred to as the world of subsistence) that we all used to inhabit until very, very, very recently, it was only community that could ensure survival. In a non-industrial world, autonomous individuals would either be killed by rivals, wild animals or hunger. It was only in his community that a man had freedom! Outside of his community he could expect a quick death. This is a very radical redefinition of what it means to be free. But we must understand that for freedom to exist, first there must be Life. So, what is it that enables Life? We must start by answering *that* question and by organizing our societies to incentivize the conditions that support the answer to that question. In the non-industrial world of subsistence that we all came from, hardly two generations ago, it was obvious to everyone that community ensured Life and that all our morality was therefore designed around the maintenance of community and the relations we had with other communities and *Bhu Devi*. Think 'truth-speaking, sharing, family values, respect for elders, hospitability, *ahimsa*, *shaurya*, talking indirectly about topics that may offend, building inter-dependencies, ritualizing possible points of friction, sacralizing rivers, land, trees etc.' This is true of traditional communities all over the world.

There are a couple of conclusions that emerge from this understanding:

1. In large parts of the agricultural, nomadic and forest-dwelling worlds, this non-industrial, community-centred life continues to exist, and we must respect the right of these communities to live as they see fit, because we can see now that their morality is a legitimate outcome of the primarily natural world they inhabit and that they are not 'backward' or 'immoral'.
2. If we feel today that our world has changed so much in the mere seventy years since WW2 that our timeless communities have been rendered irrelevant, then we must enquire into the true nature of that suspiciously rapid change. What has the coming of the Western industrial model into our urban settings done to us and what do those changes mean for us in the long-term?

I understand that autonomy is a drug that once tasted is hard to discard. But, if we are intelligent, we can see that just because we want it, it doesn't mean it's the next best thing since *kaaju katli*. We ignore community consciousness at our peril. This new-found autonomy did not drop from the sky, neither is it a fact of nature. So, where did it come from? And how did it become the moral force that it has? Why have we, in just a couple of generations, been made to feel violated if our autonomy is constrained even a little? Why do we look upon older social structures that call for the sacrifice of our autonomy as 'regressive'? As 'Evil' even?

From inhabiting the World-of-Nature for two hundred thousand long years, Man and his tools finally passed a tipping point sometime in the 20th Century. That moment in history has its roots in the Industrial Revolution of Europe but— for a vast majority of people on Earth—the ripples of the Industrial Revolution finally became waves only last century. Until that time, 80% of humanity continued to live primarily in the World-of-Nature. It was only in the last century that the World-of-Human-Artifice (earlier also referred to as the world of surplus) began to outstrip the World-of-Nature as Man's primary experiential milieu. Our vehicles and transportation networks became our legs, our JCBs and earth movers became our arms, the internet became our memory, under-sea cables and satellites became our voice and eyes. Like a giant octopus, our World-of-Human-Artifice sits upon the World-of-Nature, sucking at it and re-distributing its gifts. Each one of us, who has access to these tools, has become a superman. And supermen can indeed live all alone in pristine Individualist Autonomy. There is nothing that our traditional communities can do for us supermen, that our 'octopus' can't. So, it's clear now, it's the 'octopus' that has rendered our communities irrelevant, and granted us liberty as we know it—a technology-driven-individualist-autonomy. We have now come to be wholly dependent on the 'octopus', otherwise known as the 'system'. It is ironic that we experience this total dependency as autonomy—but I digress...

Our limited emotional selves have evolved to respond to immediacy (think 'living in the savannah amidst lions'), and we work most naturally with objects and concepts within one degree of separation from us. Inevitably then, the immediacy of the World-of-Human-Artifice that we live within today, has become our reality—asphalted roads, apartments, petrol pumps, light bulbs, TV, internet, smartphones, showers, western toilets, cars, planes, ATM cards, LPG gas, shopping malls, advertisements, universities, manicured lawns, ready-made clothes, groceries delivered. Billions today cannot even imagine that there was, and in fact, continues to be, a life free of all of this stuff. All we see is the 'octopus', we do not see the World-of-Nature hidden under its folds and tentacles—forgotten and invisiblized, but still giving without protest, our *Bhu Devi*.

Where Individualist Autonomy is Leading Us

As we have seen, the World-of-Nature *demanded* community and the World-of-Human-Artifice *enabled* individual autonomy. The White Man, who created and entered the World-of-Human-Artifice first, started to look with disdain upon the World-of-Nature—both Nature herself and the communities that inhabited that world. This is the colonial gaze that we fought against for so long and finally overthrew. Or did we?

More and more, it is becoming apparent that, as we too entrench ourselves in the World-of-Human-Artifice, we too begin to look with disdain upon the World-of-Nature. We see the same patterns of behaviour and thought that the White Man has exhibited repeat themselves in our unconscious minds. Today, a vast majority of urban, educated Hindu youth look down upon their ancestral social arrangements, their *jaatis*, their *kulas*, the traditional occupations that kept their ancestral fires burning, and on all villagers and village life in general. Individualists accusing communalists of being evil because they prioritize their inter-relationships is analogous to rich people accusing poor people of being evil because they have no money. It's absurd, but it's typical of people making the transition from a subsistence morality to a surplus morality. This unconscious state of affairs needs to be critically looked at for four major reasons.

By uncritically embracing the World-of-Human-Artifice and worshipping its hidden principle of Individualist Autonomy:

1. We fail to see, that at the **Level of Morality**
   ...this liberty-giving autonomy is merely a function of the recent emergence of a high technology-enabled World-of-Human-Artifice. It is not necessarily a 'moral good' upon which we must hang our judgements of our ancestors or other people who continue to live in the World-of-Nature.

2. We also fail to see that, at the **Level of Fragility**
   ...this state of affairs is barely a hundred years old and we still do not know its true nature, though many educated guesses can be made. Will it last? Or will it destroy us all in an explosion of climate change, nuclear war, man-made pandemic, poisoned food and resource termination? We don't know. So how can we trust it, and how can we possibly construct our morality around it?

3. We also fail to see, that at the **Level of Freedom**
   ...the technologies that give us this liberty actually enslave us in many ways. We have to constantly remind ourselves that these technologies

have been built by corporations whose primary motivation is profit and the control of humans, not our well-being. By allowing our lives to revolve around, and depend intimately on, these technologies, we become beholden to these corporations, just as we were once beholden to the Gods. They promise freedom but they demand surrender. And as we move towards a more bio-manipulative future, our addiction to liberty has brought us to the threshold of self-extinction. We are faced with existential dilemmas of our own making. Who are we (now that AI will soon do all we can)? What is our identity (now that gene editing can manipulate us before birth)? Why do we continue to live (now that Science says there is no soul/God)? We see the failure to answer these questions play out more and more, in the violent chaos of the industrial world that keeps pushing the boundaries of what we are supposed to consider "normal' & 'human'.

4. We also fail to see that, at the **Level of Well-Being**
   ...this autonomy, insofar as it turns us unconsciously against the very communities we have sprung from, leads to an inner contradiction, an unbridgeable cleavage in our psyches, a kind of self-hate. When we humans accept and embrace an intellectual position that turns us against our biological and cultural origins, we enter a world of mind-body dichotomy that leads unerringly to all the psychological ills that we encounter in the industrial world (loneliness, depression, stress, substance abuse). And many of these psychological ills eventually lead to many of the un-named and un-nameable physical ills that also plague industrial society (autism, auto-immune conditions, cancer, dementia, sociopathy). These are all ways that the body reflects the self-hate of the mind. This is not just at the individual level but also at the level of humanity itself.

The ancients knew that, for everything gained, we had to give up something in exchange. This was the sentiment that appeared in our culture as the idea of Sacrifice. Industrial society, on the other hand, like Christianity before it, believes in Heaven, a place where we can have it all and give nothing in return. Christians believed that Heaven was elsewhere. Western and Westernized Modernists believe that we can make Heaven here on *Bhu Devi*. They do not see that as our muscles grow, our hearts shrink, our nerves fray and our bones splinter.

World War II? No Problem. Holocaust? No Problem. Chemical and atomic weapons? No Problem. Shall we introspect? No way!! Let's repurpose all those fluoride factories into selling toothpaste. Let's repurpose all those chemical weapons factories into making fertilizer. Let's invent TV for thought control. Let's send people to space. Let's start the Cold War and threaten each other with annihilation. Sounds great! And in a few decades let's do gain of function research, kill ten million people with a virus, lock seven billion people indoors and transfer wealth from small businesses to global behemoths. Wow!

But what's really wow is *Us*. Watch ourselves accept every step of this mad sequence of actions as "History"...as inevitable, as "human nature"...as "progress". And every year there are more and more of us who buy into this story. Every year we take one more step towards undisguised *Matsya* 'Machine' *Nyaya*.

In my opinion, it's time to engage seriously with the true nature of the technologies and the systems of the World-of-Human-Artifice... to get a grip on the extent of psychological and sociological loss that we face in exchange for the (temporary) security it provides. It also appears that we are not in control of it and that there are many among us (politicians, scientists, technologists and artists) who wish to sacrifice humanity itself at the altar of the octopus's unknowable heart. And there are many among us who in naive enthusiasm cheer on the take-over of our human essence by the miraculous monsters of our own making.

The Metaphysics of the Machine
A Causal Map of the Western Moral Edifice

The White Man is not ignoble because he fails to follow our values; he is ignoble because he fails to follow his own. His seemingly noble ideals of Liberty and Equality have brought us only hell because they are parsed through his Active Principle (the Market) and judged in reference to his Transcendental Principle (the Machine). That is why the pursuit of Liberty perversely led to slave-driving, genocide and colonialism while the pursuit of Equality perversely led to the massacre of a hundred million people last century. As they say on Twitter—"Feature not Bug"

Many believe that the secularized world that the Western man inhabits today has no sense of the sacred because it lacks a transcendental principle, but this is a false understanding. As Elon Musk reveals inadvertently in this interview[2] (>16.30), the Western world *does* have a transcendental principle—it is the Machine. Westernized Man wants to transcend his human condition, not by striving to become divine but by becoming Machine. From this implicit, but seldom declared fact, flows the entire downstream debris of Western society.

Just like we use our Active Principle, *Dharma*, as a guide, so too does the White Man use *his* Active Principle, the Market, as his guide. And just as our actions are tempered by our association with our Transcendental Principle, *Moksha*, so too are his actions intensified by *his* Transcendental Principle, the Machine. Western post-Enlightenment Man has stepped into a *chakravyuh* of his own making from which he cannot now exit. All his art, literature and science fiction cry out the story of his pathos.

So, let me draw you a causal map with words.

i. From the enslavement of West Africans, the genocide and theft of the Americas, the robbery of Bharat, Africa, and South-East Asia, came the wealth that built the West. It is this wealth, and the power that it brought, that has served as the self-justification for the White Man's immoral actions over the past five hundred years. "Oh, if we too become like him, we too can become rich and powerful like him!" we think, "Let us simply ignore his depravity. To hell with the sacrifices made by our ancestors."

ii. From that ill-gotten wealth was built the World-of-Human-Artifice, the cities of Western Europe, the cities of North America and the winding tentacles of highways and pipelines that brought resources from all corners of the globe to keep those cities vital. *Surplus*.

iii. From the continued rape of *Bhu Devi* and the displacement of traditional peoples all over the world, the World-of-Human-Artifice has spread to every continent. Today, enormous Western-style cities exist everywhere... Mumbai, Tokyo, Shanghai, Lagos, Sao Paulo, and innumerable others. Each of these cities sits in the centre of a vast catchment area that supplies it resources and people... food, water, cement, steel, wood, lithium, coal, farmers, carpenters, sweepers. A total and complete refashioning of reality.

iv. From the ubiquity of that World-of-Human-Artifice has come the possibility that some of us can be Supermen. And, from the example of those men have come the stories, TV shows and movies that have encouraged us to internalize the idea that Individualist Autonomy is our birth-right... that each and every one of us can be Supermen... one day. *Apna time aayega*. But this is not true at all... billions languish in the cages of their unmet expectations, living their lives vicariously through the lives of TV stars.

v. From this universalization of the Western principle of Individualist Autonomy has come the widespread acceptance of the twin Western ideals of Liberty and Equality. Think about it... without the internalization of the principle of Individualist-Autonomy it would be impossible to imagine such a thing as Western Liberty. The "I want"-ness of it all. And without the ideal of Liberty, it would be impossible to imagine such a thing as Western Equality (which is nothing but a demand for equal liberties). Individuality, Liberty and Equality are a triad, they are deeply connected.

vi. With the growth of the idea of Individualist Autonomy, our ability to see relationships recedes and we start to see ourselves as atomized entities. Individuals without relationships slowly start to disengage from the idea of culture, shared values and the sacred (this is happening as we speak, in Bharat). Instead, we begin to direct our loyalties towards the Machine and the Market. Traditions fall apart and we start to generate secular ideas to bind us into groups, to make us recognizable to each other. Nationalism was one of the first such glues that the White Man invented and supplied to us. Once the borders were settled (more or less), other ideas took the place of Nationalism... ideas that are still being churned out, like 'Free-World', 'One World', 'Liberty', 'Equality', 'Social Justice', 'Human Rights', 'Progress'. These ideas are supplied as binding material, without which the system cannot maintain coherence. And as we, ordinary people, absorb these ideas, we begin to use the adherence to these ideas as a metric to judge ourselves and other people.

"What!! she agreed to *Kanyadaan*, she's sooo regressive!!"

vii. From the application of Liberty and Equality as judgemental tools has come the idea of Rights. Is my life condition 'Free' or 'Equal'? If not, I am being denied Rights and the law should move to rectify my condition. Nothing organic, evolved or naturally human can exist... all must be processed and represented. In reality, there is no such thing as Rights. It is an entirely manufactured concept upheld by a monster centralized state and based on reference to certain Western ideals which themselves grew out of industrial surplus propped up by slavery, robbery, genocide and the rape of *Bhu Devi*. To emphasize the fact that Rights are fictions, allow me to bring up a recent (April 2024) Supreme Court ruling. While hearing a case involving threats to the Great Indian Bustard from overhead transmission lines in its habitat, the presiding judge ruled on, hold your breath, "The Right to be Free from the Adverse Effects of Climate Change".[3] Just think about it. In order for this "Right" to be actualized, we would either have to tear down the entire industrial economic system, or in order to continue to maintain this fiction in public discourse, the government would have to control and surveil the entirety of human activity and all its downstream effects. The irony is not merely that this Right will never be more than a fiction, but the fact that the very industrialization that birthed the idea of Rights is now sought to be put in the dock for *violation* of those very same Rights!

This is a remarkable edifice and it's one that we take for granted today but, by prising it apart as I have done above, we see that it is just one among many routes that humanity could have taken, and indeed peoples all over the world have always travelled upon many, many roads. It is only now, at this unique moment in History, that we are being told that this Western moral road is the only legitimate path we ought to walk upon because to take any other would be immoral! Not only is that coercive and false but it obfuscates the roots of this particular moral road. Those roots, that lie in slavery, genocide and colonial robbery, should be unacceptable to any *Dharmic* person and perhaps any decent human being. Furthermore, the fact that this model rests on the expectation of continued and, indeed, eternal supply of surplus should have the sceptics amongst us alarmed.

Did you know that concrete has a lifespan of, at most, a hundred years? Every building, bridge, road, house, tank, dam... in fact the entire World-of-Human-Artifice must be built again every one hundred years, if not more often, forever! Forever being a very, very long time. Does anyone seriously think that this is going to be possible, that the world as we know it will continue to exist in status quo or in an improved condition even a hundred years from now? One only has to look at Kolkata...the shining jewel of the British Empire, to know how everything is going to be in sixty years' time. It's like sitting in Anantapur in the month of May, eating ice-cream all day and saying that it's actually not too hot... until the moment when the ice-cream runs out.

The West had Africa, Bharat and Native America to subsidize its development journey. Russia had Siberia and the 'Stans'. China had Tibet, Xinjiang and vast tracts of Africa. What do we have? Who do we ravage but ourselves? And, more importantly, what next? What most people don't understand is that the creation of the world of surplus, otherwise called 'development', is not a destination, it is merely the first step in a prohibitively expensive annual maintenance contract that we sign up to forever. Look at all the wars that America is having to fight just in order to maintain its flow of cheap oil. The more developed one is, the more maintenance one needs. Every single casino in Vegas uses more electricity that an entire Indian town. The faster the treadmill, the faster one has to run. Initially it feels like we're getting fit but, in due course, we realize that we're heading for a burst aorta.

And last, but not least, we need to pay heed to the catastrophic consequences of this model for human health and well-being... autism, Alzheimer's, Parkinson's, diabetes, allergies, dementia, bipolar, manic, auto-immune, sociopathy, psychopathy. These consequences are inherent to this model of 'progress', to living within the metaphysics of the Machine and in the slipstream of the Market. It is the price we pay for our greed and hubris. It appears to me that this edifice rests upon a very shaky foundation indeed.

A Path Diverges in the Wood

There appear to be only four ways ahead.

1. The return to Community life in the World-of-Nature.
   Many on both the Far-Left and the Far-Right favour this. Many proponents of intentional community-living imagine that this movement can be made now, consciously, or later, when we are forced to do so, post-collapse.

2. The continuation of the current trajectory into an AI-inspired, space-faring, chip-wearing, bio-manipulative future.
   The technologists and many ordinary people dream of this. Many like Elon Musk are aware of the dangers of this Matrix-like future but continue to cheer it on because they feel it is inevitable. The risks of collapse, if we blindly follow such a model, are great. Covid has already given us a glimpse.

3. A *Dharmic* cultural victory and take-over of the means of production leading to a qualitatively different set of technologies.
   This course is almost impossible to imagine at this moment.

4. Reaching a fine balance between the World-of-Human-Artifice and the World-of-Nature. This is what those with a 'Small is Beautiful' bent of mind dream of.

Personally, I know that #2 is where we are at because that's where our *Adharmic* rivals are at, and we have no choice but to go head-to-head with them. #3 seems utterly impossible at the moment. But I hope for #4 and I prepare for #1.

A Quick Recap – What's Under the Hood?

It is only with the widespread advent of the Machine-World (the ubiquitous World of Human Artifice) that the differences between people start to become irrelevant. Machines, with all their super-human capability, paper over human differences by compensating for inequalities. It is only then, for the first time, that the idea of temporal Equality becomes not just possible but also starts to be seen as an ideal. This is the root material cause for the eruption of Equality claims in modern society.

Similarly, it is only in a substantially Machine-World that the Western idea of Liberty as autonomy starts to gain traction, eventually establishing itself as an ideal. This is only possible because machines, again with all their super-human capabilities, paper over our human frailties and physical limitations. This feeds the delusion that we are capable of autonomous existence, when in fact we are further entrenched in a web of ever-expanding dependency (perhaps not directly on other humans, but certainly on more and more complex systems of economic and technological origin).

From this vantage point we can see that, when a person criticizes a society for being unequal or illiberal, he is actually criticizing it for being non-industrial or pre-machine-*vaadic* (literally, *machine-istic*). Today, when we speak on behalf of Equality and Liberty as understood in the West, we are actually subconsciously speaking on behalf of the Machine, as representatives of the Machine and the peculiar moral imperatives it engenders.

In a pre-machine-*vaadic* time, when differences were *essential* (that is, Gods-given), how a civilization dealt with difference and how justly it distributed resources and opportunity among those differences was in fact the hallmark of its decency and ethicality. Our *jaati-vyavasthaa* is a classic example.

Similarly, in a pre-machine-*vaadic* time, when autonomy was an impossibility, how a civilization assigned purpose to each individual life was in fact be the hallmark of its compassion and ethicality. Our *karmaphala* and *nishkama karma* are classic examples.

In all these matters, the uber *Sanatana* ideals of *Purusha* and *Purushaarth* stand apart.

Unfortunately, with the advent of machine-*vaad*, our heads high on gasoline, these same mechanisms that once fed us ironically come to be seen as monstrous

So, regardless of one's position vis-à-vis development and material progress, many of us need to understand that Individual Autonomy is not *automatically* the moral good that it is advertised as, that the Rights and Equalities that we fight for on the streets and courts today are not Gods-given, and the merely seventy-year-old, ever-expanding World-of-Human-Artifice that supports these ideas rests on very, very thin unsustainable ground. In other words, we must face up to the fact that Individualist Autonomy, Liberty, Equality and the idea of Rights all stand on the legs of the Machine-World, which in turn rests on the continued, unsustainable rape of *Bhu Devi*, without which the surplus generated by the ultra-technologized world would simply disappear and, along with that world, the machines and the ideals that were birthed by them too would vanish. We need to consider again that a society built on the values of community, collaboration, compassion, duties and sustainability still sounds like it will serve human interests in the long term better than the cocktail we currently have.

So let me start by setting aside the value of Individualist Autonomy and let us consider again the idea of *Community*.

References and Links

1. Jared Diamond, *The World Until Yesterday*, Allen Lane, 2012

2. Elon Musk, *The Joe Rogan Show*, https://www.youtube.com/watch?v=ycPr5-27vSI

3. Simrin Sirur, "Climate litigation has entered the room. But could Great Indian Bustards be inched out?", *Mongabay*, 2024
https://india.mongabay.com/2024/04/climate-litigation-has-entered-the-room-but-could-great-indian-bustards-be-inched-out/

Section 4 | Chapter 4.2

NO BRANCHES WITHOUT ROOTS – PART II
An Understanding of Hindu Organizing Principles from the Outside-In : Community, Collaboration, and Civilization

Maragatham, 2022

(Concepts introduced in Part I of this essay are frequently referred to, especially the ideas of the world of subsistence/the world of surplus and the six principles of social organization as manifested in the West and in Bharat. Do refer back when needed. Also, this is an extremely concept-dense essay, so feel free to read it in parts, at your leisure.)

Community
A Defence

People may imagine, upon reading my words, that I am an 'upper caste' man trying to use clever arguments in order to retain my 'privileges', but this could not be further from the truth. I came to rural Tamil Nadu two decades ago, on the run from the ugliness of America and the growing Americana in the urban centres of modern India. Of course, I had already been brainwashed by Marxist ideas and the logic of social justice movements that were sweeping the West and that would soon become mainstream even in India. I spent years trying to square the circle, to fit my ideas into the village world I experienced every day. Luckily for me, the circle was never squared and I was slowly but surely absorbed into the circle. The 'OBC' *Vanniyar jaatis* and the 'SC' *Paraiyar jaatis* who I worked with, whose kids my children played with, were to become my extended community. Their love for their traditions, their/my Gods, their many ingenious skills and, above all, their easy, non-judgemental hospitality slowly and inevitably nudged this fallen Liberal back into the Hindu fold. I do not deny that this rural Hindu life has its share of skirmishes, squabbles and entrenched problems. Millions see these issues as all-important and discuss them threadbare, but I see them as mere hiccups. Its better we focus on what has been *enabled* by our ancient systems of community organization, self-regulation and management, because all of that has been invisiblized in the shrill anti-Hindu rhetoric of the past hundred and fifty years. If we set aside our individualist eyes for a while and suspend our kneejerk application of the Western ideals of Liberty and Equality, we will reach a place of reasonable neutrality from which we can enter this familiar yet different world.

What is apparent to any neutral observer of the community-conscious Hindu world is the sheer harmony and beauty of what is happening here, every day, in plain sight but seemingly unnoticed. Our liberal eyes fail to see the *Maargazhi Kolams*, the *Aadi Thiruvizhaas*, the *Portaasi sanikizhamais*, the annual *Koozh-oothara Vizhaas*, the daily offerings to *vepamaram Vediappan*, the *vellikizhamai alankaaram* for *Puttruamman*, the easy camaraderie between communities and clans that have kept the rice paddies fertile for millennia, maintained our water irrigation systems for centuries, maintained the peace through the sharing of pasture land and the exchange of seeds... the intricate eco-system of collaborative communal life that results in the grass growing in the *yeris* becoming the roof over our heads, all happening as if by magic, with no governmental presence and no top-down 'system' or 'organization'. And, indeed, it is magic to see people being humans in a primordial sense, husbanding nature, settling their conflicts through ritual gift-giving, collaborating daily and never forgetting to thank the Gods for all this hard-won bounty. How can something as remarkable, gentle and beautiful as this be as evil as they say it is?

I stand with this vanishing world of authentic human experience. I stand with my *Vanniyar* and *Paraiyar* brothers and sisters and the world they have created, nourished and died defending. Urban Hindus, high on atrocity literature and the rhetoric of five millennia of oppression do not realize that by aiming to erase 'caste' they are teaching the children of our communities to hate where we've come from. By teaching our children to erase the beautiful and sustainable traditions that gave us Life, they are not saving us from oppression but, in fact, *subjecting* us to oppression. By 'ethnociding' us 'for our own good' the anti-caste brigade reveals itself to be a pawn of the Western Active Principle (that is, the global capitalist Market) that detests diversity, community and independence because they are inefficient and outside of its control. Don't they see how ironic it is that they want to *save* us 'subalterns' by erasing our cultures and traditions and by brainwashing our children into believing that the lives of their ancestors were inauthentic? Millions in our cities forced to do nine-to-five jobs that they detest, that they dream of escaping from every day, stuck in traffic jams for hours, breathing in noxious fumes, all that is not oppression? But simple people coming together to create a local economy, build their homes, husbanding natural resources sustainably, growing their food, feeding thousands of others, maintaining good humour and fellow-feeling over millennia—*that* is oppression?! What kind of perverse Marxist mind would look upon reality, see nothing of its beauty or intricacy, imagine a non-existent system that has neither been defined nor seen to be implemented, and then dismiss reality itself as oppression?

Some inter-tribe skirmishes are on the rise, prejudices flare up more often, natural resources are fought over more fiercely, feelings of us and them are delineated more sharply. Yes. But is this not to be expected in a land which has been fighting a war for one thousand two hundred years, where farmers were taxed 60% of their harvests for seven hundred years, where access to the Commons has been restricted and outright denied for two hundred years, where people have been denied their identities for seventy years? Is a certain level of debasement not to be expected in a land where wars, taxes and denial have resulted in the closure of indigenous education systems, the impoverishment of our places of religious expression and the erasure of pride in our ancestral work and traditions—basically everything that could have helped uplift us during the dark centuries? But still we maintained our dignity and our faith in the Gods and our customs. What stamina! What pride! What faith! Let us understand the context in which this debasement occurred. Let us start from the beginning... from a time before the debasement. Let us use that as a springboard just as the Europeans ignored the Dark Ages and looked to the Greeks, and let us build a narrative of pride. Let us use that narrative to build strength and purpose and unity and figure out how to avoid a future debasement while remaining uncompromising in our essential character.

Let us start by turning the narrative on its head. Hinduism did not *create* 'caste'. Caste, in the form of *jaati*, is nature itself. It is the tribalism that has existed in all places since the dawn of time. People banding together into comfortable groups in which trust can be verified and promises enforced, figuring out how to deal with other groups... this is *jaati*. *Jaati* gave us community, *jaati* gave us the means to survive in the World-of-Nature. Remember that until 1900 CE, our population was 80 million people living in far-flung villages spread over 275,000 square miles of heavily forested land in which roamed 40,000 tigers. This is the context for *jaati*. In this land where the rivers flowed and which the Gods blessed, our ancestors made their fires, transplanted rice, domesticated cows, harvested bamboo, maintained the peace, made art, shared stories and participated in a metaphorical life.

Let us not hate it.

Let me now offer a way to think about ourselves that will peel away the foreign onion skins that have grown to cover our self-perception.

Culture and Civilization
Looking In, Looking Out

Culture is organically evolved. It represents the urge to localization. It is the tribal aspect of ourselves. *Civilization*, on the other hand, represents the urge to universalization. It refers to a set of uber values, ideals and techniques that are capable of bringing people of different cultures together to give them a common umbrella to band under, even though the cultural ground they stand upon may not be uniform. There are thousands upon thousands of cultures, but only a handful of civilizations. Out of that handful, just a few are still with us today: Western post-Christian Civilization (the current hegemon); Han civilization (that is currently making a bid for primacy even though it is heavily race-focused); *Sanatana* Civilization (that is awakening after centuries); Islamic Civilization (that is strongly entrenched but uncreative); and Japanese and Slavic civilizations which were always race-focused and limited in their appeal. Out of these civilizations, only Western Civilization and *Sanatana* Civilization have the necessary epistemological tools to appeal to all of humanity. The other civilizations are necessarily self-limiting because of the narrowness of their worldviews.

All civilizations have grappled with the problem of how to bring the tribes together. This is the great task that civilizations perform and, in doing so, they have had to deal with all the ethical dilemmas that consequently arise. Different civilizations have approached this task differently—the out and out tough cop approach of Islam, versus the good-cop/bad-cop approach of Christianity, versus the 'take this cash and this booze and this sex while we brainwash your kids' approach of Western Liberalism. But it is only *Sanatana* Civilization that held the means to be just as important as the ends... the ethics of *how* to approach the problem was taken to be as important as the ultimate unity to be forged.

The questions that *Sanatana* Civilization asked were these: "How was the unity to be forged without erasure, without genocide, without enslavement, without the temptations of debasement, but with an invitation to nobility, in diversity, in beauty and in collaboration? How to invite, rather than demand? How to entrench the values so deep and so naturally in work, in community, in ritual and in geography, that we would not need weekly brainwashing sessions?"

That *Sanatana* Civilization engaged with these matters should be seen by all as its claim to ethical pre-eminence. Today we disparage it because we no longer have the subtlety of mind to appreciate the complexity of the task that it set itself. It would have been so much easier to have enslaved communities, committed genocide, colonized other countries, built a short-lived unity through expansionism, but our *rishis* chose to take a high road. It was obviously a much slower road, but a much more beautiful one, and a deeper process as a result. This is in evidence when we consider the diversity of culture, the beauty of tradition and the depth of philosophy that took root in Bharat. Such a human garden exists nowhere else in the world. If the Islamic invasions had not disrupted this astounding ethical experiment, we may well have reached our destination—but, alas, it was not to be.

Islamic Civilization and Christian Civilization spread under the banner of expansionism. The idea that one has to expand at all costs resulted in leading both these civilizations straight into the jaws of great evils: slavery, genocide, and colonialism. What's more, a unity forged in the fires of such evil is inherently weak. It falls apart as soon as expansionism is no longer possible. As long as the spoils of colonial loot and rape are flowing, the converted and 'united' tribes are happy. But, as soon as the flow of ill-gotten wealth and women stops flowing, the tribes fall into fighting over the spoils. We saw this in post-pagan Europe and more recently in 20th Century Western Europe. We see this throughout the Muslim world—Iran versus Iraq, Saudi versus Yemen, Turks versus Kurds, Pakistan versus Bangladesh, Sunni versus Shia etc. If one is only united when one has a common enemy, then what kind of unity is that?

Western post-Enlightenment Civilization is also expansionist, but its methods are more sophisticated. Instead of using the sword or the gun, it spreads by appealing to our baser values—greed, selfishness, and lust—and labels them as our 'true nature'. It then attempts to create a highly unstable system of control and punishment. Lust is encouraged as porn, greed is encouraged as the Market, selfishness is encouraged as individualism... but these very same values are criminalized when they cross arbitrary tipping points. So, get this, the *very values* that are the *engine* of Western life are criminalized beyond arbitrary tipping points. *This* is the schizophrenia that modern Westernized people labour under.

Sanatana Civilization, on the other hand, appeals to our nobler values, *nishkama karma*, *seva*, *dana* and *tyaga*. It posits that these values lead to the revelation of our true nature which is *aatman* and, further, that the true nature of the *aatman* is the *paramaatman*. This truth that *Sanatana* Civilization offers to us is free of internal contradictions. A society that functions as per these values is self-limiting, self-policing, self-sustaining and uplifting. It exhibits integrity. *Sanatana* Civilization invites us to step up so we can take control. Western civilization tempts us to step down so we can be controlled.

When civilization comes, it usually expects local cultures to surrender to it. Most civilizations believe that unless disparate cultures give up the ground under their feet, they will not be able to come together under the new civilizational umbrella. So, the agents of civilization indulge in ethnocide, genocide and enslavement. This was how Christian civilization spread to the Americas, Africa, Australia and Asia. This is also how Islamic civilization spread in West Asia, North Africa and Bharat. These examples of violent civilizational spread are so ingrained in our consciousness that we imagine all civilizations to be similar. It is the reason why many awakened Hindus have ironically turned into apologists for Empire. They insist that Europe 'won' because it deserved to win and that if we want to win, we must become like them. It is also the reason why 18th Century Europeans could not but imagine that there must have been a war-like *Aryan* race that came to Bharat and subjugated the indigenous people... because they simply could not imagine any other way. And the rest, as they say, is History.

The Unique Nature of Sanatana Civilization
Building a Unity in Diversity

Sanatana Civilization was qualitatively different. It was not just a force for unity, it was simultaneously also a force for balance and harmony—*Dharma*. It is for this reason that it is known as *Sanskriti*. Similarly, Hinduism as a religion is qualitatively different from the Abrahamic religions in that it represents the pursuit of *Satya* rather than the forceful implementation of commandments. It is for this reason that it is known as *Dharma*. But I will continue to use the word *civilization* and *religion* for ease of comparison with global phenomena.

Unlike the spread of other civilizations, when *Sanatana* Civilization first emerged and spread in Bharat, it did not come upon the wings of erasure, genocide and slavery. It did not come as a destructive tsunami, it came instead as a bridge. The bridge was a call to nobility. Tribes were invited to belong, to sacrifice their competitive instincts for the greater good, to honour a set of common values and participate in a great collaborative *yagna*. Tribes were encouraged to see themselves and each other as parts of a single divine body, and the divine body, or *Purusha*, was here on *Bhu Devi* to offer excellence to the Gods. This dramatic vision, manifest on *Bhu Devi*, is our collaborative effort, our coalition, the weave of the cultural fabric of this nation. Some tribes made it all the way across the bridge, some made it half way, some were hesitant and watched it from afar, but our *rishis* built that bridge and left it there for all time to come. The people who crossed the bridge continued to interact with people who didn't. The tribes who chose to stay on the periphery of the bridge, or in their forest strongholds, continued to bring their produce and skills to the bridge because the bridge was a source of work and wealth. A visit to Kutch even today will show us how the people of the bridge continue to interact with and value the nomadic *Rabaris*. A visit to Kotagiri will show us how the people of the bridge continue to interact with, and value the mountain-dwelling *Khotas* and *Kurumbas*. A look at the video *Kani tribe visits Travancore royal family*[1] will show us how the *Kaani vanavaasis* continue to relate to and work alongside the Travancore royal family. And, of course, we have the famous example of the *Bhils* and Maharana Pratap forging a unity for a common goal. Given these living examples, I find it hard to accept that the oft-referenced ill-treatment of SCs and STs was an established civilizational practice. I would rather look towards the documentation of 'caste' practices pre-17th Century to come to a reasonable understanding of how classical Hindu society used to function at a time when we still held ourselves up to the name *Arya*.

The British censuses and the institutionalization of 'caste' post 1947 have permanently closed access to our civilizational bridge. Today, many who are heirs to the values of the bridge would rather jump off onto a ship headed for foreign shores. Today, many communities who lived on the periphery of the bridge have been schooled to see the bridge as a monster. But those of us who still believe in the bridge and what it stands for need to work out how to re-open the bridge, to re-establish its noble values as aspirational, and unblock the flow of *sanskriti* for the benefit of all communities.

In a time when people were willing to wait lifetimes and *Sanatana* Civilization was willing to let the natural flow of time leave its mark on the destiny of communities, we never did develop a mechanism for *actively* bringing peripheral communities on board the bridge. In this age of speed and excess, we are not afforded that luxury. Now is the time to build the institutional mechanism for bringing all interested people on board the bridge.

If there is one task that a Dharmic-minded government along with our acharyas must collectively engage in, it is this.

Hinduism: A Confluence of the Bottom-Up and the Top-Down
Establishing an Accurate Mind-Model of Hindu Society

Civilization is indeed a top-down force but it doesn't have to be ethnocidal, as *Sanatana* Civilization has shown. It can appear as a bridge or a ladder or the branches of a tree pointing skyward. Our cultures meanwhile are bottom-up, they are the roots of the tree that connect us to *Bhu Devi* and our *Kula Devatas*. So, in order to truly understand Hinduism—as we know it in its everyday practicality—we have to see it as a confluence of the two streams, the Bottom-Up *Bharatiya* well-spring and the Top-Down *Sanatana* glacial stream. These two living bodies of water come together to create the river that is Hinduism.

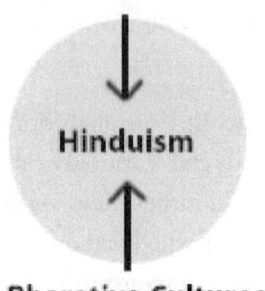

Bottom-Up Hinduism is the collective of our *Bharatiya* cultures, our *jaatis*, *kulas*, local traditions, traditional occupations, *Kula Devatas*... everything that gives us our beauty and diversity.

Top-Down Hinduism is *Sanatana* Civilization, our morality encoded in ritual, our self-perception encoded in metaphor (*purana*), our history encoded in poetry (*itihaasa*), divine alliances encoded in geography (*teertha*). And through this complex web of interlinkages run the philosophical ideas of the *Veda*, *Karma*, *Dharma*, *Purushaartha*, *Bhakti*, *Jnana*, *Moksha*... everything that gives us our commonality and strength.

People from the political Left insist that the Top-Down does not exist and that Bharat is just a collection of unconnected tribalisms. People from the political Right insist that the Bottom-Up ought to be erased and an Abrahamic-style, top-down uniformity needs to be mainstreamed that would draw from a mix of Western ideals, Islamic mechanics and *Sanatana* philosophy, but would consciously reject *Bharatiya* cultures. Both positions ignore the complexity and genius of our condition.

Without the bottom-up part of ourselves, we would be no different from the desert cults, full of arid injunctions and commandments creating zombies and relying on weekly brainwash sessions to hold the flock together. No beauty, no diversity, no tradition, no breadth. Without the top-down part of ourselves, we would be no different from the tribes of Africa and Papua— isolated, alone, and fearful of each other. No *Karma*, no *Dharma*, no *Advaita*, no *Yoga*, no depth.

The fact is, we are not this *or* that, we are this *and* that. We didn't end up like colonial Britain, ethnocidal Turkey or Nazi Germany because of the bottom-up part of ourselves that understands diversity and limits. And we didn't end up like the DRC, Rwanda and Papua because of the top-down part of ourselves that understands our commonality and our one-ness in the *Purusha* and the *Paramaatman*.

This two-headed nature of Hindu society has not gone unnoticed. The European mind, unable to see that these two heads, far from being rivals, actually had a symbiotic relationship with each other, have tended to pit the two heads against one another— *Dravidian/Aryan*, Tribal/*Brahmanical* etc. But the Hindu heart sees them as the warp and the weft of our social fabric, or perhaps the engine and the petrol of our Hindu life, if you prefer a more modern metaphor.

MVNL Sudha Mohan, in *Sivasya Kulam*, writes:

> Hindu society consists of two parallel religious systems: *Vaidikam* and *Tantrikam*. The practices of the latter are clearly *Siva-Sakti* worship, and they are the various *kulams* of South India. They have their counterparts in North India, like the *Nath* tradition. The *tantrik* practices range from simple *grama devata* practices to more esoteric ones. At the extreme end, there might be practices that can offend one's sensibilities as they involve uninhibited sex, alcohol, blood, and meat.
>
> However, in many of the common *grama devata* festivals, the traditional *Brahmins* also get involved, but the further rituals typically involve non-*Brahmin* priests. For example, in one of the villages in Telangana, in a three-day festival called *Bodurai*, a *Brahmin* initially performs some rituals and then recedes. Later, a specific community of *Chaakalis* (cloth washers) conducts the priestly rituals. Many of these temples have priests from the toddy-tapper (*Gouds*), carpenter (*vadrollu*), and other so-called 'lower castes' performing

rituals. The point is that the interface between the *Vaidikam* and the *Tantrik* methods has been ranging from indifference, to a mutual give and take, to a complete shunning (in extreme *Vamachara* practices). At no point was there a violent suppression of one by the other.²

The Mechanics of *Sanatana* Unity
The Toolkit of *Rishis*

So, if top-down *Sanatana* Civilization did not create *jaati*, what did it do with *jaati*?

How did it build unity without coercion? How did it bring diverse people to the table and make sure they all left relatively satisfied?

The *rishis* who designed *Sanatana* Civilization used a number of tools to achieve their purpose. Remember, it was a communal world they were dealing with. How communities interact and the expectations they have are totally different from how individuals behave. And as we've seen earlier in Part I of this essay, a communal world is the long-term stabilizing force; the individualist world is unstable and unsustainable. So, the toolkit of *rishis* is, in fact, *the* toolkit of solutions to human strife. As Anand Coomaraswamy writes:

> There are unities more essential and more important than any political unity; and these are based on common understandings of the ultimate ends of life rather than upon its immediate purposes, as to which there can be an almost endless variety of notions.³

What I'm going to describe will make sense only to people who appreciate that, at the social level, the value of *Harmony* is one of the highest moral goods to which a society can aspire. Not Liberty, not just mere Peace, but actual Harmony. So, let us begin to unpack the toolkit of *rishis*...

#1 Establishing an Acceptable Deal for Resource Distribution
> The first thing *Sanatana* Civilization did in order to bring lasting peace and stave off inter-tribal war, was to encourage occupational specialization within the tribes. This was the first step, without which the tribes of Bharat

would have gone down the route of the tribes of Africa. In Sub-Saharan Africa, the Bantu-speaking tribes swept across the continent, displacing all the other tribal communities, sending many to extinction and pushing many of the earliest tribes to remote pockets. This never happened in Bharat. No one *jaati* caused ethnic or actual physical cleansing of any other *jaati*. Just look at European history to see what ethnic fighting looks like. Wave upon wave of ethnic wars. It was only the access to colonial loot that stopped their fights temporarily. And even that 'peace' broke down in 1914 and again in 1938. Let us be clear that the seventy years since then do not represent the end of History, though the White Man imagines it to be so. The essential internecine nature of materialist Europe will reappear again and again.

In a subsistence world where the number of jobs as well as types of work were severely limited, the *jaati-vyavastha* granted, reserved and provided for work to every single community, creating a cultural milieu where every type of work was equally valued as a route to the divine (as per Shri Krishna Himself). And it did this, with seemingly zero enforcement. This makes it the original, decentralized, community-centred, spiritualized welfare State. It avoided every pitfall of centralized atheist Communism (soul-sucking uniformity, inhuman scale, inequality and corruption) over what is possibly a time-scale a hundred times longer.

#2 Envisioning a Metaphysical Purpose

Making sure the tribes don't fight one another over resources is one thing, but bringing them together to create an economic engine is an entirely different thing. This was accomplished in Bharat with a call to *yagna*. The *jaatis* were invited to offer excellence through their work as a sacrifice to the Gods. The *nishkama karma* of our communities was the fuel that lit the fire of our civilization. Again, Ananda Coomaraswamy writes:

> The vocation, whether it be that of the farmer or the architect, is a function; the exercise of this function as regards the man himself is the most indispensable means of spiritual development, and as regards his relation to society the measure of his worth.[4]

#3 Envisioning a Metaphysical Road while distributing Responsibility

The *yagna* is our destination, yes, but what is the road that gets us there? The road to get to the *yaaga-shaala* too was a metaphysical one. The vision offered to our communities was the vision of the cosmic *Purusha*. The thousands of disparate *jaatis* were brought together under four uber-groups representing the legs, hands, torso and head of this divine being. The mechanism that helped *jaatis* access the *Purusha* was *varna*. This is clearly an act of unity and not of division as many claim. *Shudras* represent creative excellence, *Kshatriyas* represent power, *Vysyas* represent wealth and *Brahmanas* represent dispassion. When we come together like this, we manifest the cosmic *Purusha* here on *Bhu Devi* and we have glorious Bharat.

#4 Establishing an Aspirational Value with an Inverse Relationship to External Power

All societies enshrine an aspirational value that helps people direct their ambitions, the pursuit of which leads them towards a transcendental principle that is a core civilizational ideal. In the case of modern capitalistic society, that aspirational value is the acquisition of wealth and the transcendental ideal it is supposed to lead towards is Liberty (autonomy from material constraints). In classical Hindu society, the aspirational value was dispassion, the pursuit of which led one in the direction of *Moksha*.

A Transcendental Principle is important to give society a sense of shared destination. In our case it is the idea of *Moksha*. Values that follow from that transcendental principle are what lend cohesion to society and point it in the direction of the shared destination. It is the compass, it is *the* agent that generates societal potential difference (the unseen animating force that funnels people through their lives). In every society, the people who adhere more closely to the cherished values of that society are given greater respect. This is true even today when wealth, fame, power and physical beauty are the anointed aspirational values. The Musks, the Kardashians, the Trumps lead the pack. A quick Google search of the top twenty Twitter accounts will lay out in clear terms who our heroes are and what kind of people we aspire to be like. In a different world, when *tyaga*, *dana, bhakti, nishkama karma* were the aspirational values, a different kind of paragon was held up as aspirational, as heroic.

The Greeks too had creative excellence, the Mongols too had power, Rome too had wealth, but only *Bharatavarsha* had dispassion. External Power (wealth, land, weapons, armies) draws respect automatically, so our *rishis* made sure the opposite force—internal power—was institutionalized as aspirational. Dispassion, the ability to have control over the inner world, thoughts and emotions, desire itself, was held up as the paragon. This great inversion served as the only check and balance we ever needed. Not that *nyaya* was never consulted but, by and large, communities and individuals became self-policing.

#5 Fractalizing the Uber Value-Hierarchy within all Groups

In his review of A.M. Hocart's *Caste: A Comparative Study*, Halley Kalyan points to this insight—the fractalization of our highest values made available to all. Barbers, washermen, drummers, farmers... everyone functioned simultaneously as a priest in a specific fractal part of the Hindu-verse.

Halley Kalyan observes that Hocart's foundational insight on 'caste' is the realization that, in India, every occupation is a priesthood:

> Castes are merely families to whom various offices in the ritual are assigned by heredity. To the European the barber is just a man who shaves others, the washerman a man who does the laundry. For a native, these two mean much more than that. "Practically on every occasion," says my first Tamil witness, "the barber and washerman will have to be present. They are called the children of the family". When we analyse what he means by "occasions" we find that he has in mind festivals, such as weddings, funerals etc. Thus, at a Tamil wedding the musicians (*Nattuvar*) walk before the bride-groom, the washerman spreads clothes for the bridegroom (who for the time being is God Siva) to walk upon. In the rear, other washermen assisted by barbers sing or howl blessings and praises of which he (the bridegroom) is the subject. The barber carries the *Tali* or marriage necklace (equivalent of our wedding ring), and the cloth called *kurai* for the bride. What the bridegroom wears while he is being shaved becomes the pre-requisite of the washerman and the barber. At a funeral, the barber, the washerman, and the drummer are

sent for, not the musicians... the barber prepares the fire for cremation and conducts the person who lights the fire three times round the pyre. He is like a priest on the cremation ground.[5]

Ananda Coomaraswamy makes a similar observation. In traditional society, he says:

The artist is not a special kind of man, but every man is a special kind of artist.[6]

#6 Creating Interdependencies

To further the collaborative spirit amongst *jaatis*, deep interdependencies were created, many of which had both economic as well as metaphysical dimensions.

Halley Kalyan delves deeper in his presentation *Jāti Purāṇas of Tēlaṅgaṇa*:

Pattachitra is a form of scroll paintings. *Nakashis* make such scrolls for many performing artist *jaatis*. So, the *Nakashi jaatis* make these paintings which are used by other *jaatis* in their narrative traditions. For example, you have a purana called the *Jamba Puranam* which is narrated by a *jaati* called *Dakkalis*. They narrate it for another *jaati* called the *Madigas*. Similarly, the *purana* called the *Markandeya Purana* is narrated by a *jaati* called *Kunapuli* for the sake of another *jaati* called *Padmashaali*.[7]

It is impossible to tell how such complexity was instilled and encouraged—whether it was done subtly or if it happened organically—but what is clear is that there is no historical memory of how all of this came to be. We only have our *purana* and our customs as explanations and evidence.

#7 Providing Society with a Nuanced Model for Building Hierarchy with in-built Checks and Balances

Hierarchy is one of the most difficult topics to broach today because, post-Marx, people have all sorts of false notions about it. Let me start by saying that hierarchy, especially contextual hierarchy, exists everywhere, in all societies, in *every* subset of *every* society, in our jobs and in our families. Every civilized society functions around a theory of justice overlaid upon a commonly accepted model of hierarchy. It may be unspoken, but it has to exist. The organizational structure of society coalesces around that theory. If the theory and the structure around it are strong, then people of high character will advance and occupy positions of power, but if the theory is amorphous and the structure weak, then society goes through upheavals again and again as people of low character rise to fill power vacuums. In any case, all noble systems are prone to entropic forces (as can be seen in the real-time corruption of Indian and American democracies) and need regular revitalization.

Decentralization of power was a key feature of *Dharmic* jurisprudence because the alternative – centralized state power, was a seen (rightly) as a sure recipe for *matsya nyaaya*. That both order and high moral standards were a feature of *Bharatiya* society for thousands of years is the most conclusive evidence for the ethical superiority for our systems. The health of our traditional theories of justice and hierarchy can be gauged by the fact that classical Bharat constantly threw up leaders of high character from all *varnas*—Rajendra Chozha, Raja Prataparudra, Rani Durgavati, Maharana Pratap, Gajapati Kapilendra Deva, Shivaji Maharaj, Rani Lakshmi Bai—and also by the fact that common people stood by their leaders. I'm not sure if we had even one instance of a widespread people's revolt in this land before the modern era. Communists see this as evidence of total oppression, but philosophers will know that it is evidence for a just society. Only justice can consolidate a people's self-perception over millennia; oppression can't last more than a few centuries.

See Pietro Della Valle's accounts from the mid-1600s of his encounters with *Bharatiya* royalty (Rani Abakka Devi Chowta and her estranged husband Raja Lakshmappa Arusu) to get a sense of how unassuming our kings and queens were when compared to the Marie Antoinette's and Shah Jehan's of the wider world.

> ... so it was better to go and speak to her in the field, where she was viewing her Workmen, than in the house. Accordingly I went, and, drawing near, saw her standing in the field, with a few Servants about her, clad as at the other time, and talking to the Labourers that were digging the Trenches.[8]
>
> ... we beheld the Queen coming alone in the same way without any other Woman, on foot, accompany'd onely with four, or six, foot Souldiers before her, who all were naked after their manner... one of whom carry'd over her a very ordinary Umbrella made of Palm leaves. Her Complexion was as black

> as that of a natural AEthiopian; she was corpulent and gross, but not heavy, for she seem'd to walk nimbly enough; her Age may be about forty years... was cloth'd, or rather girded at the waist, with a plain piece of thick white Colton, and bare-foot, which is the custom of the Indian Genteel Women, both high and low... From the waist upwards the Queen was naked, saving that she had a cloth tied round about her Head, and hanging a little down upon her Breast and Shoulders. In brief, her aspect and habit represented rather a dirty Kitchen-wench, or Laundress, than a delicate and noble Queen, whereupon I said within myself, Behold by whom are routed in India the Armies of the King of Spain, which in Europe is so great a matter! Yet the Queen shew'd her quality much more in speaking than by her presence; for her voice was very graceful in comparison with her Person, and she spoke like a prudent and judicious Woman.[8]
>
> Within the little Porch was a small room, long and narrow, where the King sate near the wall on the left side; and he sate upon the ground after the Eastern manner, upon one of those coarse cloths, which in Persia and Turkic are' call'd Kielin and serve for poor people; nor was it large, but onely so much as to contain the Person of the King, the rest of the room being bare, saving that it was smoothed over with Cow-dung.[8]

The *rishis* imagined all of Hindu society as being of one body—an earthly representation of the divine *Purusha*. In classical Hindu society, it was recognized that the *Purusha* is One, but also that it is comprised of the Many. When the Many realized their earthly communion by playing their parts in the divine theatre of life, the *Purusha* was made whole.

This much is clear, but what about the *Purusha* Himself? What was His nature? How was He to be envisaged?

To answer that question, the *rishis* looked to *Purushaarth*. We know that *Purushaarth* is an organizational framework for life. The *rishis* took this understanding and extrapolated it to the macro level. They applied the idea of *Purushaarth* to the transcendental *Purusha* Himself.

First, His very body, envisioned as a parliament of communities with all their varied responsibilities, was seen as being representative of four *varnas*. Varna was the simplified metaphorical projection by which the thousands of communities were mapped onto the body of the Purusha, without which the entire enterprise would probably have been impossible for the ordinary human to imagine. Next, each of the four *varnas* was linked to one of the four aspects of *Purushaarth*. The *Kshatriya* communities were imagined to reflect *Dharma*, the *Shudra* communities were imagined to reflect *Kama*, the *Vaishya* communities were imagined to reflect *Artha* and the *Brahmana* communities were imagined to reflect *Moksha*. This roughly corresponds to their traditional occupations / predilections: Power, Creative Excellence, Wealth and Dispassion. That was how the divine *Purusha* was subject to earthly *Purushaarth* and how the *Purusha* became *Purushaarth* manifest. Classical *Bharatiya* society was not feudal, it was *in-corporated*.

Two things are to be noted here: i) that all the communities (through the metaphorical mechanism of *varna*) were envisioned as being in communion as *one* divine body; and ii) that just as parts of a body are inter-dependent and inter-related, so too were the communities of Bharat. There was no mention of a pyramid-style hierarchy. We know that one cannot attain *Moksha* without the performance of *Dharma* and one cannot perform *Dharma* without the fulfilment of *Kama* and *Artha*. Each one either depends on or lends meaning to the other. So, no one *varna-conglomerate* was free of any other, and each had its sphere of influence where it claimed supremacy—a four-strand quadruple helix of our civilizational DNA that is visually elaborated upon in the figure below (S being Shudra, V being Vaishya, K being Kshatriya and B being Brahmana).

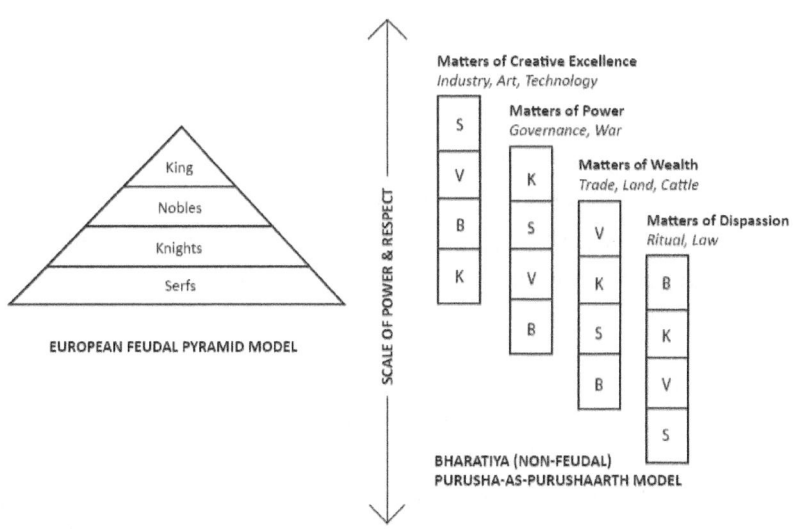

At a micro-level, through the institutions of *Kula* and *Jaati*, the *rishis* made sure that the distribution of ritual practice, material power and material wealth was heavily decentralized and multivariate, with thousands of local maxima giving every community a particular sphere of influence and dominance and therefore a stake in the whole. The inter-relationships between local maxima (as we saw in #6) also gave every community a reason to honour dependencies.

**THE CONTOUR-MODEL OF DECENTRALIZED
POWER DISTRIBUTION AND INTER-RELATIONSHIPS
BETWEEN KULAS (SPIRITUAL) AND BETWEEN JAATIS (OCCUPATIONAL)**

That our ancestors wholly and wholeheartedly embraced this vision of society (even as late as the 14th Century) is clear from a single inscription commissioned by Raja Anavema Reddi (1364-1386 CE) that read, "I the valiant member of the fourth *varna* destroyed the throngs of *mlechhas* and gathered learned *Brahmanas* at this court." [9]

Modern-day opponents of classical Hindu hierarchy who subsist on a diet of 'oppression' and 'privilege' make a number of mistakes in their misreading of it. One, they conflate value-hierarchy with material-hierarchy. Two, they fail to mention both the decentralization of power and the multivariate distribution of it within society. Three, they fail to appreciate the complexity of ritual responsibility sharing that emerged in Hindu society. All of these are indigenous mechanisms that served as checks and balances against the *adharmic* centralization of material power. Contrary to the modern point of view, we can see now that it was in fact the nature of the *rishi*-designed value-hierarchy in Bharat that prevented the emergence of a power-drunk material-hierarchy and all the immorality that would have followed.

#8 Establishing a Resonant Theory and Metaphysics of Justice

> Without a value-hierarchy there is no potential difference in society that induces movement, aspiration, inspiration, order. We are seeing in real-time what happens when value-hierarchies collapse as the USA struggles to maintain coherence between the 'Left and the 'Right'. It is true that value-hierarchies ultimately also have real-world manifestations and these have to have checks and balances (that is what the Law is supposed to do).
>
> Even in a relatively flat hunter-gatherer society, individuals do want to become the chief, or the shaman, or the matriarch, or the revered healer or the celebrated hunter. A society without ambition (and therefore hierarchy) cannot even be imagined. The only real question worth asking then is "What are the values that determine that hierarchy?"
>
> Insofar as the material-hierarchy of society represents its cherished value-hierarchy, it is the very force that animates that society. In a society that believes in wealth, the people with more wealth will be its paragons and their actions would form a moral archetype for other people to follow. On the other hand, in a society that believes in dispassion, the more dispassionate ones would be seen as paragons whose actions would direct the societal compass.
>
> But, if the societal material-hierarchy does *not* represent the value-hierarchy that people hold dear, then that hierarchy will be seen as oppressive. For example, if the people of Tibet see the *Bodhisattva* as an archetype, then Chinese rule would necessarily be seen as oppressive because it is materialist and atheist. That is, there is no synergy between the values of the people and the values of the imposed material-hierarchy. We can make the same claim for the imposition of *zamindaari* on classical Hindu society.

Feudalism, as we know it, came to India first with the establishment of the *jagirdaari* system by Khilji which was regularized into formal law by Cornwallis's *Zamindari* Settlement. The communities that aligned with the British and benefitted from *zamindari* came to be seen as feudal and the ire that 'peasants' felt against the *zamindars* was a direct reflection of how morally distant from traditional *Bharatiya* arrangements that system was.

The converse is also true—that is, a hierarchy that was once seen as just, because it represented the cherished values of a people, can come to be seen as unjust, not because it suddenly becomes oppressive but because the values of the people have changed. This is what all revolutions (including the first one, Christianity) try to do. They aim to change the values of a people (usually through education of children or media propaganda) so that the same people will begin to look upon their ancestral order as unjust.

The fact that we, today, see the social structure of our ancestors as oppressive is not evidence that our ancestors were in fact oppressed (or oppressors), it is merely evidence that our values have changed so much that we can no longer see the world as our ancestors once saw it. As we have moved from *Moksha* to the Machine, from *Dharma* to the Market and from Community to the Individual in our metaphysics, we see things differently, we judge things differently. To throw more light on this phenomenon let us investigate the Active Principle a little.

Under the Hood – How the Currency of Hierarchy Circulates

The average American flipping burgers at a restaurant makes an annual income of 22,000 dollars. Elon Musk makes 22,000 dollars every minute. That's an insane potential difference of half a million times! But we see this as normal. As *just* even. Why is that? It's only because we have accepted, unquestioningly, the Market as our Active Principle. The Market literally flows in our veins. Anything the Market does is *just* because it is perceived as *unbiased*.

There is a one-on-one correspondence between this modern worldview and the *karmic* worldview. In the old days, the Active Principle that guided our ancestors was *Dharma* (determined by *karma*). It was this *karma-*

determined-*Dharma* that flowed in their veins. It was *this* that was seen as just. It was *this* that was unbiased. It was *this* that determined whether one was born to the *punya* equivalent of a burger flipper or an Elon Musk.

The difference is that the Market assigns responsibility for life's uncertainties outside of ourselves and calls it chance, while *karma* assigns responsibility for life's uncertainties within ourselves and calls it *praarabdha*.

If the Market's currency is money, *karmic* currency is *punya*. Both metaphysical systems are clear that anyone and yes, *everyone*, can gather currency and is in fact ordained to do so. That *is* the aim of the game, to gather the currency of choice. As one gathers currency, one rises in station.

Thus, the value-hierarchy centred around dispassion had metaphoric consequences in the *karmic* plane via the idea of *punya*, and those metaphoric consequences had material manifestations in terms of a nominal ritual hierarchy. If we agree (unlike the wokes) that the emergence of material-hierarchy is inevitable, then all moral societies need to imagine a way to manage its consequences (it is for this reason that the West came up with the idea of Rights). The classical *Bharatiya* system, wedded as it was to the *Dharmic* ideal of eschewing *matsya-nyaaya*, took another route.

Our *rishis* made sure that the emergent *punya*-derived *karmic* hierarchy (which was essential to maintain morality in a decentralized society), was subverted in the material plane by linking its fruits to the value of dispassion (in order to avoid *matsya-nyaaya*). Two mutually dependent goals were thus accomplished:

1. By urging people to identify with their *aatma*-journeys (through *punya*, *punarjanma* and ritual incentives), the *rishis* ensured that society was burnished with the fire of noble aspiration.
2. By linking ritual privileges with greater levels of dispassion and self-denial in service of the common good, the *rishis* ensured that *matsya-nyaaya* was avoided. In fact, some groups with ritual privileges did not have any material privileges at all. Conversely, the people denied certain ritual privileges were granted greater societal liberties.

Even if our modern minds don't want to see this arrangement as a reflection of *satya* itself, surely, we can see that this was a decent and nuanced deal. By inverting the relationship between material power and ritual station, the *rishis* ensured that the earthly ego of any *aatma* had no earthly cause for earthly resentment or earthly arrogance.

No doubt the picture painted here is that of an ideal but, since we sit here today in judgement of the past, let us first grasp the nature and intent of the ideal instead of self-flagellating over cherry-picked instances of our *failure* to uphold the ideal. Ask yourself this: Do the Christians blame Jesus's love for the genocide of Native Americans, or do they double down on his central message, so much so that even their erstwhile West African slaves are today adherents of the very religion that enslaved them in the first place?

Unique, elegant and ethical though it was, this vision of *Bharatiya* value-hierarchy maintained with the circulation of *punya*-currency has lost its hold on people's minds.

Why?

The Reasons for our Modern-Day Disenchantment with our Ancestral Imagination

Our problem today is that, under the influence of Western memes, our value-hierarchy has been hijacked and is no longer centred around dispassion. Additionally, we no longer believe in the currency of traditional *Bharatiya* ritual hierarchy—*punya*. It is no wonder then that the entire edifice of traditional hierarchy appears monstrous and unjust to us.

And even if some of us continue to believe in *punya*, we have a problem with the idea that the fruits of *punya* are distributed at birth. This problem that we have is a function of our weakened faith in *punarjanma* and a waning of our identification with our *aatma*-journeys under the influence of secularism, but it also stems from two misunderstandings:

1. Misunderstanding how *Karma* Functions
   People misread the doctrine of *karma* in two ways:

   i. They blame *karma* for people being forced to do jobs they didn't want to do. This is false. Whenever people have been stuck in

such jobs, it's because they belonged in a particular community. A *Konaar* cowherd walking into a *Vishwakarma Aasaari* carpenter's community saying that he wants to belong there is just as impossible as a *Kurumba* person walking to the *Toda* village and saying that he wants to start being a *Toda* person. It's the old-world equivalent of a modern person asking *"Why can't I be you?"* It's simply not feasible. Both economically and culturally, and also in terms of sheer 'personhood', it would be an act of dilution. This is not a *karmic* issue, it is a tribal issue... and we have seen that the world of subsistence was tribal in nature. If change was truly desired, an entire community would have to shift profession, or a true leader would need to guide his community to a new horizon. And this did happen more often than we think. But, for the vast majority of people, for the majority of time, life within their communities doing their sacred work was more than sufficiently fulfilling.

   ii. People also make the mistake of blaming *karma* for creating a birth-based hierarchy of intrinsic worth. This is false. *Birth* is the *only* moment when the chips from one's *purvajanma* actions are encashed. It has *nothing* to do with a person's intrinsic worth in *this* life. It has *nothing* to do with a person's capacity for *Dharma* and *Moksha* in *this* birth. People of all communities who follow the higher values of *Sanatana* Civilization— *tyaga*, *nishkama karma*, *dana*, *bhakti*, *ahimsa*, *shaurya*, excellence etc.—are noble and are considered *Arya* and worthy of respect. It is simultaneously true that many of us in our debasement today have consciously and unconsciously moved away from this understanding and indulge in supremacy and/or victimhood. Both supremacy and victimhood mongering are un-*Arya*; it is nobility that is *Arya*. Wherever we have failed to stand for sacrifice, sharing and integrity, we stand accused of having forgotten ourselves and we need a course-correction.

3. Misunderstanding how non-Modern Societies Function
What most people don't realize is that, even today, when the idea of *karma* has lost its hold on people's minds, if I was to ask a *Vanniyar Gounder* or a

Vishwakarma Aasaari or a *Paraiyar* or an *Irular* if he wants to be a *Dikshitar* at the Chidambaram temple, his answer would be "No". Why is that? If he feels that his station in life is 'low' and that of the *Dikshitar* is 'high' then why wouldn't he exchange positions? In the modern West, the burger flipper would most certainly take the opportunity to exchange positions with Elon Musk. What's different here?

A few things:

i. The idea of community is still strong. One cannot simply walk away from one's extended family and into someone else's extended family.
ii. The idea that all work is sacred is still strong. One cannot abandon one's own sacred work and take on someone else's sacred work just like that without going through the grind of mental and ritual preparation for it. It would be a betrayal to one's own ritual priesthood.
iii. The ritually higher in station one is, the more difficult the life, the greater the sacrifices of pleasure, the greater the adoption of stringent rules of *saucha*. Nobody really wants this. This inversion of the relationship between value and power that we discussed earlier is deeply familiar to all *Sanatanis* and they respect its implications. To move to a higher ritual station would require the sacrifice of power and wealth as well as the discipline to sacrifice desire. No modernized Hindu really wants this, and a traditional Hindu would never dream of taking such a short-cut. So, what is it that the anti-caste warriors are fighting for? Something that neither the moderns nor the traditionalists want?

Today the ideas of equal opportunity and growing the pie are used as inducements to sweeten the Western deal, to justify the insane societal potential difference between the burger flipper and Elon, to convince us that we too can one day be Elon Musk. But it is sleight of hand. There is a thousand times more inequality today in the Western industrial world than there has ever been in classical Hindu society. We don't let it affect us because industrial surplus has given us the cushion of mixie-grinder-TV-fridge-Netflix. What kind of theory of society derives its sense of justice from the presence or absence of mechanical goods? A weak one, no doubt.

The fact is that both the ideas of equal opportunity and growing the pie are ideas of the world of surplus. They **could not** possibly exist in the world of subsistence, which is why in *that* world, the ideas of **limits** and **distribution** were the governing ideas. To turn around and blame the doctrine of *karma* for the inequalities that today's Market economics has fostered among our communities, as many revolutionized people do, is preposterous.

An Analysis of the Modern-Day Pillorying of our Ancient Categories

Question: Since the democratization of the *Veda* with the coming of the British and the printing press, has there been a history of any *Kshatriya*, *Vysya* or *Shudra* community coalescing with an intent to safeguard the *Veda*? Has there even been a single instance? If not, then we cannot, indeed must not, label the stewardship of the *Veda* by the *Brahmana* communities as a monopoly. Why do some people who do *not* want to safeguard the *Veda* care if the *Veda* is being safeguarded by some *other* people? Or more accurately, it is obvious that true *Kshatriya*, *Vysya* and *Shudra* communities have no interest in taking on *Brahmana* responsibilities, but fallen modern Indians of all communities, including *Brahmana* communities, are intent on sullying the *Veda* and our traditional arrangements for their safeguarding. With these acts, they reveal themselves to be misguided.

Only people who believe in the *Purusha*, the *Purushaarthic* interpretation of the *Purusha* and those who buy into Hindu *punarjanma* metaphysics will even see *karmic*-hierarchy as real and valid. For anyone else, it's just a bunch of nonsense. Now here is the paradox. If people have a problem with this *karma*-derived ritual hierarchy, it means they have a problem with Hindu metaphysics. If that is the case, then by what definition are they Hindu? And if they are not Hindu, then why do they care? Additionally, if they define themselves as Hindu by some other parallel metaphysics, then in true *Sanatani* style they would not bother with people who define their Hindu-ness differently from them. The principles of live and let live and tolerance, and perhaps Mutual Respect, would prevail. Parallel and often incompatible streams within Hindu society have flowed side by side for centuries in pre-Modernity without feeling the need to erase each other. It is only today after having internalized Western universalism that we are intent on foisting upon the *whole* of Hindu society a single moral code. In our righteousness, we believe that we are on the side of good but in an unbiased reality we will see that we have now become vehicles of intolerance.

This inability to appreciate the Old Way stems from our having adopted wholesale the Western Social Principle of Individualist Autonomy over the traditional *Bharatiya* Social Principle of Community. *Punya* is earned by individuals, yes, but the stewarding of *punya* via acts of *karma* was done by community. The individual and the community were tied at the hip in a subsistence world, just as the individual and the 'system' are in the surplus world.

The idea that one can walk in and out of our birth communities is a product of the world of surplus. Subsistence does not allow us that luxury. There literally was no such thing as the individual as we now know it (though we all had our personalities). The individual, as we know it today, is a creation of the machine-world we inhabit. In the subsistence world, for the many, their communities would determine what they stood for (and I want to stress that *that is perfectly ok*). But we must also acknowledge that for the few (leaders and inspired souls), their inner fires determined what they stood for. Entire communities could rise in station or great individuals could take their communities along to a new horizon, and this did happen more often than we care to recognize in our modern-day blame game. It is meaningless for the *'varna by janma'* camp and the *'varna by guna'* camp to rant and rail about this phenomenon.

Recently, online, the accusation was thrown at me that *Brahmanas* had the privilege of 'pole position' and they held on to it monopolistically. Let's take a look at what this 'pole position'" entailed. Here is Al Beruni in the 11th Century:

> The *Brahmana's* duty is to practice abstinence, to make the earth his bed, to wash himself thrice a day and make a sacrifice to the fire at dawn and dusk. He fasts a day and breaks fast the next day and is never allowed to eat meat. Whatever alms he receives, he places before his master and eats only the leftovers. During *Grihasta*, he co-habits with his wife only once a month. The brahmana lives from what he gathers on the earth or from trees. He may not participate in trade or the keeping of cattle. He must continually read, perform the sacrifices, take care of the fire which he lights, offer before it, worship it and preserve it from being extinguished, that he may be burned by it after his death.[10]

This is what privilege in the Hindu universe looks like—the privilege to lead a life of hardship and self-denial, the privilege to voluntarily humble oneself by begging for food every day, the privilege to subordinate oneself to a string of arcane rules and regulations in order to maintain the purity of being that makes one a fit vessel to approach the Gods on behalf of all society. *This* is what a 'high' station looks like. *This* is what the gathering of *karmic* currency, *punya*, will bring upon you. *This* is *not* what anybody who is not steeped in the Hindu universe actually wants.

This inversion of the relationship between material power and spiritual worth is what generates respect in the Hindu universe. It is the single reason why classical Hindu society was so stable, why it never generated resentment or revolution.

Modern Hindus whose minds have been revolutionized do not understand this at all; they mistakenly identify the inequalities that have arisen in post-1857 modern India as artefacts of the social structure that existed in classical Bharat and that is why they rant and rail against 'caste'. They know not what it really is, at all.

And it's important to realize that the *value*-hierarchy was a moral one (and therefore accepted). If the hierarchy had been based merely on wealth or strength or numbers, popular belief in the ritual leadership derived from that hierarchy would not have endured. As Francis Xavier points out in his letters in the mid-16th Century:

> If it were not for the opposition of the Brahmins, we should have them all embracing the religion of Jesus Christ... All the time I have been here in this country I have only converted one Brahmin.[11]

In the Hindu universe, the equality that was offered to all was equality of access to *Purushaarth*, equality in opportunity to do one's *Dharma* and collect *punya*, and equality in the approach of *Moksha* via the routes of *nishkama karma, bhakti* and *jnana*. In this age of surplus, we may not agree anymore with the framework that the *rishis* made for us but, unless we can again imagine an equivalent framework, we do not have the right to tear down, in a fit of ignorance and self-hate, what we are utterly incapable of building up.

Rarely referred to, but essential to point out in today's charged atmosphere, is the fact that all the great diversity of *panths* and *sampradayas* are actually irrefutable proof of the non-coercive nature of *Sanatana Dharma*. Communities or spiritual figures who disagreed with mainstream arrangements could simply up and leave, forming a new *sampradaya* or *panth* with an entirely different permutation of founding axioms culled from our ocean-like *shruti* and *smriti*. It will do us all good to recollect the example of the great Vishwakarma *kulas* who draw their *parampara* from the architect of the Gods himself. In their unapologetic self-consciousness, they instituted an entire non-Brahmanical parallel organizational structure that grants them the right to wear the *yagnopavit*, which they continue to wear with pride today. They were never persecuted. Indeed, they are only the most prominent of *Shudra kulas* who continue to wear the *yagnopavit*. Others include the potter *jaatis*, the weaver *jaatis*, and—contrary to all expectations—even the leather-working jaatis.[12]

This religion has always been all of ours to claim, as long as those claims have rested upon the embrace of greater and greater burdens of responsibility and sacrifice.

We see now that *Sanatana* Civilization, far from being the great divider that people accuse it of being, was actually the compassionate force that brought the *jaatis* of Bharat together under one grand metaphorical umbrella. And it did so without erasure, without genocide and without slavery. *Varna* was one of the spokes of that metaphorical umbrella—one that laid the foundation for the most sustainable, ethical systems of social organization ever devised on *Bhu Devi*.

(That many of us don't live by its values but continue to claim the privileges that our ancestors earned through great sacrifice is a modern problem and I will refer to it in Part III of this essay.)

The *Dharma* Tree

A Visual Representation of the Breadth and Depth of Hindu Complexity

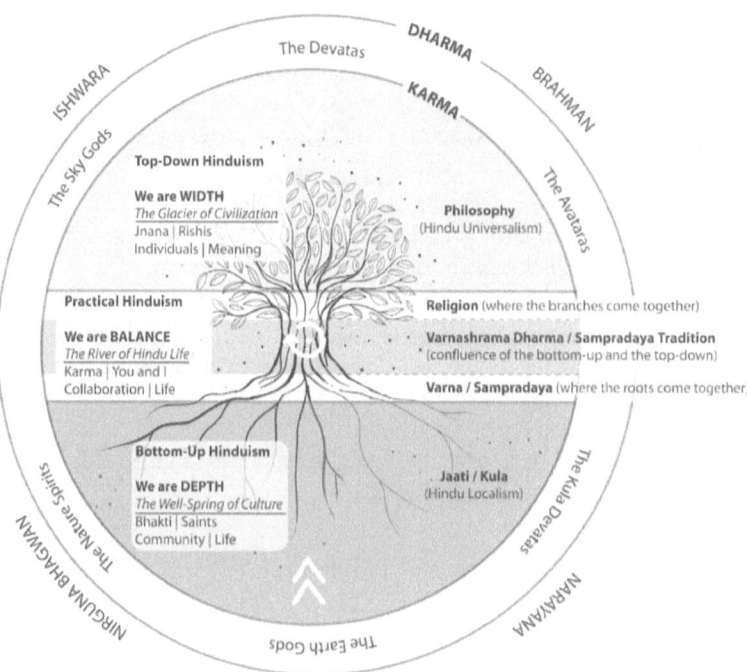

The *Dharma* Tree is why the Tamils go to Kashi and it is why the Awadhis come to Rameshwaram. It is why, in the villages of Tamil Nadu, *Vediappan* sits in regal splendour under his Neem tree, awaiting offerings of blood and alcohol, while in the same village dare-devil youth throw themselves at oil-slicked *khambams* and build seven-storey human pyramids for a taste of butter like their beloved Sri Krishna did in the *Dwapara Yuga*. It is why Malayadhwaja Pandya fought alongside the Pandavas in Kurukshetra and why his daughter Meenakshi wed the Lord of Kailasa Himself in a wedding where she was given away by her brother, Shri Vishnu Himself. It is why Tamil and Sanskrit are seen as two sides of Ishwara's *damaru*. This is *not* a competition, this is *not* 'Brahmanism', this is not a game of oppressor-oppressed for simpletons, this is not Western-style erasure, this is not any of those black and white structures that the Westernized mind is capable of understanding. This is a magnificent Banyan that only the Hindu mind and heart can appreciate.

This tree shall not die. This tree shall cover *Bhu Devi* again, when the citadels of greed have fallen.

References and Links

1. "Kani tribe visits Travancore royal family", *Times of India*, 2019
   https://timesofindia.indiatimes.com/videos/entertainment/events/kochi/kani-tribe-visits-tavancore-royal-family/videoshow/71350500.cms

2. MVNL Sudha Mohan, *Sivasya Kulam: Decoding Caste, Untouchability & The White Man's Burden*, Samvit Prakahsan, 2022

3. Ananda Coomaraswamy, *Letters*, 1942

4. Ananda Coomaraswamy, *'Christian and Oriental Philosophy of Art'*, 1956

5. Halley Kalyan, *A.M. Hocart's 'Caste: A comparative study'*, 2021
   https://pragyata.com/a-m-hocarts-caste-a-comparitive-study/

6. Ananda Coomaraswamy, *'Christian and Oriental Philosophy of Art'*, 1956

7. Halley Kalyan, *Jāti Purāṇas of Tēlaṅgaṇa – Bhāratavarṣa's Narrative Traditions*, 2022
   https://www.youtube.com/watch?v=yRHlppdYWGo (16.45 onwards)

8. Pietro Della Valle, *Travels of Pietro Della Valle in India Vol.2 (Translated by Havers G, 1892), original 1650CE*

9. Raja Anavema Reddi, *Srisailam Inscription*, 1378CE

10. Al Beruni, *Al Beruni's India*, 1030CE (translated by Dr. Edward Sachau)

11. Henry James Coleridge, *Life and Letters of St. Francis Xavier Vol. 1*, 1872
    https://archive.org/details/LifeLettersOfStFrancisXavierV1

12. Geringer and Chabrelie, *L'Inde Française Ou Collection De Dessins*, 1827
    https://archive.org/details/LIndeFranaiseOuCollectionDeDessins/page/n279/mode/2up

Section 4 | Chapter 4.3

NO BRANCHES WITHOUT ROOTS – PART III
Using the New Understanding of Hindu Organizing Principles to Clear Cobwebs

Maragatham, 2022

In Part I and Part II of this essay, I introduced a bunch of ideas:

1. The World of Subsistence versus the World of Surplus
2. A Morality of Subsistence versus a Morality of Surplus
3. The Six Principles of Social Organization as manifest in the West and in Bharat
4. Individual Autonomy versus Community Collaboration
5. Culture versus Civilization
6. The Bridge of *Sanatana* Civilization
7. Hinduism as a Confluence of Bottom-Up *Bharatiya* cultures and Top-Down *Sanatana* Civilization
8. The four *Varna*-centred Values and our Fellowship in the *Purusha*
9. Eight Tools from the Toolkit of *Rishis*

These ideas can help us radically overhaul the way we look at ourselves.

The Nature of our Battlefield

I thank my online detractors for pushing me to clarify my ideas. I do not want to come across as an apologist for the culture of debasement that exists in many parts of modern India.

Arya means noble, and nobility is the capacity for self-sacrifice for the greater common good without self-aggrandization or the demeaning of others. I defend the *jaati-vyavastha* and the *varna-vyavastha* for their ethical brilliance in a subsistence world, and the sheer beauty and diversity that they enabled. I do not defend supremacy, whether caste-based or of any other kind (religious, technological). I do not defend the belittling of people, nor do I defend obnoxious caste-based supremacy. I do not defend the determinist position that deals in IQ and race-based arguments to justify a lack of compassion. I *also* do not defend the communities that indulge in political victimhood mongering. Victimhood is alien to *all Bharatiya* cultures.

We should see the exhibition of such un-*Arya* behaviour as debasements, and these debasements as the playing out of human failings. Why the debasement occurred, I have alluded to earlier in Part II. During the course of our thousand-year war and our subsequent military and intellectual defeat by the British, the threads that bound our ethical vision started to come undone and our communities defensively reverted to the petty aspects of tribalism—pride, arrogance, greed, hunger for power, victimhood and vanity. Let me record here that *Sanatana* Civilization has, from the outset, sought to control these negative human urges and bind us into a single body dedicated to excellence, dispassion and *Moksha*. It is in the service of that uplifting harmonic vision that our religion has given us *Dhyana* (for individuals), *Samskaaras* (for families), *Rna* (for communities), *Tirtha* (for the *Rashtra*) and *Purusha* (for the wider world). It is this whole (and wholesome) understanding that has been lost to us in the long years of our debasement.

So, while we work to raise ourselves up out of this debasement, we must take great care to avoid laying the blame for it on our religion. The moral injunctions of other religions could not prevent their adherents from sinking into the great evils of slavery, genocide, re-education camps, colonialism and holocausts. Their downstream ideologies have further led us to the more recent mutated evils personified by Hitler, Stalin, Mao, Pol Pot, Abu Bakr Al-Baghdadi and the likes of Adam Lanza (the school shooter at Sandy Hook). And yet, the adherents of these religions remain miraculously unapologetic. Conversely, the ethical fundamentals of our religion are so robust that even the combined nationwide failings of ordinary Hindus did not lead to evil on any comparable scale. Yet, ironically, we remain constantly apologetic. It is very important that we keep this in mind even as we introspect. And especially as we consume international news reports that continue to somehow see fit to depict all the ills of modern India as reflections of our immoral *sociology*, while depicting modern ills of the West as reflections merely of disturbed *psychology*. Never once have the news reports alluded to either their culture or their religion as possibly being the source of those ills.

No doubt, evil has shown its face even in Bharat. We have examples such as the Kilvenmani Massacre[1] to be ashamed of. But, in my opinion, even though I am aware that many disagree, evil was never institutionalized in Bharat because of the inherently decentralized nature of our social structure that our *rishis* consciously retained *for this very purpose*.

While we may exonerate ourselves from evil, we must acknowledge that, over the last two centuries, we have allowed and continue to allow the widespread appearance of un-*Arya* obnoxiousness within our communities. Many point to *jaati*, *varna*, manipulative *banias*, wily *brahmins* and the doctrine of *karma* as the culprits for our fall into un-*Arya* habits. If we take those accusations seriously, we must ask why the ill effects of 'caste' and *karma* didn't reveal themselves for thousands of years prior to our enslavement but magically became all-pervading after the arrival of British evangelism in Bharat. We must also ask why the 'caste-less' desert religions were at the forefront of brokering evil for centuries if, after all, their 'caste-less-ness' was supposed to grant them an angelic demeanour?

It's obvious that 'caste' and *karma* are not the real reasons for our fall into un-*Arya* habits, though ignobility may use them as a template upon which to manifest (just as it would use any existing underlying structure). I suggest we look to more mundane and material reasons. What we know as 'caste' today is a photograph of the status quo of our 19th Century debasement that has been frozen in time, extrapolated forward and institutionalized indefinitely—first by the British in their cunningness, and then by the Indian State in its foolishness.

We have the 18th Century example of a Mahar introducing himself to Warren Hastings with the memorable words, "We are soldiers, Sir, and conquerors; we make war, and we also make shoes," to remind us of a time before the fall.

Starting with the Battle of Rajasthan, through the establishment of Vijayanagara and all the way up to Shivaji Maharaj, we have evidence that the idea of the *Arya* as a person who stood for every Hindu was still strong. The thousand-year war had weakened us but had not damaged us beyond all recognition. But the overwhelming military victory of the British, their take-over of our Commons, the institutionalization of *zamindari* and the closure of our indigenous schools finally sounded the death knell for the old ethical vision. We fell into the White Man's black and white world of judgementalism. The institutionalization of that black and white vision in 'independent' India, has, instead of delivering pride, self-respect and mutual respect, led us into a deep pit from which we dig up the White Man's stories about ourselves and in which we continue to water the seeds of our debasement. It is from that manufactured soil and that inauthentic pit, that the tree of 'free' India has arisen. If we want to re-shape this tree or plant a new tree, we need to overhaul our understanding of our past. Let us start by clarifying what exactly we're squabbling about in Hindu society today.

Our war is being fought on two fronts:

1. A 19th Century war to re-establish the principle of Mutual Respect, deliver dignity for all *jaatis*, and recognize every community's contribution to our continued miraculous existence and to reaffirm our communion in the *Purusha*.
2. A 21st Century war to save our traditions (and, by extension, our communities) from the poisonous onslaught of Western ideals, irreverence and individualism. Why we need to do so I have detailed in Chapters 3.1, 3.2 and 3.3 of this book.

People familiar with my work will know that my fight is the 21st Century fight. I am not fighting the 19th Century fight. So, when I defend the *jaati-vyavastha* or the *varna-vyavastha* or a simpler community-centred world, I am not doing so in order to "retain my privileges" in the status quo of our debasement. I do so because I recognize that our headlong rush into the Western hyper-technologized world with its idealistic framework of Individualism, Liberty, Equality and Rights is leading us to a level of *adharma*, ignobility and irreverence that we cannot even begin to imagine.

The champions of the 19th Century war should realize that the 21st Century war also needs to be fought. What is the use of fighting for the dignity of all communities when there will soon be no communities left at all? Unfortunately, though the 19th Century war is being fought by hundreds of millions of anti-caste warriors, they fight it under the banner of Western ideals of Individualism,

Liberty and Equality. This has perversely turned what should have been our rise from debasement into a festival of self-hate and fresh conflict. This war needs to be fought on a very different basis (which I will come to in the next section).

Similarly, those of us who are fighting the 21st Century war have to make our position on the 19th Century war clear. Our complex and subtle arguments in favour of tradition and community should not be used as a shield by supremacists and traffickers in debasement. Our fight is for the bottom-up *Bharatiya* cultures for their beauty, diversity and decentralizing impulse. Our fight is also for top-down *Sanatana* civilization, that orphaned force for Hindu unity, that continues to do its work in silence, unnoticed and un-acknowledged by intellectuals... that ancient *Arya* call to nobility that we shall not abandon.

The *Sanatana* Basis for Hindu Unity

The need for Hindu unity is recognized by many but, at this moment in time, the Indian State, as well as reformists of all hues, is hell-bent on achieving Hindu unity through the erasure of our communities. It's a bit like cutting off one's hand because the elbow is itching. Elbow itching? No problem. No hand, no itch. Problem solved!

The statement "We need to be strong" has two parts—"We" and "strong". There is a widespread belief that unity will bring us strength and the way to unity is the erasure of our communities. But almost nobody is focused on the first part of the phrase. Who are "We"? And what will the erasure of our communities do to our self-definition?

The problem is that we are firmly in the grip of three Western Principles:
The Western Active Principle: The Market
The Western Social Principle: Individualist Autonomy
The Western Interactive Principle: Ideals (Liberty, Equality and Rights)

Under the influence of these principles, we have unconsciously turned against the equivalent *Bharatiya* Principles of *Karma-Dharma*, Community Collaboration, and our *Moksha*-centred Values.

We fail to see that attempting to reach Hindu unity under the banner of un-Hindu principles will, obviously, lead us to an un-Hindu place. The evidence is everywhere. Even if we end up united, which I doubt very much, we will no longer be ourselves. So, what's the point?

If we do want to rebuild our unity in an authentic manner, we need to do it under the banner of *Sanatana* Civilizational values and mechanics. Unfortunately, the centralized secular State and the decentralized *Arya* spirituality do not dovetail very well. But the State can play a part in shaking things up.

The Indian State needs to stop looking West and start looking to the toolkit of *rishis* (described previously in Chapter 4.2) for inspiration. It needs to:

1. **Come up with an acceptable deal for Resource Distribution.**
   Reservations are acceptable to Hindus (as *jaati* has shown), but the formula should emerge from consensus among all communities. More importantly, the raison d'etre for reservations should *not* be "reparations for past sins" but rather "inter-*jaati* peace". This would literally be the modern horizontal equivalent of traditional vertical *jaati*-based reservations. De-couple this mechanism entirely from oppression-rhetoric by completely overhauling the upper caste/lower caste logic. There is simply no such thing. Obviously, this vision can only manifest if high quality schools, vocational training and colleges were easily accessible to all people (including the poorest) and we, as a society, stopped seeing only some streams of learning and work as desirable. The full diversity of human potential must be encouraged to manifest in as many diverse acts of excellence.

2. **Create the *Bharatiya* Grand Narrative**
   This will serve as the modern equivalent of the ancient *Arya yagna*. Institutionalize the teaching of this narrative in schools and in art/movies. It would include the mainstreaming of pride-filled stories from all communities. Stories of our inter-community skirmishes and betrayals should be studied for academic purposes but they are irrelevant to our purpose of unity. What we should focus on are stories of our collaboration.

3. **Institutionalize Nationwide *Purusha* Festivals**
   Create a State-sponsored series of annual festivals that would celebrate our communion in the *Purusha* where all communities come together at the *taluka*-level once a year to reaffirm their commitment to our ancestral treaty. The actual ritual form of the festival should be worked out by local *mathas*. Leverage how *Thiruvizhas*, *Kumbha Melas* and *Poorams* are organized.

4. **Decentralize and Overhaul Public Office Culture**
   Devolve more and more responsibility and control over local governance/ communal and religious tradition to communities. Emphasize *Sanatana* values of Excellence, *Nishkama Karma*, *Daya*, *Dana* and *Tyaga* in public office. Move firmly away from Liberty and Equality. Move from a discourse of Rights to a discourse of Duties.

5. **Media Control**
   Establish a responsible global news agency (like the BBC or Al Jazeera) that will speak for the Hindu people not just from a political point of view but also from the point of view of our civilizational value system. Also crucial is the need to incentivize the creation of Art (movies, music) around harmonizing *Sanatana* values instead of revolutionary Western ideals. At the moment, we have neither structure in place.

6. **Re-open the *Sanatana* Bridge**
   Create the governmental framework and the spiritual ritual mechanism in consultation with our *mathas* for the immediate and permanent on-boarding of peripheral and external communities on to the bridge of Santana Civilization for all those who want it. This will take a generation but media/education should make clear to the coming generations:

   a. that we are all one in the *paramaatman*. Leverage *Vedantic* and *Bhakti* thought to rebuild linkages that are broken.
   b. that, in the Industrial Age, the ancient social taboos have ceased to be relevant.
   c. that the communities who traditionally did taboo work should be acknowledged for their contributions to our common cause. Leverage the teachings of the *Vyaadha Gita* and the *Gita* itself.

d. that work that nobody wants to do should be done by everyone or by machines.
e. that the communities who traditionally did taboo work were well educated (as Dharampal ji[2] has shown) and continue to play economic and ritual roles in *Bharatiya* life. They are not, and in fact never were, 'other' in classical *Bharatiya* imagination. If we were to map our subsistence tribes onto a spectrum of modern categories, we would create a continuum that included Forest-Dwelling Tribes (ST), Forest Dependent Tribes (ST), Nomadic Tribes (ST), Agriculture-Dependent Tribes (SC), Settled Agricultural Tribes (BC/OBC) and Agriculture-Enabled Tribes (GC).

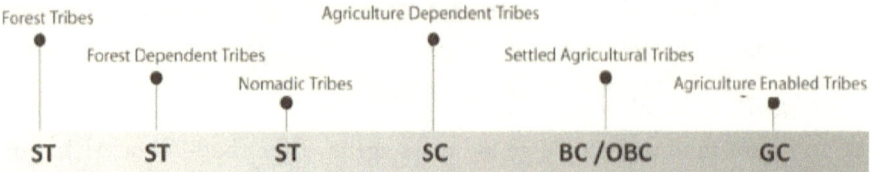

It's time we internalized that the evolution of this spectrum was not a top-down imposition—this was the play of anthropological history, technological history, community choices and compromises at work. The 'caste system', as we know it, is a photograph of this spectrum taken by the British in the 19th Century and we are now permanently locked into that photograph. We need to break free of the 19th Century photograph and start to see ourselves as a spectrum of possibilities again. We need to re-open the bridge of *Sanatana* values for all who wish to access the bridge. It goes without saying that all who do *not* wish to access the bridge are free to continue to live life as they see fit. They are all *Bharatiya* bottom-up cultures and this land is their *punyabhoomi* too.

All this sounds like science fiction today but we will be surprised how much the first principles of our systems eventually affect individual behaviour. See how the adoption of a Liberal constitution transformed us in a mere seventy-five years. All that the vast majority of people really need is a framework that delivers the right incentives.

An Accurate Understanding of the Role of Civilization in general, and the Brilliance of *Sanatana* Civilization in Particular

There is a widely held view that *Sanatana* Civilization with its 'caste system' is/was a divisive force. But to make a proper assessment we need to look at our society not from the point of view of the modern present but from the point of view of the classical past. Once we make that shift, we see that the past, far from being the one-big-happy-family-utopia that many paint it to be, was actually a thinly populated dispersed tribal reality. The further back in time one goes, the *more* diversity there is, not less. A still living example of such a world can be found in Papua New Guinea. In comparison to that antagonistic, zero synergy world, what we have had here in Bharat for millennia is a model of co-existence and collaboration... and therefore *civilization*. It is only when seen in this authentic light that we truly understand how *Sanatana* Civilization (like all others) is a force for unity and not divisiveness. The oft-repeated accusation that *Sanatana* Civilization brought divisiveness to India is patently false—the divisions *already* exist in the very nature of ancient tribal cultures. The difference between *Sanatana* Civilization and all others lies in its intent and in its method; in how it went about forging a unity out of this dispersed tribalism.

The ideal of the *Purusha* and the technology of *varna* (as the hook to bind the tribes to the *Purusha*) provided the context in which the tribes organized themselves economically into *jaati*, culturally into *kulas*, and religiously into *sampradayas*. We can see clearly that all these were mechanisms for *uniting* the thousands of dispersed tribes and not for dividing them from one ancient fictitious uniform mass. What the *continued* existence of that diversity tells us though is more remarkable. It tells us that *Sanatana* Civilization is unique amongst world civilizations in that it brought unity without erasure. In effect it acted as a compassionate steward for diversity, and it is in this adoption of the forest-paradigm for organizing human society that its claim to ethical pre-eminence lies. Our cultural diversity, far from being a reflection of the *divisive* spirit of *Sanatana* Civilization, can now be seen as *evidence* of its non-coercive, nature-inspired ethical nature—live and let live. It is in this demonstration of the possibility of simultaneous co-existence of opposing truth claims in reasonable harmony, that *Sanatana* Civilization shows the face of its universality. It is a universality rooted in a higher-order harmony and not in a lower order uniformity.

Our religion expends an extraordinary amount of effort in trying to help people figure out how to overcome the conflicts inherent in their differences without resorting to Abrahamic-style final solutions. *Jaati* was in fact one of the foremost ideas that allowed for difference to express itself without fear of reprisal, and also for collectives to safeguard the ritual and value framework that gave them self-definition. Once we accept that *Sanatana* Civilization was non-coercive and harmonic, we can finally see why it was perceived, by its adherents, as being non-oppressive and, therefore, as *just*.

An Accurate Understanding of the Events of 1857 and their Implications for what is called "Privilege"

1857 was a watershed year. It was the year we fought our last war for independence. Everything we did after that was, and continues to be, within the locus of European systems. We were not (mentally) enslaved prior to 1857 as we are told, but post-1857. Collapse of our institutions had started a hundred years before that, but that was the year we knew for sure that there was no going back to the Old Way. The entire machinery of ancient patronages collapsed and, with that, so did the old values and the communities that upheld those values. The *Shudras* communities lost control of the natural/agricultural world and could no longer maintain the means of production for creative excellence, the old markets that the *Vaishya* communities controlled collapsed and they ran out of wealth to support temples and schools, the *Kshatriya* communities were militarily defeated and no longer had the power to maintain a Hindu State and the *Brahmana* communities, without the infrastructural support of the other three *varnas*, could no longer follow the life of dispassion or teach the old values. The *Purusha* fell apart. Communities from all four *varnas* now depended directly or indirectly on the systems developed by the White Man. It was every man for himself.

A handful of communities continued to hold on to the strings that tied the *Purusha* together and we will discuss the fate of these communities a little later.

Vaishya communities that started doing business with the British became wealthy. *Kshatriya* lineages that accepted British suzerainty were rewarded with palaces and princely salaries. *Brahmana* communities that started working for the British became clerks and lawyers in the corridors of Empire. Today, it is the children of those early movers who have figured out success in the Western marketplace. And even out of this demographic, millions have only moved to middle-class lifestyles over the past two generations. Entire generations have had to work their butts off in dead-end jobs in an effort to educate their children in the White Man's ways. This hard-won 'success' is today labelled, by revolutionaries, as 'privilege'. Ok, let's call it 'privilege', but let us be clear where it originates from. This material inequality that we see in modern India originates in the Western marketplace, not in the ancient social structure of classical Bharat. In fact, it is a product of the collapse of that ancient world of equivalence.

It is fashionable in all circles, these days, to point fingers at 'caste' as if it is a magic wand that explains every socioeconomic ill that plagues us. This is both lazy and ineffective. At most, the communities and people that got ahead in the Western world can be accused of having betrayed the *Purusha* (and I think that's a valid criticism), but since everyone today is trying to make it big on the White Man's stage, and nobody truly cares for the *Purusha*, it's not really much of an accusation to make. Do the communities that fell into material poverty post-1857 need a leg up so that they too can compete in the Western marketplace? Of course. The open-hearted spirit of the *Arya* must prevail even as we live within a foreign framework. But it should be understood by all that any redistribution of resources and knowledge is from a place of sharing and an ancient understanding of our one-ness, not from a place of un-*Arya* guilt, blame or shame.

An Accurate Understanding of the *Bahujan* Circumstance

In the world of subsistence, a significant proportion of people made a livelihood directly and indirectly off the land. What are today called *Bahujan* in some revolutionized circles, even now constitute some 70%-80% of our population. These ingenious communities stewarded our natural resources, farmed the land, kept it fertile for millennia, created more than fifty thousand varieties of rice alone, husbanded our cattle, genetically bred the over one hundred native cattle breeds we have, harvested resources from forests and grasslands, were masters at creating water conservation structures, built houses, wove cloth, made baskets, utensils, weapons, ships and our temples and *murthis*. They knew the lie of the land, they were the majority, they were physically robust, they controlled the entire means of production of weaponry and industry, and they owned the land and the cattle. To claim that these communities were weak, poor or oppressed is a travesty. They were quite literally the economic engine of classical Bharat.

But, alas, the coming of the Industrial Revolution rendered all of their skills obsolete. From being *the* upholders of *Dharma*, these communities were progressively impoverished over two hundred years. The Commons, pasture lands, rivers, tanks, mountains and forests all became property of the Crown. The entire spectrum of tribes that depended on the Commons and had sustainably stewarded our natural resources for millennia found themselves without access to the basic necessities of life. Basic agriculture that used to be taxed at 15% under a Hindu monarchy, was now taxed at 60% and a system of *zamindars* was set up to interface between the British and the village folk. As the British became more and more rapacious, so too did the *zamindars* who were answerable to them. The proud *Bahujan* was broken. The agrarian rebellions all over the country were eventually brought to a bloody end.

The *Bahujan* now had to function within the Western marketplace like everybody else, but his skills were no longer valued. Every skill that was hand/land based was being mechanized. He was now obsolete in every way except the purely physical. He became labour for hire. This was a problem faced by agrarian communities all over the world, not just in Bharat. This is what the Arts and Crafts movement in England sought unsuccessfully to overturn. In Bharat, this destruction of the World-of-Nature has been ongoing now for 200 years and is still in progress, aided in part by the unconscious Indian State. The industrial World-of-Human-Artifice will not rest until every square inch of land and every vestige of traditional life is accounted for.

This, and not the 'caste system' is why the *Bahujan* is materially poor and unprepared for modern life. *This* is the reason they need affirmative action, to prepare them with the skills needed to survive in the crazy anonymous world we live in today.

Do some of these communities still face discrimination based on the fact that they are 'backward', '*gawaar*' and because some of them used to do what was once considered taboo work? Yes. Does this un-*Arya* state of affairs need remedial action? Yes. Is it a cause of their pain? Yes. Is it a cause of their material poverty? No.

As I pointed out in Part I of this essay series, as we make the move from the World-of-Nature to the World-of-Human-Artifice, we become like the White Man with his colonial gaze. *Bharatiyas* must avoid that way of being at all costs. We must internalize, once again, that we are all one in the *Purusha* and the *Paramaatman*.

The Self-Perception of Scheduled Castes

It is fashionable in revolutionized circles to draw equivalence between the communities that are today called the Scheduled Castes and the formerly enslaved West Africans of the Americas. If one belongs to an SC community, this would be one of the greatest dis-services one could do to the memory of one's own ancestors. The SC communities were never enslaved, they were a free and proud people.

An understanding of the spectrum of communities and the vision of *Sanatana* Civilization as a bridge gives us a useful framework for looking at the history and position of SC communities.

The colonial view is that SC communities were genetically ASI people who were enslaved by the genetically ANI people. The revolutionary view is that SC communities were former Buddhists who were enslaved by *Brahmanical* Hinduism. Both these views of the world have been built with zero evidence. Not only that, these views of the world are problematic because they enslave the SC communities in a narrative of victimhood in which they will never be able to take pride in their ancestors. It is, in fact, via this sleight of hand 'emancipation' that the SC communities are being enslaved, post-independence, for the very first time.

Allow me to propose instead that, in classical Bharat, the communities that chose not to cross the bridge of *Sanatana* Civilization but live instead in the near vicinity of the bridge came to occupy a cultural position that was partially *Sanatani* and partially independent. Unlike the STs who lived almost completely independent lives, the SCs were nominally people of the plough. They were partially assimilated into settled civilization but simultaneously free to follow their own customs around marriage, food, worship, alcohol, dance, art and spirituality outside the strict regimentation of *Varnashrama Dharma*.

The commonly-heard reference to Shudra *jaatis* and SC *jaatis* as communities who were to 'serve' other communities should be read from a material and not a psychological perspective. To 'serve' does not mean to be a servant, it means to *enable*. Today's service and manufacturing sectors come to mind. These communities were a free people, fiercely independent, making beautiful craftwork, building beautiful houses, making and performing Art, stewarding Nature, playing their part in agriculture, temple building, village rituals and war. History shows that the so-called 'criminal tribes' and the forest tribes fought the hardest against British occupation and have resisted conversion to Islam the longest in Pakistan.

It is true that some of these communities ended up doing taboo work because they were not fully assimilated and due to which they had to live and eat separately, but it is also true that this was such a common tribal phenomenon that it was not thought even worth mentioning by any observer of Hindu life right from Arrian all the way to Al Beruni and Domingo Paes. That the Jarawa do not eat, cohabit or inter-marry with the Sentinelese is clear. It does not mean that either of those communities is *enslaved*.

But what is most important for all of us—and especially *Dharmic* SC people—to note is that *Sanatana* Civilization never denied SC communities their spirituality (whether *Vaidik*, *Tantra* or Shamanistic), their culture, their family life, their livelihood. They were educated along with all other people of the bridge in our indigenous schools as Dharampal ji[2] has shown. They held important ritual positions[3] in bridge life. These ingenious communities maintained monopolies[4] over certain types of work, participated in agriculture, craft, stewarding natural resources, temple building and war. They were a free people, probably fiercely independent. Many of these tribes were labelled as "Criminal Tribes"[5] by the British because they fought so hard and long. Our SC communities can take a great pride in their ancestral contributions to our collective present.

People ask, why would people choose to do taboo work? I ask, why do people choose to live in the Arctic, in the Sahara, in the Amazon? In the world of subsistence, this question was irrelevant—all that mattered was community, and community defined itself around ritual, place, skills and work. Any work and any socio-ecological niche that brought survival was valued. Communities accepted what they deemed to be a good deal. Between the hardship of total freedom in the wild (like the STs) and the discipline of life around the *samskaaras* of the bridge, the SC communities, found a middle path... an economic and cultural niche in the periphery of settled agricultural life. That's all. No need to look further for arcane explanations.

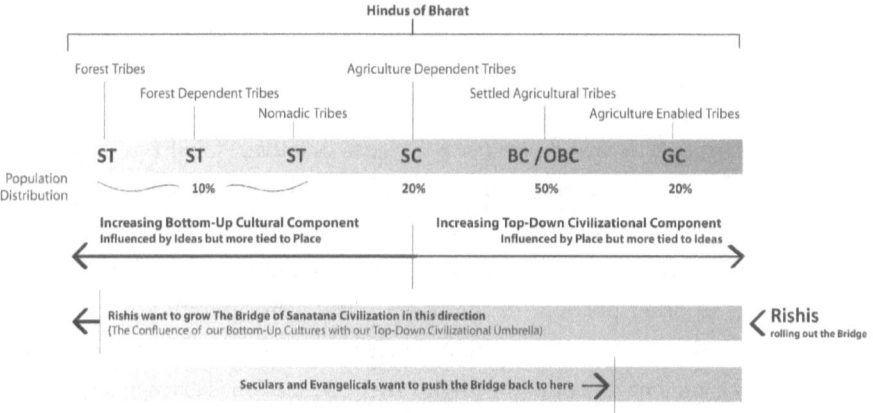

Over the past two centuries, in our debasement, have SC communities been denied entry onto the bridge of *Sanatana* Civilization? Yes. Do we need to remedy this situation immediately? Yes, because that is the very opposite of the reason the bridge was created in the first place by our *rishis*, which was to bring all the tribes of Bharat under one, united metaphysical umbrella. But let it simultaneously be known that crossing the *Sanatana* bridge is a matter of taking on civilizational responsibilities and denying oneself many of the liberties that we have come to take for granted in Western liberal Modernity. Knowing this, would people really want to take on *Sanatani* responsibilities, or is the tug-of-war in modern Indian society merely a spectre of groups cynically parsing an ancient framework through Western ideals and using the resulting mish-mash in the great game of garnering political and material wealth? In simpler terms, when people say, "We were denied the *Veda*, we want parity," are they saying that because they really care about the *Veda* or is it some other memeplex at play?

Which finally brings us to the crux of the matter—would the SC communities *actually* want to get on the *Sanatana* bridge now if such a mechanism was created? If not, do they want to continue to live just outside as their ancestors chose to? Or do they prefer the White Man's ideals and life as newly individuating Hindu liberals, or atheists, or neo-Buddhists? I don't know... this they will have to decide. But the people of the bridge need to get that on-boarding ritual mechanism ready regardless. It would be a pity if our Hindu communion comes to be forged in the irreverent fires of the modern marketplace rather than in our conscious and reverential adoption of our highest *Dharmic* ideals.

The Place of Brahmanas

Sanatana Civilization is *not* Brahmanism because *Sanatana* Civilization was *not* created by *Brahmanas*. *Sanatana* Civilization and its tools for the ethical integration of the tribes of *Bharatam* were created by *rishis*. The *Brahmana jaatis* were merely in charge of one portion of the flame, just like the communities of all other *varnas* were in charge of other portions of the flame. They were appointed to be 'living libraries' who had to learn and pass on the ancient lore, verbatim, generation after generation. The ancient lore of every single other civilization is extinguished. Only that of *Sanatana* Civilization lives on. This is entirely due to the decentralized (and disciplined) nature of knowledge keeping that the *rishis* instituted in their genius.

If the *Veda* is the fount of top-down *Sanatana* Civilization and our umbrella of unity, it is no surprise that the *keepers of the Veda* came to be seen as the *agents* of top-down Hinduism. Ordinary Hindus recognize this and have no problem with it. But recently revolutionized former Hindus have taken to calling *Sanatana* Civilization as *Brahmanism* for this very reason and accusing *Brahmanas* of being monopolists instead of recognizing them as stewards. When they use *Brahmanism* as a pejorative, as they do, what they are actually saying is that they reject top-down *Sanatana* Civilization and that Hinduism is just a bunch of tribalisms. That is the exact same formulation that Christian missionaries use as a conversion strategy. The fact that *Brahmanas* have become everybody's punching bag today shows that a substantial number of us have been converted out of Hinduism either consciously into atheism and Abrahamism or also unconsciously into Liberalism and Secularism.

Every community from every *jaati* and every *varna* has its own temples and spiritual/religious traditions but the *civilizational temples* built by our kings and queens were handed over to specialists to look after. These specialists were largely from *Brahmana* lineages. The idea that everyone can build a house but complex structures need specialist architects should be a formulation that is acceptable to all Hindus. Their expertise in memorizing the *Veda* was certainly one of the qualifications that set them apart as specialists but what they were really experts in, was *saucha*.

All ancient religions recommend the cleaning of oneself physically and ritually before presenting oneself to the Gods. Even a political religion like Islam has people do some ritual washing before prayers. Take this idea of re-presentational purity and extrapolate it backwards to include all the hours of the day, every day of the year, and not just from the beginning of a person's life, but from all his lifetimes before this current one. That's how seriously we approached our Gods in the old days. The *Brahmana jaatis* were chosen as specialists because their entire lives are filled with arcane rules and rites to maintain the ritual purity that makes them fit vessels for approaching the Gods. These civilizational specialists in *saucha* were appointed by our kings to represent *all of society* in the daily *pujas* at the civilizational temples, so that other people could go on with their normal lives bothering with *saucha* only at special times of the year.

It's not hard to understand this formulation. It has nothing to do with Equality or any other revolutionary Western fiction. If, today, we genuinely want to roll back the *saucha* requirements for approaching the Gods, we should at least sit down and have a serious discussion about it with religious experts, not simply abuse it and ignore it. Reformists should introspect on the fact that true Hindus would not be so cock-sure that the Gods would be okay with dilution.

The Old Way

If, in Greece, tomorrow, an ancient, isolated population of Apollo worshippers were to be discovered in a secret valley, would all of Europe rally around to celebrate and protect them, or would they accuse them of monopoly and inequality and take down their ritual practice? I ask this question because that's exactly what we're doing in modern India, in our reformist zeal.

This state of affairs does not apply only to *Brahmanas* in our civilizational temples in places like Tamil Nadu[6]—it also applies to bottom-up traditions of all *jaatis* regardless of *varna*. Sabarimala[7] is a case in point. The recent furore around the practices of the Madurai Adheenam[8] is another case in point. Many *Shudras* communities and some *Kshatriya* communities still maintain ancient living traditions. Every Hindu worth his/her salt should rally around to celebrate and protect these remnants of our ancient traditions, and use these springboards to revive their own traditions. Instead, what we have is a situation where these communities are being penalized simply for having survived the ethnocide of the last thousand years. This is direct evidence of our deep colonization by Western memes.

If reformist Hindus have new ideals and new ideas, the right place to manifest them is in the creation of new traditions that are built on those new foundations. That is the Hindu way. Tearing down the old to manifest the new is completely un-Hindu. We, as Hindus, build up or branch out, we do not tear down. If one cannot find the self-respect within oneself to protect the dying whispers of one's ancestors, then the least one can do is to leave what remains of the Old Way alone.

An Accurate Understanding of the Tamil Predicament

As touched upon earlier in this essay, we have to understand the original nature of the world of humans is not unity. The original nature is diversity and entropy. It takes effort and centuries of conflict resolution before tribes can be brought together under a single metaphorical umbrella, united enough so that they would maintain the peace. And in that peace, agriculture could flourish and, with that, prosperity, strength and stability would come. The places that have had agriculture the longest are the places where peace has reigned the longest—these are also the places where civilization is most deep-rooted. The nature of those civilizations will tell us something about the true nature of Man. Bharat and China are clearly the leading exemplars.

The *Dravidianists* who believe that in the *Sangam* Age there was unity and peace which the *Aryans* destroyed with their divisive caste system have got the whole thing in reverse. As one goes further back in history, we have *more* division not less. If at all there was unity in the distant past, it would have been a very localized tribal unity with no tools for touching the lives of other tribes. There is a reason why the great Tamil epics are unknown even in Chittoor district of bordering Andhra Pradesh, and indeed were all but forgotten even in *Tamizhagam*, but the *Ramayana* and the *Mahabharata* are all-pervasive. In every small hamlet of Tamil Nadu, *therukoothu* performances draw only from the *itihaasa*, not from the Tamil epics. That is because the Tamil epics were cultural (literary), not civilizational (archetypal). The values of pre-*Sanatana* Tamil culture (if there was such a thing and whatever those values may have been) were obviously not articulated clearly enough with a fully fleshed out metaphysics that would attract people from outside. If we are going to insist on seeing things through the prism of Western historiography, then we must never forget that all the great Tamil expansion in South-East Asia happened only after their complete absorption into *Sanatana* Civilization. And Tamils would do well to remember that, as with every other place, *Sanatana* Civilization came as a bridge, not as a tsunami. Sanskrit came as an embellishment, not as an erasure. The Tamil language still enchants. The Tamil epics still exist. The Tamil Gods still live. There is no cause for bitterness except within the hearts of the small-minded. Every cultural facet that exists today is a result of decisions taken by our ancestors in full consciousness. At best, Tamils can argue that their culture was one of the major influencers of *Sanatana* Civilization, and that would be a great cause for pride in itself.

Mobility in the World of Community

"Were the *Irulas* forced to catch snakes and eat rats?"

Nobody in his right mind will answer in the affirmative to that question. The thing is, things just turned out that way. *That* is the socio-ecological niche of the *Irulas*. The evolution of the spectrum of *Bharatiya* bottom-up cultures is a perfectly natural phenomenon of anthropological history. It is in fact the living manifestation of our journey from the Neolithic to the Iron Age and beyond.

In this world of Individualist Autonomy, the idea that one is stuck in one's community or in work that one does not 'choose' is anathema. But this was perfectly normal in the Old World. Community was the basic unit of life, not the individual. So, belonging in a community was both essential and personal. Whenever people have been stuck in jobs, it's because they belonged in a particular community. A *Konaar* cowherd walking into a *Vishwakarma Aasaari* carpenter's community saying that he wants to belong there is just as impossible as a *Kurumba* person walking to the *Toda* village and saying that he wants to start being a *Toda* person. It's the old-world equivalent of a modern person asking *"Why can't I be you?"*. It's simply not feasible. Both economically, culturally and in terms of sheer 'personhood', it would be an act of dilution. If change was truly desired, an entire community would have to shift profession or a true leader would need to guide his community to a new horizon. And this did happen more often than we think. But for the vast majority of people, for the majority of time, life within their communities doing their sacred work was more than sufficiently fulfilling.

The idea that one can walk in and out of our birth communities is a product of the world of surplus. Subsistence does not allow us that luxury. There literally was no such thing as the individual (though we all had our personalities). The individual, as we know it today, is a creation of the machine-world.

Mobility always existed, but it was a slow process. Getting an entire community on board a change of profession is a serious, time-consuming exercise. Also, there would be another community already doing that particular job. What would happen to them? How to avoid conflict? And what about the responsibilities that the community currently performed? How would they face their ancestors for that betrayal? All of these economic, practical and metaphysical questions would have to be answered before a community could 'move'. See how difficult it is for the *Devendrakula Vellalars*[9] to 'move' even in modern India.

Modern individuals may not understand this level of complexity, but they need to understand that these are not reasons to hate where we've all come from.

Don't Use Bad Words #1 – "Discrimination"

Discrimination is literally life itself. Without discrimination one can't do anything. Every single choice or decision that we take means that we are using our faculties of discrimination. Who to marry? What names to give our children? Which school will we put them in? What will they study in college? What to cook for dinner today? Which TV show to watch? Which friend to visit today? All of it involves discrimination.

So, what is especially discriminatory about the Hindu religion? Today, discriminatory beauty pageants are held. Discriminatory entrance exams are also held. Elections are discriminatory, corporate structures are discriminatory. But we accept all of these discriminations without a second thought.

For example, do I resent Deepika Padukone for her success? No, she deserves it, she looks better than me and is probably a better actor. Do I resent Bill Gates for his success? No, he is probably a smarter business man than I am. Do I resent Virat Kohli's success? No, he's probably a better cricket player than I am. So why do the old discriminations appear beastly today but modern discriminations appear normal? That's because, as I've pointed out in Part II of this essay series, our values have changed.

We have exchanged our traditional Hindu metaphysics that was built around *Punya, Paapa, Karma, Punarjanma* for Western principles and ideals—Liberty, Equality, Utopia and Progress. So, when we use these Western ideals to judge our traditional discriminations, of course they appear beastly, even as our new discriminations appear normal. It's not the discriminations that are at fault, it is *we* who have changed. We have adopted a Western lens to view ourselves with, and when we do that, we are filled with self-hate. The question is, if we judge ourselves using foreign ideals, *who exactly are we?*

I'm not saying, we are perfect and we don't need to change aspects of ourselves. But that change has to come from an assessment of ourselves made with respect to our own highest values and metaphysics. For example, we can argue for universal temple entry by stating that –

   a. We are all one in the *Paramaatman*
   b. We are all one in the *Purusha*
   c. We are all one in our demonstration of *Bhakti, Shaurya* and *Tyaga*
   d. We are all one in our adherence to the *samskaaras*
   e. The taboos around their traditional work are no longer relevant

Change does not automatically imply 'reform' and reform does not automatically imply the application of Western ideals such as, in this case, Equality.

Don't Use Bad Words #2 – "Oppression"

I sometime make a provocative statement online. "Anyone who believes that in a room of a hundred people, three people brainwashed and oppressed the remaining ninety-seven people, believes that their ancestors were either dumb or weak."

The response usually is that the British did exactly that in India. I reply that the British, when they came to India, were a full generation ahead of us in weapons technology and defeated us militarily. The *Brahmanas* (who are cited as the agents of oppression) since 5000 BCE, on the other hand, had only a cotton thread. The land, the cattle, the armies, the weapon-making technology, all lay in the hands of the *Shudra jaatis*. It is obvious that they were not oppressed.

If this doesn't close the discussion, I ask, "Why did Dheeran Chinnamalai,[10] the great *Vellala* hero, fight the British till his last breath, but never raise his sword against the *Brahmanas* of Srirangam?"

There is usually no answer to this question, but the answer is obvious. The great *Vellala* hero obviously saw the British as oppressive but *not* the *Brahmanas* of Srirangam. This action of his also makes clear that he was *capable* of recognizing oppression when he saw it, and also proves the corollary—that if he didn't raise his sword against the *Brahmanas*, it was obviously because he did not see their actions as oppressive. Today, the cultural descendants of the great hero consider themselves 'oppressed', have taken on the moniker of 'backward caste' and work for the atheist parties at power in the state. Ironically, these people, under the influence of Marxists and Christian inversion, call out the British as great emancipators and the *Brahmanas* as oppressors. But, History tells us a different story. In the time before our morality was abducted by the West, it was the West that was seen as oppressive and the *Brahmana* as emancipatory through his personal demonstration of the spirit of dispassion...*vairagya*.

It's time then to clearly define the word 'oppression'. Let's start by reminding ourselves that the practice of *saucha*, that stratified ritual space in Bharat, may appear to the modern mind as obnoxious, but it was a common technique used across the classical world as a way to approach the Gods. And, more importantly, we must also remind ourselves that obnoxiousness is *not* oppression. Genocide, slave-trading, colonialism, mass rape, re-education camps, holocaust, paedophilia... all of that is what counts as oppression. Let's not allow the real oppressors off the hook simply because they have invented the washing machine and the internet. Immorality cannot be allowed to hide behind a self-justificatory veil of machinery.

The Individual in Community and in State

The reason community is important, apart from all the reasons mentioned in Part I of this essay, is because communities are self-policing and intimate. An individual makes promises, but it is his community that helps him keep those promises. Without his community, an ordinary man will waver and likely lurch from one new year resolution to the next, but rituals of constancy performed in community hold a man to the hard, disciplined, connected and worthwhile life. *That* is the inner logic of the *samskaaras*.

All society is built on the lives of such men and women. In their absence, society quickly falls apart. That is cultural entropy at work. Hedonism and nihilism soon come knocking.

It is only with community that we have tradition and it is only with sacred tradition that we have self-governance. And it is only with self-governance that we have the possibility for decentralization that is the hallmark of the kind of liberty required to create a *Dharmic rajya*. In the absence of that self-governance, we are forced to have a monster centralized State. And, because the State is not an organic entity but something created, we are forced to *define* what it stands for. That brings us to the threshold of ideals, constitutions, laws and punishment. No longer is the nation aligned with the people, it is the people who are expected to align with the nation. This is a form of un-freedom and creates tremendous strain within society which now needs constant policing and surveillance.

It is clear that *community* does half the work that states do, all without an ounce of effort or policing or punishment. That is why a *Dharmic* State prefers to govern over communities rather than individuals. But the Western State, with its focus on the Machine and the Market, prefers individuals who can be controlled and manipulated instead.

Today, we live in a Western State but our social life is still reasonably communal. In my opinion, it is vital that we protect and retain that way of being for as long as we can, because our communities are *the* buffer against the runaway State. Without our communities, we are mere individuals who can be spied on, threatened and manipulated into serving the will of the State, which today, unfortunately, bends to the will of global corporations... those non-human entities who serve the profit motive and ultimately the metaphysics of the Machine and the Market.

Where to Point Fingers – Bottom-Up or Top-Down?

The understanding that Hinduism is a confluence of Bottom-Up and Top-Down is very useful for clarifying where our interventions are needed.

There was a recent hullabaloo about a dance maestro in Kerala[11] who was excommunicated by his artist community because his son married a Muslim woman. People blamed the community for failing to support the man in attempting to *ghar-wapsi* his daughter-in-law like Abrahamic communities may have done.

What internet Hindus fail to understand is that this is not a bottom-up problem at all. Communities, since time immemorial, have maintained their customs by excommunicating people who broke the rules. That's the way communities maintain coherence. If at all there is a problem, it is a top-down problem. *Sanatana* Civilization has still not mainstreamed the mechanism for dealing with situations like this, for on-boarding non-Hindu people who enter our families through marriage and also for providing ritual direction to Hindus who have been excommunicated by their communities.

Similarly, 'caste'-centred violence, like the Jat protest[12] for governmental quotas, is not a top-down problem at all. Blaming *Sanatana Dharma* for these problems, as Abrahamics do, is an obfuscation. These are bottom-up tribal problems that *Sanatana* Civilization has, in fact, been trying to resolve in an ethical manner at all levels—social, religious and psychological, since the dawn of Hindu time.

A Final Word

On a trip to Rajasthan some years ago, I had hitched a ride in a jeep. The other people in the jeep were the driver-owner of the vehicle (a *Rajput*), a *Gurjar* shepherd, and a woman who was catching a ride home. Suddenly, the woman exclaimed that she had left her keys behind at her workplace. The owner of the vehicle was reluctant to drive all the way back to get the keys, but the *Gurjar* shepherd goaded him on. "Oh, you are a *Rajput*, it's your duty to help her." He then turned to me, and by way of explanation said, "You see, he is *Rajput*... without his ancestors, none of us would be alive here today. He has to live up to their name."

The expressionless *Rajput* gentleman turned his vehicle around and drove back to the woman's workplace where she could pick up her keys and we started our journey afresh.

People still have a memory of how things ought to be and some of the resentment against the so-called 'upper castes' stems from the fact that many continue to claim the respect that was due to their ancestors while failing to honour the higher values that earned that respect in the first place. Ordinary people see that birth-*Brahmanas* today do not live up to the value of dispassion, birth-*Kshatriyas* no longer demonstrate the *Dharmic* use of power, birth-*Vaishyas* no longer demonstrate the *Dharmic* use of wealth, and birth-*Shudras* no longer demonstrate creative excellence in the enablement of *Dharma*. It's no wonder that ordinary people start to doubt if there is such a thing as *Arya* nobility at all. Ordinary people will only accept a *Dharmic* value-hierarchy once again if they can see demonstrably that our *Purusha* is truly alive.

What can we make of this? How can we pick ourselves up? In *Light In The Forest – A Dharmic Landscape for Hindu Kids and their Parents*, I write:

> If our modern-day work is not dedicated to the Gods, then it does not qualify us to belong to any *varna*. If we want to reclaim the pride and nobility that was associated with work in ancient Bharat we need to properly honour the idea of *varna* in today's world, we need to develop a vision of work that goes beyond just job and salary. Work must be seen as collaborative sacrifice. When we dedicate, together, to the Gods in this way, pride, quality, inspiration and respect will automatically follow. This would be a first step in redefining *varna* for the modern world. If we don't restore this unique *Bharatiya* understanding of work as dedication, our *Purusha* will remain incomplete, ragged and broken, while we, far from being the fitting heirs to a great tradition of work, will merely be well paid but Westernized slaves in a chaotic global marketplace.[13]

References and Links

1. https://en.wikipedia.org/wiki/Kilvenmani_massacre

2. Dharampal, *The Beautiful Tree*, 1983
   https://archive.org/details/TheBeautifulTree-Dharampal

3. Halley Kalyan, *A.M. Hocart's 'Caste: A comparative study'*, Pragyata, 2021
   https://pragyata.com/a-m-hocarts-caste-a-comparitive-study/

4. Sonalee Hardikar, Ashish Dhar and Shivam Mishra, "The Real Cost of Leather: Chamars, Cow, and Colonialism", *Pragyata*, 2021
   https://pragyata.com/the-real-cost-of-leather-chamars-cow-and-colonialism/

5. Pandit Satish K. Sharma, *Caste, Conversion, A Colonial Conspiracy*, Indic Talks, 2021
   https://www.youtube.com/watch?v=bpervnxyZYQ

6. Pramod Madhav, "Tamil Nadu: Row over appointment of non-Brahmin priests in temples by DMK govt", *India Today*, 2021
   https://www.indiatoday.in/india/story/tamil-nadu-dmk-temples-appointment-non-brahmin-priests-subramanian-swamy-1842003-2021-08-17

7. "Sabarimala Case: What The 'People For Dharma' Lawyer, Who Left The Supreme Court Spellbound, Had Argued", *Swarajya*, 2019
   https://swarajyamag.com/news-brief/sabarimala-case-what-the-people-for-dharma-lawyer-who-left-the-supreme-court-spellbound-had-argued

8. Pramod Madhav, "TN palanquin row: Madurai seer claims harassment by ruling party, threat to his life", *India Today*, 2022
   https://www.indiatoday.in/india/story/tn-palanquin-row-madurai-seer-claims-harassmentruling-party-threat-life-1945607-2022-05-05

9. Aravindan Neelakandan, "This Community In Tamil Nadu Wants To Be Taken Out Of The SC List; On Friday, It Moved A Step Closer To The Mission With A Major Victory", *Swarajya*, 2020
   https://swarajyamag.com/politics/this-community-in-tamil-nadu-wants-to-be-taken-out-of-the-sc-list-on-friday-it-moved-a-step-closer-to-the-mission-with-a-major-victory

10. Ratnakar Sadasyula, "Dheeran Chinnamalai", *History Under Your Feet*, 2018
    https://historyunderyourfeet.wordpress.com/2018/04/17/dheeran-chinnamalai/

11. Rickson Dommen, "Poorakkali artist in Kerala banned from temple ritual over daughter-in-law's religion", *India Today*, 2022
    https://www.indiatoday.in/india/story/kerala-poorakkali-temple-ritual-kannur-artist-banned-religion-non-hindu-house-muslim-daughter-in-law-1926114-2022-03-16

12. Deeptiman Tiwary, "Jat quota stir turns into inter-caste violence: 4 non-Jats killed, shops burnt as per owner caste", *Indian Express*, 2016
    https://indianexpress.com/article/india/india-news-india/jat-quota-stir-turns-into-inter-caste-violence-4-non-jats-killed-shops-burnt-as-per-owner-caste/

13. Maragatham, *Light In The Forest – A Dharmic Landscape for Hindu Kids and their Parents*, 2022
    https://notionpress.com/read/light-in-the-forest

Section 5

PURVA PAKSHA

Section 5 | Chapter 5.1

My cynical outlook on high technology and the centralized State may not resonate with many Hindu Revivalists. But I would invite them to read this piece nonetheless so that we, as the *Sanatani* people, may become more conscious and introspective about these matters, hopefully leading us to a pragmatic semi-*Dharmic* compromise.

The Mechanics of our Journey from the *Dharmic* Tree of Life to the Western Tech-State

Maragatham, 2022

The worldly life is full of competing truths. Things that make some people happy can also make other people unhappy. Things that make us happy now can also make us unhappy at some other time or place. It was apparent to our *rishis,* and continues to be apparent today to us, that worldly truths are both subjective (dependent on the perceiver) and subject to change themselves over time and space.

These days it has become a habit to assign quantitative values to subjective truths in an effort to 'measure' them and make them 'objective—GDP, happiness index, religious freedom index etc. But just because some subjective truths are quantifiable along arbitrary metrics it does not actually make them objective. Any metric used to quantify truths, apart from being limited, also fails to take into consideration the second and third order downstream effects of these truths which are themselves un-measurable and subjective. For example, politicians and bureaucrats widely use GDP as an 'objective' measure of a subjective truth called 'progress'. Progress is irrationally linked with the idea of an increase in human well-being but, paradoxically, it is simultaneously engaged in poisoning our food, giving us cancer, putting us in a surveillance State etc. all of which are the exact opposite of well-being! What do we make of that?

It becomes apparent that, while subjective truths may be quantifiable along one metric, quantifiability does not automatically lead to greater clarity along any other metric.

Acknowledging this all-pervasive State of inter-related chaos, all our *darshanas* called this interplay of subjective truths as *Maya*. Only the unchanging and eternal absolute truth was termed objective and therefore real.

This recognition of *Maya* came very early to Hindu civilization but it took until the late 20th Century for the Western mind to perceive it. The Western mind perceived this phenomenon in the physical world as quantum physics and in the social world as *post-modern-relativism*. Until that slow realization, they struggled under irrational Christian supremacist beliefs that led them down the road to the Dark Ages, slavery, genocide, colonization, World Wars and Holocaust. It's not clear if they have fully emerged from this suicidal mindset yet but there are clues that many morally-minded academicians and common folk do realize that they have to step away from supremacy. Unfortunately, they have conflated supremacy with hierarchy, and the road they have taken since the fall of Modernity post WW-2 has been even more spectacularly irrational.

While the Hindu mind responded to *Maya* with *Moksha* and *Dharma*, the Western post-modern mind continues to struggle with it and most frequently responds with hedonism and/or nihilism (everything is meaningless). The Western understanding follows the line of thought that if all worldly truths are subjective then they must all be equal because they are all equally false. This leads directly to the idea that nothing is sacred and therefore life is meaningless. This leads logically to the adoption of hedonism and nihilism as guiding principles in Western anti-culture.

At the institutional level, the adoption of the worldview that all truths are equally false has led the West (and increasingly us) to the door of revolutionary Equality—the idea that if every subjective truth is equally false, then all hierarchy is inauthentic. Our task then is to coercively erase any hierarchy that may organically emerge among subjective truths, and all hierarchies that have arisen in the past must be replaced by newer systems which would ideally be mathematical or technological so that the impulse to hierarchy inherent in the human touch is effectively obliterated.

The application of this ideal is currently tearing apart human social fabric and is being pursued desperately in both India and the West as a means to what Jordan Peterson calls Equality of Outcome.[1] This approach elevates an artificially (and sometimes coercively) imposed Equality as *the* touchstone against which every other value has to be measured and to which they must all eventually submit. This ideal is the foundation of wokeism. See legislation in California[2] that aims to ban the teaching of advanced mathematics in schools because not everyone is equally good at it! See education policy[3] in Scotland that allows schools to assign gender to students as young as four without parental consent! See the beginnings of a fresh erosion of traditional morality as professors at major US universities start to normalize paedophilia![4] After all, if all truths are equal, then what's the value-metric one can possibly use to define morality?

Traditional *Bharatiya* society, on the other hand, did not follow the route taken by the West. Instead of taking the untenable position that all truths are equal, we took the position that subjective worldly truths must be arranged into a hierarchy of truths. Those truths that were seen as leading us towards the absolute truth were considered higher truths and those truths that led us away from the absolute truth were deemed lower truths. This is the fundamental understanding that leads to the development of values and social institutions that are based on those values. There *is* a hierarchy of values. Sometimes, the values are closely mapped and it's difficult to choose between them—which leads to what is called a *Dharam-sankat*. "Should Bhima respond to Draupadi's pleas or should he keep his elder brother's promise?" But, for the most part, in normal life, the traditions have already parsed and sorted our values into a hierarchy that is designed to lead us closer to the absolute truth. We don't have to go through this process every day, ourselves. We can lean on the collective wisdom of the ancients. We can also add to that repository of wisdom as we work our way through newer *Dharam-sankats*.

It is, therefore, that in daily life tradition acts as a roadmap and a decision-making machine for human communities and individuals. It takes the stress of living away from us so we can all simply focus on living.

I now invite you all to think of the traditions as the sticks that form a nest for humans within the wider natural world. Traditions form a human nest. Life outside of the nest was not recommended for ordinary people lest they go mad. The individual is simply not mentally and emotionally equipped for life alone. The sheer physical difficulty of survival and emotional difficulty of being face-to-face with a raw and disinterested natural world will drive an individual dead or mad. Such a life was reserved only for the adept few who had outgrown the human condition... the masters.

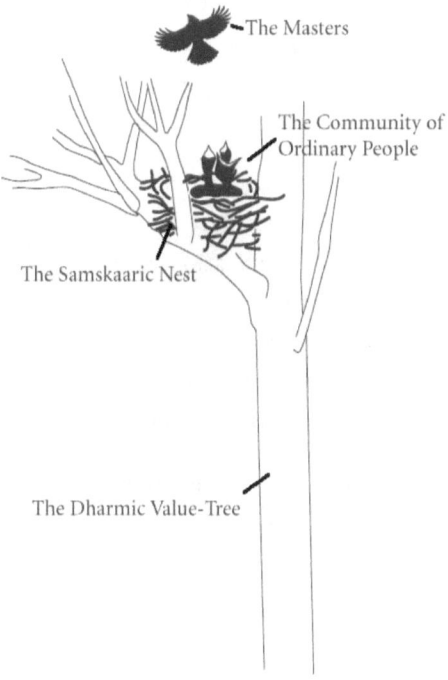

THE TRADITIONAL WAY

In the Hindu world, the sticks that make our nest are the *samskaaras*. The tree that holds the nest up represents our values (derived from the *Purana* and the *Itihaasa*). Both the tree and the nest prepare us for that moment in life or in coming lifetimes, when we are ready for flight... a journey towards the absolute truth. Until then, our essential work in life is the *maintenance* of our nests and the *watering* of our tree.

What happened with the advent of Western Modernity in the West is that even the last vestiges of Christian 'traditions' were discarded and individuals fell from their human nests and hurtled towards the ground. Western 'experts' had to hurriedly create an intellectual net to catch their falling selves. This net they called *Humanism*. In reality, it was nothing but a post-rationalization of the final fall of Western Man from the human nest.

A detailed description of the strands that wove the net of Humanism was provided by Sigmund Freud. He explained its essential character in psychological, emotional and sexual terms. This study of imploded Man through the Freudian lens came to be celebrated as 'our real selves' while the original human nest was derided as 'regressive'. The fall from the nest into the net was celebrated as 'freedom'.

As one can imagine, a net woven together by strands of emotional and sexual indulgence was not the ideal basis for the formation or maintenance of civilization. As a foundation for civilization or even culture, the Freudian net was, and continues to be, an utter failure. It has to be held up by something more robust. It has to rest upon a structure that would perform the role that the value-tree originally performed. That structure, which replaced our traditional values, was the *technological State*... our new tree of values.

The Tech-State is an enormous global system of machines, connecting pipes and processes that organizes and propels resources (humans, energy and material) at ever more dizzying speeds around the world (and more recently to outer space). The Tech-State generates enormous surplus and it is this surplus that is the life-blood of the Freudian web. Without this surplus, the emotional and sexual indulgence of the web would become prohibitively unsustainable and the strands of the web would simply snap, sending the modern human hurtling to the ground. We can now see why the Western Man needs the Tech-State (also called the 'system') so desperately. We can see why it must be saved at all costs. Because without it, the fuel for our self-indulgence would dry up. The entire intellectual edifice of Humanism would crumble and we would be left with the unappetizing option of having to return to our regressive traditions. To prevent or postpone this eventuality, we offer ourselves up as resources to the Tech-State... as fuel to its fire, to keep the engine going. We trade our Liberty for its surplus. The Tech-State does not want community, it does not want religion, it does not want tradition or *meaning*. All it wants is for us to conform to the 9 to 5, and in return it offers us distractions and addictions.

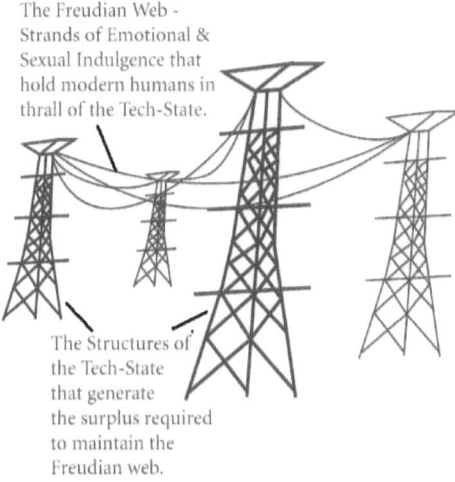

THE MODERN WAY

Look how the national leaders in the UN have stopped representing their cultures and have started representing their economies and the interests of their corporations. We humans, and our exuberant manifestations of life have been rendered obsolete. Here in India, these fears may seem alarmist because we are still on the way up and we still have our grandparents and our festivals, but Westerners understand what they have lost. They lament but are powerless to recover themselves in the face of the Machine that they themselves have created. As we observe the West, we need to tone down our optimism for their vision and spend a lot more energy building intellectual and institutional dams to control the flow of their wild river. We need to put our heads down, practice our *samskaaras* and connect with our children. We need to make sure that when this foreign flood has abated, we will have retained some 30% of our *Bharatiya* selves. More than that I am pessimistic about.

Watching *Wild Wild Country*[5] recently reminded me again of how frail the individual psyche is—that when left rudderless it simply implodes. Osho *bhakts* and other New-Ageists may call it self-discovery or seeking or whatever, but it is merely the human individual imploding outside the nest of community and tradition—a flightless bird spiralling towards the ground. It leads absolutely nowhere. We must keep our eye on the fact that no *ashram* of any master (whether real or pretend) has ever created a superior human being, let alone another master. Modern *ashrams* provide solace to rudderless individuals but they have all failed at regenerating themselves. That is why the *ashrams* of yore were not places of self-discovery but places where students learned the skills of 'nest-maintenance'. From the *sapta-rishis*, to Gautama to Ramana, we see that it was only contact with raw Nature and/or silence that taught true self-discovery and, in fact, opened up channels for higher-order knowledge flow (if one survived the encounter and retained one's faculties).

So, what then is the true nature of this new tree of values that many of us have adopted and have grown more and more addicted to?

1. The Tech-State is Universalist.

It wants us *all*. It wants to control our dreams. It wants to replace our Gods.

This characteristic was not so obvious or disturbing to many of us until recently because we were still largely surrounded by the natural and traditional world. This is no longer true and, as post-geographic technologies have grown, the universalist nature of the Tech-State can find its way into every nook and cranny of our world. The COVID years have shown that mind and body control of literally the entire human population is now a possibility. The more people get on TV, the more they get on the internet, the more they get on to the international banking system, the more they get on the slipstreams of Big-Pharma and Big-Agri, the more susceptible we all are to being manipulated.

Did you know that farmers in Europe are not allowed to grow and share seeds?[6] Did you know that the Government of Tamil Nadu has stipulated that no private person can own an unlicensed indigenous bull[7] nor use it for breeding?

People cannot be left alone. If you are not a super-elite (Gates, Rothschild etc. who actually control the State), then you are either:

a. Held in permanent suspension by the State through subsidies, dole etc. that keep one forever in the State's debt. Such a person can never resist or rise against the state because the State is his/her *mai-baap*.

   OR

b. Taxed by the State until you are essentially in chains. Any smidgeon of freedom that an independent-minded person may discover will, in due course, attract the State's attention and that activity will be taxed and licensed.

Here is the great paradox, the State which was created ostensibly with the intent to protect people's liberties cannot accept a single free person/community within its borders. It is apparent that our *independence* is not its concern. Our *dependence* upon it, on the other hand, is very much its concern. It wants to be the final arbiter of our destinies. Unfortunately, most humans are not concerned with Liberty if they are granted TV/fridge/Netflix in exchange. This is the dehumanised condition we find ourselves in today, a far cry from the mindset of the heroes who composed the *suktas* of the *Rig Veda*.

2. The Tech-State is Bottom-Feeding

Holding us all in a Freudian web of 'equally false' relativist truths, the Tech-State uses our negative emotions (that have been post-rationalized as 'our real selves') to both feed us and control us. Its engine runs on human greed, lust, pride, selfishness, fear and victimhood. All these are leveraged to push us harder and, when we slip, to hold us to ransom.

3. The Tech-State is Anti-Liberty (and for once, I use the word Liberty in its original sense.)

Like all other Abrahamic religions before, the Tech-State too wants total conformity. The question to now ask is "What does the Tech-State want?"

It's not entirely clear but, for all practical purposes, its goal appears to be Efficiency with a capital 'E'. To this new Efficiency God, anything that does not result in greater and faster flow of resources, energy and money will be deemed worthy of sacrifice and elimination.

Humans are definitely slated for elimination when the time comes but, until then, the Tech-State finds it necessary to control them as far as possible and for this it is essential to have them all operating under a single OS. The culture of post-geographic social media systems provides the perfect template for creating that single OS. Traditions, religions, families, old loyalties, borders... all of these constructs are obstacles. They come in the way. It is against this backdrop that we should read the elimination of families, traditions, communities, gender etc.

In one word: hyper-secularization. Not just separation of State and religion, but elimination of human assemblies by the State and its replacement with technological assemblies. Humans are downstream of these assemblies. Do you control the social media presence in your life or does it control you? The borders are already fuzzy. Expect that those borders will entirely collapse in the coming decades. As Musk says, "If we don't become cyborgs, we risk irrelevance."[8]

Succumbing to total control by a vastly more superior un-human system with its own unknown end goals is anti-Liberty.

The Tech-State is not interested in Human well-being and in fact may be aligned with a post-human world. The Tech-State is our new value-tree but it has a radically different character from our old value-tree. The old value-tree and our *samskaaric* nest were designed for *humans* to realize their full potential and aim for transcendence towards the Divine Absolute.

Though the Tech-State's character is not entirely clear yet, it appears to be approximately aligned with a mechanical urge to realize pure efficiency... and we, the obsolete humans, are to serve as resources to that end. As we move towards an AI and bio-manipulative future, the techno-elite push to a post-human future is becoming more and more apparent.

And the madness doesn't stop here. We must know that the quasi-religion of the super-elites, Longtermism, asserts that "there could be so many digital people living in vast computer simulations millions or billions of years in the future that one of our most important moral obligations today is to take actions that ensure as many of these digital people come into existence as possible."[9]

What!!??

So, no, it's not important that we leave a clean and abundant world for our children but it is important that we subsidise the lives of billions of digital people on other planets! If we think this is funny, remember the joke's on us.

4. The Tech-State is Asuric

When looked at closely, the Tech-State's post-human vision maps very closely to say, the *Aurobindonian* worldview which sees humans as part of a play by the Absolute to rediscover Herself. That is, humans are but a short-term pit stop in the grand journey to evolve into a higher consciousness. But the great difference between the *Aurobindonian* view and the Tech-State view is that the former places humans at the centre of its metaphysics, as entities who have agency to evolve, while the latter views humans as disposable resources who will play a part not in reaching the Divine but in enabling the Machine to supersede them.

One striking aspect of the Tech-State which gives away its essential *asuric* nature is its increasing focus on negative human emotions to run its engine (greed, pride, lust, envy, fear etc). In sharp contrast, all *Dharmic* systems focus on our higher emotions—happiness, courage, altruism, service etc.

Further evidence of the Tech-State's *asuric* nature is to be found in its constant movement towards the theft of human liberty via total surveillance and eventual bio-manipulation. It promises that will lead us to greater happiness. It is clear that it is sleight of hand. We know that greater convenience that the Tech-State promises requires the sacrifice of liberties, but beyond a point the convenience to liberty graph does not lead to greater happiness and may, in fact, lead to what any sane person would classify as Hell (see the light grey graph in comparison to the medium grey and dark grey graphs below).

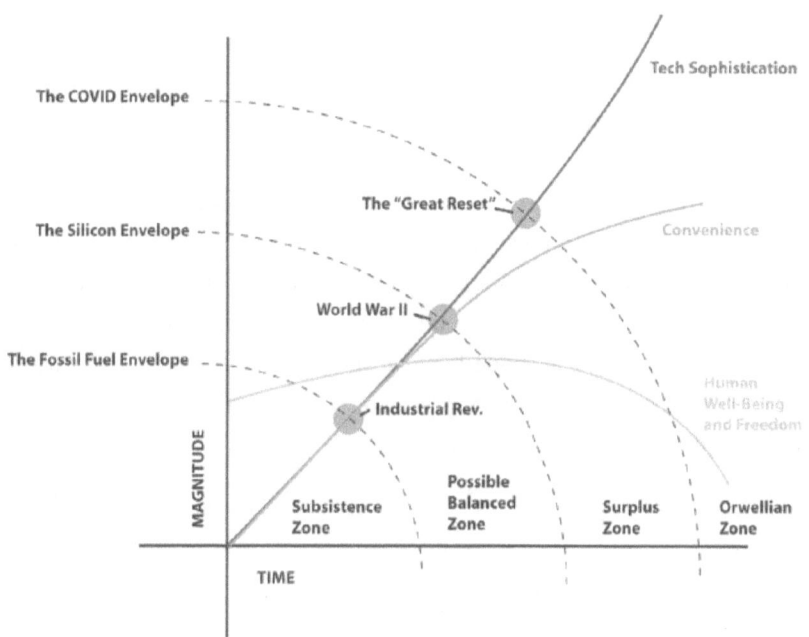

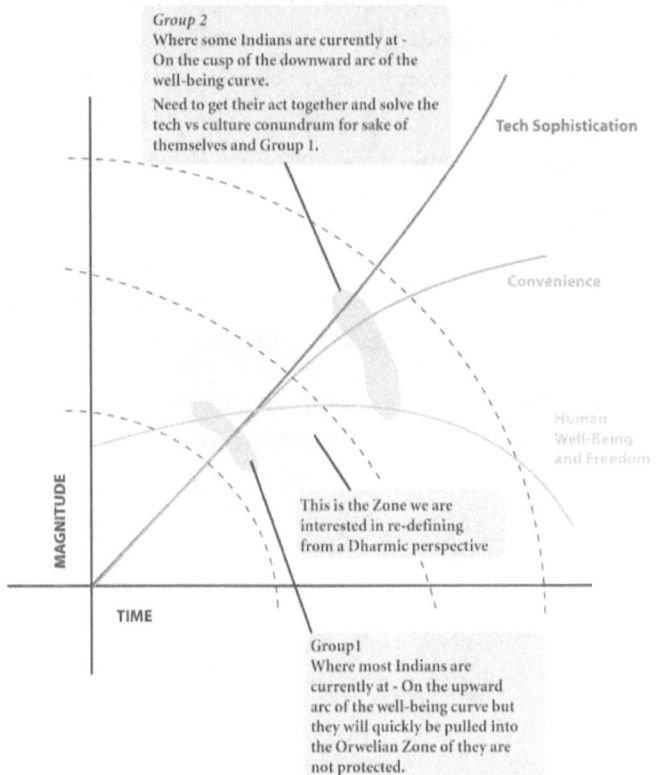

The Tech-State couches its intentions in words like happiness and well-being and, more recently, sustainability, but though it was created by humans and is ostensibly run by humans has an interest in human welfare only as long as it can be convinced that we are useful resources. The human body, human behaviour, our children are all resources, not agents of divinity as our *rishis* imagined, but resources like minerals and petrol. I don't think we are paying enough attention and even when we do we ignore the matter because it is too horrific to contemplate. But that attitude is what allows the system to take baby steps without pushback until pretty soon we are way over the horizon of what we would have considered normal and human.

The game is well underway. See the statements linked to below that give their game away.

> ...it's all about scale. By overcoming the imprinting problem, the world is their oyster as far as genetic engineering is concerned.[10]

The essence of the current incarnation of capitalism is "surveillance capitalism," as Shoshana Zuboff has demonstrated in her book of that name. High-tech companies profit by sucking up oceans of information from their customers and using it to compile behavioural portraits that they sell to advertisers. The more sophisticated these behaviour portraits become, the more they will be used to predict and control behaviour.[11]

Autonomous weaponry is the third revolution in warfare, following gunpowder and nuclear arms. The evolution from land mines to guided missiles was just a prelude to true AI-enabled autonomy—the full engagement of killing: searching for, deciding to engage, and obliterating another human life, completely without human involvement.[12]

The woman said the other black car had taken Ruth's two daughters away, into emergency state care. And she told Ruth to hand over her two older sons to be taken away, too. The following day, two black cars appeared again. The couple assumed it had all been a terrible mistake and the children had been brought back. But, they were wrong. Four policemen got out. And took the baby.[13]

Hindus who believe that we can create a *Dharmic* Tech-State are, in my opinion, being too optimistic and perhaps naive. Yes, we have to deal with our *asuric* rivals, but let us not drink their *asuric* kool-aid and imagine that it will lead to a Hindu destination.

If and when our *asuric* rivals collapse, or in the unlikely eventuality that we overcome them (while keeping our sense of self intact) and a true *Dharmic Rashtra* is established in Bharat, we must pay close attention to two key formulations that our *rishis* instituted—**decentralization** (the equivalent of *jaati* and *sampradaya*) and **spiritualization** (the equivalent of the *Sanatani* ritual and ascetic tradition). Without these two impulses being consciously embedded in our State apparatus, we will end up in an un-Hindu—and, indeed, in an un-human—place.

Post Script 1

People have pointed out that my use of Tech-State falsely accuses innocent technology of all kinds of evils. I partially agree that it is the impulse to a centralized State with a mandate to impose and control a global centralized culture that is primarily at fault. This proselytizing universalism is a Christian impulse and it continues in the modern West in various secular forms.

But, at the same time, giving a clean chit to high technology does not seem entirely fair. It's like arguing that the gun didn't shoot the children at Sandy Hook, it was the gunman. True, but also a little bit like the 'Ashwattama is dead' kind of truth. If the gun wasn't available, the crazy gunman could not have done as much damage as he did. The fact is that humans are not at the level of consciousness that allows for harmless access to technologies of such enormous consequence. It is high technology (especially geography/body eroding technologies, starting with the telegraph, locomotive, air flight, radio waves, internet, ICBM, nuclear warheads, CRISPR) that pushed us past the tipping point. These technologies empowered the West's post-Christian urge to total dominance. It is these technologies that give this post-Christian urge the means to actualize its evil intent. If we weren't so 'frog in the boiling water' about this phenomenon, we would recognize that the journey from the genocide of European Jews in the Holocaust to COVID has been one helluva wild gallop for the Global State riding the Technological Horse. At this moment in history, I think it's fair to call this phenomenon, the Tech-State, a symbiotic double-headed beast.

People who are still gung-ho about high technology have to demonstrate how they intend to subordinate it to a higher human value system and how they will create the necessary institutional circuit breakers to protect their human appliances from voltage surges in the system.

Post Script 2

We see now that the actual nuts and bolts of modern society are machines and technological assemblies, not human groups and human inter-relations. Humans are merely button pushers at best, and raw material at worst. Neither of these roles is in need of any metaphysics of communion. Apart from the selfish narcissism that Modernity encourages us to indulge in (and which is the basis of Freudian psychological description of the "true nature of Man"), we have no need for any other deeper explanation of life and living. Everything is **already taken care of** by the technological assemblies that organise our lives in the Tech-State. In this petri dish of self-indulgence, all that is needed by way of metaphysics, therefore, is a psychological post-rationalization of the fall from the human nest—the what's and the how's of coping with the un-human place we moderns find ourselves in. The attempted codification of that sense of loss and our subsequent search for higher meaning has come to be mapped (over the past 150 years) by a set of ideas and practices that today go by the name New Age. By cherry-picking ideas and practices from Hinduism, Buddhism and Shamanism modern 'seekers' have created a decontextualized assemblage religion that is wholly and self-indulgently modern. That is why no traditional person has any interest in New Age at all, because he/she already exists in an unruptured vision of self, society and universe. New Age exists where both rupture and a search for re-connection co-exist.

If this underlying context is understood, Hinduism can act as a guide for New Age, and New Age can be an ally of Hinduism in the modern age. Unfortunately, adherents of New Age often see themselves as superior to adherents of traditional Hinduism (because they have evolved beyond it). We can see now that this is merely a function of New Age being a child of Modernity and moderns invariably *have* to believe that Modernity is superior to any other way of being. Anything less would undermine one of the cornerstones of Modernity—Progressivism.

References and Links

1. Jordan Peterson, *Equity: When the Left Goes Too Far*, 2019
   https://www.jordanbpeterson.com/political-correctness/equity-when-the-left-goes-too-far/

2. James Varney, "Is Mathematics Racist? California could blaze pathway with woke math", *The Washington Times*, 2021
   https://www.washingtontimes.com/news/2021/jun/6/is-mathematics-racist-california-could-blaze-pathw/

3. Daniel Sanderson, "Scottish four-year-olds can change gender at school without parents' consent", *The Telegraph*, 2021
   https://www.telegraph.co.uk/news/2021/08/12/scottish-four-year-olds-can-change-gender-school-without-parents/

4. Joshua Rhett Miller, "Virginia prof under fire after saying sexual attraction to children isn't always immoral", *New York Post*, 2021 https://nypost.com/2021/11/15/allyn-walker-says-attraction-to-children-isnt-immoral/

5. *Wild Wild Country*, Netflix Mini Series, 2018 https://www.imdb.com/title/tt7768848/

6. Guy Castler, "Seed Laws in Europe: Locking Farmers Out", *Grain*, 2005 https://grain.org/article/entries/541-seed-laws-in-europe-locking-farmers-out?print=true#:~:text=The%20European%20law%20only%20allows,unable%20to%20maintain%20a%20variety.

7. Devanathan Veerappan, "Tamil Nadu Farmers Worried about New Breeding Act", *The Times of India*, 2020 https://timesofindia.indiatimes.com/city/madurai/tamil-nadu-cattle-farmers-worried-about-new-breeding-act/articleshow/73079245.cms

8. Olivia Solon, "Elon Musk says humans must become cyborgs to stay relevant. Is he right?", *The Guardian*, 2019 https://www.theguardian.com/technology/2017/feb/15/elon-musk-cyborgs-robots-artificial-intelligence-is-he-right

9. Emile P Torres, "Understanding 'Longtermism': Why this suddenly influential philosophy is so toxic", *Salon*, 2022 https://www.salon.com/2022/08/20/understanding-longtermism-why-this-suddenly-influential-philosophy-is-so/

10. Shelley Fan, "Scientists Use CRISPR to Condense a Million Years of Evolution Into Mere Months", *Singularity Hub*, 2022 https://singularityhub.com/2022/09/11/scientists-use-crispr-to-condense-a-million-years-of-evolution-into-mere-months/

11. Adrian Wooldridge, "China's Surveillance State will be the West's Future Too", *Bloomberg*, 2022 https://www.bloomberg.com/opinion/articles/2022-09-12/china-s-surveillance-state-will-be-the-west-s-future-too?leadSource=uverify%20wall

12. Kai Fu Lee, "The Third Revolution in Warfare", *The Atlantic*, 2021
    https://www.theatlantic.com/technology/archive/2021/09/i-weapons-are-third-revolution-warfare/620013/

13. Time Whewell, "Norway's Barnevernet: They took our four children... then the baby", *BBC*, 2016
    https://www.bbc.com/news/magazine-36026458

Section 5 | Chapter 5.2

A (T)Radical Critique of Modernity
Sanatana Exceptionalism in Light of Modernity

Maragatham, January 2023

Coming to Grips

The family is in steep decline, but nobody knows it. On the contrary, we have been fed, and we have accepted wholeheartedly, the subliminal message that we are 'progressing' and 'well-settled'. Who has fed us those messages, and why, is a deep and complex topic that I have tangentially explored in the essay *The Mechanics of our Journey from the Dharmic Tree of Life to the Western Tech-State* (Section 5, Chapter 5.1).

But one doesn't need to understand complex arguments to witness the obvious. My paternal grandfather was one of eight siblings, my paternal grandmother was one of eight siblings, my maternal grandfather was one of five siblings and my maternal grandmother was one of eight siblings. My father, growing up, had *thirty-eight* first cousins and siblings. I had twelve. My children have exactly three first cousins (all abroad). But this is not merely a matter of making more babies (though it is deeply connected to the other thing I want to discuss)... this is, for many families of my socio-economic profile, the bleeding edge of a genetic and cultural extinction being played out in real-time.

What could we—with our wealth, foreign connections and grasp of Dickensian English— possibly have in common with Boro and Boa,[1] the last of the Great Andamanese tribe? Well, it appears that we share their fate of cultural and genetic extinction (at the very least, our branches of our family trees do).

When we die, we will die alone (or very nearly so). No clansmen from far-flung villages will drop their livelihoods and rush to our funerals. Our bodies will not have to wait until the last troupe of relatives, from the most distant branch of the family, arrives bearing flower-garlands and tears. Our final journey will be from the aseptic environs of the ICU to the eerie silence of the electric incinerator. Not for us the final march through the paddy fields, not for us the final blessing as we are borne away on bare shoulders past our *Kula Devata*, one last time through the streets we played in as children. Not for us the long final pause, waiting for the sound of drumbeats to subside before we are consigned to the flames.

Ram Naam Satya Hai...

I refuse to be the last man standing.

I refuse to be the dead-end of my ancestral tree.

I refuse to be the man who presides over the final extinction of his ancestral culture, preserved with such passion through war, famine, death and disease by generation upon generation of great men and women who came before me.

What is it I have to do to turn this tide?

If these sentiments mean nothing to you and if this last question does not evoke a resonance in your heart, then the rest of what I am about to discuss will also be of no importance. But for those of you to whom the answers to this question matter, we have a long and complex journey ahead of us. The routes we take may be many, but the general direction of our journeys will be the same.

I was twenty-eight when Luis, a Mexican-American friend, declared that different parts of the world belonged to different peoples, each of whom have their own colours, flavours and stories. I had just come to my own personal conclusion that all the stories I had been fed throughout my boyhood were false and that, in order to shed that old identity, I had to climb beyond the constraints of geography, history and culture. I had come to believe that the only *real* identity I could have would be one that I gathered through the breadth of my personal experience... a singular set of stories that would define 'Me'. To be able to 'live anywhere', 'do anything', 'be anyone' had become my emancipatory personal credo. Not surprisingly, I had laughed at Luis's suggestion. But he was adamant. He said we were free to visit other places and build friendships, but we were not free to claim other lands and cultures as our own or appropriate them like Modernity does for tourism and entertainment. He seemed to suggest that there was something *essential* about culture and place that served a deeper purpose, and that that impulse needed to be respected.

Though opposed to that limiting point of view at that time, that conversation stayed in my mind, probably because I too had embarked subconsciously on a journey to recover my roots. I had turned my back on America and 'progress'. I was to return to India where I would, inevitably perhaps, soon grow disenchanted with urban life, seeing it as a pale shadow of the life I had consciously rejected in America. I would turn to rural Tamil Nadu for a sense of the authentic. And there I would attempt to rediscover and pick up the weave of broken ancestral strands.

It has taken me twenty years since then to finally understand Luis's position and build an intellectual bridge between my position and his.

I have come to see that, indeed, everything is just a story that we tell ourselves but some stories ring truer than others because they are *our* stories, they tell the tale of how we came to be born, how we are connected to our parents, and through them to their parents and to all those who came before them, and how that long chain of people is connected ultimately to this land, the stars, the *Kula Devatas* and the deeds and words that were passed on like precious jewels from mother to daughter, father to son. All other stories start to fade into inconsequence.

Central to this point of view is the understanding that if those precious words and deeds were not passed on and were not stewarded (often at great personal cost) by successive generations, then there would be nothing *living* to connect us with our ancestors, creating the equivalent of a still-birth for our personal life stories. This results in a rootlessness that has profound implications for our understanding of identity and purpose and ultimately for the well-being of both humans and the natural world.

This is the great schism between the two worldviews—the 'Way of Maintenance' and the 'Way of Experience'. The Way of Maintenance is the traditional way; it posits that *culture* is what defines our identities and what we choose to do as individuals is just the *tadka* on top. The Way of Experience is the modern way; it posits that what we choose to do is what defines our identities, and our cultures are merely the *tadka* on top. The Way of Maintenance is a responsibility-centric vision of human purpose, where our life experiences, in the service of tradition, lead to greater depth. The Way of Experience, on the other hand, is a desire-centric vision of human purpose. It surrenders the idea of responsibility to the Tech-State while urging people to explore 'Life'. Such an exploration leads to a great breadth of shallow experience, but not to depth.

So, when we say we are modern people, just who are we saying we are? Are we mere consuming individuals composed of multiple chains of carbon molecules as Economics and Science tell us? Does this hedonist-materialist description ring true? What if we were to stop for a minute and truly internalize this self-perception... how then would we behave?

How would we understand morality, family, children, love, honour? In a purely material world what would be the *basis* to determine *value*?

How would we place value on ancient, unspoken, positive human needs such as purpose, belonging, connection, love, participation, sharing, contribution, fulfilment, well-being?

Why are those needs valued?

To *whom* are those needs valuable and *what* is the nature of that being?

It has become obvious in the modern world that we can't and we don't ask these questions. *That* is our hypocrisy. We want the fruits of the materialist worldview, but we think we can avoid bearing the true physical, emotional and spiritual costs of such a worldview.

Take for example the ridiculous Happiness Index,[2] the announcement of which has become an annual farce. The countries that regularly rank at the top of this index also rank at the top of global anti-depressant[3] usage. So, what does it even mean? Quantitative metrics have replaced qualitative metrics and we have started to define ourselves by access to a set of curated experiences provided by the Tech-State rather than by who and how we *are*.

Oh, you have access to a club with a swimming pool, then surely you must be happy.
Oh, you have access to a hospital with MRI facilities, then surely you must be happy.
Oh, you have access to a road without potholes, then surely you must be happy.

The sheer reductive nature of these suppositions shows us clearly the limitations of the materialist worldview that assumes that we can take apart an organic, complex and dynamic system such as culture and put it back together more efficiently using a set of quantitative markers.

Wendell Berry's primal question remains as relevant as ever: *"What are humans for?"*

What is it that lends our lives Meaning, that gives us connection and contentment? He writes:

> People use drugs, legal and illegal, because their lives are intolerably painful or dull. They hate their work and find no rest in their leisure. They are estranged from their families and their neighbours. It should tell us something that in healthy societies drug use is celebrative, convivial, and occasional, whereas among us it is lonely, shameful, and addictive. We need drugs, apparently, because we have lost each other.[4]

In the old world, it was the traditions (the manifest structures that held and supported abstract cultural values) that performed those tasks. They connected people backwards in time with their ancestors, forward in time with their descendants and sideways across geography with their community. In other words, traditions held us steady in the matrix of space-time. In the ocean of life, the traditions were a raft, the rituals were the poles and our *shraddha* the rope that bound the poles together. Without that raft, we experienced a metaphorical drowning... a loss of Meaning with profound emotional and physical consequences.

Modern cultural artifacts such as Hollywood movies or TV shows regularly explore this 'drowning' theme, but instead of focusing on how to rediscover our cultural rafts, they cloak the 'drowning' itself within a garb of romanticism. For example, in the stress-laden, depression-soaked, un-human worlds that they conjure up (see New Amsterdam, Real Detective, House of Cards or literally any contemporary series), the everyday normalcy of trusting another human being would be shown as the most heroic act one can possibly perform, or the act of having a baby or family would be depicted as some sort of holy grail rather than the absolutely normal and natural thing that it is in the traditional mind. We are all familiar by now with the protagonist who chooses to remain human in an alien world, who maintains sanity in an insane world, or who shows love in a loveless world. None of these shows/movies ever questions the baseline assumption that the world is inevitably alien, insane or loveless. Twenty years ago, such movies were called dystopian (remember *American Beauty*?), today they are the norm, the accepted backdrop for all 'human-interest' stories. Every generation severed from its cultural roots takes us further and further into a world where rootlessness is normalized and loss of Meaning becomes the baseline human state. The sane begin to be seen as insane, the authentic as weak and the rooted as alien. When most people are broken, they are no longer seen as broken. Instead, anyone who displays even a smidgeon of wholeness comes to be treated as a pitiable curiosity who hasn't experienced 'real' life. All across the modern world today, people bond not over what connects them but over the extent of their dysfunctions. The threads that have bound the world since the dawn of Time have started to unravel, and our systems of law and governance, far from resisting this descent into chaos, are primed to incentivize that unravelment.

See a recent example from The Guardian: "Why a shortage of Mr. Rights means single mothers hold the key to the falling birthrate"[5] No family? No problem! The author advocates that the government must incentivize children growing up without their fathers. Sheer dystopian genius. In such a world, every band-aid for the now broken crystal we inherited from our ancestors *must* be seen, in due course, as *more* beautiful than the crystal itself, because maintaining psychological coherence in the modern world, requires that we *post-rationalize* the disruptive processes of Modernity and normalize our personal dis-integrations.

And so, it comes to be, that all attempts at nurturing the ancestral crystal or putting back together its broken pieces are labelled as either quaint or downright evil by the self-justificatory intellectuals and artists of Modernity. They say tradition must die because it is oppressive, that family must end because it is fascistic, that civilization must fall because it is patriarchal. Instead, they celebrate as 'freedom' the depression, the addiction, the loneliness, the dis-connect, the discontent, the mal-content, the inhuman scale, the enslavement to corporations and the profit motive, the belittling of human purpose and spirituality and the actual cultural and physical suicide that modern life represents, as if all that was not oppressive, fascistic and 'patriarchal'.

Wendell Berry recognizes this delusionary self-sabotage when he writes:

> We all come from divorce. This is an age of divorce. Things that belong together have been taken apart. And you can't put it all back together again. What you can do, is the only thing that you can do. You take two things that ought to be together and you put them together. Two things! Not all things.[6]

Yuval Noah Harari recognizes this delusionary self-sabotage when he writes:

> Modernity is a deal. The entire contract can be summarised in a single phrase: humans agree to give up meaning in exchange for power.[7]

Ananda Coomaraswamy recognized this delusionary self-sabotage when he wrote:

> The contentment of innumerable people can be destroyed in a generation by the withering touch of our (Western) civilisation; the local market is flooded by a production in quantity with which the responsible maker of art cannot compete; the vocational structure of society, with all its guild organisation and standards of workmanship, is undermined; the artist is robbed of his art and forced to find himself a "job"; until finally the ancient society is industrialised and reduced to the level of such societies as ours in which business takes precedence of life. Can one wonder that Western nations are feared and hated by other people, not alone for obvious political or economic reasons, but even more profoundly and instinctively for spiritual reasons?[8]

If we are not already at a point of no return, it's high time our systems of law and governance modified their stated purpose from the maintenance of an *Ideal-Based Morality* to the incentivization of an *Outcome-Based Morality*. The difference in intention between the two systems is stark.

1. An Ideal-Based Morality is one that is focused on holding up as sacrosanct, a set of unrealizable maxims (usually of foreign origin, such as Liberty, Equality, Fraternity and Progress) that the people are forced to un-

naturally measure themselves up against, automatically setting themselves up for constant failure and punishment.

2. An Outcome-Based Morality, on the other hand, is one that is focused on incentivizing societal outcomes that are positively judged as per their adherence to actual indigenous cultural values that already live within the minds and hearts of the people by virtue of their organic development over millennia. This type of morality caters to authentic human needs of connection, contentment, beauty and purpose.

In other words, Law, definitionally, must re-establish its ancient compact with the culture of the land over which it holds sway. Law cannot stand removed from the people, it must *not* be allowed to bear first allegiance to reformist ideals instead of the value system of the people it is beholden to serve.

Questions such as "What kind of world do we want our children to live in, and how do we get there?" are more important to ask and answer than blind participation in a check-box culture of ideals, outcomes be damned!

Let us recognize that the ideal of Liberty has led us to broken families,[9] loneliness[10] and OnlyFans pages;[11] that the ideal of Equality has led us to drag queen story-hours[12] and puberty blockers,[13] that the ideal of Fraternity has led us to NATO-determined regime change[14] and the mass graves of indigenous children in Canada.[15] I'm sorry, but "No". These three Western ideals and their spin-off values systems may sometimes appear to us to be reasonable ideas (not ideals), and context-permitting, they may sometimes be implemented, but we have to make sure that they are held subordinate to higher *Dharmic* values such as harmony, contentment, beauty, cultural coherence and metaphysical Meaning. I have explored the fork in this moral road in Part I of the essay *The Hindu Traditionalist: Culture Morality and Reform* (Section 3, Chapter 3.1).

Many modern Hindus do not connect these dots because they grew up in a traditional world. They already have their pockets full of Meaning. Their parents, extended families and grandparents still loom large in their consciousnesses. In other words, they can afford to turn their backs on Tradition because the labours of their ancestors continue to subsidise their cultural profligacy. The question to ask such modern Hindus is "Can they provide their children with what their parents provided them and their grandparents provided their parents?". If the answer is "No", then their attitude is culturally (and genetically) unsustainable. This inter-generational attrition will lead to erosion and finally to extinction, both cultural (memetic) and genetic. It is only when the old guard has passed and the old world has disappeared that we will realize the worth of all that we have taken for granted and that we can never hope to recover.

Tradition and Community

From an anthropological perspective, the idea and practice of Tradition does not have a spiritual goal, though the Gods are an indelible part of it. The actual aim of Tradition is communal. To repeat, Tradition is that socio-cultural force that holds people together by connecting them vertically in time with their ancestors and descendants, and horizontally in space with their fellow traditionalists. Tradition literally holds and defines us in space-time.

Take for example, the annual *koozhu oothara vizha* celebrated by many farming communities in Tamil Nadu. The *koozhu* (a fermented rice and *ragi* drink) that is cooked in each home is carried by the women of every house to the *graama devata*. There, the *koozhu* cooked by each family is presented as *naivedya*. A divination ceremony is held and the Goddess is invoked to reveal if the rains will be on time this year and if any misunderstandings or illnesses that plague the community will be resolved. Later, the offerings of *koozhu* from every household are poured into a large common container and all of the *koozhu* is mixed together and redistributed among the community, symbolically cementing their togetherness under the protective gaze of the Goddess.

We see now, that any person speaking in favour of Tradition must at once become aware that he is also speaking in favour of those connections that it fosters, in other words *Community* (of which *family* is a subset). One cannot exist without the other. It is only communities that have traditions—individuals by themselves only have habits.

Though *individuals* per se, are not definitionally opposed to Community, the question we ask of them is whether they see themselves as belonging to a community (in which case they accept the demands of Tradition) or to no one but themselves (in which case they are adherents of Individualism).

It now becomes important to recognize that the minute one speaks in favour of Tradition, one has to engage in a dialogue with its arch enemy, *Individualism*. Any person with a traditional bent of mind will immediately see that what one stands to lose with the loss of Tradition (Connection and Meaning), carries far more weight than what one stands to gain by the wholesale adoption of Individualism (Autonomy and Self-Gratification). And even though, in these modern times, we will accept a compromise between the two worlds, this realization of loss logically leads us, *at the very least*, to acknowledge the importance of community life. This is a fair beginning to make for any supporter of Tradition. From this stage, we can start to view post-industrial human history as a tussle between the forces of Community and Tradition on one side and Individualism and Modernity on the other. This can be essentialized as a tussle between the forces of *identity* and *Meaning* and the forces of *convenience* and *efficiency*. Even the iconoclastic Abrahamic religions, that stood against Tradition for so many centuries, are now forced to fight this fight.[16] In the face of the structures of Western Modernity, they suddenly find themselves in the same boat they once put pagan cultures in: *Convert or Die*.

Once we recognize that Tradition is rooted in Community and Individualism in Modernity, a closer look at the structures of Modernity brings us clarity on how it functions, *how* it *enables* Individualism and *why* it *promotes* Individualism as a great value. More dangerous, from our point of view, is Modernity's Western origin with its Christian baggage of having to compulsorily 'save' the world. This stance leads it to demonize its opponents and attempt to destroy them by all means at its disposal. This explains why Modernity is not just pro-Individualism which we could ignore, but actively anti-Community and anti-Tradition, which we cannot afford to ignore.

Western Modernity came to Bharat with the spread of the East India Company and more urgently post-1857. It was accompanied by the wholesale conversion of our political elite into the creed of Liberalism, via the process of secularization. What was done then in the not-so-distant past through direct colonization continues today through schooling, academia, movies, regime change and NGO-led 'social reform'.

Swami Vivekananda nailed it very early on:

> The child is taken to school, and the first thing he learns is that his father is a fool, the second thing that his grandfather is a lunatic, the third thing that all his teachers are hypocrites, the fourth, that all the sacred books are lies!... We have learnt only weakness.

> A single generation of English education suffices to break the threads of tradition and to create a nondescript and superficial being deprived of all roots—a sort of intellectual pariah who does not belong to the East or the West, the past or the future. The greatest danger for India is the loss of her spiritual integrity. Of all Indian problems the educational is the most difficult and most tragic.[7]

Sure, individualists may also claim to be religious and devout believers in God but their conception of both religion and God is vastly removed from the traditionalist's conception of religion and the Gods. For the individualist, religion is personal and God exists merely as a mechanism by which he can self-rationalize his degeneracy – the "God made me this way" argument. For the traditionalist, the Gods exist as a mechanism of self-control and surrender – the "I will hold myself up to the standards set by the traditions so my actions will please the Gods" point of view.

The Communal Foundations of Liberty (in its original sense)

So, for those willing to take the next step, for those who see that it is not possible to speak in favour of Tradition without simultaneously speaking in favour of Community, we have to understand that it is not a simple thing. Community is not mere neighbourhood. Community is not that dilute word that is bandied about on American TV. Community is real, flesh and blood people you are connected to through birth, marriage and shared Tradition. It is the people who will be by your side when you are down and out, who will cry at your funeral and who will take in your children if something were to happen to you. It is those people in whom you see a reflection of your ancestors... co-stewards of those precious inherited jewels.

Most people in the Western world have forgotten that such a thing ever existed. They are now in the grip of 'social security', city 'services' and child 'care', all of which are available upon submission of one's sovereignty entirely unto the writ of the State. For those among us over whom Liberty (in its original sense) still exerts a tug upon the heart, it becomes important to see that the Individual has no Liberty within the confines of the Tech-State. The modern surplus-driven cage may be golden but it is still a cage. We have exchanged *true* Liberty for the conveniences that the Tech-State has brought us—TV, Internet, Fridge, AC and the three-week paid vacation.

So, is this it? Life?

We fail to see that as the convenience graph moves *up* to include surveillance, bio-manipulation and so-called Artificial Intelligence, the Liberty graph moves *down*, until pretty soon we find ourselves in an Orwellian zone (which of course is 'for our own good').

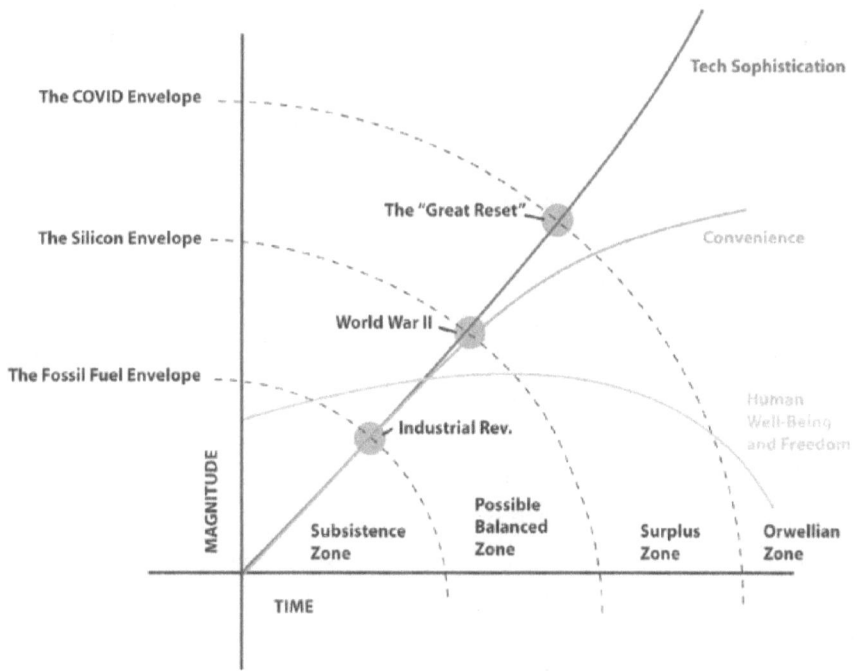

For the Liberty-minded who get this, there is only one alternative to the Tech-State, and that is a revitalization of Community. A human-scale grouping of individuals whose ability to help each other creates a bubble in space-time where survival becomes possible, where camaraderie and contentment become possible, where a degree of autonomy becomes possible because even though we consciously sacrifice for the good of the whole, we are among brothers and sisters. And, as I've said elsewhere, yes, we are yoked, but we are yoked not to corporations, advertisements, revolution, negative emotional roller-coaster rides, foreign cultural tropes and chemicals, but to the archetypes of our ancestors who gave us Life, and the words and deeds of our sages who fill our lives with positive thoughts and constructive actions—this is integrity. *This* is living with Tradition and Community and, in fact, the only true and responsible definition of Liberty. A limited but authentic Liberty set within the boundaries of responsibilities to our fellow-brothers and sisters.

Which brings us to asking what that means for us today

Unfortunately for the West, in its great future-worship delusion, it has burned all its bridges with Tradition and Community. Today, the fringe of both the far-Left and the far-Right of Western society recognizes this deep structural problem at the heart of their culture and are attempting to course-correct by exiting mainstream Capitalist society and establishing new intentional communities, either Environmental,[18] Christian,[19] or New Age[20] in their outlook. These communities, many founded by well-intentioned people, soon find they have nowhere to go, no template they can fit into, no fertile cultural earth they can still till that will bear fruit, where their children can find affirmation and belonging. They end up being islands in both time and space, separated from the lineage that birthed them and unconnected to their neighbours. Inevitably, such groups start to define themselves by who they are not, rather than by who they are. And so the cycle of rootlessness is passed on to the next generation, a kind of reactionary rootlessness. The documentary *Wild Wild Country* is probably the best study of how the attempt to create community ultimately implodes. Without the organic, historic, genetic and cultural ties that actually bind people together, such attempts *will* fall apart. As true solution-seekers, we must stop thinking in terms of decades, and return to considering centuries and millennia as the true test of the suitability of ideas.

In America, the far-Left, unable to escape its obsession with the idea of Rights, finds itself tied at the hip with Big-Government, because only Big-Government has the wherewithal to enforce the idea of Rights. The far-Right, on the other hand, unable to escape its obsession with the idea of Autonomy, finds itself tied at the hip with Big-Tech, because only Big-Tech can maintain the illusion that we have autonomy and control in this increasingly complex world.

We see now that the apparently *liberal* idea of *autonomy* can, ironically, only be guaranteed by a further and deeper *dependence* on Big-Tech, and the apparently *humane* idea of Rights can, ironically, only be underwritten by an ever larger, more *un-human* Big-State. So, even though these two factions literally define themselves in opposition to the Modern State for entirely different reasons, they find that they are irretrievably bound with that very same universalist, centralizing, Tech-State because it gives them the things that they need most. This is the source of the deep inner contradictions that plague these factions. Their enemy *is* their oxygen! Big-Tech, Autonomy, Big-Government and Rights are all tied at the hip. We cannot have one without the other.

As N.S. Lyons writes in his essay "Four Big Questions for the Counter Revolution":

> ...the more completely the sphere of autonomy is secured, the more comprehensive the State must become.[21]

In India, such factions seeking autonomy from the Tech-State (whether social-work collectives, alternative schools or neo-religious cults), all display a similar kind of schizophrenia. They denounce Capitalism but they continue to survive on subsidies distributed from within that very system. They dally with Communism but fail to understand that the minute a true Communist government was to come to power, they would immediately be shut down and packed off to some gulag factory. They rant and rail against Big-Government but fail to understand that the very Rights they so extol are fragile creations of Capitalist surplus (they cannot exist outside of that surplus) and can only be upheld by a governmental structure that is so humungous that it has its tentacles in every crevice of human society, something that they themselves would, ironically, find unacceptable. Most damagingly, they fail to see that they are able to live the rural, connected and sometime beautiful lives they lead because they live among traditional *Bharatiya* communities which provide the warmth, context and support necessary for them to feel human. If not for that traditional context, these intentional communities would simply be strangers in a strange land eventually succumbing to loneliness and in-fighting. They owe a debt of gratitude to *Bharatiya* hospitality and social structure that could adapt so easily to provide a space for them in their midst.

Unfortunately, not only do they fail to see this obvious truth, they also fail to acknowledge the essential *traditional* nature of those communities. They choose not to belong in those communities by living aloof, and they fail to honour those communities by helping *strengthen* them in their traditionalism, working, instead, in cultural blindness, to *undermine* them with ham-handed attempts at 'helping', 'educating', 'reforming' and 'teaching' them about 'oppression' and Rights. These anti-Capitalist rebels, ironically, far from helping create an alternate model for living, end up becoming the sword arm of the Tech-State in remote parts of the country that were, until they arrived, relatively independent and self-sufficient!

As the Tech-State has grown in India with the spread of the Industrial Revolution, traditional communities have been broken down by a series of State-led technological and economic interventions. Common folk hailing from communities which were remarkably autonomous till just a couple of generations ago, have become more and more tied to the State and to corporations for their livelihoods. This happened a hundred years ago in the USA as Steinbeck documents in his writings, and is happening in India right now, as we speak. It was in this context of growing State power that the idea of Rights was originally envisioned, to protect individuals from the excesses of the ubiquitous, impersonal State. Ironically today, the media arms of the Tech-State have us convinced that the idea of Rights is not for our protection from the State, but rather for our protection from the last remaining vestiges of traditionalism (which are repackaged and sold to us as bastions of oppression). We are now taught to stand against our own grandparents. This has been one of the foremost master strokes of Tech-State duplicity.

The plain and irrefutable fact is that individuals don't have traditions, only communities do. And communities are always, in the final balance, birth-based (but they don't have to be, and never were, permanent). Even if we were to form new communities today, they will soon become birth-based. Children born in intentional communities or even in neo-religious cults end up marrying within the fold, creating new birth-based communities with new (albeit dilute and flimsy) traditions. The great advantage that we Hindus have over these Western and Westernized free radicals is that we still have our tribes and cultural homes reasonably intact that we can return to and spruce up. We still have authentic thoughts to think and Gods to worship.

How will a world that is focused away from the toxins of Capitalism, Individualism and Irreverence look? What kind of social and metaphorical organization could form the scaffolding of a world focused on Sustainability, Community and Reverence?

Sanatana Exceptionalism

The only remaining, and in fact most-successful, model for such a world is *Sanatana* Bharat. *Sanatana* society, though recovering from a thousand-year war and under constant siege by the secular government suffering from deep coloniality, still continues to display the genius of its ancestral vision. Away from the twin Western poles of Tribalism and Individualism, *Sanatana* Bharat offers a third, ethical, humane path—that of the *Purusha*, the coming together of the tribes to create the one divine individual (the *Purusha*). This is the deep source of our diversity in unity (a phrase often used (in reverse), but seldom understood). Wendell Berry writes:

> There can be no such thing as a "global village." No matter how much one may love the world as a whole, one can live fully in it only by living responsibly in some small part of it.[22]

But, millennia before Berry put pen to paper, our *rishis* had intuited this human and humane truth. They consciously rejected both an unregulated, Papua-style pagan diversity, as well as a totally regulated Abrahamic-style unity. Instead, they created the unique vision of the *Purusha*, where the many come together in the divine form of the one *Purusha*. The observation that human society is constantly falling apart was not resisted but was built-in to the model. *Jaati* is the mechanism that allows for different points of view to co-exist in good neighbourliness, for groups of people to break away and start again and for new groups to join in and collaborate. *Jaati* gives us the compassionate framework to hold together the explosive entropic quality of human society without erasure. The more this quality is resisted, the more explosive society becomes. The more unity is *sought*, the more unethical become our actions in its pursuit (see European and Middle Eastern history). While the rest of the world has engaged in constant ethnic and ideological warfare for millennia, it is only *Sanatana* Bharat that has avoided that fate, and there is only one reason for this miracle: *Jaati*. If this is not cause enough to celebrate our social structure, I don't know what is.

Jaati served as a pressure valve (as seen above), gave us human-scale identity, professional monopolies, economic predictability and, therefore, inter-community peace. If *Jaati* was the 'yin', a framework for containing the explosive urge to universalism, then *varna* was the exact opposite, the 'yang', a framework for containing implosive urge to tribalism. *Varna* was the mechanism that helped us avoid internecine warfare by mapping the thousands of *jaatis* onto the one *Purusha*. It is the mechanism that took the many and made them one, gave them purpose and nobility while simultaneously retaining their uniqueness. That was genius, the genius of a forest-based civilization that could say, "Yes, we are all different trees but we make up one forest," and "Yes, we are all different limbs, but we make up one body."

Now imagine this two-dimensional mapping onto the *Purusha* drawn out in a third dimension where the sharp edges of the divisions start to blur—*jaati* becomes *kula* becomes *sampradaya* becomes *darshana* becomes *rashtra*. This telescopic vision of our society was created by our *rishis* and maintained and tended to by our ancestors. This remarkable framework for division of human society in physical space while simultaneously providing the framework for their unity in metaphorical space has had its limitations in the face of external monotheistic aggression and internal issues of human ego, but there is no doubt, when it is compared with other civilizational systems, that it has been the most ethical system for human organization ever devised. It has helped us avoid tribal insularity, genocide, ethnocide, slavery, dictatorship, irreverence, fragility and unsustainability. Every question we may have today about the human condition has already been asked, every answer already given—the seers have seen deep into our hearts and the future.

We have a tendency, ever since our brush with Western Modernity, to think that open, universalizing systems (for example Abrahamism and Modernity) are automatically more ethical than partially-closed, particularist systems (for example Paganism and Hinduism). Indeed, this has become the de facto lens we use while analysing (and inevitably denigrating) our own culture. But history shows us today in dazzling clarity that it was not *we* but the universalist, open systems that enslaved Africans, that brought genocidal death to Native America and Bharat, colonialism to Asia, and Holocaust to the Jews; that plunged the world into World Wars and eventually into the hundred million deaths of Communism. Today, under the shadow of Capitalist unsustainability and rising de-spiritualized irreverence, we are careening towards an Orwellian world of mass surveillance and bio-manipulation. If the horror of Auschwitz couldn't shake us, if the poisoning of our food supply couldn't shake us, if Mao, Stalin, Pol Pot, napalm and the nuke codes couldn't shake us, if COVID can't shake us, if the terrifying possibility of the surveillance State and the bio-manipulative State cannot shake us from our slumber, then I don't know what will.

It is argued that slavery and genocidal wars have been part and parcel of human history since the time of the pharaohs of Egypt and of the Roman empire, and that consequently it is unfair to hold Western Europe especially accountable for these phenomena. Indeed, many even argue that it was Western Europe that put an end to these phenomena. These arguments are problematic for three reasons. One, Bharat never had slavery and never participated in genocidal campaigns. Therefore, these phenomena are *not* universal and an absolutist moral claim for *Bharatiya* ethical pre-eminence can be made. The capture of combatants in war is to be morally distinguished from the capture, sale and purchase of innocent non-combatants. Two, it was *not* the West that first outlawed slavery. Similar proclamations were made in multiple places, such as in Haiti and by Shivaji Maharaj in Maratha-held territories, much earlier than in Britain. And three, the specific reason why so many see the West as an oppressor instead of merely as a rival is because they are forced to live within its hegemonic space. Even if we wanted to revert to our traditional lives today, we couldn't, because all the structures that once held that life up have been destroyed. We have no interest in the morality of ancient Egyptian and Roman civilizations because we are not forced to live under Egyptian, Roman or even Arab suzerainty now, but we *are* forced to live under Western suzerainty, which is why it is fair that we hold Western morality accountable for its lapses. Both Christianity and Modernity were foisted upon the rest of the world with the promise that they were morally superior to what came before. Not only did these new entrants into our societal space break that promise but, through cynically carrying out their campaigns of genocide, ethnocide, slave-driving and colonial extraction under the banners of Liberty, Equality, Progress and 'Jesus Loves You', they showed themselves to be far more unethical than anything that had come before. The West and Christianity continue to impact us. Their institutions and media arms continue to pontificate about the moral decrepitude of our ancestors in order to mould the minds of our children against them, and in doing so, force our societies to accept the moral road of their history as that of "all of our histories". It is this peculiar mix of hypocrisy and universalism that rings hollow to us. Well-meaning anti-establishment people in the West who see that there are problems but believe that the solution lies in some other form of open-ended universalism (New-Age, One World, One Love etc.) have not fully understood the root of the problems. The root of the matter is not Capitalism, it is what Capitalism represents—the anti-Tradition, anti-Community place where it comes from. If we are too afraid to point out that the root of Capitalism is Individualism, then we will never speak the truth, let alone act upon it. Individualism is the pursuit of the fatal idea that our freedom lies in the final severance of our bodies and minds from the connections we share with *Bhu Devi* and our communities. From this utter absence of relationship-consciousness comes its callous destruction of everything our ancestors held dear. More damagingly, the origins of the cult of Individualism can be traced to the rise of Protestantism and Humanism in Europe,[23] and ultimately to the birth of Christianity itself which severed, for the first time, our sacred compact with the ancestors and their living traditions, in favour of a fresh compact with a "Father who art in Heaven". The West has too much invested in these historical processes to set its house in order. It *cannot* introspect because doing so would call into question its very foundation. It *will not* introspect. The solution to our crises has to come from elsewhere, from a place that still understands Tradition and Community, and has the intellectual tools to steward inter-community dynamics. Unfortunately, that place, *Sanatana* Bharat, far from taking on a leadership role, is caught in a multi-level whirlpool of colonial self-hate.

A Visual Comparison of Civilizational Models

Where all my words have failed, perhaps a diagram will better capture Sanatana Exceptionalism and what it stands for at a deep, organizational level.

 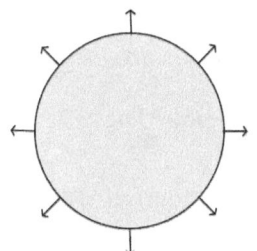 

SANATANA	ABRAHAMISM	MODERNITY
ANTI-FRAGILE	SEMI-FRAGILE	VERY-FRAGILE
AGGREGATIONAL MODEL	VIRAL MODEL	TREADMILL MODEL
STABLE - CONCENTRIC - FRACTAL	EXPLOSIVE - BALLOON	UNSTABLE - MOVING - ARROW
FIRELINED	UNCONTROLLED SPILL-OVERS	GLOBAL RISKS
INTROSPECTIVE	HEAVEN-FOCUSSED	PROGRESS-FOCUSSED
ETERNAL - SUSTAINABLE	PLUNDER - UN-SUSTAINABLE	MYOPIC - EXTRACTIVE
DIVERSE THALI	AVERAGING OUT MELTING POT	DISCRETE VENDING MACHINE
HUMAN COMMUNITY SCALE	UN-HUMAN "HOLY BOOK" SCALE	UN-HUMAN MACHINE SCALE
CONTROLLED VIOLENCE	UNIVERSALIZED VIOLENCE	PERMANENT INTERIOR VIOLENCE
		CYCLIC CATACLYSMS

References and Links

1. Priscilla Jebora, "Andamanese Tribes, Languages Die", *The Hindu*, 2010
   https://www.thehindu.com/news/national/Andamanese-tribes-languages-die/article16573196.ece

2. https://en.wikipedia.org/wiki/World_Happiness_Report

3. Servet Yanatma, "Europe's Mental Health Crisis: Which Country uses the most Antidepressants", *Euronews*, 2023
   https://www.euronews.com/next/2022/11/27/europes-mental-health-crisis-in-data-which-country-uses-the-most-antidepressants

4. Wendell Berry, *The Art of the Commonplace – Agrarian Essays*, 2002

5. Martha Gill, "Why a shortage of Mr. Rights means single mothers hold the key to the falling birth rate", *The Guardian*, 2023
   https://www.theguardian.com/commentisfree/2023/feb/11/why-a-shortage-of-mr-rights-means-single-mothers-hold-the-key-to-the-falling-birthrate

6. Wendell Berry, *The Art of the Commonplace – Agrarian Essays*, 2002

7. Yuval Noah Harari, *Homo Deus*, 2015

8. Ananda K. Coomaraswamy, *Christian and Oriental Philosophy of Art*, 1956

9. Barbara Dafoe Whitehead, "The Divorce Culture", Interview in *The Atlantic*, 1997
https://www.theatlantic.com/past/docs/unbound/bookauth/divorce/sake.htm

10. Elena Renken, "Most Americans are lonely and our workplace culture may not be helping", *NPR*, 2020
https://www.npr.org/sections/health-shots/2020/01/23/798676465/most-americans-are-lonely-and-our-workplace-culture-may-not-be-helping

11. Matilda Boseley, "Everyone and their mum is on it: OnlyFans boomed in popularity during the pandemic", *The Guardian*, 2020
https://www.theguardian.com/technology/2020/dec/23/everyone-and-their-mum-is-on-it-onlyfans-boomed-in-popularity-during-the-pandemic

12. Christopher F. Rufo, "Drag Queen Story Hour's radical origins and the subversive sexualization of our kids", *Fox News*, 2022
https://www.foxnews.com/opinion/drag-queen-story-hours-radical-origins-subversive-sexualization-kids

13. Christopher F Rufo, "San Francisco Unified School District facilitates secret child sexual transitions, lets kids identify as 'it'", *Fox News*. 2022
https://www.foxnews.com/opinion/san-francisco-unified-school-district-facilitates-secret-child-sex-transitions-kids-identify-it

14. Mikah Zenko, "The Big Lie about the Libyan War", *Foreign Policy*, 2016
https://foreignpolicy.com/2016/03/22/libya-and-the-myth-of-humanitarian-intervention/

15. Tracey Lindeman, "Canada: Remains of 215 children found at indigenous residential school site", *The Guardian*, 2021
https://www.theguardian.com/world/2021/may/28/canada-remains-indigenous-children-mass-graves

16. Jovan Tripkovic, "Columnist Rod Dreher talks Orthodox Christianity and Nationalism", *Religion Unplugged*, 2022 https://religionunplugged.com/news/2022/10/28/qampa-rod-dreher-talks-orthodox-christianity-and-nationalism

17. Swami Vivekananda, *The Complete Works of Swami Vivekananda, Volume 3, Lectures from Colombo to Almora*, 1964

18. https://acorncommunity.org/

19. https://www.koinoniafarm.org/about-koinonia-farm/

20. https://www.ananda.org/ananda-communities/

21. N.S. Lyons, "Four Big Questions for the Counter Revolution", *The Upheaval*, 2021 https://theupheaval.substack.com/p/four-big-questions-for-the-counter

22. Wendell Berry, *The Unsettling of America*, 1977

23. Nassim Nicolas Taleb, *On Christianity*, 2022 https://medium.com/incerto/on-christianity-b7fecde866ec

Section 5 | Chapter 5.3

MAN, WOMAN AND MACHINE – PART I
Ardhanareeshwara to Oppression

Maragatham, 2023

Man, Woman and *Ardhanaareeshwara*

We are not enemies. We are allies.

Ours is no battle-ground... What we have is a common-ground.

And the terms of that common ground have been laid out for us by the *devatas* themselves.

In *Kailasam*[1]

In *Vaikuntam*[2]

and in our *Devaalayas*[3]

The nature of our common ground has been further clarified by the archetype of *Ardhanaareeshwara*[4]

This is not an archetype of trans-genderism as sexual revolutionaries claim, but an archetype of complementarity between Man and Woman—the great coming together that is the basis of all life and living since the dawn of human time.

The baseline material aim of every traditional community is the imagination and incentivization of an institution whose aim is genetic and memetic bequeathal. That is, the creation of a socio-cultural scaffolding for the responsible making of babies and the subsequent maintenance of a stable and safe environment for those babies to grow up in, imbibing the cultural values of the community. Such an institution fosters, first and foremost, survival, but also commitment, will and the spirit of sacrifice in adults; and predictability, cultural affirmation, and positive role models for children. The breakdown of this scaffolding is invariably accompanied by degeneracy, falling birth-rates, societal collapse and widespread sociopathy, narcissism and, eventually, the erosion of the anima (the will to live) itself. These problems are visible everywhere today in the non-traditional world—treadmill economics,[5] societal control through the encouragement of addictions,[6] broken families,[7] mass shootings,[8] selfishness,[9] abandonment of the aged[10] and the young[11] and depression.[12]

And as Modernity eats and continues to eat into the last remaining islands of tradition, these problems will become universal. Youth today, who have grown up in the broken world are simply unaware that another, wholesome world once existed. What they do know is that the angst they feel is real, but they have no articulation of the cure because they have never witnessed it.

Unfortunately, for us, many cheer on this cultural predation because we are under the tutelage of the modern propaganda machine which tells us that tradition is bad because it is irrational, and that it is irrational because it does not enshrine the ideals of Liberty and Equality.

This universal application of the ideals of the French Revolution at random and ad nauseum upon every organizational structure is now epidemic. Since many unconscious Hindus today cheer on this Universalism without being able to see the problems it poses for family and religion, let's take another example.

Presuming that the organizational meaning and role of the Indian Army is still clear to most people, we can ask a few questions:

Q. What is the use of the army?
A. To best protect our borders.

Q. Does it do the job well?
A. Yes.

Q. Will it help the army do its job better if there were more women jawans fighting Pashtun adversaries?
A. No.

Q. Will it help the army better maintain focus and internal discipline if women and men shared locker rooms?
A. No.

Q. Will it help the army do its job better if there were more transgenders stationed at Nathu La?
A. No.

Q. Then why in the name of the Gods is the army expected to answer to the summons of Radical Equality?[13]
A. Silence. Apparently, that's an out of syllabus question.

(Note: There could well be a separate Rani Lakshmi Bai battalion of the army readied to form a second line of defence if and when the frontline falls, but that would not be equal enough for the equalists. Equal representation is now a credo; it has been severed from its connection to outcomes and social reality altogether.)

Bringing the logic of this argument back to our traditional social structures, we now find ourselves at the ridiculous historical crossroad that asks us to raise up the law-book of the French Revolution and use it to judge and condemn community, tradition, family and the very processes that gave us life and love. This is a grave case of making a category error. We must ask instead what is the *use* of family and marriage, and if, in its current form, it already performs those functions well. If the answer is yes, then why must the institution of family answer to the clarion call of the ideals of the French Revolution?

Will these ideals make the family stronger? More successful in achieving its aims? More capable of dispensing its responsibilities? Bring more children into the world? Bring more stability for those children? Transmit knowledge of the *samskaaras* more efficiently to the next generation?

Looking at current evidence from the West,[14] the answer on all counts is an unequivocal "No". Then what is it we are doing to ourselves?

Let us ask instead, what is it that traditional marriages *enable*? In fact, what is it that they have enabled since the dawn of human time? Do we have a problem with the lives and efforts of our fathers and mothers? Or that of their parents before them? Don't you and I stand here today not *in spite* of the 'fascist' institution they were sworn to, but *because* of it. What does it mean ontologically for us to not just criticize but to actively undermine the very structures that gave birth to us?

What we are secretly and unconsciously being encouraged to participate in today is *revolution*. We are encouraged to let go of the past and put our entire faith in the future (and the structures that hold that futuristic future). Every revolution becomes a re-enactment of the very first rupture, that of Christianity's break with our pagan ancestors in exchange for the '"Father who art in heaven", an imaginary relationship in the elsewhere.

As Hindus, we cannot allow this monstrosity to overtake us. *Sanatani* thought abhors ruptures and instead cultivates the idea of tradition as a bridge. It tells us that the future, that is *Moksha*, can be grasped only in conjunction with the past—that is, by paying off our *Rnas* and our *karmic* debt from lives previous. Furthermore, it posits that the future is not a future at all but is in fact the radical present, the here and now! The Western ideas of progress—whether of the material, technological kind, or the we-are-becoming-more-moral, idealist kind—are both reflections of *maya*, as far as the Hindu is concerned. Our deliverance is inextricably linked to the past and is redeemable only in the present (if and when we are ready). If at all we use the word 'progress', it has a radically different implication than anything the Western mind has imagined.

Coming back to the meaning of marriage, it's not that we stand *against* romance and consent and 'following our dreams', but we can understand their relative importance only when we recover our ability to use our indigenous value framework for judgement. Of course we celebrate romantic love; our classical literature is replete with references to it. Of course we understand consent; it is the fulcrum around which the Ramayana revolves. Of course we appreciate the impulse to follow one's dreams; we have been the land that pursued excellence for millennia. But, the overarching idea that guided the deployment of these ideas was not the self-gratification of the ego and the senses but the honouring of the Gods and the pursuit of *Dharma*. That is why they have limits and are subordinated to *samskaaric* duties, without which we would have a society in free fall, held up only on the backs of immigrants who will soon outbreed and outnumber us. The most dramatic example of such a fate is America, which is today 57.8% white,[15] losing 18% points in three decades of dramatic internal cultural polarization.

Success or failure in a Hindu marriage is not to be judged upon the anvils of Equality or Liberty but upon the *samskaaric* scales of the *Ardhanaareeshwara* archetype. So, let us not confuse our sporadic failure to uphold that archetype with the legitimacy of the archetype itself.

Let's start from first principles.

What's our aim? *Moksha*.

How do we get there? By performing *Dharma*.

What is *Dharma*? *Dharma* is many things but it has been distilled for the ordinary person into a set of ideals, the *pancha rna*; and a set of actions, the sixteen *samskaaras*.

The performance of the *samskaaras* is linked to an uber framework, the *purushaarth*, and given a context, which is the idea of life as a series of four *ashramas*.

Now, from this indigenous vantage point, we ask, "What is the *use* of marriage?"

Marriage, or *vivaaha*, it turns out, is the central lynchpin around which this indigenous cosmos revolves (for us ordinary people). A full thirteen of the sixteen *samskaaras* are directly connected to *vivaaha* and child-bearing/child-rearing. Additionally, one of the *pancha rnas*, *pitru rna*, enshrines *vivaaha* and child-bearing/child-rearing as sacrosanct. Another of the *rnas*, *rishi rna*, tangentially upholds the *samskaaras* and *aashramadharma* as sacrosanct.

Vivaaha, therefore, it becomes clear, is no mere mechanism for companionship or vehicle for romantic love and, though it could be both of those things, that is not its purpose. Its purpose is to function as the bulwark for the protection of our ideals by means of the traditions, and as the crucible for the emancipation of the individual *aatman*.

The Hindu view of marriage then does **not** say 'women must not work' or 'women must cover their heads' or that 'children must do as they're told' or that 'children must not follow their dreams' or that 'men should provide for and protect their families' or 'men should never do housework'. The Hindu view of marriage merely asks that we ask one question. "Will the performance or non-performance of an action lead to *better maintenance **and** more effective transmission of the samskaaras or not?*"

If the answer to that question is "No" then we must consider compromising upon or modifying that particular action. Every family's context is different and each one's range of acceptable actions will be different. There are no prescribed universal rules, but our reading of the common cultures of this land should stem from this deep understanding, not from the kneejerk application of the Western tropes of Equality, Liberty, consent and free-will, while being permanently fixated on the mirror of Marxism and its reflection of patriarchy.

The tug-of-war, then, is not between *men* and *women*, as the Marxists would have us paint reality, but between men and women of honour on one side and men and women of dishonour on the other. And what is honourable has already been demonstrated for us by our civilizational archetypes. It is up to men and women of honour to hold each other up to our civilizational standards of behaviour, not to engage in a tug-of-war over who has more liberty and why we don't have equal access to the tools of Western Liberty—that is sex, porn, cigarettes, booze, drugs, and enslavement to corporations. Alas, in these modern times, the latter case is far more common than the former. Additionally, the growing ubiquity of men and women of dishonour in our social and media environments has created a steep potential difference in our minds, and especially in the minds of our children, over what is the right way to live. The only way this problem will be resolved is if the systems of governance align themselves with the *samskaaras*. As long as our ideals are culled from Western Liberalism, we will continue to incentivize civilizationally-adverse behaviour, inevitably creating generations upon generations of deracinated children.

Simultaneously, it cannot be that men have more liberty than women, and women respond by demanding more equality than men. Both Hindu men and Hindu women need to eschew the call of Western Liberty and Radical Equality. Our Hindu freedom lies not in the rejection of tradition but in the rejection of corporate enslavement and sensory addictions. Our equality lies not in the profiles of OnlyFans and the corridors of the divorce courts but in our shared *remembrance* of the archetype of *Ardhanaareeshwara*.

Man, Woman and Oppression

A view from the other side

I will now walk us through a series of excerpts from Feminist classics (both First-Wave and Radical) to give us a sense of the Feminist understanding of how their perceived oppression is progressing, and how they aim to emerge from that oppressive state. (The excerpts are long, but do take the time to read them because getting a sense of the progression of thought is crucial. Every Wokeism we are faced with today has roots in Feminist theory.)

At the end of this segment, I will use the traditional view to counter that narrative, point by point. All claims that the Feminists make are indeed true, but they are also false. What we are concerned with, as traditionalists, is not the logical framework of their worldview but the unstated assumptions that underpin that worldview. If we take at face value their materialist, individualist assumptions about the world, then we have no option but to reach the same man-hating, God-denying, civilization-negating conclusions as them. But, if we start with fundamentally different axioms, we will arrive at a different and, in my opinion, more authentic, useful and beautiful destination.

Biology

Simone de Beauvoir, in her 1949 classic *Second Sex*, traces some of the roots of what she calls women's subordination to Biology. She identifies female physical weakness, hormonal instability and the yoking of women's' bodies uniquely to the "needs of the species", i.e. population growth as primary causes for the current condition of women.

De Beauvoir writes:

> On the average she is shorter than the male and lighter, her skeleton is more delicate... Muscular strength is much less in woman, about two thirds that of man; she has less respiratory capacity... Instability is strikingly characteristic of woman's organization in general... and on this account women are subject to such displays of agitation as tears, hysterical laughter, and nervous crises.[16]

She continues:

> It is obvious once more that many of these traits originate in woman's subordination to the species *(here Beauvoir is referring to woman's role as the primary maintainer of the human population, which she sees as a burden unfairly thrust solely upon women)*.[16]

She stresses that the human female is unhappy with her femininity:

> ... woman is of all mammalian females at once the one who is most profoundly alienated (her individuality the prey of outside forces *(that is the needs of the*

species)), and the one who most violently resists this alienation; in no other is enslavement of the organism to reproduction more imperious or more unwillingly accepted.[16]

She goes on to label menstruation as a "curse" and compares the life of a woman unfavourably with the life of a man, "In comparison with her (the woman) the male seems infinitely favoured: his sexual life is not in opposition to his existence as a person"[16]

De Beauvoir then goes on to say that bodily weakness is not sufficient cause to explain women's subordination and that we must look to history:

> ...the body of woman is one of the essential elements in her situation in the world. But that body is not enough to define her as woman; there is **no true living reality** except as manifested by the **conscious individual through activities** and in the **bosom of a society** (*that is, reality is social and not just physical*).[16]

For such an individualist who primarily draws his/her personhood from their ability to act free of biological constraints, menstruation, instead of being a doorway into the unique and Gods' given creativity of womankind, is seen as *horrific*, the arrival of femininity as a *descent* and the destiny of woman as *disgusting*.

> ...menstruation horrifies her only because it is an abrupt descent into femininity. She would also take her young eroticism in much more tranquil fashion if she did not feel a frightened disgust for her destiny as a whole...'[16]

History

De Beauvoir acknowledges the need for masculine protection in a low-tech world.

> ...from the most ancient records of prehistory, we see man always as armed. In times when heavy clubs were brandished and wild beasts held at bay, woman's physical weakness did constitute a glaring inferiority.[16]

She also imagines a time before the plough when women's contributions were as valued as men's. She sees that as civilizational complexity increased, work outside the house began to be far more lucrative than work done in the house and so women were progressively subordinated.

She makes the argument that in the Stone Age "land belonged in common to all members of the clan".[16] In such a world, she imagines:

> ... the two sexes constituted in a way two classes, and there was equality between these classes. While man hunts and fishes, woman remains in the home; but the tasks of domesticity include productive labour – making pottery, weaving, gardening – and in consequence woman plays a large part in economic life. [16]

But, as human society grew in complexity, she theorizes that the physical strength of men became more and more valued in an expanding civilizational wave—agriculture and architecture and technology. She sees that as Man became master over Nature, so too did he become master of Woman.

> Private property appears: master of slaves and of the earth, man becomes the proprietor also of woman. This was 'the great historical defeat of the feminine sex'... The same cause which had assured to woman the prime authority in the house – namely, her restriction to domestic duties – this same cause now assured the domination there of the man; for woman's housework henceforth sank into insignificance in comparison with man's productive labour – the latter as everything, the former a trifling auxiliary.[16]

She then looks to Historical Materialism and seeks solidarity from within the camp of the socialists and rationalists whose work speaks of eradicating systems of oppression. Women and workers both become subjects ripe for emancipation. She recognizes that the equality of women that she seeks is *dependent to a large extent on a high-technological world* without which Equality is an impossibility, but she *does not* critique that fact. Readers familiar with my earlier work will see this as a crucial step in the movement away from values (which are human, humane and organic) and towards modern ideals (which are mathematical, unhuman and only achievable through a monster State). She was naïve enough (as were many other intellectuals of that era) not to see that the monster State they dreamed of was nothing if not the super-magnification of all the masculine traits that she so reviled:

The theory of Historical Materialism has brought to light some most important truths. Humanity is not an animal species, it is a historical reality. Human society is an antiphysis – in a sense it is against nature; it does not passively submit to the presence of nature but rather takes over the control of nature on its own behalf. This arrogation is not an inward, subjective operation; it is accomplished objectively in practical action.[16]

No longer, in her view, could women be considered "simply as a sexual organism". Instead, the self-perception of women was a function of the economic and technological organization of society as a whole (in other words, a function of progressive history).

> Woman's awareness of herself is not defined exclusively by her sexuality: it reflects a situation that depends upon the economic organization of society, which in turn indicates **what stage of technical evolution** mankind has attained.[16]

From there to a total surrender to the Tech-State was only a step away. She asserts that:

> Woman can be **emancipated** only when she can take part on a large social scale in production and is engaged in domestic work only to an **insignificant** degree. And this has become possible only in the big industry of modern times, which not only **admits** of female labour on a grand scale but even formally **demands** it...[16]

So, the demand that women enter the "workforce" (as if they have not been working since the dawn of human time) that we see everywhere today in modern India is actually an old industrial idea using feminism to achieve its own ends— that is, the surrender of family, community and decentralized control over the means of production at the altar of the centralized mechanical monster. Unable to see this grand arc, she doubles down on support for the socialist state and says: "Thus, the fate of woman and that of socialism are intimately bound up together, as is shown also in Bebel's great work on woman. 'Woman and the proletariat,' he says, 'are both **downtrodden**.' Both are to be **set free through the economic development** consequent upon the **social upheaval brought about by machinery**."[16]

High technology is seen as the emancipatory tool, **"Woman regains in the modern world her equality with man"**[16] she continues. And finally, "... when the socialist society is established throughout the world, *there will no longer be men and women*, but only workers on a footing of equality."[16]

Her surrender to the idea of *Machine-vaad* is complete. Her acknowledgement that it is only the Machine that can deliver her cherished Equality is also undeniable. She even goes so far as to agree that modern industry should formally *demand* female participation in the workforce, revealing how far she is willing to sacrifice even Liberty at the altar of Equality. But she was foresighted enough to see that the situation of women and the situation of 'workers' were not one and the same, and that women had unique requirements that could not be wished away simply by marching to the notes of Mother Russia.

> No more does Engels account for the peculiar nature of this oppression. He tried to reduce the antagonism of the sexes to class conflict, but he was half-hearted in the attempt; the thesis is simply untenable.[16]

She points out that "woman cannot in good faith be regarded simply as a worker; for her reproductive function is as important as her productive capacity, no less in the social economy than in the individual life."[16] For all her surrender to communist tropes, she finds it within herself to speak up for Liberty and Individuality when she writes: "A truly socialist ethics, concerned to uphold justice without suppressing liberty and to impose duties upon individuals without abolishing individuality, will find most embarrassing the problems posed by the condition of woman."[16] And then she shows her discomfort with where these trains of thought are leading: "No State has ever ventured to establish obligatory copulation... for it is impossible to bring the sexual instinct under a code of regulations."[16]

But the intellectual die had already been cast. There would be no escape from its consequences now.

An Inflexion Point in Feminist Discourse

Simone de Beauvoir's work represents a watershed. Behind her is the old kind of Western woman, and ahead of her the new kind. You will see, from the last two paragraphs, that she is still trying to make peace, to define a modern common ground between men and women. She elaborates in a reconciliatory tone:

> ...to emancipate woman is to refuse to confine her to the relations she bears to man, not to deny them to her; let her have her independent existence and **she will continue none the less to exist for him also.**[16]

She probably sees that her approach would signal the end of all romance and she makes a last-ditch attempt to build a bridge. The reciprocity of man-woman relations, she says, "will not do away with the **miracles** – desire, possession, love, dream, adventure – worked by the division of human beings into two separate categories; and the words that move us – giving, conquering, uniting – will not lose their **meaning**." She sees the abolishment of "**slavery of half of humanity**" will reveal "its **genuine significance, and the human couple** will find its **true form**."[16]

She wants female equality without the baggage of femininity, but she still wishes for the possibility of "love, dream and adventure" with a man. She wishes, in her own way, for the *Ardhanaareeshwara*. But the traditionalist asks, without the dipoles of masculine and feminine, what is that attractive force that will hold the two "working individuals" together? Will the complexities of raising children and upholding culture be accepted wholeheartedly in the absence of a sense of duty by two individuals whose fundamental focus is their own ambitions? It's a fragile dream... possible maybe, but fraught with dangers.

In a mere three decades after de Beauvoir's ground-breaking work was published, Radical Feminists (Rad-Fems), while being sympathetic to her position, had already dismissed her as belonging to the old guard who made common cause with men by referring disparagingly to her relationship with her husband.

> Why did Simone de Beauvoir adhere to the misogynist Jean Paul Sartre?[17]

Obsession with Sex and the Perversion of the Road Ahead

By the 1960s, the invention of birth control had opened up a Pandora's Box for the West from which it has still not recovered. The act of sex was finally severed from its sacred and social dimensions. Sex now emerged as one of the fundamental forces that drove the Western person. Success and Identity became tied up with it. Ethics became defined by it. One-half of the Feminists insisted that free sex had made them equal to men. The other half argued that free sex had enslaved women even more to patriarchy. Sheila Jeffries writes:

> What part does sexuality play in the oppression of women? Only in the system of oppression that is male supremacy does the oppressor actually invade and colonise the interior of the body of the oppressed.[18]

She sees all forms of sexual behaviour as a code for "dominance and submission", "power and powerlessness" and "conquest and humiliation". Why, she asks, does "every sexual reference, every sexual joke, every sexual image serve to remind a woman of her invaded centre and a man of his power."[18]

She asks "Why all this fuss in our culture about sex?"[18] and responds "Because it is specifically through sexuality that the fundamental oppression, that of men over women, is maintained."[18]

The "fascist" heterosexual family lay broken, true, but advertisements, movies and pornography now manipulated female self-perception on a much grander scale than family expectations ever had. Rad-Fems began to theorize that an understanding of the problem could not be limited merely to the structures of Man, but had to be expanded to include Man himself. Jeffries continues with an incendiary paragraph:

> The heterosexual couple is the basic unit of the political structure of male supremacy. In it each individual woman comes under the control of an individual man. It is more efficient by far than keeping women in ghettoes, camps or oven sheds at the bottom of the garden. In the couple, love and sex are used to obscure the realities of oppression, to prevent women identifying with each other in order to revolt, and from identifying 'their' man as part of the enemy. Any woman who takes part in a heterosexual couple helps to shore up male supremacy by making its foundations stronger.[18]

She asks why "are more and more women, at younger and younger ages, encouraged by psychiatrists, doctors, marriage guidance counsellors, the porn industry, the growth movement, lefties and Masters and Johnson to get ****** more and more often?"[18] And she provides her answer. She sees penetration by the penis as a form of dominance and control. As more and more women earn money and are economically freed from men, she hypothesizes that the only way men can continue to control women is through the act of sex, which is why the whole capitalist industry is hell-bent on telling young girls to "get ******".[18]

She rejects the idea that the sexual revolution was a leveller. "Every man knows that a ****** woman is a woman under the control of men, whose body is open to men, a woman who is tamed and broken in."[18] She continues, "Before the sexual revolution there was no mistake about penetration being for the benefit of men.

The sexual revolution is a con trick. It serves to disguise the oppressive nature of male sexuality and we are told that penetration is for our benefit as well."[18] She sees all acts of penetration as a means for sucking a woman's confidence and building a man's mastery and strength.

Woman, it was deemed, could never be herself as long as she had men in her life. When asked if heterosexual women were the enemy, she replies that "Men are the enemy."[18] but "Heterosexual women are collaborators with the enemy."[18] In her view, a woman who goes out to work in the day and comes back to look after home at night is working at cross purposes. All the good work that heterosexual feminists do is cancelled out by the fact that they continue to maintain relations with men.

> Being a heterosexual feminist is like being in the resistance in Nazi-occupied Europe where in the daytime you blow up a bridge, in the evening you rush to repair it.[18]

Destination Dead

And finally, we are at the end point where this kind of hyper-sexualized, individualistic thinking leads. It is inevitable. There may be a whole range of feminists out there today but rest assured that if they were to examine their intellectual positions, they would all end up here. In this neo-religion, like all others, the spectrum of feminists is only an indication of how devout one is. Both Sheila Jeffries (in the first quote) and Marilyn Frye (in the second) insist:

> We *do* think that **all feminists can and should be political lesbians**. Our definition of a political lesbian is a woman-identified woman who does not **** men. It does not mean compulsory sexual activity with women. The paper is divided into two parts. The first cover the reasons why we think serious feminists have no choice but to abandon heterosexuality.[18]

> For instance, women with **newly raised consciousnesses** tend to **leave marriages and families**, either completely through divorce, or partially, through unavailability of their cooking, housekeeping and sexual services. And **women academics tend to become alienated from their colleagues and male mentors** and no longer serve as sounding board, ego booster, editor, mistress or proofreader. Many **awakening women become celibate or lesbian**.[19]

Sex is no longer a sacred act between a married man and a married woman. The family is no longer the worldly remaking of a fundamental truth in the image of a sacred archetype. Child-bearing and child-rearing are not glorious acts of care and optimism that repay our ancestors by paying forward the miracle of our own births. Nope. None of that nonsense that was designed to "fool women into voluntary enslavement" is acceptable anymore at the table of the human condition. Jeffries and Frye continue to push their case:

> We know that for some women, for example those with children, those with no easy access to the movement, and those without the experience of living on their own, the break is more difficult than for others and they need more time and practical support. We know how difficult it is to find a women's house to move into and what it is like to feel like a 'new girl' at the women's disco'. But part of the support must be in explaining as clearly as possible the political reasons for our own choice and talking honestly about all the difficulties with the women who are making it.[18]

> Matters pertaining to marriage and divorce, lesbianism and abortion touch individual men (and their sympathizers) because they can feel the relevance of these to themselves—they feel the threat that they might be the next. Hence, **heterosexuality, marriage and motherhood,** which are the institutions which most obviously and individually maintain female accessibility to males, **form the core triad of *anti-feminist* ideology.**[19]

Yes, we read that right. Heterosexuality, marriage and motherhood are the core triad of anti-feminist ideology! When motherhood itself is considered anti-feminist, we have to conclude that Feminism is anti-Woman. Clearly, this is no longer about rights or respect or love. This is pure, unhinged 'Me, Myself and I' revolution—license masquerading as Liberty getting its foot in the door under the cover-fire of Equality.

By abandoning everything ancestral, organic, decent and customary, Rad-Fem has embarked on a revolutionary, emancipatory path that elevates the sexual act to the status of a political messiah into whose crossroads, ultimately, all kinds of deviant pathways have converged: Gender as a social construct;[20] Queer Theory;[21] Transgenderism;[22] Pedophilia;[23] Bestiality;[24] Incest;[25] BDSM;[26] and the hijacking of children from their parents for Trans-indoctrination.[27] Because, after all, these are all self-expressions of "oppressed categories of people" by the same catholic definition of oppression that the feminists have used to define their own oppression. Feminists today decry the usurpation of their language[28] and societal gains by Trans-activists but it was a scaffolding that they themselves erected, as Marilyn Frye expounds:

> Oppression is a system of inter-related barriers and forces which reduce, immobilize and mould people who belong to a certain group, and effect their subordination to another group (individually to individuals of the other group, and as a group, to that group).[19]

Any ordinary human will see that the above sentence is total nonsense, not because it is untrue, but because it is so generic that it could mean anything at all to anyone at all. But, for the traditionalist, this whole scaffolding is a problem, a big problem. It cannot be countered at the level of logic; it can only be countered at the level of a priori assumptions.

Rebuttal

There are some fundamental a priori assumptions made by feminists which need to be called out. Both Modernity and its subset, Feminism, believe that:

1. Materialism is Truth
2. Individualism is Good
3. Sexual Expression and therefore Sexuality is a key component of a person's identity

All three of these assumptions are false.

It is *Brahman* that is True and all material is imbued with its divine intent.

It is community that is good and family that is the most fundamental societal unit. Ordinary individuals without community and family are incomplete and therefore act in ways that are at odds with the divine intent, thereby accumulating *karmic* debt.

A person's major identity comes from his community and family whose *Dharma* he has to fulfil. His minor identity comes from his personal acts. And in the case of exceptional people, identity is drawn from the sacrifices for the greater good that they make in their journeys towards *Moksha*. Sexual expression is either irrelevant or limited to the *kama* part of a person's *purushaarth*, which in turn is subordinated to *vivaaha* and *Dharma*.

Aside from the Hindu metaphysical critique made above, we can also look at the internal contradictions and lacunae in the feminist stance from the perspective of an ordinary Hindu:

1. *The feminist stance abandons the Gods*
   By rejecting the unspoken but obvious truth, that by making men and women different, the Gods intended them to be different and complimentary, feminists automatically declare themselves as atheists and are in contravention of *deva rna*. A feminist is forced to ask, "Why did God make women weaker than men?" or "Why did God give women menstruation and pregnancy?" or simply "Why didn't God make men and women equal?" which is no different from asking "Why did God make women at all?!" It is an attitude of self-denial. As a corollary, no believer (in the traditional sense) can be a feminist.

2. *The feminist stance abandons culture, tradition and the ancestors*
   By summarily rejecting the traditional ways of the ancestors (instead of at least attempting to evolve or consciously expand them with changing civilizational complexity), feminists are in contravention of *rishi rna* and *pitru rna*. As a corollary, no traditional Hindu woman can be a feminist.

3. *The feminist stance abandons the civilizational imperative and the need for a stable model of survival and growth*
   How do they expect the human species, their own civilization and even the economy to survive without the bearing and bringing up of children? Besides, who do they believe will fight our civilizational enemies? For all their 'understanding' of history, they seem incredibly naive with regard to historical forces. Perhaps wars *are* Man-made problems but their effect on women cannot be wished away. Also, it is important to note that women in power do go to war too (think of Indira Gandhi and Golda Meir). So, I have to ask, are they really endorsing the Matrix solution of extra-corporeal wombs with exclusively female cloned foetuses?

4. *The feminist stance abandons the needs of children*
   Children need to grow up in stable households with male and female role models. Additionally, the more cultural affirmation there is around them the better it is for kids. A fragmented society results in fragmented psyches.

5. *The feminist stance ignores one million years of history*
   ...during which honourable men have loved honourable women, lived and died for them, protected them from wild beasts, creepy crawlies, and marauders.

6. *The feminist stance ignores ten thousand years of history*
   ...during which honourable men and honourable women have put their energies into putting food on the table and freeing humankind from the vagaries of nature. It is upon that foundation that the Rad-Fems stand today. By defining all the social structures that evolved over those millennia as 'oppression', Rad-Fems fail to acknowledge that foundation. That is self-contradictory.

7. *The feminist stance ignores three hundred years of recent history*
   ...during which it was industrial surplus that created the appliances and devices that freed women from domestic physical work and gave them the time and space to articulate a demand for Equality. It ignores the fact that equality as demanded by Feminists is only possible in the presence of that surplus. And equality in the workplace that seems so obvious to us today is only possible in the presence of so high a technological society that all the physical, navigational and analytical advantages of men are nullified by machines that can be run by any human regardless of sex.

8. *The feminist stance ignores the fact that the continued present-day maintenance of that entire engine of human artifice is carried out largely by men*
   ...in the armies, in the mines, on the electric poles, in the sewers, in the machine shops, on the oil rigs, on the construction sites.

9. *The feminist stance does not introspect enough*
   ...about the meaning of such an Equality that is predicated on a surplus that has been earned off the oppression of others (colonialism and slavery), the work of others (inventors and manufacturers), that is contingent

upon the continued goodwill of others (maintenance staff) and requires us all to surrender our agencies to the Tech-State that orchestrates it all. This late-Modernist Autonomy does not come for free. As a corollary, no true adherent of the Sustainable, Agri-Cultural or 'Small is Beautiful' worldviews can be a feminist.

10. *There is a fundamental paradox here that puts feminists in a bind, but about which most refuse to speak*
In order to live autonomously *without men*, feminists have to embrace the hyper-technologized world and all its structures that are built and maintained by men, BUT if they reject those structures (because they are built by men) and choose instead to return to a low-tech world built and maintained by Mother Nature, they are ironically forced to go back to relying on men (who they use as a shield to ward off the dangers and difficulties of the outer natural world).

In conclusion, I would like to point out that there are feminists like the Jungian, Clarissa Pinkola Estes, author of *Women Who Run With The Wolves*, who take a different route. She is unwilling (as all Westerners are) to abandon Individualism, but she does abandon Materialism. And that makes a huge difference to the conclusions that she draws about the role of women in society and the nature of their relationship with men. Here she writes:

> If women want men to know them, really know them, they have to teach them some of the deep knowing. When men show that willingness, then is the time to reveal things; not just because, but because another soul has asked. [29]

"In mythos, as in life", she sees that there is nothing better that a "wildish woman" loves more than a mate who can be her equal, but the "dual nature" of woman causes heartburn.

> Understanding the dual nature of women sometimes causes men, and even women themselves, to close their eyes and hail heaven for help. The paradox of women's twin nature is that when one side is more cool in feeling tone, the other is more hot. [29]

Therefore, she continues, the dual-natured woman seeks a man with an attitude that finds "valuable, courtable and desirable" the "mysterious and numinous double in woman's nature."[29]

As Hindus, neither individualism nor materialism is an acceptable starting point. For us, the basic societal unit is the family and not the individual. Moreover, the family is held in the protective embrace of community and tradition. As Hindus, our focus is not on identifying ourselves with gratification of the senses, but with breaking from desire and addiction. As Hindus, our interest is not in elevating sexuality to the pinnacle of human experience but in binding it within *Purushaarta* limits.

It is very important for us all to break with the Western lens and see clearly again the true nature of our reality. For the Hindu traditionalist, both the Marilyn Frye view of all men as toxic oppressors and the Rollo Tomassi counter-view of all women as hypergamous, alpha-male magnets, are false. Such perverse views arise in a culture that has severed its links with the Gods, *Prakriti*, Community and Tradition. In such an anti-culture, the individual is bereft of many of the vital links that make for his optimal flowering and he descends into various shades of narcissism. It is this narcissism, which has been taken by post-Freudian Western society to represent the truth of what humans *really* are. Their entire societal and legal framework has been designed based on this erroneous understanding. All Western structures are merely extremely complex mechanisms by which the State aims to control and manipulate this narcissism. The Western States (and by association, all other modern States) are riding a tiger, and an illusory (*maayic*) one at that.

Wendell Berry captures this phenomenon in this anecdote from his friend Wes's farm in Salinas:

> Wes pointed to a sunflower growing alone apart from the others and said, "There is a plant that has realized its full potential as an individual" and clearly it had: it had grown very tall, it had put out many long branches heavily laden with blossoms and the branches had broken off, for they had grown too heavy and long. The plant had indeed realized its full potential as an individual but had failed as a sunflower. We could say that its full potential as an individual was its failure. It had failed because it had lived outside an important part of its definition, which consists of both its individuality and its community. A part of its properly realizable potential lay in community, not in itself.[30]

And, more recently, even though he is unwilling to use the word community, the staunch individualist Jordan Peterson too reiterated the same sentiment during his interview of Vivek Ramaswamy.

This is a terrible thing that the radicals on the Left have done to people psychologically... to tell them that that "you are *only* what you claim to be". It's like well...No! that's not true...You are what you've been able to negotiate with other people...and that's a damn good thing for you too because...isolated and alone, there's no indication at all that we'd be other than, you know, maximally sinful in the direction of our greatest weaknesses. We *need* other people, and part of our identity is the ability to integrate ourselves with other people and use them as signalling devices for our own orientation. [31]

Men asking for more Liberty than women will lead to more of this:

> South Korea's total fertility rate – the number of children a woman is expected to have in her lifetime – dropped to 0.98 in 2018, far below the 2.1 needed to keep a population stable.
>
> – From the 2019 Straits Times article *Till death do I stay single: South Korea's #NoMarriage women* [32]

Similarly, women, by asking for more Equality than men will lead to more of this (observe the difference in the way the two titles are worded):

> MGTOW believe that women are extremely likely to make false accusations of sexual or domestic violence, in order to damage men socially, steal their money or even have them jailed.
>
> – From Laura Bates's 2020 article in The Guardian, *MGTOW-Men going their own way: the rise of a toxic male separatist movement* [33]

And both men and women, by embracing Individualism, get more of this:

> The truth as I see it is that contemporary marriage is a wretched institution. It spells the end of voluntary affection, of love freely given and joyously received. Beautiful romances are transmuted into dull marriages, and eventually the relationship becomes constricting.
>
> – From Mervyn Cadwallader's 1966 article in The Atlantic, *Marriage as a Wretched Institution* [34]

This modern disharmony *cannot* be resolved within the framework of even more Western Idealism. It is only when Western Idealist-Morality is replaced by a value-centric Outcome-based Morality that harmony can be restored. Unlike the West which has long abandoned harmony as a value and believes that the problems of disharmony can be resolved by technology, we Hindus continue to be deeply invested in the value of harmony. We are less interested in abstract ideals that end up causing disharmony and more in shared values that result in harmonic, *Dharmic* societal outcomes.

Hindu women can and must hold their men up to the ideal of Shri Rama just as men hold their women up to the ideal of Savitri. It is not tenable that women are held up to the archetype of Savitri while men are free to model themselves on Ravana. The Hindu solution to the man-woman dichotomy lies not in both sexes clamouring for more and equal access to Western ideals but in aligning with the *samskaaras* under the grace of the archetype of Ardhanaareeshwara.

References and Links

1. Image Credit Traditional Image reworked by Author
2. Image Credit Traditional Image reworked by Author
3. Image Credit Traditional Image reworked by Author
4. Image Credit Traditional Image reworked by Author
5. Leah Collins, "Job unhappiness is at a staggering all-time high, according to Gallup", *CNBC*, 2022
   https://www.cnbc.com/2022/08/12/job-unhappiness-is-at-a-staggering-all-time-high-according-to-gallup.html
6. "Untreated & Unheard: The Addiction Crisis in America", *CBS News*, 2022
   https://www.cbsnews.com/video/untreated-unheard-the-addiction-crisis-in-america/
7. *The American Family Today*, Pew Research Centre, 2015
   https://www.pewresearch.org/social-trends/2015/12/17/1-the-american-family-today/

8. "150 days, 263 mass shootings reported in U.S. so far for 2023", *CBS News*, 2023
   https://www.cbsnews.com/video/150-days-263-mass-shootings-reported-in-us-so-far-for-2023/

9. Ashley Humphrey and Ana Maria Bliuc, *Western Individualism and the Psychological Wellbeing of Young People: A Systematic Review of Their Associations*, MDPI 2022
   https://www.mdpi.com/2673-995X/2/1/1

10. Jacob Ausubel, *Older people are more likely to live alone in the U.S. than elsewhere in the world,* Pew Research Center, 2020
    https://www.pewresearch.org/short-reads/2020/03/10/older-people-are-more-likely-to-live-alone-in-the-u-s-than-elsewhere-in-the-world/

11. NCSL Report, *Youth Homelessness Overview*, 2023
    https://www.ncsl.org/human-services/youth-homelessness-overview#:~:text=Each%20year%2C%20an%20estimated%204.2,by%20a%20parent%20or%20guardian.

12. National Institute of Mental Health, *Mental Illness Information*
    https://www.nimh.nih.gov/health/statistics/mental-illness

13. Sruthakeerthy Sriram, "The Battle for Gender Equality in the Indian Armed Forces", *nyaaya.org*, 2022
    https://nyaaya.org/guest-blog/the-battle-for-gender-equality-in-the-indian-armed-forces/

14. Kay S Hymowitz, "A Nation Dying in Despair and Family Breakdown Is Part of the Problem", Manhattan Institute, 2019
    https://manhattan.institute/article/a-nation-dying-in-despair-and-family-breakdown-is-part-of-the-problem

15. William H Frey, "New 2020 census results show increased diversity countering decade-long declines in America's white and youth populations", *Brookings Institute*, 2021
    https://www.brookings.edu/research/new-2020-census-results-show-increased-diversity-countering-decade-long-declines-in-americas-white-and-youth-populations/

16. Simone de Beauvoir, *The Second Sex*, 1949

17. Marilyn Frye, *The Politics of Reality*, 1983

18. Shiela Jeffries, *Love Your Enemy?*, Leeds Revolutionary Feminist Group 1981

19. Marilyn Frye, *The Politics of Reality*, 1983

20. Jessica Murphy, "Toronto Professor Jordan Peterson takes on gender-neutral pronouns", *BBC News* 2026
    https://www.bbc.com/news/world-us-canada-37875695

21. Gayle S Rubin, "Thinking Sex: Notes for a Radical Theory of the Politics of Sexuality" in *Pleasure And Danger: Exploring Female Sexuality* edited by Carole S. Vance, 1984
    https://sites.middlebury.edu/sexandsociety/files/2015/01/Rubin-Thinking-Sex.pdf

22. Douglas Murray, "Has Trans-Activism gone too far?", *UnHerd*, 2019
    https://unherd.com/2019/11/has-trans-activism-gone-too-far/

23. *French Petition against Age of Consent Laws*, 1977
    https://en.wikipedia.org/wiki/French_petition_against_age_of_consent_laws

24. Michael Roberts, *The Unjustified Prohibition against Bestiality: Why the Laws in Opposition Can Find No Support under the Harm Principle*, SSRN 2009
    https://papers.ssrn.com/sol3/papers.cfm?abstract_id=1328310

25. Jeff Jacoby, "Hypocrisy on Adult Consent", *Boston.com News*, 2005
    http://archive.boston.com/news/globe/editorial_opinion/oped/articles/2005/08/28/hypocrisy_on_adult_consent/

26. Neil McArthur, "It's a Travesty that BDSM isn't technically legal", *Vice*, 2016
    https://www.vice.com/en/article/vdqem4/its-a-travesty-that-bdsm-isnt-technically-legal

27. Hannah Grossman, "Washington bill to allow medical transgender interventions on minors without parental consent", *New York Post*, 2023
https://nypost.com/2023/04/17/washington-bill-to-allow-medical-transgender-interventions-on-minors-without-parental-consent/

28. Allie Griffin, "Two 'radical feminist' groups support GOP bill to ban trans women from women's sports: report", *New York Post*, 2023
https://nypost.com/2023/04/20/two-feminist-groups-support-gop-bill-to-ban-trans-women-from-womens-sports/

29. Clarissa Pinkola Estes, *Women who Run with the Wolves*, 1992

30. Wendell Berry, *Men and Women in Search of Common Ground*, 1986

31. Jordan Peterson, *Vision Restored*: Ep. 380,
https://www.youtube.com/watch?v=rlTY7VzqBwc (1:19:10 onwards)

32. "Till death do I stay single: South Koreas #NoMarriage women", *The Straits Times*, 2019
https://www.straitstimes.com/asia/east-asia/til-death-do-i-stay-single-south-koreas-nomarriage-women

33. Laura Bates, "Men going their own way: The rise of a toxic male separatist movement", *The Guardian*, 2020
https://www.theguardian.com/lifeandstyle/2020/aug/26/men-going-their-own-way-the-toxic-male-separatist-movement-that-is-now-mainstream

34. Mervyn Cadwallader, "Marriage as a wretched institution", *The Atlantic*, 1966
https://www.theatlantic.com/magazine/archive/1966/11/marriage-as-a-wretched-institution/306668/

Section 5 | Chapter 5.4

MAN, WOMAN AND MACHINE – PART II
Equivalence to Equity

Maragatham, 2023

Prologue

I have a feeling some kind of disclaimer is due. My fight is not the 19th Century fight for Mutual Respect; my fight is the 21st Century fight for the continued existence of Community, Tradition, Cultural Identity and, ultimately, Humanity as we know it. As far as I am concerned, Mutual Respect is a given, whether I am talking about inter-community dynamics or man-woman dynamics. I am not endorsing supremacy of any kind. This is a call for a return to sanity.

People pointing out that Hindu society suffers from many of the same problems that the West does should realize that human weakness, and subsequently societal sickness, is a universal phenomenon. The difference lies in intent. *Sanatana* values stand *against* moral descent and societal disintegration—*Daya, Dana, Ahimsa, Aparigraha, Vairagya, Ashrama Dharma, Purusha, Pancha Rna*. Our values are invested in the maintenance of self-control, synthesis and harmony. This intent is reflected in our longevity and our ability to renew ourselves even after periods of internal decay or external aggression. So, whatever societal decay we see in Bharat today is *in spite* of our values, not *because* of them.

Western Modernity, on the other hand, is openly entropic in nature. Its outcome, if not its explicit aim, is to erase all forms of true community in order to supplant people with machines, and all culture with a technology-supported centralized State, which I have earlier referred to as the Tech-State. It does this by glorifying what have come to be known as Western values—Individualism (in the form of self-indulgence), Materialism (in the erasure of the idea of the sacred) and Progressivism (of both the technological and moral kind). So, unlike in the case of Bharat, the civilizational decay we see in the West and in Westernized segments of our own population is not because *humans have failed*, but because the *system has succeeded!* The Tech-State, and the elites who run it, see the inherent inefficiency and messiness of human interactions as justification for control or erasure. Yuval Noah Harari points to this reality in his interview with Chris Andersen:

> A lot of people sense that they are being left behind and left out of the story, even if their material conditions are still relatively good. In the 20th Century, what was common to all the stories—the liberal, the fascist, the communist—is that the big heroes of the story were the common people. If you lived, say, in the Soviet Union in the 1930s, life was very grim, but when you looked at the propaganda posters on the walls that depicted the glorious future, you were there. You looked at the posters which showed steel workers and farmers in heroic poses, and it was obvious that this is the future.
>
> Now, when people look at the posters on the walls, or listen to TED talks, they hear a lot of these big ideas and big words about machine learning and genetic engineering and blockchain and globalization, and *they* are not there. *They* (ordinary people) are no longer part of the story of the future.
>
> Now, fast forward to the early 21st century when we just don't need the vast majority of the population because the future is about developing more and more sophisticated technology, like artificial intelligence [and] bioengineering, Most people don't contribute anything to that, except perhaps for their data, and whatever people are still doing which is useful, these technologies increasingly will make redundant and will make it possible to replace the people.[1]

The only error in Harari's observations lies in his tracing of the origin of this problem to post-modern times when, in fact, the roots of this problem lie in the source code of Modernity itself, in the worldview that cut the thumbs of Bengali handloom weavers in order that the machines of Lancashire could triumph.[2]

Feminism too, as a child of Western Modernity, exhibits a predilection for all these impulses: Individualism, Materialism, Liberalism, Centralization, Technologization and a disdain for Traditional Community. Many women (and men) proclaim that they are feminists without really knowing what it is they mean by that statement. What they really want is a world of Mutual Respect, that is *Ardhanaareeshwara* but, in the absence of intellectual clarity, they latch on to the term Feminism, which is a mistake, as we shall see below.

Every degeneracy we see today has its roots in four layers of cultural sub-soil (each progressively leading to the next):

1. Abrahamism, from which came the destruction of the ancient *Dharmic* value of Mutual Respect and the exaltation of the idea of a uniform, monotheistic Universalism in its place. That is, the idea that what is good for me should also be good for you and I will proactively impose my vision upon you regardless of what you want because I know better than you about you. This is violent supremacy (*matsya nyaya*).
2. Western Modernity, from which came the glorification of Individualism as self-indulgence; Materialism as the erasure of the idea of the sacred; and *Technological Progressivism* as represented by the subordination of human interests to the logic of machines and the impulse to Centralization via the Tech-State.
3. Marxism, from which came the exaltation of the oppressor-oppressed lens for viewing human history, the institutionalization of perpetual victimhood and the commandeering of the Tech-State as the vehicle of *Moral Progressivism*—that is, the belief that human society can be consciously redesigned to represent higher and higher moralities.
4. And, ultimately, Feminism, from which originally came
    a. the intellectual separation of Sex and Gender
    b. the inclusion of Sex and Sexuality as categories of oppression
    c. the idea that the body itself is a site for political action and ultimately technological tinkering

It's important that Hindus start making the connections between the complex matrix of the many 'isms' out there, their Abrahamic/Western roots, and their final surrender at the feet of the un-human centralized, machine-aligned Tech-State.

Hindus are not opposed to anyone's personal choices, or even any group's collective choices and self-perceptions, as long as the person or group finds a suitable ritual space in which to belong and limit itself. But, unfortunately, under the prevalent universalist zeitgeist, the choices that *some* people have made have become political battlefields upon which the *whole world's* culture and morality are now imagined to hinge. And Hindus in their current weakened State find themselves drawn, like moths to a flame, into these battlefields. The idea that there must be a single moral code by which every human in all nations upon the world, should abide, is Abrahamic universalist supremacy in its most distilled and potent form. We have seen it before, we have fought it before; we must recognize it again now in its newest *avatars*, and resist it at all costs.

The early 21st Century culture wars in America and the UK have found their way, in a remarkably short time, to our shores as well. Here are some excerpts that give us the lay of the land:

> (You) know what is not a problem for kids who are seeking a good education? Drag queens…Drag queens are entertainment. And you know what I'll say that was totally not poll-tested, I'd say this, 'A drag queen for every school.'
>
> – Michigan Attorney General Dana Nessel at a Summit in Lansing, hosted by the Michigan Department of Civil Rights, as reported by Craig Mauger in, *AG Dana Nessel jokes 'a drag queen for every school,' attacks 'fake issues'*, Detroit News 2022 [3]

> Research suggests that children as young as two recognize their trans identity, yet many nurseries and schools teach a binary understanding of pre-assigned gender. LGBTQ-inclusive and affirming education is crucial for the wellbeing of all young people…Young children should be able to play, explore and learn about who they are, and the world around them, without having adults' ideas imposed upon them.
>
> – UK LGBT advocacy group Stonewall, as reported by Joanna Williams in, *The Truth about Trans Teaching in Schools*, The Spectator 2022 [4]

> Today, from the tiniest village primary to large academy trusts, schools teach about sexuality, relationships and gender identity. They have written policies on gender identity or transgender pupils. Most are identikit statements, but the practices they engender should concern us all.
>
> – Joanna Williams, *The Truth about Trans Teaching in Schools*, The Spectator 2022 [5]

> In a week-long conference last fall, titled "Standing with LGBTQ+ Students, Staff, and Families", Los Angeles Unified School District administrators hosted workshops with presentations on "breaking the [gender] binary", "providing children with free gender affirming clothing", understanding "what your queer middle schooler wants you to know", and producing "counter narratives against the master narrative of mainstream white cis-heteropatriarchy society". Los

> Angeles Unified has gone all-in on "trans-affirming" programming. The Human Relations, Diversity, and Equity department has flooded the district with teaching materials, including, for example, videos from the consulting firm Woke Kindergarten encouraging 5-year-olds to experiment with gender pronouns such as "they," "ze," and "tree" and to adopt nonbinary gender identities that "feel good to you." The district requires teachers to use a student's desired name and pronoun and to keep the student's gender identity a secret from parents if the student so desires. In other words, Los Angeles public schools can facilitate a child's transition from one gender to another without notifying parents.
>
> – Christopher F. Rufo, *Sexual Liberation in Public Schools*, City Journal 2022 [6]
>
> California Moves Toward Giving Therapists Unconditional Power To 'Emancipate' 12 Year Olds From Their Parents.
>
> – Susannah Luthi, The Washington Free Beacon, 2023 [7]

And back home in India –

> Drag Queen Story Hour was organized by @keshavsurifoundation at Tagore International School, Vasant Vihar on 14th Oct for campaign members of classes IX and XI where a drag queen @hiten.noorwal read out a story sending our message on gender fluidity and promoting queer models to impact student minds.
>
> – Vedica Saxena as reported by K. Bhattacharjee in, *Efforts underway to mainstream 'Drag Queen Story Hours' in India*, OpIndia 2020 [8]
>
> This training material is designed for sensitization of teachers and teacher educators regarding aspects of gender diversity keeping gender-nonconforming and transgender children at centre stage. The mandate is to integrate these children in the school system and provide them an appropriate learning environment. Teachers' sensitivity is above all to reach the desired goal because they are the major change makers who are in constant and close touch with children.
>
> – NCERT, *Inclusion of Transgender Children in School Education: Concerns and Roadmap*, Training Material 2020-21 [9]
>
> As a talented writer and performance artist, Alok V Menon is paving the way for societal acceptance and visibility for transgender and gender non-conforming individuals. Let's cheer for Alok and the beautiful change they're creating #WithPride.
>
> – US Embassy in India, via Twitter 2023 [10]

Drag, Trans, Genderism, Queer, Woke, Cis...whatever does all this mean? If the aim is to stop schoolyard bullying of kids who are 'different' and to build toilets for *actual* inter-sex kids, then let's do just that without losing a single moment. But let us simultaneously know that everything else we hear about these matters is hogwash. We don't need a worldwide moral revolution in order to do those things. When we allow these matters to become political and cultural movements, we are playing into the hands of a poisonous branch of Western Liberalism that wants to put sex at the centre of human identity and use Western Equality as a crowbar to prise apart not just tradition but identity itself.

Here is the high priest of sexuality himself (celebrated French philosopher and self-confessed pedophile,[11] Michel Foucault) stating this in no unclear terms:

> It is through sex – in fact, an imaginary point determined by the deployment of sexuality – that each individual has to pass in order to have access to his own intelligibility... the whole of his body... to his identity.
>
> – Michel Foucault, *The Care of the Self*, 1984 [12]

The right way for Hindus to intellectually process these phenomena they are being sucked into is set out below.

The Hindu View

The erasure of the idea of the Sacred and the fall of Community in the West is generating a vast pool of unhinged individuals who, in the absence of a sense of purpose and self, latch on to either sexual gratification or the latest social theory as their holy grail, under which banner they find a sense of belonging and purpose and begin to organize moral revolutions. But, without an overarching theory of Meaning and Balance, these revolutions quickly descend into more and more perverse manifestations of victimhood mongering and special pleading. And, unfortunately, the universalist State, hamstrung by its inability to tell the difference between mainstream and periphery, ends up locking peripheral demands into universal law.

The Abrahamic idea of a prophet with a bunch of commandments that should be foisted upon every single human has been inherited lock stock and barrel by

Western elites under the delusion that they are harbingers of a more moral world. Not only is this attitude unethical and supremacist, but the morals themselves are suspect.

At the societal level, the *Dharmic* counter to Abrahamic Universalism is Community-held Tradition, and it manifests in a two-sided framework:

1. *Jaati-Consciousness*, the idea that difference and diversity can be ethically managed by dividing up time, space and ritual into community-specific parcels, and
2. *Purusha-Consciousness*, the idea that diverse groups can be brought together by designing the terms for their interaction on the metaphorical plane.
3. It is obvious to Hindus that communities have as much of a right to pass on their ancestral values to their children as individuals have to pass on their personal ideals to their children. A *Traditional* State would take that into account. In such a State, not all values and ideals would be seen as equal. Values, such as self-sacrifice, harmony and sustainability that are stewarded by the *stable cultural mainstream* via the performance of *duties*, would be incentivized. At the same time, graded levels of liberty would be provided to the unstable periphery. In a direct counter to this approach, the post-modern Tech-State does exactly the opposite. It incentivizes the unstable periphery and uses peripheral values to slowly but surely criminalize and disincentivize the stable cultural mainstream. It does this in order to discourage the processes of organic community formation, enabling it to gain greater central control over alienated individuals.

We see evidence for this in the hard sciences (technological progressivism), in liberal arts (moral progressivism), and in public policy (both technological and moral progressivism). Here, Janna Anderson, Lee Rainie and Emily A. Vogels present their analysis of Pew Research Data generated by 914 innovators, developers, business and policy leaders, researchers and activists:

> As these experts pondered what was happening in mid-2020 and the likely changes ahead, they used words like "inflection point," "punctuated equilibrium," "unthinkable scale," "exponential process," "massive disruption" and "unprecedented challenge." They wrote about changes that could reconfigure fundamental realities such as people's physical "presence" with others and people's conceptions of trust and truth.

They wondered, too, if humans can cope effectively with such far-reaching changes, given that they are required to function with "paleolithic emotions, medieval institutions and god-like technology," in the words of biologist E.O. Wilson.[13]

Not only is the very idea of Balance *lost* in the pursuit of this insane model of 'progress', but it could also very well be argued that the developmental model we seem to have chosen by default, actively *seeks* imbalance.

Man, Woman and Equality

People don't want Liberty, what they want is Purpose. People don't want Equality, what they want is Respect.

Many calls for Equality are usually calls for respect. A solution to the problem of disrespect is usually better served by introspection and conversation mediated by spiritual gurus, **rather** than by revolution. Alexander Solzhenitsyn exposes the fallacy at the heart of modern ideologies in a speech delivered at Les Lucs-sur-Boulogne in 1993:

> The French Revolution took place in the name of an intrinsically contradictory and unrealizable slogan: Liberty, Equality, Fraternity. But in social life, Liberty and Equality tend to exclude each other, are antagonistic to each other! Freedom destroys social Equality – this is even one of the roles of Freedom – while Equality restricts Freedom, because otherwise it cannot be achieved. As for the Fraternity, it is not of their family. It is only an adventurous addition to the slogan and it is not social dispositions that can make true brotherhood. It is spiritual.[14]

Most people are aware, at the back of their minds, about this conundrum. Equality and Liberty are antithetical to each other. The more externally-imposed Equality we institute, the less free we are all going to be in the long run and, beyond a tipping point, that loss of freedom leads to immoral outcomes and violent reactions. Wendell Berry writes:

> It makes no sense, for example, to equate equality with freedom. Equality in certain circumstances is anything but free. If we have equality and nothing else,

no compassion, no magnanimity, no courtesy, no sense of mutual obligation and dependence, no imagination, then power and wealth will have its way, brutality will rule. In order to survive, a plurality of true communities would require not egalitarianism and tolerance but knowledge, an understanding of the necessity of local differences, and respect. Respect, I think, always implies imagination – the ability to see one another, across our inevitable differences, as living souls.[15]

... and as *Purusha*-Consciousness would have us understand, to see those living souls as forming part of a greater divine living soul.

And yet, we are captivated by this idea of Equality.

Equality is a very persuasive idea because it has mathematical simplicity. It appeals to our sensibilities even though every fibre of reality screams I N E Q U A L I T Y and difference.

In Part I of this section, extracts from Simone De Beauvoir's book *Second Sex* gave us a fairly objective, materialist understanding of how man-woman relationships evolved. But I object to her misreading of agricultural society. She is mistaken when she lays the blame for Abrahamic misogyny and the tech-derived problems of early Modernity at the doorstep of Agriculture. A truly agricultural polytheist society provides equally important work for men and women. If men are ploughing, then women are planting. If men are threshing, then women are winnowing. If men are milling, then women are cleaning the grain. If men are repairing the roof, then women are maintaining the floor. If men are building and maintaining the family's bridges within the community at large, then women are building and maintaining the family's bridges within the extended family. The men placate *Munishwaran*. The women placate *Mariamman*. This is a kind of equality and, in fact, it is the traditional Hindu view of equality. That is, **Equality as Equivalence**. This view differs dramatically from the Western model that is being pursued today, which is **Equality as Equity**, or the equality of outcome. This ideal forces upon us the remarkable view that if men and women are not equally represented in all activities and end goals, and if men and women are not equally involved in all decision-making, then it must be because women are being oppressed.

Man, Woman and "Equality as Equivalence"

Just recently, something that I had been aware of for two decades, but that I always looked at with limp Western eyes, suddenly jumped out at me in all its ancient intricacy. In my line of work, building construction, there are always teams of men and women who do different jobs. Even when they are involved in doing the same job, the work is divided into masculine sub-jobs and feminine sub-jobs. Try as I might I could never convince a woman to do a man's job even when I knew that she had the strength to do so and neither could I convince a man to do a woman's job even when I knew he had the delicacy to do so. My attempts were always met with derisive laughter..."How can I do that sir? That's a man's job." Or "What sir? That's a woman's job." This is not unique to construction of course, it extends to agriculture and all traditional occupations. The entire traditional population of this country lives in an entirely gendered landscape! Their *entire* world is gendered—language, clothes, ritual, work, family, even space itself.

If we step out of the modern, urban, framing of this scenario as "Oh that's just patriarchy" and instead we enter the world of *Ardhanaareeshwara*, we would be overcome by a delicate sense of beauty, as if walking past a night-queen in full bloom on a moonless night. Something would grab hold of our senses and turn our heads against our will in a direction we had no intention of going. This is not about power... this is about *beauty* and *balance* and the acknowledgement of the will of the Gods. This is thus... and thus it must be.

Traditional Hindu society, like all other traditional societies, has grappled with the conundrum of Equality. But unlike the Abrahamic religions that chose to impose Equality through violent genetic and memetic homogenization, *Sanatana* Civilization chose to define Equality in abstract terms. Divining, already five millennia ago, that any attempt to impose Equality from the top-down would lead to unthinkable immorality (genocide, ethnocide, surveillance, centralized control), it accepted instead that the great diversity of community life and spiritual expression in this land should not be erased, and that every person would find Equality—not in homogeneity, but in equal access to *Purushaarth*, to the tools of *Dharma* and to the road to *Moksha*. This lofty ideal also had material implications. It required that a tribal society be organized in such a way that *all* communities and, by extrapolation, all individuals within each community, would have access to the means to garner *Artha* and *Kama* (the foundational elements of *Purushaarth*). It was this that gave birth to *jaati*. *Jaati* was, and in many places continues to be, the unique, self-regulated and decentralized Welfare State of traditional *Sanatana* society.

Our understanding of gender difference was no different. The differences between man and woman were patently obvious. It was apparent to our ancestors that they were intended to lead different lives, and had different routes to self-fulfilment and self-realization. Throughout history, in all traditional societies, whether the Native American long house or the Hindu autonomous village, women and men led entirely different lives—women with other women, and men with other men. Women cooking, weaving, storytelling, singing, cleaning, looking after children and animals, agricultural post-production, medicine making. Men hunting, ploughing, building, negotiating, trading, jousting...

In *Exploring the longhouse and community in tribal society*, Jodie A. O'Gorman reveals:

> Although the boundary is ambiguous and permeable, activities typically involved women in agriculture and gathering, while men were engaged in warfare and hunting (O'Gorman 1996; Skinner 1926; Wedel 1986). In much of their daily lives adult men and women occupied distinct spatial realms, and their practices and interactions with gendered groups shaped experiences of community. Associated patterns of behaviour would be focused on the longhouse, natal, and village communities for women and the longhouse, natal, and marital communities for men. In the wide range of activities that women engaged in, the community of the longhouse would have provided support in child rearing, protection, and pooled labour for harvesting and processing a wide array of wild and domesticated foodstuffs. Shared labour relationships in the longhouse community would have been particularly important during the fall months, when many of the important wild and domesticated storable crops had to be harvested and processed for storage.[16]

Similar descriptions are seen in *The Remembered Village* by M.N. Srinivas:

> During the post-harvest rain-free period, women busied themselves with making dried foods and pickles which brought some variety to the routine diet of cooked balls of *ragi* dough and hot sauce. Strips of mutton were covered

with a paste of spiced chillies and hung out to dry and then stored. These were roasted and eaten as a relish during summer when the appetites of even men working in the fields needed to be coaxed. *Happala* (*paapads*) and *sandige* (relishes made with cooked rice-flour), and green mango and lime pickles were made and stored in mud pots or stone jars. In the richer and upper caste households these activities consumed a considerable amount of the time and energy of the women-folk. Work parties of women and girls rolled out *paapads* and made different kinds of *sandige* during summer afternoons. If there was going to be a wedding in the house, then these tasks were begun weeks ahead of the event.

The man had other jobs besides the work on the farm and caring for the bullocks, sheep and goats, He had to attend to all the maintenance and minor repair work in the house, bring fuel and chop it, do all the big shopping in the towns. If he had a teenage son, the latter relieved him of such jobs as taking the bullocks twice a day to the pond or canal, providing green fodder for the sheep and goats, and chopping dry sorghum stems for cattle fodder. It was the man who exercised control over the domestic economy. He made the annual grain-payments at harvest to the members of the artisan and servicing castes who had worked for him during the year.[17]

Does it really seem accurate or honest then to assess these descriptions of life as forms of 'patriarchal oppression'? Or should we see them as the organic organization of life in pre-industrial times? The emergence of a sense of oppression and a reactionary felt need for emancipation are both modern phenomena. To be precise, they are reactions to the Jane Austen phase of Western history. We are being disingenuous when we lay blame for them on tradition or pre-industrial times. But the modern mind has always needed a fall guy to help justify its excesses.

Pinkola Estes has this to say about the uniqueness of the woman's being, her soul-journey and how it fundamentally differs from the soul-journey of a man:

> A woman's issues of soul cannot be treated by carving her into a more acceptable form as defined by an unconscious culture, nor can she be bent into an intellectually more acceptable shape by those who claim to be the sole bearers of consciousness.[18]

She continues, "When women reassert their relationship to their wildish nature, they are gifted with a permanent and internal watcher, a knower, a visionary, an oracle, an inspiratrice, an intuitive, a marker, a creator, an inventor and a listener who guide, suggest and urge vibrant life in the inner and outer worlds."[18] When women are in touch with this inner nature, she says, "the wild teacher, wild mother, wild mentor" support them in their inner and outer lives.

More insightful is her description of the phases in women's' lives. In the first half of her life, she says, a woman moves from instinct to bodily knowledge. And in the second phase to a sort of soul-consciousness:

> The body becomes an internal sensing device almost exclusively and women become more and more subtle. As a woman transits through these cycles, her layers of defence, protection, density become more and more sheer until her very soul begins to shine through.[18]

Taking off from this insightful description of female reality, we can answer questions posed by modern Hindu women about why they were traditionally 'denied' ritual fitness. The fact is the very opposite is true. Women were and still are free to create any number of ritual structures, but they *never do*. Why? Because it's simply *not their scene* (to use a colloquial phrase). Women already have access to eternity via their bodies and birthing. It was man who had to labour to create an exteriorized scaffolding (tradition) to enable him to touch eternity (all the while lovingly holding women as central and indispensable to those traditions). So, when a modern woman claims equal space in the ritual world, she is disrespecting her own spiritual ladder while unconsciously occupying rungs in her man's ladder. Nithin Sridhar, in his book *Menstruation Across Cultures*, has this to say about how and why the *rishis* divined the ritual world into male and female aspects:

> Men do not undergo menstruation and hence they do not have access to this self-purifying process. Instead, the scriptures suggest a variety of rules and ritual practices...Activities like *samskaaras*, *mantra japa* and *sandhyopasana* etc. have all been prescribed for men to attain purity and be free from *adharmic* actions. But women do not have to perform any of these spiritual activities to attain purity. They become pure simply by undergoing menstruation. What comes by special effort to men, comes as part of a natural process to women.[19]

Sinu Joseph elaborates further in her book Varna Vidya:

> Any girl/woman of menstrual age who has been made to chant *Vedic mantras* or perform *agnikriyas* as prescribed in the *Vedic karmakanda* for six months

or more has a high probability of experiencing problematic menstruation... ovarian dysfunction, endometriosis... difficulty while attempting to conceive... an indifference towards *samsara*... from worldly duties... severe psychological effects, and cause disturbed mental states.[20]

Anyone who has witnessed Hindu coming-of-age rituals for boys and girls will be struck by the difference in intent. The boy is initiated *externally* into *mantra* and ritual acts by a fraternity which focuses on word and metaphysics, whereas the girl is initiated *internally* into her moon cycle by a sorority which focuses on her body and her beauty. It is clear again, as it was clear to our ancestors, that a woman's path to self-realization is interior, through the body and intuition, and the man's path lies in the exterior, through the mind and action. Women's lives, therefore, have as much of a rich interiority as men's lives have a rich exteriority. Both aspects represent one-half of consciousness, *Prakriti* and *Purusha*. It has been the job of traditional culture to find and institutionalize the perfect balance. Doesn't mean that a man cannot be intuitive or a woman cannot be analytical. Doesn't mean that women never fight or trade. Doesn't mean that men never clean or look after children. But it does mean that, by and large, society acknowledged and honoured the differences between the two sexes while leaving the framework loose enough to support circumstance and genius.

Deep in the heart of this understanding of the world lie the following two questions. If a man does a woman's work, then what are women for? And, if a woman does a man's work, then what are men for? If a sense of being put to full and wholesome use in the service of a larger cause (*kutumba, kula, rashtra*) is one of the fundamental requirements for human contentment, then one can point to the continued failure of Western Modernity to answer the above two questions as one of the root causes of the all-pervasive dissonance in modern Western/Westernized relationships. Both men and women feel useless, and they bring the stress associated with having to constantly prove their value (to themselves and to each other) into their relationship.

Man, Woman and "Equality as Equity"

Just as the growth-based economy puts us all on a ladder of ever-increasing expectation of efficiency and performance, so too does the Equity meme pull us into a tighter and tighter matrix of ever-increasing micro-friction and self-validation. Every household activity/decision becomes a site for negotiation, where husband and wife have to make sure that there is an even distribution of victories of opinion. Children growing up in such an intimate battlefield have no experience of the contentment that comes from a life where everything fits in place. Wendell Berry writes:

> The sacrament of sexual union which at the time of the household was a communion of workmates, and afterward tried to be a lover's paradise, has now become a marketplace in which the husband and wife represent each other as sexual property. Competitiveness and jealousy, imperfectly sweetened and disguised by the illusions of courtship, now become the governing principles, and they work to isolate the couple inside their marriage. Marriage becomes a capsule of sexual fate. The man must look on other men and the woman on other women as threats. This seems to have been particularly damaging to women; because of the progressive degeneration and isolation of their "role", their worldly stock-in-trade has increasingly had to be "their" men. In the isolation of the resulting sexual privacy the disintegration of the community begins. The energy that is the most convivial and unifying loses its communal forms and becomes divisive.[21]

But quaint interests of mine, such as the mechanics of marital disharmony and the Abrahamic roots of misogyny, don't even register in today's stratospheric discourse centred around gender dysphoria[22] and artificial wombs.[23] We've gone from figuring out very simple solutions to inter-personal frictions to a very complex dismantling of all we hold dear in a matter of a mere five decades.

Just as modern factory schooling forced children, for the very first time in history, to spend an unprecedented amount of time every day locked up exclusively with other children of their own age group in a state of near-incarceration, it is also for the first time in human history that men and women are being thrust into the same physical spaces over such long periods of time every day, forced to do the same things and compete over the same resources, all the while maintaining a studied asexuality in their interactions. There is absolutely no precedent for this brand-new and presumably un-natural phenomenon.

We have to understand that it is *this* artificially contrived dynamic between man and woman in the context of the industrial Tech-State that is the context for the modern understanding of Equality. Let us also understand that this new form of Equality bears no relation to the traditional idea of Equality as Equivalence and has no interest in the idea of Balance. It is from within the mindset of the growth-based economy, un-moored from the idea of natural limits and in the absence of a theory of Balance, that Equality takes the form of Equity.

So, what is Equity?

Equity is today defined as Equality of *Outcome*. It carries within it the seed of the idea that if outcomes are not equal, it is because there is systemic bias which is a form of oppression. Western feminists were the first to chart and mine this intellectual territory and now their Catholic definition of oppression has spread like a virus across the academic and legal terrain. Today anything organic and normal is considered oppressive simply because it exists. They say:

> Oppression is a system of inter-related barriers and forces which reduce, immobilize and mould people who belong to a certain group, and effect their subordination to another group (individually to individuals of the other group, and as a group, to that group).[24]

According to this definition, all of reality is imagined as a hydra-headed weighing scale occupied by an ever-expanding set of special interest groups. The weights are supposed to be controlled by an ever-expanding lexicon of law to ensure that each hydra-head is at the same level as every other. Karl Marx has, like Jesus before him, risen from the dead to claim all of society for himself and his insane oppressor-oppressed binary.

In the West, when the concept of systemic bias first started to become widely prevalent, potentially explosive reactions to this seemingly all-pervasive injustice were sought to be contained by the state within newly theorized educational and economic structures that were promoted as delivering *equality of opportunity*. But by the 1980s, Critical Race Theorists had extended the critique not just to education and knowledge production but also to the previously off-limits categories of community and family. Richard T. Schaefer writes in his 2008 *Encyclopedia of Race, Ethnicity & Society*:

> Indeed, as one of the most overarching concepts animating Critical Race Theory (CRT) thought is the critique of liberal, color-blind ideology. Universal

> principles associated with color-blindness – such as non-discrimination, formal equality of opportunity, and the rule of law – are lauded for their potent mix in bringing down the Jim Crow laws of legalized segregation. Yet these same principles are found limiting in the post-segregation context...The formalistic conception of equality expressed in color-blind strictures of equal treatment can remedy only the most blatant forms of discrimination, such as refusal to employ a person of color, but cannot address processes based on equality of outcome.[25]

By the 1990s, Queer Theory (QT) had extended the critique further to include Nature itself. Judith Butler, in her 1990 classic, *Gender Trouble,* writes:

> Expressed differently, the new understanding of heterosexuality as an economic and reproductive regime denaturalizes the classification of human bodies into men and women. Henceforth, it would no longer be possible to think of sex as prior to gender, or as a sign on which the latter is written: on the contrary, sex indistinguishable from gender, a category that is "fully politically invested, naturalized but not natural".[26]

The intellectual arc of this worldview has led to scarcely believable movements in America that intend to forcibly equalize outcomes by law. If CRT and QT remained but topics of academic interest, or the guiding principles of a community of believers, then we could simply ignore them and carry on with our lives. But, under the one-size-fits-all umbrella of Western Universalism, CRT and QT, catalyzed further by Intersectionality, have become revolutionary ideologies that want to upend society altogether. Their adherents will not rest until we are all converted. See the Quentin De Kock "Taking The Knee" episode for a public example involving a celebrity.[27]

Given the pusillanimous nature of the Indian State, we ignore these movements in America at our own peril. Already 'anti-caste' groupings in India have gleefully jumped on this gravy train of university positions and published papers.

The Trans-movement is just one of the symptoms of this way of thinking, but has quickly become its most prominent face given its penchant for indecency[28] and perverse interest in manipulating children.[29] Many first-wave feminists like J.K. Rowling have a problem with the Trans movement, but they probably realize that it was a can of worms that they themselves opened. She writes:

> I've read all the arguments about femaleness not residing in the sexed body, and the assertions that biological women don't have common experiences, and I find them, too, deeply misogynistic and regressive. It's also clear that one of the objectives of denying the importance of sex is to erode what some seem to see as the cruelly segregationist idea of women having their own biological realities or – just as threatening – unifying realities that make them a cohesive political class. The hundreds of emails I've received in the last few days prove this erosion concerns many others just as much. It isn't enough for women to be trans allies. Women must accept and admit that there is no material difference between trans women and themselves.
>
> But, as many women have said before me, 'woman' is not a costume. 'Woman' is not an idea in a man's head. 'Woman' is not a pink brain, a liking for Jimmy Choos or any of the other sexist ideas now somehow touted as progressive. Moreover, the 'inclusive' language that calls female people 'menstruators' and 'people with vulvas' strikes many women as dehumanising and demeaning.[30]

First-wave feminists are discovering, like it or not, that feminist thought is indeed tied at the hip to all the radical post-feminist movements that are in play today. As a last throw of dice, such feminists have even created an entirely new category of Feminism called TERF (Trans-Exclusionary Radical Feminism).

Other, more extreme, feminists are willing to bite the bullet and embrace the end-game of their journey. They recognize that the moment sex and gender were intellectually separated, and gender was made into a 'social construct', it was no longer about equal rights, but about something else altogether: the final and complete destruction of cultural, social and biological identity. Carol Hay writes in *Who Counts as A Woman?*:

> By demarcating feminism's subject matter — by articulating a concrete category of harms that deserved feminist attention — feminists inadvertently defined womanhood in a manner that implies that there are right and wrong ways to be a woman. "Identity categories are never merely descriptive," she (Butler) insists in "Gender Trouble," "but always normative, and as such, exclusionary.

Any attempt to catalog the commonalities among women, in other words, has the inescapable result that there is some correct way to be a woman. This will inevitably encourage and legitimize certain experiences of gender and discourage and delegitimize others, subtly reinforcing and entrenching precisely those forces of socialization of which feminists claim to be critical. And what's worse, it will inevitably leave some people out. It will mean that there are "real" women whom feminism should be concerned about and that there are impostors who do not qualify for feminist political representation.

The women who are accused of being impostors these days are often trans women.[31]

This way of thinking about the world has led to outcomes both amusing and abhorrent. I quote now from various news reports and radical academic sources to give us a picture of what's really happening deep in the American heart and a sense of things to come.

1. The acknowledgment that feminist autonomy would *not* exist in a low-tech environment and is therefore *predicated* on a world of high technology leads cutting-edge feminists to make a public show of loyalty to a dystopian, cyborgian future. Laboria Cuboniks writes in her manifesto *Xenofeminism: A Politics for Alienation*:

    The construction of freedom involves not less but more alienation; **alienation is the labour of freedom's construction**… Anyone who's been deemed 'unnatural' in the face of reigning biological norms, anyone who's experienced injustices wrought in the name of natural order, will realize that **the glorification of 'nature' has nothing to offer us.**[32]

    She goes on to denounce "Essentialist Naturalism" as theological, a religion that has no place for the queer, the trans, the differently abled, or the pregnant!

    She casts her lot with "technoscience" where "nothing is so sacred that it cannot be reengineered and transformed so as to widen our aperture of freedom, extending to gender and the human."[32].

She cancels everything sacred and transcendent, stressing that everything is open to being tinkered with and hacked.

Pushing further out, she defines her movement:

> Xenofeminism indexes the desire to construct an alien future with a triumphant X on a mobile map. This X does not mark a destination. It is the insertion of a topological-keyframe for the formation of a new logic... In the name of feminism, 'Nature' shall no longer be a refuge of injustice, or a basis for any political justification whatsoever![32]

And finally, her clarion call:

> If nature is unjust, change nature![32]

2. Compared to that cutting edge, some older and more prosaic battles are still being fought:

> The Marine Corps' longstanding tradition of having two-tiered fitness requirements for men and women aims to ensure fairness, but a growing chorus of critics say it creates a double standard and implies that female Marines are not as physically capable as men.
>
> Many **experts** say the Marines' current policy makes sense. There's **clear scientific evidence** that men on average are physically stronger than women.
>
> – Jeff Schogol, *New concerns that lower fitness standards fuel disrespect for women*, Marine Corps Times 2017 [33]

3. The commandeering of the Trans movement as a stepping stone towards making the species extinct and creating 'super-humans' or Cyborgs:

> Nathanson told Ingraham that trans and non-binary movements have sprung up because "feminists challenge the notion of gender" and this has evolved into the development of feminist ideology.
>
> In response, Ingraham said: "Their goal ultimately is the destruction or elimination of the traditional family, though, is it not? That's what we really want to get at here. That's really what's going on."
>
> "I think that the trans people have taken it one step further because by abandoning gender altogether, not simply re-writing it, they're basically trying to use social engineering to create a new species. Which is what, in fact, the

transhumanists have been doing for the past half century. Using medical and other technologies to develop a new species."

– Ewan Palmer, *Laura Ingraham Guest Says Trans People Will 'Destroy' Gender Norms to Create 'New Species'—'Human and Part Machine'*, Newsweek 2019 [34]

4. The colonizing of all branches of knowledge with Marxist theory. Teaching the "Equitable Math" curriculum is law in California today:

> White supremacy culture shows up in math classrooms when…The focus is only on getting the "right" answer.
>
> Instead…The concept of mathematics being purely objective is unequivocally false, and teaching it is even much less so. **Upholding the idea that there are always right and wrong answers perpetuates objectivity as well as fear of open conflict.**
>
> – *A Pathway to Equitable Math Instruction*, 2021 [35]

5. The emergence of a new Theology. Radical sexual movements take Marxist theory to its illogical end. It feels like 50 CE all over again. The Christians are at the gates of Rome… Only, this time, the Christians themselves are Rome! And like the early Christians who infiltrated Rome two thousand years ago, it's not really Rights that the new bearers of victimhood want, it's the entire world remade in their image. Normal *itself* is oppression:

> Queerness is not yet here. Queerness is an ideality. Put another way, we are not yet queer. We may never touch queerness, but we can feel it as the warm illumination of a horizon imbued with potentiality. We have never been queer, yet queerness exists for us as an ideality that can be distilled from the past and used to imagine a future. **The future is queerness's domain.** Queerness is a structuring and educated mode of desiring that allows us to see and feel beyond the quagmire of the present. The here and now is a prison house.
>
> – José Esteban Muñoz, *Cruising Utopia*, 2009 [36]

> Carruthers suggests that bringing a Black queer feminist lens to political thought and praxis **renounces the middle-class notion of the public sphere** as a place where identity should be abandoned to maintain the myth of universality. Even more, her vision of activism decenters queerness; she demands that multiple types of oppression, types that will not be experienced the same way

> or even at all by the entire LGBTQ+ community, must be acknowledged to imagine and enact a **truly transformed, justice-oriented social world**.
>
> Instead of asking, How can we include queers in the existing social world, he (Joshua Chambers-Letson) asks, **How can we queer the existing social world** to make it habitable by queers?
>
> – Jennifer Miller, *Thirty Years of Queer Theory*, UT Arlington Curriculum 2020 [37]

> Longtime Rubin collaborator Pat Califia, who would later become a transgender man, claimed that American society had turned pedophiles into "the new communists, the new niggers, the new witches." For Califia, age-of-consent laws, religious sexual mores, and families who police the sexuality of their children represented a thousand-pound bulwark against sexual freedom. "You can't liberate children and adolescents without disrupting the entire hierarchy of adult power and coercion and challenging the hegemony of anti-sex fundamentalist religious values," she lamented. All of it—the family, the law, the religion, the culture—was a vector of oppression, and all of it had to go.
>
> – Christopher F. Rufo, *The Real Story Behind Drag Queen Story Hour*, City Journal 2022 [38]

6. And, most damagingly, they know they can't have/bring-up kids of their own, so they want ours. Akin to countries with inverted population pyramids encouraging immigration, unsustainable lifestyles are constantly looking to be subsidized by people who take the trouble to live sustainable lives. How long are we going to allow our children to subsidize the economic and cultural profligacy of the West?

> Drag Queen Story Hour (DQSH) as a form of queer imagining in an early childhood context. Through this programme, drag artists have channelled their penchant for playfully **"'reading' each other to filth"** into different forms of literacy, promoting storytelling as integral to queer and trans communities, as well as positioning queer and trans cultural forms as valuable components of early childhood education.
>
> DQSH creates spaces for young children and families to immerse themselves in LGBT-themed stories, and does so in ways that seem to genuinely reflect queer ways of being and relating – rather than as a neatly marketed product. We believe that this makes DQSH worthy of closer study. We argue that the

programme creates a pathway into the imaginative, messy, and rule-breaking aspects of drag for children without necessarily watering down queer cultures.

– Harper Keenan, *Drag pedagogy: The playful practice of queer imagination in early childhood*, 2021 [39]

The professional vision of educators is often shaped to reproduce the State's normative vision of its ideal citizenry. In effect, schooling functions as a way to straighten the child into a kind of captive alignment with the current parameters of that vision," Kornstein and Keenan write. "To state it plainly, within the historical context of the USA and Western Europe, the institutional management of gender has been used as a way of maintaining racist and capitalist modes of (re)production.

To disrupt this dynamic, the authors propose a new teaching method, "drag pedagogy," as a way of stimulating the "queer imagination," teaching kids "how to live queerly," and "bringing queer ways of knowing and being into the education of young children." As Kornstein and Keenan explain, this is an intellectual and political project that requires drag queens and activists to work toward undermining traditional notions of sexuality, replacing the biological family with the ideological family, and arousing transgressive sexual desires in young children. "Building in part from queer theory and trans studies, queer and trans pedagogies seek to actively destabilize the normative function of schooling through transformative education," they write. "This is a fundamentally different orientation than movements towards the inclusion or assimilation of LGBT people into the existing structures of school and society."

– Christopher F. Rufo, *The Real Story Behind Drag Queen Story Hour*, City Journal 2022 [40]

7. And if our children's minds were not enough, they want their bodies too. The younger the better, often for obviously deviant reasons. These processes are now law in California:

> (Under Bill AB 957) California courts would be given complete authority under Section 3011 of California's Family Code to remove a child from his or her parents' home if parents disapprove of LGBTQ+ ideology.[41]

Many of these 'oppressed' groups imagine that they are fighting Universalism with their attempts to bring down 'cis-white-hetero-normative' culture. They do not see that they themselves wish to impose their values universally upon society, thereby becoming a Universalism themselves.

It may well be that people have different capabilities and desires and if these groups want to stand against Universalism, they will find, once they have exhausted all other paths, that the only logical and ethical way to do this is via the means of *jaati*—different strokes for different folks. It is at that point in human societal evolution that people will ask, "Then what is it that will hold us together?" And they will find that there is only one answer—the concept of the *Purusha*. The West currently is not focused on defining its own *Purusha* because centuries of wealth accumulation and military superiority are keeping the wheels of their civilization turning. But make no mistake, as the wealth runs out and their military superiority is challenged, they will either have to discover a way out of the intellectual quagmire they are in, by defining the terms of a modern *Purusha*, or they will endure total collapse. Marxism and Postmodernism are Western Civilization's greatest fault-lines. Their ship has finally run aground on these two icebergs of their own making.

In Bharat, it was the idea of the *Purusha* and the institution of *jaati* that allowed for difference to gain expression while simultaneously protecting us from revolution. Christianity-led Western Universalism and their pyramid model of seeing the world, on the other hand, has traditionally seen differences as threats that needed to be enslaved or exterminated. Today, under the influence of Marxist oppression theory, the West pushes the pendulum to the other extreme by taking these differences and foregrounding them in their politics and society, effectively creating an inverted pyramid. They do not realize that their problem is not how the pyramid is organized, their problem is the idea of the pyramid itself. There is only one solution to Pyramid-Thought and it is Purusha-Consciousness—the honouring of difference through separation and resource distribution, and the honouring of similarity through collaboration and the fractalization of civilizational values.

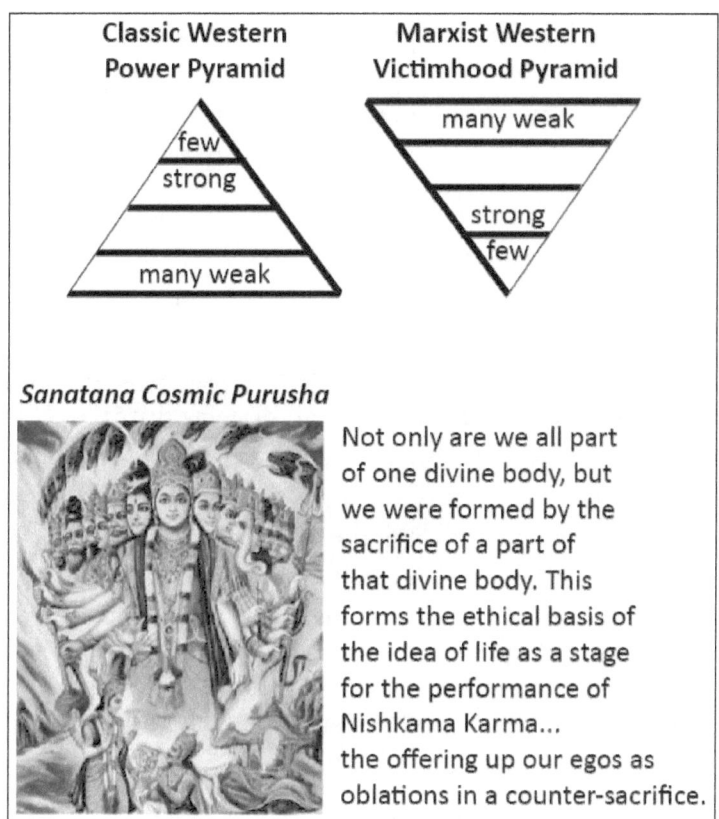

So, where does that leave Hindu men and women?

It can be nobody's contention anymore that women can't do what men can do. In all walks of life, from science to business to the toughest physical tests, women have shown that they are eminently capable. Just recently, Kirsten Neuschafer became the first woman to not just sail in, but to actually *win* the Golden Globe Race.[42] All we can say with certainty is that, within the wide spectrum of modern jobs/activities, some are more suited to men and some are more suited to women, but the vast majority of jobs are suited to both sexes. Our problem is not whether Equity can be achieved or whether it is a noble goal; our problem is the *outcomes* of Equity for our families, our children, our communities and out traditions. Equity kills, because it has no nuance. The excerpts in the previous section should alert us all to the dangers of the world that is coming. Just like equality between religions in India has come to mean that everybody belongs equally to all religions, so too does equity between sexes end up meaning that all people belong equitably to both sexes and everything in between. Where the traditional mind sees Balance through diversity and mutual respect, the Modern Western mind sees Equity through uniformity and erasure.

For all of us who value the culture we grew up in and have a desire to pass on that flame to future generations, we have to realize that that world did not emerge from a vacuum. It emerged from the lived reality of certain values and civilizational priorities. We have to start thinking about how we can engage with the modern world while retaining that core, and a big part of doing that is for Hindu men and women to figure out a new status quo. We may not be traditionalist but we can choose to be traditional. That involves making conscious choices and sacrifices for each other, the children, the extended family and the ritual acts we are called upon to maintain. This requires a taming of the individualist spirit that Modernity has engendered in us all... not an extinguishing, but certainly a taming.

In my mind, until the coming of *Ram Rajya* in the unforeseeable future, we have three options:

1. Return to the Traditional world.
   This is difficult at two levels. One, no one wants to do it for economic reasons; and two, that once-vibrant world is now a lonely place.

2. Invest a portion of our family lives in the low-tech world.
   That low-tech world could either be agricultural or organized around one's traditional hands-on occupation. This investment of time and effort in cyclic activities will build cyclic consciousness and automatically traditionalize our inter-relationships.

3. Consciously bi-genderize the modern world.
   Since we don't have the capacity to bi-genderize work and space in the modern world, we can choose to bi-genderize time. For example, in the first fifteen years of married life, when the man and his active capabilities are on the ascendant, he could work outside the home while the woman does limited creative work from home where the kids are at an age when

they need her. In the next fifteen years of married life, when the woman and her intuitive capabilities are on the ascendant, she could work outside the home while the man does limited creative work from home, where the kids are at an age when they need him. If possible, live with grandparents and home-school the kids.

Obviously, this is not a solution for couples who want to climb the corporate ladder; this is a rough and partially tested idea for Hindu couples who are genuinely looking for a way to manage the conundrum of Western Modernity without having to retreat entirely into Option No. 1. It's possible that this approach will minimize disharmony, outsourced childhoods, value erosion and emotional/sexual problems that we have come to associate with marriage in modern times.

References and Links

1. Yuval Noah Harari, "Interview with Chris Andersen", *Breitbart*, 2022
   https://www.breitbart.com/economy/2022/08/10/wef-adviser-yuval-harari-we-just-dont-need-the-vast-majority-of-the-population-in-todays-world/

2. William Bolts, *Considerations on India Affairs*, 1772
   https://archive.org/details/in.ernet.dli.2015.195631/page/n7/mode/2up

3. Michigan Attorney General Dana Nessel at a Summit in Lansing, hosted by the Michigan Department of Civil Rights, as reported by Craig Mauger in "AG Dana Nessel jokes 'a drag queen for every school,' attacks 'fake issues'", *Detroit News*, 2022
   https://www.detroitnews.com/story/news/politics/2022/06/15/nessel-jokes-a-drag-queen-every-school-speech-against-fake-issues/7639375001/

4. Joanna Williams, "The Truth about Trans Teaching in Schools", *The Spectator*, 2022
   https://www.spectator.co.uk/article/the-truth-about-trans-teaching-in-schools/

5. Ibid.

6. Christopher F. Rufo, "Sexual Liberation in Public Schools", *City Journal*, 2022
https://www.city-journal.org/article/sexual-liberation-in-public-schools

7. Susannah Luthi, "California Moves Toward Giving Therapists Unconditional Power To 'Emancipate' 12 Year Olds From Their Parents", *The Washington Free Beacon*, 2023
https://freebeacon.com/california/california-assembly-bill-665/

8. K Bhattacharjee, "Efforts underway to mainstream 'Drag Queen Story Hours' in India, 'volunteers' from classes 9 to 12 being trained to further gender identity politics", *OpIndia*, 2020
https://www.opindia.com/2020/07/drag-queen-story-hour-gender-identity-politics-tagore-international-school-nazariya-qfrg/

9. NCERT, *Inclusion of Transgender Children in School Education*, Training Material 2020-21
https://archive.org/details/inclusion-of-transgender-children-in-school-education_202111

10. US Embassy India, *via Twitter*, 2023
https://twitter.com/USAndIndia/status/1672454503965294593

11. Noah Percy, *The Age of Consent and Its Discontents: French Intellectuals and the Reform of Sexual Violence Law, 1968–1982*, Thesis, 2022
https://history.columbia.edu/wp-content/uploads/sites/20/2022/05/Percy-Noah_Senior-Thesis-Update.pdf

12. Michel Foucault, *The Care of the Self: Volume 3*, 1984
https://archive.org/details/historyofsexuali03fouc

13. Janna Anderson, Lee Rainie and Emily A. Vogels, *Experts Say the 'New Normal' in 2025 Will Be Far More Tech-Driven, Presenting More Big Challenges*, Pew Research Centre 2021
https://www.pewresearch.org/internet/2021/02/18/experts-say-the-new-normal-in-2025-will-be-far-more-tech-driven-presenting-more-big-challenges/

14. Alexander Solzhenitsyn, *Speech delivered at Lucs-sur-Boulogne*, 1993 http://la.revue.item.free.fr/nouvelles_de_chretiente141_090808.htm

15. Wendell Berry, *Sex, Economy, Freedom and Community*, 2002

16. Jodie A.O'Gorman, "Exploring the Longhouse and Community in Tribal Society", *American Antiquity*, 2010 https://go.gale.com/ps/i.do?p=AONE&u=googlescholar&id=GALE|A234934200&v=2.1&it=r&sid=AONE&asid=008dfed7

17. M.N. Srinivas, *The Remembered Village*, 1976 https://archive.org/details/rememberedvillage0000srin

18. Clarissa Pinkola Estes, *Women Who Run With The Wolves*, 1992

19. Nithin Sridhar, *Menstruation Across Cultures*, 2021

20. Sinu Joseph, *Varna Vidya*, 2023

21. Wendell Berry, *The Unsettling of America*, 1977

22. Emily Bazelon, "The Battle over Gender Therapy", *New York Times Magazine*, 2022 https://www.nytimes.com/2022/06/15/magazine/gender-therapy.html

23. "The world's first artificial womb for humans", *BBC News*, 2019 https://www.bbc.com/news/av/health-50056405

24. Marilyn Frye, *The Politics of Reality*, 1983 https://archive.org/details/encyclopediaofra0001unse_o0i9/page/344/mode/1up

25. Judith Butler, *Gender Trouble*, 1990

26. Tim Wigmore, "Quinton de Kock will take the knee – and explains his U-turn", *The Telegraph*, 2021 https://www.telegraph.co.uk/cricket/2021/10/28/quinton-de-kock-will-take-knee-explains-u-turn/

27. @KateShemirani via Twitter posting video from Los Angeles https://twitter.com/KateShemirani/status/1665762669792489472

28. @DrLoupis via Twitter posting a video of Jeffrey Marsh
    https://twitter.com/DrLoupis/status/1669624172786462732

29. J.K. Rowling, *J.K. Rowling Writes about Her Reasons for Speaking out on Sex and Gender Issues*, 2020
    https://www.jkrowling.com/opinions/j-k-rowling-writes-about-her-reasons-for-speaking-out-on-sex-and-gender-issues/

30. Carol Hay, "Who Counts as a Woman?", *The New York Times* 2019
    https://www.nytimes.com/2019/04/01/opinion/trans-women-feminism.html

31. Laboria Cuboniks, *Xenofeminism: A Politics for Alienation*, 2015
    https://laboriacuboniks.net/wp-content/uploads/2019/11/20150612-xf_layout_web.pdf

32. Jeff Schogol, "New concerns that lower fitness standards fuel disrespect for women", *Marine Times*, 2017
    https://www.marinecorpstimes.com/off-duty/military-fitness/2017/05/21/new-concerns-that-lower-fitness-standards-fuel-disrespect-for-women/

33. Ewan Palmer, "Laura Ingraham Guest Says Trans People Will 'Destroy' Gender Norms to Create 'New Species'—'Human and Part Machine', *Newsweek*, 2019
    https://www.newsweek.com/laura-ingraham-podcast-trans-people-species-machine-paul-nathanson-1377906

34. *A Pathway to Equitable Math Instruction Dismantling Racism in Mathematics Instruction*, Equitablemath.org Curriculum, 2021
    https://equitablemath.org/wp-content/uploads/sites/2/2020/11/1_STRIDE1.pdf

35. José Esteban Muñoz, *Cruising Utopia*, 2009

36. Jennifer Miller, "Thirty Years of Queer Theory" in *Introduction To LGBTQ+ Studies*, University of New York Press, 2022

37. https://milnepublishing.geneseo.edu/introlgbtqstudies/chapter/thirty-years-of-queer-theory/

38. Christopher F. Rufo, "The Real Story behind Drag Queen Story Hour", *City Journal*, 2022
https://www.city-journal.org/article/the-real-story-behind-drag-queen-story-hour

39. Harper Keenan and Lil Miss Hot Mess, "Drag pedagogy: The playful practice of queer imagination in early childhood", *Curriculum Enquiry*, 2021
https://www.tandfonline.com/doi/full/10.1080/03626784.2020.1864621

40. Christopher F. Rufo, "The Real Story behind Drag Queen Story Hour", *City Journal*, 2022
https://www.city-journal.org/article/the-real-story-behind-drag-queen-story-hour

41. Tony Kinnet, "BREAKING: California Bill Would Charge Any Parent Who Doesn't Affirm Transgenderism With 'Child Abuse'", The Daily Signal, 2023
https://www.dailysignal.com/2023/06/09/california-bill-would-charge-any-parent-doesnt-affirm-transgenderism-child-abuse/

42. Lauren Sloss, "Meet the first woman to sail the 'Voyage for Madmen'", *The New York Times*, 2023
https://www.nytimes.com/2023/06/14/travel/kirsten-neuschafer-golden-globe.html

Section 5 | Chapter 5.5

MAN, WOMAN AND MACHINE – PART III
Tech-State and Machine Consciousness

Maragatham, 2023

Prologue

Readers who have read my earlier essay, "The Mechanics of our Journey from the Dharmic Tree of Life to the Western Tech-State" (Section 5, Chapter 5.1), will have a sense of what I mean when I use the term Tech-State. It represents the totalizing impulse of Western Modernity, when high technology, global corporations and willing nation-States form a nexus of totalitarian control over the lives of individuals and communities. In return, it offers us addictions that serve as distractions and the annual week-long holiday at the beach. We are all so steeped in this version of reality that we find it hard to recognize or question. While it has us, men and women, fighting over rights, responsibilities, alimony and patriarchy, the truth of what is happening to us is very different indeed (which I will come to shortly).

This worldview of the Tech-State has been institutionalized and propagandized for more than a century by the Western system that many of us now pass through. Samo Burja writes in his 2021 essay "The End of Industrial Society" how school as we know it was invented to prepare children in advance for the shock of the un-natural conveyor-belt industrial world that they are being primed to join:

> The new proceduralized organizations of the 19th-century industrial city further increased demand for human capital of the industrial type. This necessitated mass schooling, which tried to proceduralize some of the same cultural and physiological shock experienced when entering an industrial city.[1]

Today, most of us believe implicitly that we are more free, that our lives are infinitely better than those of our ancestors and that the high-tech world we live in is an inherent good. We also tacitly acknowledge that though the journey to this place was littered with immorality it was all worth it because it was for the ultimate common good of mankind. By taking to heart this sentiment, we have become the zombies of Progress. To us, the slavery of Africans, the genocide of Native Americans, the re-education camps of Australia, the theft of entire continents through manifest destiny, the pillaging of entire countries through colonialism, the gassing of Jews in the Holocaust, and the rape of *Bhu Devi* that made it all possible are all part of the 'normal' course of history, a 'phase' we had to go through. We assume that we have outgrown that period of adolescence and that we will never have to pay an emotional price for that journey.

Today, the results of this pernicious sequence of events (that has resulted in the high-tech corporatized world we live in) are so ubiquitous that the worldview they represent has been universalized, even in our minds, not just as the brutal history of the West, but as the history of *all* humankind. When the word civilization is used in casual conversation, we implicitly mean Western civilization. And indeed, the longer we unquestioningly feed from the bowl of goodies that this immoral history has made available, we too become complicit in its actions (though our own ancestors were its victims) and will face its *karmic* consequences. The Hopi people refer to this current condition of ours as *Koyaanisqatsi* or 'world out of balance'.

As heirs to other civilizations and ways of being, we cannot limit ourselves to merely being satisfied with running in the White Man's race and aiming to do better than him (as China aspires to). It is important that we find a reasonable way to incorporate our traditional life patterns as a major part of our lives even as we find a way to participate in Western Modernity while shaping it from within, away from its genocidal roots, and towards a genuine *Dharmic* end, so as to ensure that all that suffering was not in vain.

This, in my opinion, is the only possible justification and course of action we *Dharmics* can adopt that is even halfway noble and honest.

Man, Woman and Tech-State

A recent reference to Child Rights in a conversation got me thinking about Rights in general. I had already been thinking along these lines by the time I wrote

"No Branches without Roots — An Understanding of Hindu Social Structure from the Outside In" (Chapter 4.2 of this book), and my thoughts have since been further clarified. Despite what our brainwashed minds are led to believe in today's world, there is, in fact, no such thing as a Right. There is the Gods' given world and that's all there is. Everything else has been made up by us. In the traditional way of seeing things, we have duties that we perform in gratitude and reciprocity for having been graced with Life. When we perform our duties, we gain the respect of our peers and social privileges are accorded to us by our fellows. This was basically how the world functioned for a hundred thousand years at least.

All of a sudden, some three hundred years ago, under the influence of industrial surplus, the idea of Rights started to gain traction. But it is only in the last eighty years (post the Nuremberg Trials) that this strange idea has come to be universalized. In fact, it is through the idea of Rights that Western society attempts to come to terms with the horror of its own depravity and institutionalized rapaciousness. Rights are a mechanism by which the State is supposed to protect us culturally naked, ordinary citizens from the excesses of the industrial behemoth we live within. Unfortunately, this idea of Rights that was supposed to protect us from the excesses of the industrial system are today used undemocratically to take down what little remains of our regressive traditions and communities, while the State itself is unabashedly hand in glove with the military-industrial complex it is supposed to maintain a check on. This lens for viewing our predicament is, unfortunately, almost non-existent in India, and the idea of Rights is now second only to the IPL in its hold over people's minds. Today, no matter where in India one goes, one will be faced with this idea that people have Rights, and when those Rights are denied, revolution is a legitimate response.

A serious person has to ask two questions:

1. Where did these Rights come from?
2. What are the underlying values that determine the nature of those Rights?

Robert H Bork writes in his 2003 book, *Coercing Virtue*:

> This book, however, will concentrate on what seems to me the single most powerful influence aiding and abetting all other forces: the recent ascendancy

almost everywhere of activist, ambitious, and imperialistic judiciaries. Oddly enough, the role of courts in displacing self-government and forcing new moralities has not triggered a popular backlash. Courts have been and remain far more esteemed than the democratic institutions of government, even though the courts systematically frustrate the popular will as expressed in laws made by elected representatives.

It is apparent even to a casual observer that, everywhere, democracy and indigenous moral traditions are in retreat. Even as more nations adopt democratic forms of government, reforms are undermined by other internal developments. This is particularly noticeable in older, advanced democracies. Increasingly, the power of the people of Western nations to govern themselves is diluted, and their ability to choose the moral environment in which they live is steadily diminished.[2]

Imagine, if this is how Western Conservatives feel about their current state of affairs (knowing full well that the undemocratic laws they are subject to are an off-shoot of their very own historical and religious evolution), how much more pathetic must be the situation of the traditionalist citizens of countries such as India, who far from being able to articulate an intellectual response to the internationalization and liberalization of law, are unable, in their illiteracy, to even understand the consequences of the constitutional values that they have been led to foist upon themselves.

So then, where do these Rights come from?

The obvious answer is that they come from the entity that is willing to enforce the maintenance of those Rights (we can call this entity the patriarch). So, what is that entity in modern times? It is the centralized Tech-State. We are now left with the conclusion that the centralized Tech-State is our patriarch in modern society. This super-patriarch will obviously accept no upstarts who challenge its diktat, whether individual men or women (in families) or community leaders (in communities).

And what is the nature of that Tech-State? Apart from being technological, centralized and prone to surveillance of individuals, the overwhelming feature of the Tech-State is its propensity for Liberalism and Universalism. It stands against the particular, the organic, the human and humane. It stands against Tradition and Community. It stands against Culture and Identity itself.

Again, Robert H Bork provides an explanation:

> It may not be immediately obvious why the New Class should be overwhelmingly liberal in outlook. Perhaps the best explanation was offered long ago by Max Weber – Intellectuals characteristically display a strong desire for meaning in life, and for them meaning requires transcendent principles and universalistic ideals. These qualities were once conferred by religion, but religion is not an option for intellectuals; the only alternative is the utopian outlook of the Left. Once the hard-core varieties of the Left were put out of favor by World War II and the Cold War, the intelligentsia turned to the softer and eclectic socialism of modern liberalism.
>
> As a political and cultural philosophy or impulse, conservatism or traditionalism offers no comparable transcendentalism, no prospect of utopia. Conservatism is infrequently an option for the intelligentsia; the New Class despises the few conservatives to be found in its ranks more than it does those whom it regards as the retrograde "unwashed"—the general public. Conservative pragmatism, especially its concern with particularity—respect for difference, circumstance, tradition, history, and the irreducible complexity of human beings and human societies—does not qualify as a universal principle, but competes with and holds absurd the idea of a utopia achievable in this world.[3]

I guess this is all old-hat for people in the social sciences but for my own clarity let me recap.

The entity that is willing and able to enforce the maintenance of Rights can be called the patriarch. The super-patriarch in modern times is the Tech-State. The Tech-State is fundamentally liberal and universal in nature. It uses high technology, surveillance and an increasingly centralized bureaucracy to disintegrate traditional community and local economies while maintaining its stranglehold on atomized individuals by controlling the airwaves, providing pleasurable distractions and establishing its value system through the Rights-based discourse. The Rights-based discourse is interesting in that it gives people the impression that they are being cared for and their interests are being protected, while in fact the entity that is doing the protecting is the one undermining our communities, monitoring our actions, breaking our local economies and indoctrinating our children. It's a bit like the Tamil Nadu government providing free home appliances to women subsidized by the money it makes from selling booze to their husbands. It's a sleight of hand, that at first sight looks like a win-win, but in fact is a lose-lose. And eventually the realization hits that the entity which is willing to enforce the maintenance of Rights has (ultimate) ownership over people who accept those Rights.

In the case of children, this matter is most unresolved. Now that patriarchy is defined around the idea of maintenance of Rights rather than the performance of duties, are we actually saying that the State, as super-patriarch and the entity willing to enforce the maintenance of Rights, has more ownership over our children than parents (who perform the duties)? If the answer is yes, it represents a tectonic shift in how humans have thought about the nature of human life and human relationships. Even if not stated in such clear terms, the existence of governmental institutions such as Child Care Services in the West makes clear what the tacit assumptions of the Tech-State are—that parents are merely guardians of their children and the State reserves the right to claim ownership[4] over them at any time based on an alien value system of its own making.

Now, we ask some hard questions.

Is it better that 'ownership' of actual human people lies with other human people who are capable of compassion and with whom we have a symbiotic relationship, i.e.: Community? Or, is it better that it lies with an un-human and indifferent entity over whom we have zero emotional control? If there needs to be a system in place to serve as a check against the worst forms of human debasement (violence, trafficking, rape etc.) is it not better for the long-term benefit of the human soul that these checks and balances are provided by community and not the State? That's exactly how our ancients imagined society. Individual excesses are checked by family, family excesses are checked by community and community excesses are checked by a multi-community *panchayat*—and only after that does the State come into the picture.

Today, American Conservative voters nod in agreement as Vivek Ramaswamy's war cry resonates across city halls. "The nuclear family is the best form of governance known to Mankind." But what Vivek fails to do is to extrapolate this maxim further to include community and super-community, all of which are responsible for bringing stability, peace, prosperity, continuity and well-being. This was the matrix that classical Bharat developed— *kutumba, kula, jaati, sampradaya*—all of which were free from direct State control. We have been schooled to see these social formulations as constraints when in fact they are the guarantors of our liberty and the guardians of our identities. Sohrab Ahmari writes in his review of Josh Hawley's *Manhood: The Masculine Virtues America Needs*:

> Hawley reiterates the paradoxical wisdom, common to both the classical tradition and historic Christianity, that freedom and restraint aren't enemies, but friends. Or as he puts it, that "order and self-command are not opposite to liberty but are liberty's prerequisites. Freedom and character go hand-in-hand."[5]

In other words, making a promise may well be the work of an individual but, very often, the keeping of that promise is a community's work.

This idea of Liberty being linked to Community and Duty ties in directly with what have come to be known as Women's Rights. Women today derive their Rights from the State, not from their community or tradition. There is a sense among women that they have been freed from the control of men and society. But this is a shallow reading of the situation. They have traded a certain type of intimate and symbiotic relationship with their men and their communities for an indifferent and mechanical relationship with the State. Is this what they want? Do they want to live in a patriarchy of this un-feeling, un-human entity? Have we come to such a pass that we trust the State (with its foreign values) to be more just than our communities and families?

Men, of course, have no Rights because men are supposed to make their own way in the world. In fact, an optimistic reading of this arrangement is that those groups who have no Rights are groups which are free. The State may screw with them, but they are, in fact, free (in limited but real ways). Any groups that demand Rights or are given Rights by the State are groups which are expected to surrender their autonomy to the State. They start behaving like vassals of the State who will never rise up against it because they derive their personhood from it. One can see this all over rural Bharat. Formerly fiercely autonomous groups today behave like puppy dogs seeking governmental favours, unwilling to even raise a finger to fix the roads and drains in their own villages. Their entire raison d'être now is no longer their traditional work, or the upholding of tradition, or the upkeep of their sacred spaces, but the search for the latest holy grail—the governmental job with incentivized laziness and perpetual pension.

In recent times (with the widespread availability of appropriate high technology), the Tech-State apparatus has realized that this is an easy way to quell dissent. This is why the State is constantly trying to expand its sphere of influence by dishing out dole, subsidies and special privileges to more and more groups who it chooses to define as 'victims'. This is the way it subjugates us; this is the way it buys our loyalty, votes, compliance and silence. Of course, this process is a two-way street. The more the State subsidizes and incentivizes victimhood, the greater the tendency there has been among human groups to claim victimhood status.

Thinking (and feeling) women need to reconsider this situation. If it is liberty (in the original sense) they want, it has to be earned in conjunction with—and by making a fresh compact with—men. What they have now is *not* liberty; it's a gilded cage erected by a mechanical master who will not even enquire their name, let alone love them or give their lives for them.

Perhaps women are not interested in true liberty and find that they prefer the distant tyranny of the State better than the sometimes-intimate tyranny of men.

Even if this is the case, we have to ask what the State stands for? Why should Hindu women agree to be the subjects of an entity that stands for Western values built on the backs and blood of our Hindu ancestors, on the colonization of our lands, on the enslavement of our ancestors, on the genocide of entire continents worth of people, on the violence of the World Wars, on the skeletal remains of Jews killed in Germany? Is this the nameless entity our women want to side with?

The centralized Tech-State is an entity that functions to privilege two fundamental principles—Machine and Market. All women (and men) who align with it will find themselves pulled into its slipstream, slaves to efficiency and money, willing to sell and be sold, with none of the uplifting, human, humane, divine impulse of a Savitri or a Nachiketa.

Our shift from the natural communal world to the world of laws and systems has not just changed our physical and institutional life, it has caused an epistemological upheaval. Who are we? Who do we owe loyalty to? Who do we protect? Who do we turn to for protection? Who do we love? Who do we bring up? Where does our life force come from? how do we imagine ourselves in connection with each other and the universe? Mary Harrington writes:

> We need to re-imagine marriage as the smallest possible unit of resistance to overwhelming economic, cultural, and political pressure to be lone atoms in a market. Households formed on this model can work together both economically and socially on the common business of living, whether that's agricultural, artisanal, knowledge-based, or a mix of all these. This is an essential precondition for the sustainable survival of human societies.[6]

She then goes on to opine that the biggest obstacle to this vision is an outdated mindset that looks down on all duties beyond personal fulfilment and sees our relationships as transactions and means for ego gratification rather than as "enabling conditions for solidarity."[6]

Her words resonate with many of the things I've been saying when she points out that what looks like progress is only seen as positive because we are ignoring the costs. The comforts we have gained over the last 300 years were built on the "backs of plundered, colonized, and enslaved peoples, and at the cost of incalculable environmental degradation."[6]

On a positive note, she urges that:

> ... we're not powerless. We don't have to stumble blindly into an age of technological upheaval with a worldview shaped by a set of industrial-era memes that are now making things worse. Just as we have in the past, we can and must once again re-evaluate how men and women can be human together.[6]

We have entered a radically new and un-human way of being with each other, if we surrender our sovereignty to the nameless State. We need to think of Rights and restrictions again, if need be, but also the nature of the entities that will enforce them. We need to humanize those entities. In the old days that system was called community and family, and the restrictions were called *samskaaras* and promises—of humans, for humans, and by humans. Nathanael Blake writes in his 2019 essay, "The Romance of Ordinary Marriage":

> Our freedom is not realized in the possibility that we might **do anything**, but in doing what we have **said we will do**. Human freedom is consummated in the voluntary self-limitation of the promise made and fulfilled.[7]

The global Tech-State has long passed beyond the pale. It is too humongous, too homogenous, too indifferent, too disloyal (as COVID has shown) to represent us for anything essentially human.

A Clarification: People who are not very familiar with my work may conclude that, by advocating against the idea of Rights, I am a supporter of a world where *matsya nyaya* prevails. That is not what I intend. As Hindus, we need to draw a distinction between the Western idea of Rights granted to us by a supervising authority (thereby becoming a force against Liberty, Tradition and Community), and the *Sanatana* vision of a decent society which has been passed on to us by our ancestors and received directly from our civilizational archetypes. It is by asking ourselves "What would Shri Rama do?", "What would Sita Mata do?", "What would Shri Krishna do?", "What would Durga Mata do?", "What would a Mahaperiyava advise?", "What would a Raja Bhoja have done?" that we generate ethical action. Our ethical failures in recent times are not because our culture is bad (as our rivals are keen to imply), but because the threads that bind us to our archetypes have grown frayed over the last three hundred years. I have covered the Hindu approach to ethics in an earlier essay, "The Hindu Traditionalist: Culture, Morality and Reform" (Section 3, Chapter 3.2 of this book).

The Hindu response to the liberal, globalized Rights-based order is in fact a deeply civilizational State that incentivizes archetypal behaviour. Without that, we literally do not have access to our indigenous ethicality and all the lies they have made up about us will indeed come to pass. A civilizational State is thus not merely a means for protecting ourselves, it is a means for us to actually *be* ourselves—our best selves.

Man, Woman and Machine

Very simply, the industrial dynamic describes a turn in human affairs when the vast majority of human activity changed from being cyclical to being linear. Our age-old impulse to **Maintenance** was replaced by an impulse to **Progress**. Our fundamental ontology shifted from Balance and Contentment to Imbalance and Disruption, and our self-perception from Divinity to Materiality, the world no longer alive to the breath of the Gods but to the scream and buzz of the Machine.

Men were the first to fall into the slipstream of this paradigm. High on crude oil, they imagined it was they who controlled the machines of their own making, little realizing that, as the machines grew in sophistication, they were being replaced altogether. All the special powers of men were superseded in one dramatic century. Their physical capability, their analytical capability and their navigational capability were all superseded by machines, ironically of their own making. Man now has the power of the Gods at his disposal but he himself is no more than a pusher of buttons. No longer useful in any primal way, no longer spiritual in any essential way, he is unable to exercise his Gods-given agency. And if he does not have a job as a pusher of buttons, he lies around like an obsolete piece of machinery, no longer valued, sometimes exploited, sometimes ignored, always growing in resentment. This is what we find in vast swathes of the discontented masculine world today. The world no longer needs men *as men*. Mary Harrington writes:

> There are plenty of articles out there about the mental health crisis among men, but invariably the prescription is that men should behave more like women and then perhaps they'd be less miserable. That's getting it completely backwards. The reason men are miserable is because they are told not to socialise like men... [8]

She clarifies her stance further when she urges women to step back and "let men have their own spaces."[8] Our failure to do so, she predicts, will just lead to men getting "more miserable, lonelier, more resentful, and then more hostile towards women."[8] And ultimately, she warns:

> There is, I think, a strong feminist case for women just stepping back. Otherwise, we don't stand a chance of ever recovering solidarity between the sexes, which is a vital precondition for surviving cyborg theocracy together, as embodied human persons.[8]

The age of the Machine was no doubt birthed by men. But these men were not men in the traditional sense. They no longer saw themselves as protectors of a world in balance, making vows and performing deeds dedicated to the Gods. Instead, human history witnessed the emergence of a peculiar kind of man who aimed to be a God by stamping his authority over a defeated *Bhu Devi*. From the traditional point of view, it would not be accurate to label such a creature as man. A man is not merely his biological self, but also his cultural self. So, let us call this new creature Machine-Man. And in the Machine-World, Machine-Man is but a subset, a cog, a resource... but he accepts his lot because he is offered a seemingly limitless surplus (of exploitative origin) in exchange.

The story of women *is* a little different, but ultimately the same. For a brief while (in the West) women found themselves closeted in their husband's homes, cut off from the sorority of agrarian, communal life that existed earlier and unable to join the exterior fraternity of Machine-Men. This is the Jane Austen phase of Western history. This unsustainable and un-natural situation boiled over and women too slowly, but steadily, started streaming into the imbalanced world of machines. It certainly did not make sense that Machine-Men had limitless surplus at their command, while women were expected to live a life of domesticated limits.

This entry by women into the exterior Machine-World had important consequences.

1. Women became Machine-Women.
2. The old world of Balance and the idea of Equality as Equivalence was rendered extinct.
3. The old type of communal sorority and femininity as we knew it was over.
4. The empowerment of women in a world of increasing technological sophistication was underway. And as machines grew in sophistication, all of men's special powers were neutralized by them, thereby creating a level playing field for women in the exterior world. After all, anyone, regardless of sex, could be a button-pusher.
5. Women, who still had their special powers (birthing, nurture, intuition, relational intelligence, dexterity) intact, began to believe that they had won the battle of the sexes, or at least could sense that victory was near, and that they would soon rule both the interior world and the exterior world.

"Women have won, and men just need to learn to deal with it," screams the feminist on social media.

But have they really?

Consider first, the paradox of women's entry into the Machine-World. It was the emergence of the Machine-World that helped create the level playing field for women in the exterior world. It is also due to that Machine-World that the old world of balance and the communal, feminine world of the interior was lost. The Machine-World is therefore, ironically, simultaneously responsible for both the apparent emancipation of women and the obliteration of woman-ness. As happened with men, women too will become Machine-Women. And since there is no apparent difference between Machine-Men and Machine-Women, we can simply say that men and women have been replaced by Machine-People.

Consider also the trajectory of technological growth. As the 20th Century was the graveyard for the special powers of man (physical, analytical and navigational), the 21st Century will be the graveyard for the special powers of women. Birthing, nurture, human relational intelligence and dexterity will all be superseded by the coming machines of biotech and AI. External wombs are already being tested[9] as are conversational AI and companion robots.

When these technologies finally take off, later this century, we will know that neither men nor women have won. We will have both lost, and the Machine-World will have won.

Only two options remain for human-minded people:

1. A return to a low-tech world of Balance, or
2. A conscious effort to bring Balance into the Machine-World by setting limits, figuring out roles and creating space for the use of our sex-specific special powers.

If the Machine-World is not consciously humanized and bi-genderized, it will de-humanize and de-genderize us all.

Within the Machine-World, honourable men and women have abandoned Balance and surrendered all their special powers to the Machine. They are now, literally, equal. We are all equal button pushers. The arrival of this stage of Modernity has had some very interesting physical and physiological effects. Human fertility has dropped.[10] Homosexuality has risen.[11] Transgenderism has risen.[12] A culture of hermaphroditism is slowly metamorphosizing into a hermaphrodite species. This entire process of transformation is catalyzed by Machine Consciousness. The hermaphrodites *need* the Machine because they have lost all their special powers. They can now no longer survive without the Machine-World. This turn is expectedly enshrined in the value system of such a society. Technological progress is deified. Babies themselves will be made either through cloning or incubated in artificial wombs with their genes adjusted for equal IQ and equal beauty.[13] The line between Man and Woman grows dim just as surely as the line between Human and Machine grows dim. Again, Mary Harrington is accurate, when she writes:

> What I mean by 'cyborg theocracy' is the moral and political order which emerges from the belief that we are most emancipated when our condition of freedom is underwritten by technology.[14]

The "cyborg era", she says, is a push by the powers that be to eliminate human nature altogether through technology. At this current point in history though, those efforts haven't been fully successful, they have merely "reordered human nature to the market, frustrating it in the process, leaving it neutered and commodified."[14]

She explains that the "Ground zero of the cyborg theocracy" is the cancelling of all possible bodily integrity. The Trans phenomenon, she says, is not to be read as a malign conspiracy but as evidence for the disembodied nature of the world we live in today.

> ... people so radically dissociated from their own bodies that they've come to believe that they can only reach any sense of fulfilment by re-modelling their bodies to bring them in line with identities which they imagine they've concocted ex nihilo, but which more often than not are the products of some f*cked up online Girardian mimesis.[14]

Decades ago, Wendell Berry was already describing this phenomenon, albeit from a slightly different starting point:

> It is obvious how much skill and industry either partner may put into such a household and what good economic result such work might have, and yet it is the kind of work now frequently held in contempt. Men in general were the first to hold it in contempt as they departed from it for the sake of the professional salary or the hourly wage, and it is now held in contempt by feminists.[15]

He points with characteristic clarity to how farm wives who help run a household economy are often asked by feminists "But what is it that you do?"[15] by which they tacitly imply that there is something "better" to be done out there than caring for and managing a household and a farm.

Pointing beyond the obvious to the structural framework that holds that derisive worldview in place, he asks, "What is the purpose of this technological progress? What higher aim do we think it is serving?"

And he answers provocatively with a series of negatives:

> Surely the aim cannot be the integrity or happiness of our families, which we have made subordinate to the education system, the television industry, and the consumer economy. Surely it cannot be the integrity or health of our communities, which we esteem even less than we esteem our families. Surely it cannot be love of our country, for we are far more concerned about the desecration of the flag than we are about the desecration of our land...[15]

The higher aim of progress, he pinpoints, is more money and more ease. And our greed for these two goods we have disguised and justified by a "cultish faith in the 'future'"[15]

In contrast to that worldview, he stresses that

> A good future is implicit in the soils, forests, grasslands, marshes, deserts, mountains, rivers, lakes and oceans that we have now, and in the good things of human culture that we have now. We have no need to contrive and dabble at "the future of the human race"; we have the same pressing need that we have always had – to love, care for & teach our children.[15]

Obviously, a person such as Wendell Berry advocates for a rejection of the industrial logic altogether and a return to the logic of agriculture and the idea of Equality as Equivalence. Given that such an outcome is never going to happen in the medium term, we must ask what are the strategies we can use to bring the idea of Balance into the Industrial Age. It's funny that the same question that I have been asking with regard to economics and the environment should find expression again when I'm thinking about Man-Woman relationships. Ultimately, it's all about what is sustainable and what type of human behavioural patterns are aligned with sustainability (economic, cultural and well-being).

It is in the presence of natural limits that the idea of roles and the honouring of difference appear to us to be decent, beautiful, balanced... and, indeed, equal. In the absence of those natural limits, set adrift in a world of *apparent* limitlessness, those same constraints start to appear oppressive, obscene... and unequal. And within the morality of this apparently limit-free world (the morality of surplus as I've called it before), humans start to seek Equality in homogeneity, in the erasure of difference, in the abandonment of their roles and identities.

"We are equally free from constraints" and "We are equally oppressed" are the grand themes of the Machine-World's zeitgeist.

Epilogue

I recall reading and noting the following:

> Do not allow mere ideas to supersede the sanctity of your vision. You must do what it takes to achieve your vision and generally it calls for sacrifice. This is an ancient understanding of the world that pervades all human endeavours including marriage. And marriage is also the building block of culture and civilization all of which are visions too. Damage to the vision of family and marriage causes damage to the grander vision as well.[16]

In this vivid call to action, we see a reflection of how our ancients saw *swadharma* as that sacrificial fire where the dictates of the ego and the desires of the body are offered in order to appease the transcendental principle of the ultimate reality. In Hindu thought, real is not that which 'materially exists' but is 'that which is eternal and immutable'. Therefore, even in our time here on *Bhu Devi*, society is organized to point towards, to celebrate and to mimic that higher reality. The long term is always given precedence over the short-term. That which is stable is always given precedence over that which is fickle. That which has wide benefit is always given precedence over that which benefits the few. Actions that lead to the extinguishment of our egos and the emotional roller-coaster are given precedence over actions that fan those flames. It is in this perspective that we, as Hindus, must view marriage. *Vivaaha* is a force for stability, a place of security for children to grow up in, a vehicle for the performance of specified rituals that provide purpose and sharpen resolve, a crucible where the couple's commitment to the idea of commitment is tested, a metaphorical space where a man and a woman not only bring forth new life but also aim to establish, here on *Bhu Devi*, over multiple lifetimes if need be, *that* which exists in *Kailasa* and *Vaikuntha*.

References and Links

1. Samo Burja, "The End of Industrial Society", *Palladium Mag*, 2021 https://www.palladiummag.com/2021/03/24/the-end-of-industrial-society/

2. Robert H Bork, *Coercing Virtue*, 2003

3. Ibid.

4. Upala Sen, "Cradle. Snatched.", *The Telegraph Online* 2022 https://www.telegraphindia.com/culture/cradle-snatched-indian-couple-in-berlin-had-their-child-taken-away-by-german-protection-services-the-telegraph-talks-to-them-and-other-parents-about-a-disturbing-first-world-trend/cid/1877423

5. Sohrab Ahmari, *A Nation in Search of Men*, 2023 (paraphrasing Josh Hawley, *Manhood: The Masculine Virtues America Needs*, 2023) https://www.theamericanconservative.com/a-nation-in-search-of-men/

6. Mary Harrington, *Counting the Cost of Progress*, 2023 https://www.plough.com/en/topics/justice/social-justice/counting-the-cost-of-progress

7. Nathanael Blake, "The Romance of Ordinary Marriage", *The Public Discourse*, 2018. https://www.thepublicdiscourse.com/2018/03/20926/

8. Mary Harrington, "The Reactionary Feminist Fight against Cyborg Theocracy", *The European Conservative*, 2023 https://europeanconservative.com/articles/interviews/the-reactionary-feminist-fight-against-cyborg-theocracy-mary-harrington-and-sebastian-morello-in-conversation/

9. "What if women never had to give birth again", *BBC Reel*, 2022 https://www.bbc.com/reel/video/p0bmqfk9/what-if-women-never-had-to-give-birth-again-

10. Nicola Davis, "Humans could face reproductive crisis as sperm count declines, study finds", *The Guardian*, 2022
    https://www.theguardian.com/society/2022/nov/15/humans-could-face-reproductive-crisis-as-sperm-count-declines-study-finds

11. Samantha Schmidt, "1 in 6 Gen-Z adults are LGBT. And this number could continue to grow", *The Washington Post*, 2021
    https://www.washingtonpost.com/dc-md-va/2021/02/24/gen-z-lgbt/

12. Azeen Ghorayshi, "Report reveals sharp rise in transgender young people in the US", *The New York Times*, 2022
    https://www.nytimes.com/2022/06/10/science/transgender-teenagers-national-survey.html

13. David Cyranoski, "The CRISPR-baby scandal. What's next for human gene editing?", *Nature*, 2019
    https://www.nature.com/articles/d41586-019-00673-1

14. Mary Harrington, "The Reactionary Feminist Fight against Cyborg Theocracy", *The European Conservative*, 2023 https://europeanconservative.com/articles/interviews/the-reactionary-feminist-fight-against-cyborg-theocracy-mary-harrington-and-sebastian-morello-in-conversation/

15. Wendell Berry, *Feminism, the Body and the Machine*, 1989 https://religioustech.org/wp-content/uploads/2019/09/Berry-Wendell-Feminism-the-Body-and-the-Machine.pdf

16. Unfortunately, I've lost the attribution to this quote. I can't find it anywhere on the Internet either. There is a possibility that it may be something I myself wrote earlier (given that this essay has been three years in the making), but upon reading it, some of the word choices are a little bit off my style. If there is another author of this quote, Thank you.

SECTION 6

ENQUIRY

Section 6 | Chapter 6.1

ARTHA, KAMA, MOKSHA AND A GAPING HOLE IN THE MIDDLE – PART I
So, which way Modern Hindus?

Maragatham, 2023

The correct, non-contradictory way to live is to accept the existential truth that *if we love something, we must also support the structures that make that thing possible.* If we claim to love the *Sanatana* religion, we have to inevitably also love the traditions that give shape to that religion. And once we love those traditions, we also have to inevitably support the social structures that are the vehicles for the maintenance of those traditions—that is, *Sanatana* Community.

It cannot be that we claim to love the *Sanatana* Religion but at the same time work to undermine *Sanatana* Tradition and *Sanatana* Community.

We would do well to remember this diagnosis, which has been accurate for 190 years:

> Our English schools are flourishing wonderfully...The effect of this education on the Hindoos is prodigious. No Hindoo who has received an English education ever continues to be sincerely attached to his religion. Some continue to profess it as a matter of policy. But many profess themselves pure Deists, and some embrace Christianity... It is my firm belief that, if our plans of education are followed up, there will not be a single idolater among the respectable classes in Bengal thirty years hence. And this will be effected without any efforts to proselytise, without the smallest interference with religious liberty, merely by the natural operation of knowledge and reflection. I heartily rejoice in this prospect.
>
> – Thomas Babbington Macaulay, *Letter to his Father*, 1836[1]

Connecting the Dots #1

What is *Sanatana* about something that keeps 'evolving'?

For the word *Sanatana* to have any meaning, either it must refer to a set of practices that are capable of standing the test of time, or a set of values or principles that are immutable even as practices change. So, if, as many of us believe, our practices have to 'evolve' in order to 'keep up with the times', then is it not vital that we state and define what the *rock-bottom un-changeable Dharmic values* are that we use as a metric to judge whether a change in practice can be considered evolution, or adjustment, or adaptation, or plain surrender?

Achcha chalo, let's assume that we have in fact defined a set of *Dharmic* values and principles that we hold dear and will never compromise with. Would we not now use those values to judge the times that we live in? When we do that, will we continue to 'keep up with the times' if the times themselves are revealed to be *adharmic* under the lens of our values? Would we not ask where 'the times' have arisen from, and what the core values of 'the times' are? Would we not enquire if those core values are foreign or *Dharmic* and, even if they are foreign, whether they are complimentary to *Sanatana* values or antithetical to them?

Some key questions remain unasked and unanswered in our mad rush towards the Western river.

If our religion is constantly evolving, and if our traditions are mere superstitious weakness, then we have to ask ourselves what the contours of this evolving religion are in the absence of our traditions. What would give it shape, form, exceptionality, definition and differentiation? Going further, if we are serious we have to ask what kind of post-traditional social institutions we need to design, and how we would ensure that they continue to reflect *Sanatana* metaphysics and aesthetics while holding its morality at the core?

For example, Ganapathy Sthapathi—who came from an ancestral lineage of *shilpis*, entered the modern educational universe and eventually founded the Government College of Architecture and Sculpture—is Mahabalipuram. Bharat now had an institution designed by a real practitioner to hold and nurture his ancestral knowledge. Any person with interest could now join the university and learn the art. So far so good. But what happened to that institution immediately after Sthapathi's death? The five-year course was reduced to a three-year course. All Sanskrit learning was scrapped (even though all the ancestral literature is in Sanskrit). The university has become a hotbed of political one-upmanship.

These are not my personal observations; these are observations made by a graduate whom I spoke to. There are two problems here that I instinctively see—one, the secularization of the knowledge tears it apart from its original intended context making it nothing more than a technical manual; and two, the steep drop in quality as a consequence of turning a sacred body of knowledge over to a set of politicians, technocrats and careerists.

So, how do we propose to tackle, very seriously, this issue of Hindu institution building in the modern world? How do we retain context without birth-based tradition, and how do we maintain excellence without community? Super important questions to answer.

Unless we answer these questions and demonstrate our solutions in practice, we have no business interfering with traditional social structures. On the other hand, if we don't even think it is important that we ask and answer these questions, well then... we modern Hindus are simply no longer Hindus in anything akin to the old way. We are all converts, either into Christianity Lite or some shade of Atheism (no matter the Ganesha *murthi* in our *puja* rooms).

If Tradition is to be erased, then we have nothing that holds Community together. In fact, many of us, depending on which shade of modern we are, already believe that *Sanatana* Community is evil, or backward, or regressive. So, we have now decided that along with Tradition, Community too must go. This brings us to the question "How do we, the adherents of this evolving religion, plan to transmit reverence for the contours of that religion to the next generation in the absence of Community?" What is going to be the institutional mechanism by which our values are going to be bequeathed to the next generation? Because, without that mechanism, we are looking at extinction in one generation. Are we going to design a Hindu Church or are we going to have once a week congregations and daily calls to prayer? Or are we smart enough to design something totally original here and now?

The phrase 'We must be strong' has two parts—'We' and 'Strong'. If we let go of the 'We' in our mad rush to be strong (or united, or to 'keep up with the times' or whatever), then what exactly would it be in aid of, if we are now no longer ourselves? If we are anyway going to stand against our ancestors' traditions and beliefs, then why not simply convert and be strong Muslims or united Christians? What's the difference? It is obvious that self-definition is the first step in this journey to strength. *Who* is it that wants to be strong? *Why* is it that entity wants to be strong?

Let us gather the courage to define the terms of our self-belief. Why do we care if we are Hindu or not? Raghava Krishna of Brhat Culture Engine writes:

> A moral conviction about the empathy of ancestors is the fundamental building block of a civilization. To know that our inheritance is a moral one.
>
> A sense of Gratitude. Gratitude creates the desire to preserve, belong and pass on.[2]

There are many among us today, well-wishers and *bhaktas* even, who claim to love the religion but not the traditions and communities. It has been argued that this new conception of our religion is essential for our adaptation to the modern world of technology and Individualism. Maybe it is, but let us be clear that it has nothing whatsoever to do with the religion of our ancestors.

The idea of Chesterton's 'fence' is useful at this juncture.

> "Do not remove a fence until you know why it was put up in the first place."
>
> Chesterton went on to explain why this principle holds true, writing that fences don't grow out of the ground, nor do people build them in their sleep or during a fit of madness. He explained that fences are built by people who carefully planned them out and "had some reason for thinking [the fence] would be a good thing for somebody." Until we establish that reason, we have no business taking an axe to it. The reason might not be a good or relevant one; we just need to be aware of what the reason is. Otherwise, we may end up with unintended consequences: second – and third-order effects we don't want, spreading like ripples on a pond and causing damage for years.[3]

To understand, therefore, the *use* of traditions as ancient as *Sanatana* traditions (and the need for social structures that held those traditions) requires much *sadhana* and insight. It is far better that we follow the lead of our *acharyas* on these matters rather than engage in individual-driven laissez-faire chop and change. It may well be that we fail to follow the traditions in this *Kali Yuga*, but let us not claim that whatever we do under the influence of Western memes of equality and choice, that suits our convenience, is in fact sanctioned by Tradition. It is not.

Traditions do change, but under the guiding hand of fully-engaged masters and practitioners, not you and me. How can someone not fully invested in a tradition be allowed to bring about changes in that tradition? It makes absolutely no sense. But the phenomenon of people who don't believe in the traditions but are ironically intent on appropriating or erasing the same traditions is a growing phenomenon. In the *Sanatana* world, where invitation rather than imposition prevails, if one has a problem with a particular tradition, one is free to leave, create a new tradition or engage in dialogue. That's exactly what *jaati* and *sampradaya* are for. But, unfortunately for us, *jaati*-nature is fast fading from our consciousness and the idea of change, instead of being accretional as it used to be, has become viral.

Take for example the Sabarimala issue where changes in a practice were demanded by people who had no *bhakti* in the practice (let alone knowledge of). So, were they believers or not? If they were believers, would they not want to show their belief by following the traditions? And if they were non-believers, then why do they care? This self-contradictory stance is taken by disruptors and a number of quasi-Hindus of the reformist bent of mind (including the Liberal Indian legislature and judiciary).

See the latest incursion into a purely Hindu religious space:

"Madras High Court : No more elephants for Tamil Nadu temples"[4]

If we are constantly using *foreign* ideals to judge and manipulate our *indigenous* traditions, then we really have to ask, "Who the hell are *we*?" If we were conscious *Sanatanis*, shouldn't this process of judgement be the other way around? Shouldn't we be judging Western ideals using *Dharmic* values and outcomes as benchmarks?

I have attempted to start this *purva paksha* in the essay *The Hindu Traditionalist – Culture, Morality and Reform Part II* (Section 3, Chapter 3.2 of this book).

Change—or evolution (if you will)—has to be positioned with respect to *Dharmic* archetypes, *Dharmic* values and/or *Dharmic* outcomes. It is only then that we can weigh what we are likely to lose against what we are likely to gain when we make those changes. And it is only then that evolution takes the form of *revitalization* rather than the erasure that goes by the name of *reform* today.

So, let us start to look at the unconscious and unconsidered changes that Hindu *samaj* has been subjected to in the last two centuries as 'Adaptation to Modernity' and not as 'Reform of Hinduism'. This simple verbal and mental trick will help change the way we approach these changes. We will start to see that adaptation may be necessary but it doesn't have to be packaged as 'progress' or 'reform'. We will start to see that adaptation has a purpose higher than merely serving as a doorway to Westernization... and that purpose is the long-term protection of all that is beautiful and eternal about our religion. No matter the compromises we may have to make, they all become worthwhile only if we retain a sense of that higher purpose, otherwise, we're on a one-way road to deracination. This requires the State to enter into a sense of its true purpose and become the upholder and builder (along with *Dharmic* private parties) of cultural institutions that hold and protect different parts of our essence.

From such a position of self-belief, *all* the issues that plague us will find resolution or compromise. But, if we start (under the influence of Western memes) with the assumption that *Sanatana* Community is an irredeemable evil, as many on both the Left and Right of the aisle do, then all attempts at 'reform' ultimately sow the seeds of erasure.

We are today on the brink of such an extinction.

The far-Left wants to deny *Sanatana* unity in their imagined pursuit of diversity, little realizing that it is that civilizational unity that has resulted in the continued survival of the diversity they so feverishly pursue. The far-Right, on the other hand, wants to erase *Sanatana* diversity in the pursuit of nationalist unity, little realizing that it is the maintenance of that diversity that has been at the heart of our *Sanatana* self-definition, and it is that identity that has lent us our differentiation in the face of Abrahamic cultural desertification. Only the ordinary Hindu knows that "we are one, but we are not the same, and we've got to carry each other."[5]

Connecting the Dots #2

Why are Christian and Islamic saints never called great *reformers*?

Why is this dubious honour reserved only for Hindu saints? From Gautama to Sai Baba, every one of our saints has been burdened with this distinction. Is *Sanatana Dharma* the only world religion that is in constant need of 'reform'? When a religion has been reformed for 2600 years (even as per Western timelines) would one not expect that it should be reformed by now? Have the reformers been so inefficient? Or the people so intransigent? So much so that we apparently even need a reformist constitution and a reformist judiciary! What gives?

If one starts with the a priori assumption that *Sanatana Dharma* is *inherently* oppressive, then one is left with no option but to reform the religion into extinction. This White Man's burden has unfortunately been internalized by generations of well-meaning reformist Hindus.

I have covered the entire phenomenon of *Reform* in an earlier essay: *The Hindu Traditionalist – Culture, Morality and Reform Part III* (Section 3, Chapter 3.3 of this book).

But one curious anomaly remains. The reformists do not want to *explicitly* extinguish the religion—they appear to want to usurp the mantle of the religion while cleansing it of its essence. They want ownership over our symbols without the responsibilities of the symbolisms. They want, for example, a Shri Rama without His *Ram Rajya*; a Mahaperiyava without his *Deivathin Kural*; a *Yoga* without '*Chitta Vritti Nirodah*'; they want control over our ancient *tirthas*, not for devotion but for tourism; they want control over our ancient temples, not to offer service as per the will of the Gods but to offer them as examples of social justice as per the will of American academia; they want the beauty of our traditions without the social structures that hold and honour those traditions. These are the people, on both sides of the political aisle, who want a freedom from direct British rule without freedom from British ideals and structures of governance that impose those ideals upon our communities. What they want, quite plainly, in the case of the Right, is a Hindu Rashtra without Hinduism... and, in the case of the Left, a Hinduism without Hindus. Now why would this be?

In my opinion, the answer lies in the curiously brainwashed state that modern Hindus find themselves in, post our final military defeat in 1857, a watershed year. What has come to be known as our *first* war for independence was (quite obviously) actually our *last* war for independence... and this curious inversion of nomenclature is at the heart of the paradox that is the modern Hindu.

For people who have internalized the universality and supremacy of Western ideals, we didn't become independent because we overthrew the British military and political yoke, but because we adopted their ideals in our Republic! For this set of people, obviously, 1857 became a starting point (and it is they who are responsible for the inversion of nomenclature). For them, it was in 1857 that we finally started to become 'free' by changing ourselves into proto-Europeans and imbibing the best ideals of that continent. For the rest of us ordinary Hindus, on the other hand, 1857 represents the final throw of dice (so far) for our indigenous aspirations.

Given our current lack of material power and intellectual clarity, everything that can possibly come now (at least in the medium term) is a hybrid solution—some Western beast with Hindu characteristics. Our battles today are about defining and protecting red lines. How much of this hybrid creature can we allow to be occupied by the West before we lose all sense of Self? It is in the light of this hybrid creature that we must see the efforts by reformists to usurp the mantle of *Sanatana Dharma* as an empty shell in which to fill the ideals of the French Revolution. For seventy-five years, the idea of India has been held up as superior to the idea of Pakistan, not because it was more original or more moral, but simply because it more closely adhered to Western ideals. Think about that. This is an absurdity that is well past its sell-by date.

Connecting the Dots #3

Why does the UK get to keep its monarchy and its State religion (Christianity) while telling us that they are great evils?

Why do Christians and Muslims get to keep control over their religious institutions, schools and proselytizing arms, while Hindu temples and schools remain shackled by social justice considerations and State control? Why are their holy books above reproach while our *shrutis* and *smritis* are not?

Why do we accept these power asymmetries like zombies, even seventy-five years after 'independence'?

There is only one answer—Secularism. And not any Secularism, but the peculiar definition of Secularism that was adopted in this country. In Europe, Secularism in its original context meant 'the separation of religion and State'. It was born in a very specific Christian context to end the constant wars between the papacy and the monarchies of Europe. It has nothing whatsoever to do with *Bharatiya* history. We never had wars between our religious institutions and political institutions. Nonetheless, Nehru adopted a peculiar Secularist stance that was supposed to mean 'the State shall respect all religions equally'. Any thinking person can see that this is an impossibility because all the religions are mutually exclusive to each other. If you respect one religion, you are bound to disrespect another. For example, if the State were to truly respect Islam and Christianity, it would have to respect their need to convert the whole of Bharat into their creed and subjugate Hindus in the process. That would automatically imply a disrespect for Hinduism. The Indian State has voluntarily walked into this explosive Catch-22. Stunningly, instead of walking out, it doubled down on actualizing this paradox.

For the Indian State to be able to respect all religions equally, it would literally have to reform all religions into submission, until they were force-fitted into the Liberal template of the State. At that point, indeed, all religions would be equal and therefore equally respected by the State. But since the two Abrahamic religions—Islam and Christianity—have powerful backers, financial conduits, established institutions of dominance (proselytizing arms backed by a universalist mandate and a clear understanding of who their enemies are), clear uncompromisable theological injunctions, and a propensity for violence, the weak Indian State can do nothing about them (unlike the very different route that the Chinese State has taken). Inevitably, the Indian State resorts to appeasement of the two Abrahamic religions and unleashes its reformist agenda solely upon the Hindu religion (which, due to its decentralized, 'live-and-let-live' nature, has no in-built institutions of domination).

No stone was left unturned. From usurping control[6] of Hindu religious institutions to reforming our social structure[7] to ensuring that every ritual practice would comply with Western Liberal ideals,[8] the Indian State has poured an enormous amount of energy 'educating' and legislating away the Hindu religion.

We are taught from birth that 'caste' is a social evil. I have deconstructed this in an earlier essay: *Drawing the Line: A Comprehensive Rehabilitation of 'Caste' in the Bharatiya Imagination* (Section 2, Chapter 2.4 of this book).

We are kept unaware that the money we put into the *hundis* at temples is used by the government for whatever purpose it desires,[9] including secular causes and the appeasement of 'minorities'. Think about that, our prayers and contributions are possibly being used to strengthen the very forces who want to erase us from face of the Earth. Watch Sai Deepak's eye-opening primer *Freeing Hindu Temples from Government Control*.[10]

Our ancient rituals, judged today in secular courts of law and in the legislative assemblies of corrupt, atheist men, are banned from being performed like they were in the time of Allauddin Khilji. The very latest such incursion— citing the Animal Protection Act—is the banning of *Sarpa Kavadi*[11] for Muruga devotees. Of course, the gazillion goats and turkeys slaughtered during Abrahamic festivals will elicit not a whimper from the honourable men in uniform.

Secularism has morphed from 'separation of State and religion' to 'State is the only God'. But mind, this tasty lollipop is only for Hindus.

Secularism has addled our minds by separating us from the *essential* nature of our religion. It has convinced many of us that religion is but a small part of our identities that we can practice in private. It has also convinced many of us that there is a neutral space out there where all religions can come together in equality. In reality, none of the other religions believes this sleight of hand—it is only Hindus who have bought it hook, line and sinker. The other religions bide their time until the moment we are too weak to resist. Additionally, the secularization of our minds has opened our doors to the degeneracy of Liberalism, a third-order religion which has entered our lives like a Trojan Horse. We continue to believe that we can be Liberal Hindus while, in reality, we are converted Hindu-flavoured Liberals. We continue to believe that Liberalism is a neutral creed while failing to comprehend that it has only one mission—the destruction of the traditional world. We believe that our lives are better now, that we are more open now—but open to what? What are the social and political outcomes of that betterment and that openness for us and our children? For our families? For our communities? For the continued existence of our religion? Yesterday Kashmir, today Kerala and Assam, tomorrow Andhra, Tamil Nadu and Punjab. The war is upon us and here we are, unable to take our eyes off the shiny toys and petty freedoms that Liberalism has offered us. We have lost more ground to Abrahamists post 'independence', due to our dalliance with Liberalism, than we did in the thousand-year war. For a break-through that will give us parity with other religions, we have to first extricate ourselves from the *maya* of Liberalism and from the structures of Secularism.

Halley Kalyan has laid bare the nature and effects of Secularism in his essay "On Secularism, Modernization and Hinduism".[12]

I have explored the operating system of Liberalism in an earlier essay *Self-Sacrifice: Hindu Sheep in the Liberal Church* (Section 1, Chapter 1.1 of this book).

Connecting the Dots #4

How come all the 'great' world religions are always 'victims'?

How come the Christians who occupied all of Europe, Russia, Africa, the Americas and Australia are 'victims', but the Romans, the Greeks, the Celts, the Gauls, the Yoruba, the Guarani, the Maori and the Sioux are not?

How come the Muslims who occupied Arabia, Persia, North Africa, Indonesia and half of Bharat are 'victims', but the Berbers, the Bedouins, the Parsis, the Malay and the Sindhis are not?

It's very important for Hindus (and other traditional people all over the world), who come from a nobility-inspired template, to understand the nature of revolutionary groups who come from a victimhood-inspired template.

Instead of building unity around a shared constructive purpose, revolutionary groups coalesce around a founding event of victimhood where they were wronged.

In the case of the Christians, it was the crucifixion of Jesus of Nazareth; in the case of the Sunnis, it was the flight of Mohammed to Medina; in the case of the Shias it is the death of Husayn at Karbala; in the case of the Jews it was the exodus from Egypt, etc. This perverse self-perception prevents them from working constructively to strengthen their own houses, pushing them instead to primarily work destructively at weakening the houses of others (who are classified as 'oppressors'). This template has been usurped by all modern revolutionary creeds, starting with Communism which is literally founded on the idea of permanent oppression and has grown to include every single Left-Liberal cause.

To understand how these groups function, an analogy will help.

There is a house. It has been built over time by people with a constructive and therefore noble bent of mind. Over time, groups arrive, either from outside or rebels from within. They claim they are suffering and it is the house that has made them suffer. They demand 'Rights' (but offer to perform no duties). The keeper of the noble house is amazed that his constructive work could possibly be the cause of suffering and immediately agrees to grant Rights. He is unable to imagine that there could actually exist people who will not perform their share of duties. A room in the house is made available for the suffering group. The suffering group, because their very self-definition is suffering, is never appeased. It begins to say that the whole house is rotten and needs to be either torn down or handed over to them to run because they are 'more moral'. The keeper of the noble house, at this point, offers a few more rooms and concessions. He even starts to make the suggestion that perhaps the group may benefit by building their own house. He may even offer his expertise in house building. But the group grows more and more intransigent. Building their own house will mean that they are no longer suffering, their very identity would then be at stake. How could they possibly accept such an oppressive proposition? They redouble their clamour for more space in the house and for the house to be torn down.

The keepers of noble houses actually have no problem sharing rooms with any group that is willing to take on house duties and help build more rooms. This is the fundamental logic behind the *jaati-vyavastha*. A reflection of this is clearly seen in medieval and modern times when *Bharatiya* hospitality was extended to groups like Parsis and Tibetans. It was also seen when native Americans helped

White settlers through their first winter, with gifts of corn. The problem lies with groups who do not acknowledge this unspoken covenant of noble houses, spurn their generosity of spirit, claim entire houses for themselves and do so with a self-righteous claim on the moral high ground. All traditional cultures see the diversity in human affairs as a reflection of the diversity in *Prakriti* herself—it is something to be worked with, not erased. This is the baseline reason why the polytheist claim on ethics has far greater legitimacy than that of revolutionary cults.

The keepers of a noble house have only four options now:

1. Send the revolutionary group out of their house (this is a Catch-22, as they will once again have to bear the accusation of being 'oppressors').
2. Build a wall between the rooms they have given to the group and the rest of the house (in other words, Partition).
3. Leave the house themselves and build a new one (Emigration... but where?).
4. Take to victimhood mongering themselves.

All options are losing propositions. Consider now what fate will befall the noble house if, even post-partition, members of one of the revolutionary groups continue to remain in the noble house, members of another revolutionary group are put in charge of education of the children of the noble house, and members of yet another revolutionary group are granted the constitutional right to expand indefinitely within the house. Eventually, formerly noble children of the house, seeing how lucrative the victimhood template is, start to claim victim status.[13] Nobility falls.

It must be obvious to all Hindus how these scenarios resonate with their lived experience.

The case of America is curious too. America was built by a quasi-noble people. They oscillated between constructive and destructive action (and perhaps that continues to be their national characteristic). As time has gone by, the noble aspect of that society has retreated under the onslaught of two revolutionary groups (risen from within)—the far-Right Christian groups and the far-Left Liberal groups. Both have entered into a victimhood tug-of-war. As the two main political parties are forced to align exclusively with these two groups, all other options have faded into inconsequence, and the State, unable to find self-definition, has started to flail its arms and legs all over the world. There is no doubt that the rise of victimhood (and Rights) signals the end of nobility and the great structures built by a sense of Duty.

Thus, was it in Rome. So shall it be, in America and in Bharat.

Connecting the Dots #5

How come Marxists who fought revolutions 'for the common people' ended up killing 100 million common people in the 20th Century? That's one followed by *eight* zeroes.

How come the White Man who invented the ideals of Liberty and Equality perversely ended up enslaving and genociding entire continents? "*I will enslave you so you can be free and I will kill you so we can be equal?*" Sheer genius.

As they say in tech: "*Feature not Bug*". The connections are a bit abstruse, but I'll do my best.

Many of us Left-Liberals have bought into the inevitability of Modernity and Individualism. It is not something many of us question. But, as sensitive people, we have an intuition that something is wrong with the world we live in. It is this intuition that puts us on a collision course with the zeitgeist. This is true for all of us, whether anti-developmentalists, environmentalists, songwriters, artists, social activists, socialists, alternative educationalists or organic farmers. We want a different world which is, in our minds, a more just world. But we have not truly understood the nature of the Capitalist world and our relationship with it.

Let's start with the understanding that Capitalism is merely the economic arm of a way of being and thinking of Self that goes by the name Western Modernity. It is a totalizing system that arose from the Bessemer furnace of the Industrial Revolution and unleashed the forces of Individualism, Materialism and Progressivism upon society. I say 'totalizing' because, like its Abrahamic predecessors, it wants to control everything. It cannot leave a single object or person untouched because it sees all as resources to be processed and transformed. It abhors alternate loyalties—family, community, nation, religion, beauty, spirit, Gods. All must, in the medium term, either be consumed or erased.

Halley Kalyan's neologism "Machine-*vaad*" (Machine-ism) is an apt descriptor for the end-game of Western Modernity. It refers to the 'way of the machine'... a self-perception of ourselves and *Bhu Devi* as *resources* whose end goal is *efficiency* and whose self-worth is measured by metrics of *quantifiable productivity*. Whereas in the past we humans saw ourselves suspended between Animal-nature and Divinity, we today see ourselves suspended between Animal-nature and Machine-ness, or what has come to be called 'The Matrix' in popular discourse. This has been clear to thinkers and writers for a little over 200 years now.

> Men have become the tools of their tools.
>
> – Henry David Thoreau, 1817[14]
>
> Instrumentality is considered to be the fundamental characteristic of technology. If we inquire, step by step, into what technology, represented as means, actually is, then we shall arrive at 'Revealing'. Technology is therefore **no mere means**. Technology is a way of 'Revealing'. If we give heed to this, then another whole realm for the essence of technology will open itself up to us. It is the realm of 'Revealing', i.e., of Truth.
>
> And yet the revealing that holds sway throughout modern technology does not unfold into a bringing-forth in the sense of poiesis (poetry). The revealing that rules in modern technology is a challenging (it makes demands) which puts to nature the unreasonable demand that it supply energy that can be extracted and stored.
>
> If man is challenged, ordered, to do this, then does not man himself belong even more originally than nature within the standing-reserve (becomes a resource)?
>
> – Martin Heidegger, *The Question Concerning Technology*, 1954[15]
>
> Today all things are being swept together into a vast network in which their only meaning lies in their being available to serve some end that will itself also be directed toward getting everything under control.
>
> – William Lovitt, *Introduction to Heidegger's "The Question Concerning Technology"*, 1976[16]
>
> And, for an instant, she stared directly into those soft blue eyes and knew, with an instinctive mammalian certainty, that the exceedingly rich were no longer even remotely human.
>
> – William Gibson, *Neuromancer*, 1984[17]

> Cyberspace is colonising what we used to think of as the real world. I think that our grandchildren will probably regard the distinction we make between what we call the real world and what they think of as simply the world as the quaintest and most incomprehensible thing about us.
>
> – William Gibson, 2010[18]

> It is easy for me to imagine that the next great division of the world will be between people who wish to live as creatures and people who wish to live as machines.
>
> – Wendell Berry, *Life is a Miracle: An Essay Against Modern Superstition*, 2001[19]

These three forces—Individualism, Materialism and Progressivism—accomplish much in the world and transform our lives and the world itself in totality, but let's focus our attention on four major things they enable:

1. Individualism breaks apart Community (and Family).
2. Materialism provides the de-spiritualized and de-socialized Self the psychological foundation for the guilt-free ravaging of the Earth.
3. Progressivism provides the capability (high technology), the logic (efficiency) and the morality (propaganda) for the centralization of all power and wealth.
4. Universalist Propaganda—The entire system then foists the blame for injustice, inequality and il-liberality inherent in Modernity upon traditional systems! It does this to encourage people to break with the past, with all that was organic, beautiful, independent and spiritual in their lives. We start to look with disgust at who we were and turn instead to embrace this whisperer of lies. We are now the converted.

From this traditional point of view, there is zero difference between Capitalism and Communism. Both use the three forces to enable the above disintegration. Under their pernicious effect and the propaganda of their media and educational arms, we, the intellectuals, have today unconsciously accepted Modernity as a given. Some of us mistake Modernity for mere Capitalism and we fight it, but we never question Modernity itself or its legitimacy.

We struggle against the rupture of Community by attempting to recreate Community in some intentional way. We rant and rail against centralized power and wealth, we denounce billionaires, we support independent news sources, we root for the small guy, we fight for Rights, little realizing that these are all contradictory causes. The very idea of Rights springs from industrial surplus and Big-Tech. Rights cannot exist without Big-Government, and Big-Government cannot exist without Big-Tech, and Big-Tech cannot exist without Big-Business, in that order.

One cannot live in Capitalism and fight it. One can only try to avoid it and avoid being enslaved by it in little ways that French philosophers Deleuze and Guattari described over forty years ago in their magnum opus – *A Thousand Plateaus: Capitalism and Schizophrenia*:

> Our Capitalist "societies exhibit a marked taste for all codes, codes foreign and exotic...this taste is destructive and morbid. While decoding doubtless means understanding and translating a code, it also means destroying the code as such, assigning it an archaic, folkloric, or residual function."
>
> Schizophrenics "escape coding, scramble the codes, and flee in all directions... [they are]: orphans (no daddy-mommy-me), atheists (no beliefs), and nomads (no habits, no territories)". Deleuze and Guattari's schizophrenic will not be trapped by the power-laden and despotic webs of signifiers.
>
> Deleuze and Guattari see the schizophrenic as Capitalism's exterminating angel. For them the schizo is a radical, revolutionary, nomadic wanderer who resists all forms of oppressive power. They believe that radical political movements should "learn from the psychotic how to shake off the Oedipal yoke and the effects of power, in order to initiate a radical politics of desire freed from all beliefs".
>
> Deleuze and Guattari see schizophrenia as a central part of a subversive postmodern politics with the radical potential to bring down Capitalism.
>
> – Johnah Peretti's analysis *Towards a Radical Anti-Capitalist Schizophrenia*, 2010 [20]

For Hindus, these deductions are an abomination. Read the last line again: "a politics of desire, freed from all belief". This is the exact opposite of the goal of Hindu tradition, which is "the politics of belief freed from all desire".

Deleuze and Guattari recognize the *anti-Liberty* aspect of totalitarian Capital just like Marx recognized the *anti-Meaning* aspect of it. Marx responded by taking away Liberty altogether and centralizing Meaning-production in the State, creating an anti-human hell. Deleuze and Guattari take another route. Instead of going head-to-head with Capitalism, they attempt to recover Liberty by advocating schizophrenia! The fundamental thesis of their work implies that, as long as one has identity, one will be enslaved by Capital. Conversely, if one doesn't have identity then one is 'free'. One cannot be pinned down by advertisements or controlled by corporations and the logic of consumption. To be 'free' in Capitalism, one has to shed one's identity. In such a world, identity-less-ness is valourized. We are encouraged to break all forms and become formless. Indeed, this way of being can be seen as a form of *Advaita*, but without the twin anchors of *Brahman* and *Atman*. But, unlike the *Advaitin*, the Modernist is stuck trying to manifest this vision of formlessness in the material plane. The evidence for the accuracy of Deleuze and Guattari's reading comes from the patterns we are seeing develop in modern society today—Transsexualism, Gender as a social construct, Deepfake, Cloning, Cyborgism, Social Media 'Handles', Artificial Intelligence... these all represent the breakdown of the last vestiges of authentic human form and identity. Authenticity itself will come to be seen as untruth.

When *adharma* becomes *Dharma*, we know that we are well and truly in the throes of the *Kali Yuga*.

Deleuze and Guattari's thesis is the very antithesis of Tradition and the Old Way where metaphysics helps create Form and Meaning and aids us in our yearning for eternity and immortality.

Many of us have parts of the puzzle. Some of us have left conventional society and live in rural areas and grow our own food. Some of us are involved in re-wilding parts of the Earth, some in singing resistance songs, some of us start alternate schools to turn kids away from factory schooling... this is all well and good but none of it makes a whit of difference. The logic of Capital will simply appropriate and commodify all our rebellious actions. To truly critique the Capitalist engine, we need to see that Capitalism is only a symptom, a manifestation of a deeper underlying dis-ease. That disease is Western Modernity itself, and it rests upon three legs: Individualism, Materialism, and Progressivism.

When we really start to make this critique, we see that only Traditionalism and Polytheism have the solutions to our problems. The move to a Low-Tech world demands Community. The retreat of Big-Government opens up space for

Tradition. And the withdrawal from Machine-*vaad* opens up space for Spirituality and the re-enchantment of *Bhu Devi* (polytheism).

But, as individuals within Capitalist society, we find that we are unable to accomplish anything. Our 1969 Student Revolutions are a failure, our Woodstock is a failure, our Hippie movement is a failure, our Vietnam protests are a failure, our Occupy Wall Street is a failure. Instead of re-turning to real Community among real people, we look to High Technology to fill that hole in our lives. Similarly, as Moderns, we are bereft of life-ordering mechanisms. Instead of turning to Tradition, we look to Big-Government and Big-Business to order our lives with dole, subsidy, law, punishment and the '9 to 5'. Fine. But do we not see the inner contradiction here? We refuse to take a single step towards true solutions (Community and Tradition); instead, we throw our lot in with Big-Tech and Big-Government and then we complain about corporate control, globalism, environmental damage, end of small business and Art and Craft? It is inevitable that we will fall into the grave that we dig for ourselves.

The acceptance of this line of thinking brings us to the threshold of a portal. What does Community and Tradition mean for us? What has it meant for our ancestors? What are *our* communities and traditions? How do communities get along? How are traditions transmitted? What does it take to keep that world alive? How can I reconnect? How can I start to see *Sanatana* Community and Tradition as something incredibly wise that fulfilled essential human needs instead of as the evils that modernist propaganda had fooled me into thinking they are?

(I've covered these ideas in detail in Chapter 5.2 of this book under the section Sanatana Exceptionalism)

References and Links

1. Thomas Babbington Macaulay, *Letter to his Father*, 1836
   https://franpritchett.com/00generallinks/macaulay/txt_letters_later.html

2. Raghava Krishna, *via Twitter*, 2023
   https://twitter.com/Anviksiki/status/1631142885272977411

3. "Chesterton's Fence: A Lesson in Second-Order Thinking", *Farnam Street*, https://fs.blog/chestertons-fence/

4. Kaushik Kanna, "Madras High Court: No More Elephants for Tamil Nadu Temples", *Times Of India*, 2023 https://timesofindia.indiatimes.com/city/madurai/madras-high-court-no-more-elephants-for-tamil-nadu-temples/articleshow/98320396.cms

5. Bono, *One*, 1991 https://www.azlyrics.com/lyrics/u2band/one.html

6. Hindu Religious and Charitable Endowment https://en.wikipedia.org/wiki/Hindu_Religious_and_Charitable_Endowments_Department

7. Hindu Code Bills https://en.wikipedia.org/wiki/Hindu_code_bills

8. Arun Dev, "What you need to know about Karnataka's anti-superstition bill", *The Quint*, 2017 https://www.thequint.com/explainers/all-you-need-to-know-about-karnatakas-anti-superstition-bill#read-more

9. Utkarsh Anand, "Why can't temple funds be used for public purpose? Supreme Court observes", *Hindustan Times*, 2022 https://www.hindustantimes.com/india-news/why-can-t-temple-funds-be-used-for-public-good-supreme-court-observes-101662054215497.html

10. J Sai Deepak, *Freeing Hindu Temples from Government Control*, 2016 https://www.youtube.com/watch?v=BA_VQdUMdeY

11. Dina Thanthi, *Pilgrims performing Sarpa Kavadi banned from entering the Thiruchendur Subramanya Swami temple*, 2023 https://www.dailythanthi.com/News/State/to-tiruchendur-subramanya-swamy-templebring-sarpa-kavadiprohibition-for-devotees-878179

12. Halley Kalyan, "On Secularism, Modernization and Hinduism", *Pragyata*, 2022 https://pragyata.com/on-secularism-modernization-and-hinduism/

13. "Lingayats are not Hindus", *The New Indian Express*, 2015 https://tinyurl.com/lingayatsIssue

14. https://www.goodreads.com/quotes/461550-men-have-become-the-tools-of-their-tools-money-is

15. https://archive.org/details/questionconcerniooheid

16. Martin Heidegger, *The question concerning technology and other essays*, 1977 https://archive.org/details/questionconcerniooheid

17. William Gibson, *Neuromancer*, 1994 https://archive.org/details/neuromanceroooogibs/page/n5/mode/2up

18. https://www.brainyquote.com/quotes/william_gibson_589658

19. Wendell Berry, *Life is a Miracle: An Essay against Modern Superstition*, 2001

20. Johnah Peretti, *Towards a Radical Anti-Capitalist Schizophrenia?* (An Analysis of Gilles Deleuze and Félix Guattari's, *A Thousand Plateaus: Capitalism and Schizophrenia*, 1980), CLT 2010

Section 6 | Chapter 6.2

ARTHA, KAMA, MOKSHA AND A GAPING HOLE IN THE MIDDLE – PART II
Questions

Maragatham, 2023

The *Sanatana* Map of Recent History

Here's a diagram to give us a low-resolution picture of how the river of Sanatana Civilization has narrowed over the centuries until it has, more recently, split into six prominent distributaries, all with their own ideas of what it means to be a Hindu, and many with their own ideas of why *not* to be a Hindu. Do take a moment to understand the flow.

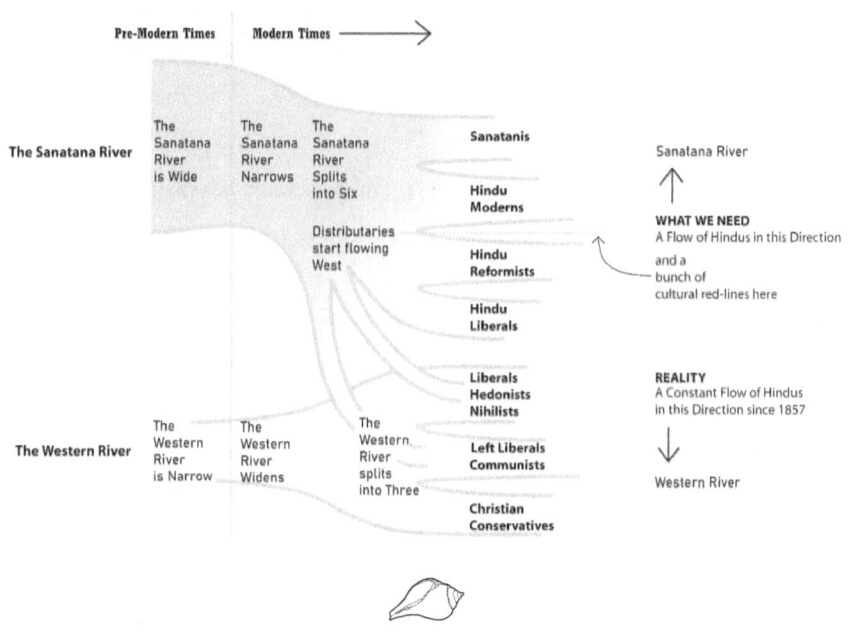

Questions for each of the Six Distributaries of the *Sanatana* River

Questions for Hindu Left Liberals, Communists (Politicized Revolutionary Types)

By self-identifying as Leftists and Left-Liberals, are we conscious that we are choosing to stand on the side of Mao, Stalin, Pol Pot and violent Abrahamic Universalism that has caused the hundred million deaths of the 20th Century, the genocide of Native Americans, the enslavement of Africans, the colonization of Asia and your own ancestors, the baby-snatcher camps in Australia and Canada, the Holocaust of Jews and the Globalist empire of materialist irreverence? I know that many of us are unconscious about the ramifications of our allegiances, as I once was, so really, "Are we *sure* this is where we want to invest our life force?" We cannot be against imperialism and simultaneously stand with the very same religions and ideals that gave birth to that imperial spirit. It's incoherent.

Simply take for example the "secular" parties. When we support them, we imagine that we are taking an anti-hegemonic, pro-diversity, pro-pluralism stance which will lead us all to a better place. But the truth is, we are being manipulated by powers beyond our comprehension into standing against the very ideals that we imagine we are standing for (not to mention our own grandparents). These are all statements made by our "secular" leaders:

> There is no religion called Hindu, Hinduism is just a hoax.[1]
>
> Hindu religion is the biggest menace not only to India, now it becomes menace to the entire world....[2]
>
> There is a saying that some are beggars by nature while others are beggars by circumstance. The ********* ****** here are beggars by nature.[3]
>
> The (********* *****) workers should be taught to live with what they receive as wages.[4]
>
> How can Hinduism be a religion? The word Hindu originates in Persian, which means thief, despicable and lowly.[5]
>
> ...we want to destroy god... we want to destroy Congress... we are against them (Brahmins)... we want to destroy religion. In short, the Self-Respect Movement shoulders the responsibility to crusade against god, religion, Congress, Gandhi and Brahmins.[6]

Mosquitoes, dengue, flu, malaria, corona, we should not oppose these things. They've to be eradicated. The same is the case with Sanatan.[7]

No one is educated in Uttar Pradesh and Bihar because of Sanatana Dharma. They are brainless. They don't have rational thinking about life.[8]

Ask them who made India a slave. Those who put Tika on the forehead made India a slave.[9]

Remove the Police for 15 minutes! Be it a thousand, a lakh or even one crore impotent (Hindus), even if they try collectively, they will not be able to give birth to a single one.[10]

Would these statements be acceptable to us if they were made about any religion other than the Hindu religion? Why not? No doubt, it's a free country, but brothers and sisters, let's think again who we want to be aligned with.

Questions for Hindu Hedonists (Deracinated Nihilistic Youth)

Have we truly internalized the worldview that humans are merely consuming individuals composed of multiple chains of carbon molecules as Economics and Science tell us? Have we truly internalized that everything is a matter of random chance dependent solely on the interplay of impersonal physical laws and chemical reactions?

If yes, then Why cry when our fathers die? Why exult when we fall in love? Why be proud of the work we do? Why kiss our babies goodnight? Why not commit suicide right now as Leo Tolstoy once urged?

> If a man lives, then he believes in something. If he didn't believe that one must live for something, then he wouldn't live. If he doesn't see and doesn't understand the illusoriness of the finite, he believes in the infinite; if he does understand the illusoriness of the finite, he must believe in the infinite without which one cannot live.
>
> – Leo Tolstoy, *A Confession*, 1880 [11]

If suicide is not an option for us, then perhaps in our heart of hearts we can start to acknowledge that not everything is meaningless and there is an un-named, unspoken thing that lends Meaning, whatever it may be. When we celebrate meaninglessness, we are being disloyal to that unspoken thing that animates us and urges us to wake up every morning and live. Perhaps we can agree that we have some responsibility towards that thing?

Questions for Hindu Liberals (Deracinated Middle and Upper Class)

I asked, in an earlier essay *Self-Sacrifice: Hindu Sheep in the Liberal Church* (Section 1, Chapter 1.1 of this book):

> Why is it that when a Hindu youth enters the doors of a *madrasa*, and stops believing in his traditional Gods, the worldview of the *Veda*, in *Karma*, in multiple births, in the sanctity of life itself, we say that he has converted, but when the same youth enters the doors of a university, stops believing in his traditional Gods, the worldview of the *Veda*, in *Karma*, in multiple births and the sanctity of life itself, we ignore his conversion and go on to praise his accomplishments and call him scientific and liberal? Why do we fear our children entering the former door but not the latter when, in fact, their effects are exactly the same?

I now have an answer for us. The reason why Hindus are able to distinguish between Hinduism and Islam but not between Hinduism and Liberalism is because Hindus are a free people. We resist dogma. It is this trait that we share with Liberals. It is this commonality that leads modern-day Hindus to confuse Hinduism with Liberalism and end up undermining and diluting their own faith. This is the reason why it is not Abrahamism, but Liberalism which is the single greatest threat to Hinduism. It is a Trojan horse that has entered each of our families on the silent wings of 'education' and Netflix.

Freedom from dogma is indeed a commonality we share with liberals but our paths diverge sharply immediately after that. Liberalism sees freedom as a 'Freedom to', while Hindus have always seen freedom as a 'Freedom from'. Liberal freedom is Liberty, Hindu freedom is *Moksha*. Liberty says we are free only when we can fulfil our every desire. *Moksha* says we are free when we are free from desire itself. Self-indulgence for individual gratification is the Liberal way. Self-control for the greater common good is the Hindu way. Liberal happiness is pleasure. Hindu happiness is contentment. If only we know this consciously, we can live as authentic Hindus even within the Liberal world.

Do the Muslims in our lives practice Islam? Yes. Do the Christians in our lives practice Christianity? Yes. Do the Liberals in our lives espouse Liberty? Yes. Do the Communists in our lives espouse Equality? Yes. Do we, as Hindus, practice or espouse *Dharma*? No. Where's the self-respect in that?

If we find it hard to step away from the ideals of the French Revolution at such short notice, there is one easy and unfailing way to reorient our priorities, and that is to abide by the Principle of Reciprocity. Observe how other religions including Liberalism treat Hinduism, and give back as good as we get. Not asking for hatefulness, just for fairness and equivalence. The Principle of Reciprocity automatically requires us to embark on a process of self-definition. This slow return to *Swayambodh*[12] may take a few years, but it is unfailing.

Questions for Hindu Reformists and "Conservatives" (Politicized Middle-Class)

"What is it that Hindu Conservatives want to conserve?" If we believe that we are conservatives, we have to answer this question clearly, because it is our answer to that question that will determine why and how we are different from Hindu Liberals (if at all).

I know, and I understand that we believe that our desire to reform our religion stems from a deep love of it. We believe that we need to reform ourselves in order to be united so we can survive the Abrahamic and modern onslaughts. We believe that we need to be united in order to be strong. Some even believe, subconsciously, that we need to reform ourselves so our society is so moral in the eyes of the West that no questions will ever again be raised about our 'regressiveness'. No more *Sati*-this, Dowry-that. We want to be seen as one among the 'progressive' nations. Do any of these courses of action look like they have been initiated by a people with self-respect?

Sociologist A.K. Saran calls it the *Nilakantha* Syndrome:

> The synthesis ideology, or the *Nilkantha* Syndrome which has continued to possess the Hindu consciousness from the days of Muslim and British domination down to the present time, is the Hindu way not only of paying the fatal price for some kind of survival, but also of masking the fact that such a tremendous price is being paid.[13]

So, ask not if we are good enough to belong in their world. Ask if they are good enough to belong in ours. Ask not what it takes to survive in their *adharmic* world. Ask what it takes to turn the world towards *Dharma*.

And if our OCD does not allow us to look ahead without first resolving every inter-tribal skirmish that plagues this land, then by all means let us establish *taluka*-level inter-*jaati sambhashan* committees, let us design annual *Purusha* festivals that will travel the length and breadth of the country bringing the *jaatis* together in shared ritual, and let us build those nationalized temples at every *taluka*, where our new ideas of social organization can be tested.

But let us do so in humility, knowing that the *Sramanic* paths have been around for three thousand years, *Vaishnavism* has been around for one thousand years, *Sikhism* for five hundred years, the *Arutperumjyothi* for one hundred and fifty years... and yet... and yet, it doesn't look like the 'depressed classes' have the least bit of actual interest in Radical Equality. They have continued to hold fast to their identities, only riding the coat-tails of Western idealism in order to gain their share of power in the modern world.

Let's give them, and indeed all of us *together*, less French Revolution and more *Dharma*...more *Purusha*. The parched earth yearns for rain.

Questions for Hindu Moderns (Ordinary Middle-Class)

Can we provide our children what our parents provided us and what our grandparents provided our parents? If not, then what will our children be able to provide their children? Will our descendants represent us as we represent our ancestors?

I know the Western world is upon us, and it's increasingly impossible to make ends meet, let alone keep track of outside influences in our children's lives, but it is time to start blocking out the noise and pay heed to that voice at the back of our heads. If, as parents, we intuit that there is something wrong with the way the world is set up, then we're probably right. The flow of culture is a one-way street. With every new generation, the new normal is always pushed further West. If we want to stop feeding the Western river and generate a flow back towards the Sanatana river before it runs dry, we cannot simply accept everything that comes our way as *zamana badal gaya hai*.

Arre, zamana kyun badal raha hai? It's not the times that change, it is always we who choose to change. We determine the times, either consciously or by doing nothing.

It is true that the old world has passed. We do not live in a Hindu ethno-scape anymore. In this new mixed world, one *has* to understand the idea of the cultural 'slippery slope'. When we leave our traditional structures, we don't enter a neutral ground. We enter a ground that has already been prepared for us by Western Modernity, a conversion ground. We get to keep the superficialities of our religion but we are forced to abandon the depths. All of us, today, exist in this liminal state. The Western structures we live within are openly entropic, they are constantly incentivizing the breakdown of all structures of Maintenance in favour of the structures of Experience. If we don't Stand for Something, we will pretty soon Stand for Nothing. There is no neutral ground where we can exist without culturally falling apart. There is no safe space our children can grow up in where they will automatically turn into *Sanatani* adults. It is in this context that the idea of Tradition becomes important as a set of red lines—uncompromisable practices and values—that we, as a society, collectively defend (like our ancestors did) from the slippery slope. They serve as footholds for committed people to hold their ground and perhaps even begin the climb up to the heights our ancestors once occupied.

> It is necessary to have "watchers" at hand who will bear witness to the values of Tradition in ever more uncompromising and firm ways, as the anti-traditional forces grow in strength. Even though these values cannot be achieved, it does not mean that they amount to mere "ideas." These are MEASURES... Let people of our time talk about these things with condescension as if they were

anachronistic and anti-historical; we know that this is an alibi for their defeat. Let us leave modern men to their "truths" and let us only be concerned about one thing: to keep standing amid a world of ruins.

— Julius Evola, *Revolt Against the Modern World*, 1934 [14]

The traditions themselves are cultural red lines but more and more we are realizing that, in the mentally-colonized Republic, the very *idea of Tradition itself* has become a red line.

What traditions will be allowed to remain in the Republic? What traditions will be reformed? Who will be allowed to honour their traditions? Who will not? Are traditions a weakness that needs to be eliminated? Or do traditions define our sense of self? Can they be changed? By whom? Who has the *adhikaara*? Are those *adhikaaris* themselves to be replaced? On what basis? Will traditionalists be allowed to define a reasonable part of our future? Or will they be exterminated in a wave of self-righteous Western idealism? Can we reach an Israel style arrangement between the orthodoxy and the liberal establishment, where tradition will be protected as a refuge and a library? If not, can traditionalists at least hope to be left alone to carry on in the footsteps of their ancestors?

We *must* ask all those questions.

And we *must* answer this one: "*Why* did our ancestors resist the invaders?"

Was it to uphold the ideals of the *French Revolution*? Come on now...

What is it they were fighting to preserve and protect? *What* was so precious that they were willing to sacrifice their lives for, to have their eyes gouged out for, to have their skin flayed for, to be boiled alive for? Does the nation/society we have today suitably honour those sacrifices and their wishes, or do we make common cause with their enemies and send our best and brightest to pay taxes in their lands and swell their coffers? Too many Hindus have unthinkingly bought into the 'End of History' argument which is nothing but a euphemism for our acceptance of a foot-stool at the table of Western Liberal hegemony.

I am aware that it is inevitable, in this age, that a vast majority of us move to a Westernized way of life, but what is the price we are willing to pay in terms of self-respect and self-perception?

If such vast and uncontrollable change is upon us, then we have to address the crux of the matter:

1. What is the model of Hinduism that Hindu Moderns will follow? What are the bare minimum cultural red lines that would comprise this new 'Hinduism Lite' so as to help differentiate its practitioners from their Abrahamic peers?
2. What kind of relationship will the Hindu Modern have with traditional practitioners—Adversarial, Respectful, Symbiotic or Live-and-Let-Live?

Surely it can be nobody's contention that the civilizational hole created by the retreat of the *samskaaras*, the *kula devatas*, the *pancha rnas*, the *yamas*, the *niyamas* and *varnashrama dharma* can simply be filled by more and more elaborate celebrations of *Deepavali* and *Holi*.

Does it not make sense that the last remaining islands of classical Hinduism be protected and nurtured by us all so they continue to serve as a refuge and a library, and maybe when we're ready, even as a civilizational mirror and inspiration?

Questions for Sanatanis (Self-Aware Practitioners)

What vision of inter-relatedness are we willing to offer all the other various shades of Hindus? What model that will suit our needs, the demands of the Gods and our ancestors, and give them all a noble purpose? Here is one way to imagine a model.

The Kurmaha | Hard Shell. Soft Core.

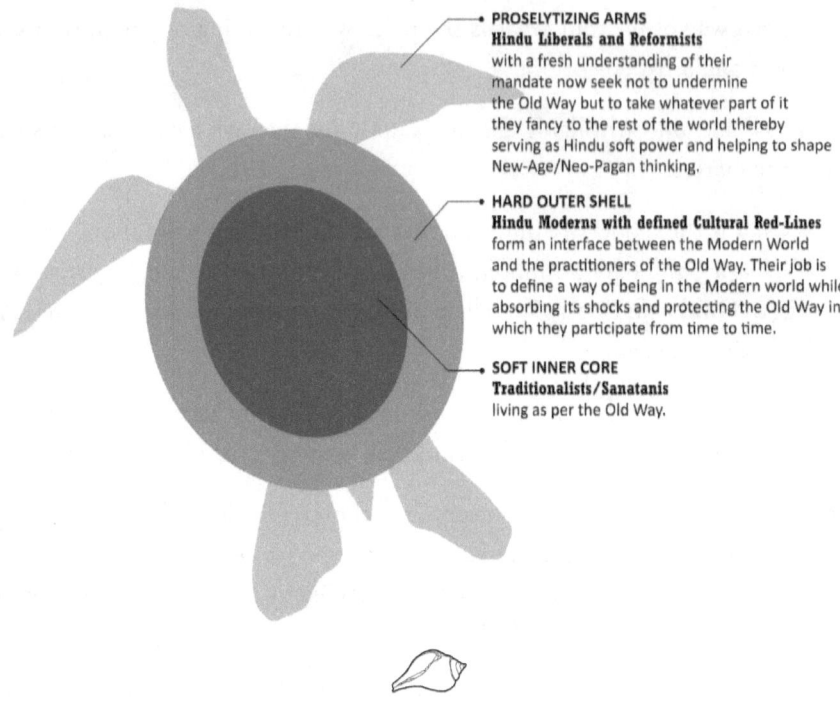

References and Links

1. OpIndia Staff, "'Hinduism is not a religion but a hoax': Samajwadi Party leader Swami Prasad Maurya rants again", *OpIndia*, 2023
   https://www.opindia.com/2023/08/hinduism-is-not-a-religion-but-hoax-samajwadi-party-leader-swami-prasad-maurya-rants-again/

2. B. Sreelakshmi, "BJP leader shares A Raja's remarks on Hindu religion: 'creating hatred'", *Hindustan Times*, 2023
   https://www.hindustantimes.com/india-news/bjp-leader-shares-a-rajas-remarks-on-hindu-religion-creating-hatred-101694519170119.html

3. OpIndia Staff, "After TMC leader Sujata Mondal Khan labels Dalits as 'beggars', BJP writes to National Commission of SC, demands inquiry", *OpIndia*, 2021
   https://www.opindia.com/2021/04/tmc-sujata-mondal-khan-dalits-beggars-bjp-national-commission-of-sc/

4. Aravindan Neelakandan, "Ten Things About Periyar Dravidian Parties Don't Want You To Know", *SwarajyaMag*, 2018
https://swarajyamag.com/politics/ten-things-about-periyar-dravidian-parties-dont-want-you-to-know

5. OpIndia Staff, "Swami Prasad Maurya, infamous for his comments on Hinduism, resigns as General Secretary of Samajwadi Party, claims discrimination", *OpIndia*, 2024
https://www.opindia.com/2024/02/swami-prasad-maurya-samajwadi-party-general-secretary/

6. E V Ramasamy, *Collected Works Of Periyar E V R*, 1971
https://archive.org/details/CollectedWorksPeriyarEVRamasamy CollectedWorksOfPeriyarEVRThePeriyarSelfRespectPr/page/n167/mode/2up?q=destroy

7. OpIndia Staff, "'Sanatan is like dengue, malaria, corona that needs to be eradicated': I.N.D.I.A. bloc partner DMK's Udhayanidhi Stalin at 'Eradicate Sanatan Conference'", *OpIndia*, 2023
https://www.opindia.com/2023/09/dmks-udhayanidhi-stalin-talks-about-destroying-sanatan-like-germs-at-eradicate-sanatan-conference/

8. OpIndia Staff, "PM Modi in MP says I.N.D.I Alliance has a hidden agenda of finishing Sanatan Dharma, the traditions that kept Bharat together for 1000 years: Watch", *OpIndia*, 2023
https://www.opindia.com/2023/09/pmmodi-bina-madhya-pradesh-address-says-i-n-d-i-alliance-wants-to-destroy-sanatan-dharma/#google_vignette

9. OpIndia Staff, "Another assault on Hinduism by I.N.D.I. alliance: Bihar RJD chief Jagdanand Singh says Tilak-wearing Hindus enslaved India", *OpIndia*, 2023
https://www.opindia.com/2023/09/how-tilak-wearing-enslaved-india-rjd-bihar-chief-jagdanand-singh-bjp-denounces/

10. OpIndia Staff, "Watch: Akbaruddin Owaisi's Anti-Hindu hate speech for which he got acquitted", *OpIndia*, 2022
https://www.opindia.com/2022/04/akbaruddin-owaisis-anti-hindu-hate-speech-for-which-he-got-acquitted/

11. Leo Tolstoy, *A Confession*, 1889
    https://www.arvindguptatoys.com/arvindgupta/confessions-tolstoy.pdf

12. A.K. Saran, *The Crisis in Hinduism*, 1971
    http://www.studiesincomparativereligion.com/public/articles/The_Crisis_of_Hinduism-by_AK_Saran.aspx

13. Pankaj Saxena and Raghav Krishna, *Shatrubodh and Swayambodh*, Young Thinkers Conclave 2022, https://www.youtube.com/watch?v=G-AyMIoZA_E

14. Julius Evola, *Revolt Against the Modern World*, 1934

Section 6 | Chapter 6.3

WORK. LIFE. BALANCE

Maragatham, 2025

Many younger Hindu intellectuals, faced with the convert-or-die choice that Western Modernity has brought to our doorsteps, have come to the conclusion that the idea of defining ourselves through limits is, well... limiting. No doubt, putting limits on oneself when your rivals do not, is a recipe for defeat, but to be unable to see that the ideal of an existence without limits is a recipe for all kinds of immorality is equally problematic.

The idea of limits is a fundamental idea in all societies, both Traditional and Abrahamic. The limits themselves may be different for different cultures, but all self-definition is engineered through the embrace of limits and the drawing of red-lines. *Yama* and *Niyama*. How much to eat? What to eat? What not to eat? How much to drink? What to drink? What not to drink? How much pleasure is to be pursued? How many spouses to have? How many children? How many clothes, vehicles, houses? How many genders? How many Gods? How much to talk? How to talk? How much to keep? How much to share? With whom to share? When accepted limits around these (and many other) questions are breached, societal judgement falls upon us.

The idea that life can be lived without limits is a peculiar and very recent innovation in human thought, and it has been made possible by the availability of enormous surplus to some of us. Children, from a young age, are no longer taught to curb their desires, but to indulge them... to 'dream'. And when some of those dreams do come true, that approach stands vindicated.

The vision is that we will invent/discover our way out of the need to follow those pesky limits – new energy sources will be tapped, new efficient technologies created and new sources of mineral wealth will be opened up, either here or in Mars. Hell, the last three hundred years are proof that this way of thinking about the world is legitimate even in the eyes of the Gods. *Look, how they've rewarded us for our audacity!* If the techno-optimists do indeed figure this stuff out, then Manifest Destiny is indeed their birthright and the traditionalists with their limits and lines were wrong all along – dinosaurs from an age when those limiting ideas were useful to maintain quaint anachronisms like community and identity.

BUT, what if those problems are never solved? What if we are living off the future, subsidized by the world and resources that our children were destined to inherit? And I mean that not just from a resource and pollution point of view, but also from a culture and well-being point of view. We're blowing the accumulated cultural and knowledge capital of a thousand generations of ancestors in a mere hundred years, all in order to underwrite a bet placed in the future. When individuals do that and succeed, they are heroes, and when they fail, they are fools.

At the very least, we must enquire into the alternate point of view.

The ideal of limitless-ness, like its sister ideals of Liberty and Equality, can only be pursued when subsidized by extreme surplus, which itself can only be produced by extreme mechanization of all aspects of human society. In such a society, any "inefficient" process must be replaced with a more efficient process. This is the only way that limitless-ness can be approached in the material world. So, the sequence is clear – initially machines help get a job done, then as their sophistication grows, they start to do the work of people, until eventually, they replace people altogether. The complex, high-efficiency world that this level of mechanization creates still finds a place for people, but the nature of work that a vast majority of people get to do has changed in four significant ways.

1. It is no longer communal
2. It is no longer sacred
3. It is no longer connected to identity
4. The person no longer has a sense of ownership over the work

These losses are huge losses, the psychological effects of which we no longer comprehend because we simply don't know any better.

So, we're seeing two major shifts – one, traditional human work starts to be done by machines, and two, people are herded more and more into working 'arid jobs'. Now, because of the higher efficiency of the system as a whole, surplus is generated which gets distributed among *some* people as higher and higher salaries. This may appear to be a win (to some), but by the standards of the old world (access to community, the sacred, identity and ownership), it is clear that we are *all* spiritually impoverished when we accept this Faustian bargain (not to mention that very many of us do not even see the economic benefits of this move). It may be possible to reach a sweet spot with regard to mechanization of society – a compromise between the ease of the new model and the soul of the old model. This is what I call the 'small is beautiful dream'. For this to happen organically, people who have lived their entire lives within a mechanized world have to be re-introduced to the old-world ideal of work not merely as an activity to earn money, but as a self-definitional activity that simultaneously connects one to both community and the sacred.

The Accusation of Drudgery

The Public Relations arms of the mechanized world paint low-tech work as "drudgery", but anyone who has worked in a paddy-line singing harvest songs with her comrades, or on the roof of a house stitching thatch with his neighbours, knows that it is far from true. In any case, I am not calling for the establishment of a nation-wide Gandhigram. What I am calling for a conscious appraisal of machines and their place in our lives.

Beauty and Perfection

Ontologically speaking, the greatest loss we face with greater mechanization is the loss of ownership over Beauty and the Pursuit of Perfection. Both these activities are now firmly in the grasp of the Machine. With the coming AI revolution, even the formerly lionized artists, designers and musicians will find their worlds devastated. We have relinquished control over the very well-springs of daily spirituality. In the old-world, our pursuit of perfection was in fact a prayer, and the result of that pursuit was a product of beauty that was literally an offering to the Gods, a *naivedhyam*.

Sociologist Venkat Rao provides the vocabulary for us to describe this phenomenon more clearly. He uses the terms "inscriptional cultures" to describe cultures that externalize cultural memory in surrogate bodies outside of the physical human body (from books to chips to databases), and "mnemo cultures" to describe cultures that put the human body to work constantly and persistently in order to retain memory in embodied, performative and inactive modes[1] (from *shlokas* to *asanas* to *hasthas*). Limitless mechanization can thus be seen as the manifestation of a greater and greater externalization (of memory, of work, of all production and therefore of the cultural-human himself). Until eventually, with the AI revolution, we are staring at a complete abduction of human agency by surrogate bodies (albeit nominally "controlled" by humans). This trajectory brings us back to Wendell Berry's primal question – "What are humans for?"

Prosperity

True that the old world had less surplus. But the real human question is not how *much* surplus, but *what* does that surplus get us in terms of well-being? To get a sense of what that question means, we can ask a few questions – "Why is it that we can no longer afford to keep cows?", "Why is it that bulls have to be killed?", "Why is it that we can't afford to maintain a thatched roof?", "Why is it no longer possible for us to build traditional temples without busting the bank?", "Why can't we afford to maintain our water bodies (*kulams* and *kalyanis*)?", "Why do the costs of performing a yajña today feel astronomical?"

This is not entirely a question of priorities. Even people with the right priorities find that doing any of these things is prohibitively expensive. So then how come our "dirt-poor", subsistence farming ancestors were able to do all of these things without batting an eyelid? How did they bring up six, seven, eight children when we struggle to put one through school? No doubt, our expectations around life have changed, but there is a kind of prosperity here that we have entirely lost track of today – a quiet prosperity. And it wasn't all at the micro scale. Even the macro could manifest this sensibility. Between the 11th and 12th centuries CE, the Chozha rulers and their subjects built upward of fifty grand temples in a 50 km radius around just one town, Kumbakonam. If the modern Indian state was to embark upon such a project over a similar timeline, it would go bankrupt. Even attempting to maintain these temples in pristine condition today would be a recipe for bankruptcy. So, who is richer – the Chozha Empire or the Modern Indian State? Europeans acknowledge this reality too. The Notre Dame could not be built today. Neither the skills nor the wealth exist.

Treadmill

What we are unwilling to acknowledge is that what goes by the name of development today is not a destination, it is the first step in the embrace of an extremely expensive annual maintenance contract that we pay in perpetuity. Add to that the requirement of the 'growth-based economy' and we have a recipe for disaster. It is not only a treadmill by definition, but a treadmill that is supposed to go faster and faster every year to maintain what is known as 'growth'. How such a thing would even be possible without the greater and greater utilization of limited resources or outright robbery in the short term, remains a mystery. War, therefore, become the inevitable end-game in this model of development. America, for example, has entered into twelve overt wars and nine covert wars in the mere seventy-five years since WW2. That's how it maintains its resource flow. The roads and services that the American taxpayers think they pay for, are also funded by the blood-stained oil and lithium from these twenty-one wars.

Security to Insecurity

What the Old Way provided, at least in Bharat, was direct access to the sacred, to identity, belonging, and *purushaarth*. Every individual was guaranteed family, community, tradition, daily work, and if they were willing, a spiritual path. The fundamental psychological fruit of this system was to bestow upon the individual an inviolate sense of stability, and therefore security. One can still see this in people from remote villages, their utter lack of anxiety. The modern person, on the other hand, is marked out by anxiety, a high frequency nervousness, a whirring neurosis, a need to perform and present a mask to manipulate emotional outcomes in inter-relationships. You can tell a city guy from a villager simply from the way they stand or sit. You can tell an American from an Indian simply from the self-consciousness inherent in the way they talk. You can tell your grandma from your mother simply from the look in their eyes. The neurotic vibration induced in us by modern living is a thing of everyday experience for most of us. We just choose to ignore it. The autistic spectrum today claims one in every twenty American children. We can't be far behind. Civilizational insecurity resonates.

Claustrophobia

The fall of the Old Way and its replacement with a foreign system that hinges on individuals having to constantly prove their supremacy over their colleagues on a treadmill owned by a faceless economic entity that also happens to believe them to be dispensable, brought material riches, but also psychological hell. Not only were all the old identities passe, but all the new identities were ephemeral and profane. The psychological cost of this change is still being measured in stressful lives, broken families, suicide, depression, inverted population pyramids, drug abuse, autism and lost childhoods.

But, this model is today so ingrained in the minds and lives of modern people that we can't imagine that any other way could possible fulfil our needs. Add this to the constant barrage of propaganda that the media arms of modernity spew out in order to keep us all convinced that this journey is essential, the destination is vital and all other ways are too painful to contemplate. Imagine a world without internet, they say. Well, some of us don't have to imagine such a world, it was reality a mere heartbeat ago, and life then was perfectly fine. Anyway, that's just to illustrate how the fear is bred into us. The "past" has been cast as a cage, and any thought of it is designed to evoke claustrophobia.

The irony of course is that no person who actually lives in the "past" feels claustrophobic, it's the people who live in the future (in their heads), who do. Why is that? The answer to that question becomes clear when we recognize the sleight of hand that we are being presented with— Modernity first creates a problem and then offers itself, that is 'even more Modernity', as the only solution to the problem.

The sense of claustrophobia we feel, is generated not by traditional structures, but by the despiritualized, atomized, anonymity of Modernity itself. The agents of Modernity (media and education) are then deployed to shift the blame onto traditional structures for that all-encompassing sense of dis-ease, and to offer "the Future" as our one and only remedy, an escape hatch. But, "the Future", as we all know, is just more of the same. Do we expect to feel more or less claustrophobic in the coming world of bio-manipulation and total surveillance? We already know the answer to that one, we just have to think back to life in 2020.

Escape from Claustrophobia, the Western Way

The Western way of dealing with this largely self-imposed insecurity and claustrophobia is to project all human emotions onto the future. The future becomes a sanctuary, a place of escape, where the limitations of the "past" can be overcome, where the tight feeling in our chests will find release. The "future" comes to be imbued with religious overtones. The idea of "Progress" is deeply connected to this imagination of the future.

"Progress Theology" is a virtual credo now among all the peoples of the world. The almost feverish need to be involved in anything "Progressive" is now a global phenomenon, only resisted by the most recalcitrant of cults. The fear of being "left behind" is a visceral entity that exists in the pits of all our stomachs.

The "Future" and its inevitable Marriage with the idea of Material Sophistication

Inevitably then, this imagination of the "future" as "progress" comes to be inextricably linked with an ever-upwards sloping trajectory of material sophistication. After all, what else could possibly be a visibly manifest representation of our progress? It has to be something physical. Something more complex than what existed before. Something that visibly and experientially manifests a *quantitative* improvement from what existed yesterday – faster, stronger, bigger, more efficient... simply more.

The Hindu View

The Hindu view, on the other hand, does not anchor on time or on material sophistication, but on *Dharma*. Any era that is more *dharmic* is aspirational. Any era that is less *dharmic* is less aspirational. Whether that era lies in the past or the future is irrelevant. Whether that era has more machines or less is irrelevant.

Anybody who buys into the idea that the present is always better than the past, must per force also buy into the idea that the future will be always be better than the present. This is Progress-Theology and it's a very pernicious religion. It excuses every depravity of history as a mere aberration that must be ignored because it was a step on the ladder to the "future". For a true Hindu, what is better or worse can never be determined by the impartial flow time, nor by its proxy – increasing material sophistication, but by the widespread establishment of *Dharma*. If *Dharma* was more widely established in the 9th Century, than today, then certainly the 9th Century is more aspirational than today. The same logic would apply for say, 3000 BCE or 2400 CE.

Mortality and Novelty

The reason for this deep psychological need to hang our hopes on something other than what we currently have, seems to have something to do with our sense of personal mortality. The fact that we start dying from the moment we are born seems to be embedded deep in our *koshas*. Sure, we look back at the past as a time when we were younger and more vital, but the paradoxical corollary of this is that we also look to the future as a domain where we can be young again, where we can resist the passage of time by doing something new and re-inventing ourselves, thereby manifesting a psychological rebirth. Of course, it's not real and its ephemeral, but that's the reason why we have to go looking for this feeling again and again. The very ephemerality of every invention is the engine that drives the next cycle of re-invention. Boom and bust. It's the same reason why individuals pursue new lovers, new travel destinations, new clothes, new restaurants, new jobs etc. It's the same reason that Western civilization pursues "Progress". Every re-invention, or new location or relationship is a piece of space-time temporarily carved out of the inexorable march of our mortality towards its pessimistic end, where we can pretend that we are young again. That's why the Novelty-Treadmill is so important in the Western self-imagination (that we have all now bought into). The Novelty-Treadmill is the modern stand-in for immortality, a crutch of the utmost psychological importance. It can't be let go off, lest we are "left behind".

Magic and Tragic

For example, let's take an institution or even place (like a house). If it is associated with new-ness or growth and youth, we feel alive when we are part of it – its Magic. When the exact *same* place is associated with old-ness, stasis and age, we feel depressed when we are part of it – it becomes Tragic. Like, I would never go back to my college again, it's just too anachronistic an experience to subject myself to... the buildings are decayed, the people that made up that place in my imagination are all gone, the ideals that it represented, I no longer find aspirational. In other words, it feels like death. And I do understand that this is how most people feel about the "past".

Some part of it is connected to the wrestling match each of us is involved in with our mortality, but another part of it is how our minds have been conditioned from holding an essentially Hindu *darshana* (to the problem of mortality) to what is essentially now a Western perspective – Progress Theology.

Renewal of Eternity as Rebirth

So, how did traditional Hindus tackle this problem of mortality? For one, they did not believe that the creation of temporary distractions to help us ignore the problem, was a viable solution. The problem was much too serious for this kind of ad-hoc and shallow response.

All traditional communities, looked at time quite differently from Abrahamics (and Modernists). The passage of time is seen as a play of divinity. Our role here is to align ourselves with archetypes. Our sense of immortality comes then, not from generating novelty, but from the Renewal of Eternity that happens when we play our parts. Just as our communities are fractal fragments of the whole, so too are the fractal fragments of Time the reflections of divine time. Every moment is not one in a line of moments stretching unto the horizon of some dystopian Einsteinian shore, but a flash of divine possibility, representing *all* of Time in the Here and Now. We, Hindus, are alive *now*, not in the hereafter. We are connected to the Now because the Now is a fragment of Eternity, not merely a step on the way there.

Consciousness Theory and Eternity in the Here and Now

This brings us to the doorstep of Consciousness Theory which sees every moment as brand-new, born from the fire of eternity and pregnant with life. The more conscious we are, the more we are able to exist in the Here and Now in full awareness. Of course, wise Hindu men and women, in every era have embodied this phenomenon in the traditional way, including more recently, a sage like Shri Ramana Maharshi. But, modern sages like Shri Aurobindo too shone light on this phenomenon, generating an entire metaphysics around it. His optimistic vision posits consciousness as the light that will defeat time and therefore death. When we are fully aware, we are *alive* in the Here and Now and we drink straight from the fount of Eternity. Every passing moment carries within it the possibility of rebirth and therefore, of eternal youth. All we need to unlock this mystery is the key of consciousness. The more awareness one is capable of bringing to bear on a moment (whatever its nature), the more immortality that moment carries. Hindus have been granted four access codes as keys to the Now, *jnana, dhyana, nishkama karma* and *bhakti*. *Now*-Consciousness is the panacea for the claustrophobia induced by mortality and time-consciousness.

Of course, all of us have to live in the world at large and we have to remember the past and plan for the future, but we can see life as a series of *Nows*. The more we are able to do this, the more we free ourselves from the anxiety of the Future-Mind and its child, the Novelty-Treadmill. This was done at the community level, in Bharat, through the traditions. The traditions are mechanisms for communities to renew Eternity year after year, thereby tying themselves to the grand movements of Nature and stepping outside of their own fleeting egoistic emotions. The Western model, on the other hand, takes those fleeting egoistic emotions very seriously and put the entire weight of a centralized structure behind physically manifesting those emotions. Unfortunately, the emotions are never satisfied and more and more has to be generated every year on that imaginary ladder to self-fulfilment. So much so, that even contentment has come to be seen as a cop-out, and the restless pain of modern living painted over with a brush of romanticism.

Take the recurring celebration of festivals or even daily cooking for instance. These are activities that have been performed since the dawn of cultural time, but we never tire of them. Why? Because they are acts of consciousness harnessed towards honouring the love we have for our families and the Gods. So, it is possible that the same activity can escape the shroud of Time when the conditions are right (that is, in the presence of Consciousness and Connection). And it is those conditions that Hindu metaphysics seeks to create within Hindu society, so that all Hindus and Hindu communities may forever have the keys to Forever.

Here are two diagrams to help us visualize how differently the individual is cradled in the traditional Hindu worldview and the modern Western worldview.

Traditional & Stable
Hindu View of Human Identity

Revolutionary & Unstable
Modern View of Human Identity

References and Links

1. D. Venkat Rao, *Critical Humanities Elsewhere: Towards Pathways of a Responsive Reception*, Presentation at Stanford University, 2025 https://www.youtube.com/watch?v=ulCeK4-O1e8

Epilogue

Re-Imagining Hindu Unity

I have no intention of getting too political, though the project at hand is indeed political. Instead, I'm going to string together some ideas and leave them hanging. Some of these excerpts and ideas have already been encountered earlier in the book, but they are presented again here as a final consolidation that helps cast a new light upon one of the major demands of our time—Hindu Unity.

> There is hardly a village, great or small, throughout our territories (British territories in India), in which there is not at least one school, and in larger villages more.
>
> – G.L. Prendergast, 1820 [1]
>
> It has generally been assumed that the education of any kind in India...was mainly concerned with the higher and middle strata of society (the *Brahmins, Kshatriyas* and *Vaishyas*). However, as will be seen, the data of 1822-25 indicates more or less an opposite position...in the Tamil-speaking areas the twice-born (in schools) ranged between 13% in South Arcot to 23% in Madras... while the *Soodras* and the other castes (later to be labeled as SC) ranged from about 70% in Salem and Tinnevelly to over 84% in South Arcot.
>
> Dharampal, *The Beautiful Tree*, 1983
>
> – (Quoting from William Adams's reports on Education in the 1830s) [2]
>
> It is true that the greater proportion of the teachers came from the *Kayasthas, Brahmins, Sadgop* and *Aguri* castes. Yet, quite a number came from 30 other caste groups also, and even the *Chandals* had 6 teachers. The elementary school students present an even greater variety, and it seems as if every caste group is represented in the student population, the *Brahmins* and the *Kayasthas* nowhere forming more than 40% of the total. In the two Bihar districts together they formed no more than 15 to 16%. The more surprising figure is of 61 *Dom*, and 61 *Chandal* school students in the district of Burdwan, nearly equal to the number

of *Vaidya* students, 126, in that district. (As per Adam) only 86 of the 'scholars belonging to 16 of the lowest castes' were in the (British) missionary schools, while 674 scholars from them were in the 'native schools'.

Dharampal, *The Beautiful Tree*, 1983

– (Quoting from William Adams's reports on Education in the 1830s) [3]

And yet, we are led to believe that education in Bharat was limited and exclusive to a few 'elites'. Worse still, we are led to believe that these 'oppressor elites' hoarded their knowledge and refused to share it with everyone else, and that the vast 'oppressed' masses were deliberately kept in ignorance so they could be 'exploited'.

Let's also remember that these statistics are from the 1820s and 30s, almost five hundred and fifty years *after* Allaudin Khilji instituted a 60% tax on the peasants. Allaudin Khilji, the Mughals, and the British are all famed for having instituted 'administrative reforms', which is code for efficient systems of extraction. Seen in this light, the *zamindari* settlement introduced by Lord Cornwallis in 1793 was merely the further streamlining of the existing *jagirdari* system introduced by Khilji.

Imagine having 60% less resources to run your families, places of worship, festivals, social organizations and schools, not just for a year or two, but for five hundred years! *Bharatiyas* had been paying 60% tax all the way from 1300 CE and the British made sure that they continued to collect that level of tax all the way till 1947 CE! Our ancestors paid that kind of tax for no return. It was extortion at the point of the sword. It was the cause of all the famines we read about. It continues to be the cause of our physical stunting. Few of us know these facts, and we are led to believe, by 1970s Bollywood masala movies, that exploitation of our fellows is somehow innate to Hindu society. The evil *Thakur* and the wily *Brahmin* are recurring tropes in the stories we tell ourselves about ourselves. This is madness. It's important for all *Bharatiyas* interested in resolving the problems of our present to look with clear eyes at our collective past.

Imagine what dedication was shown by *all* our ancestral communities to keep our temples and *gurukulas* open through all those long, war-filled centuries, even when they had hardly any resources to spare after having paid the extortionist taxes.

EPILOGUE

Imagine how *Bharatiya* life was organized and how prosperous our communities would have been before the arrival of the Turkic and Anglo colonizers. Imagine a time before the Commons were usurped by the State, before the *zamindari* systems were put into place, before the 60% tax was instituted, before the handful of colonials were put in charge of extracting produce from the 'peasants' and shovelling it into the colonizers coffers with annual expectations like modern insurance agents with quotas to fulfil... before all that, how was our society organized? How did our communities get along? How prosperous were they?

Here are some descriptions from an earlier time...

> ...for whereas among other nations it is usual, in the contests of war, to ravage the soil and thus to reduce it to an uncultivated waste, among the Indians on the contrary, by whom husbandmen are regarded as a class that is sacred and inviolable, the tillers of the soil, even when battle is raging in their neighbourhood, are undisturbed by any sense of danger, for the combatants on either side in waging the conflict make carnage of each other but allow those engaged in husbandry to remain quite unmolested.
>
> – Megasthenes, *Indika*, 3rd Century BCE [4]
>
> The fourth (out of seven) caste consists of the Artizans. Of these some are armourers, while others make implements which husbandmen and others find useful in their different callings. This class is not only exempt from paying taxes but even receives maintenance from the royal exchequer.
>
> – Megasthenes, *Indika*, 3rd Century BCE [5]
>
> ...that there is not a year but it costs our State to furnish into India, 50,000,000 Sesterces, (fifty millions of Sesterces.) For which the Indians send back Merchandise (luxury goods including cloth, spices and jewellery), which at Rome is sold for a hundred times as much as it cost.
>
> – Pliny the Elder, Natural History, 77CE [6]
>
> Every nation that ever traded to the Indies has constantly carried bullion (gold and silver) and brought merchandise in return... Their climate demands and permits hardly anything that comes from ours. They go in a great measure naked; such clothes as they have the country itself furnishes; and their religion, which is deeply rooted, gives them an aversion for those things that serve for our nourishment. They want, therefore, nothing but our bullion to serve as a

medium of value; and for this they give us merchandise in return, with which their frugality and the nature of the country furnish them in great abundance... and in every period of time those who traded with that country carried specie (gold and silver coins) thither and brought none in return.

– Baron de Montesquieu, *The Spirit of Laws*, 1748 CE [7]

This is that moment when I urge you to contemplate *who* it was that was making all these luxury goods. Who was making the steel, weaving the cloth, growing the spices and crafting the jewellery? What happened to all those communities? What happened to their prosperity? And more pertinently, what has brought about the current degeneration in their self-perception?

Here is an excerpt from A.S. Altekar's 1927 book, *A History of Village Communities in Western India*. Observe carefully the collaborative aspect of traditional *Bharatiya* life.

> ...it appears that settlement of village disputes by mutual understanding through the friendly intervention of some influential relatives was quite common in Maharashtra down to the middle of the last century. Elphinstone refers to this practice, and Pratapsimha observes in Section 1 of his code that it is a time-honoured custom in his dominions. Failing to arrive at a mutual understanding, the villagers used to refer the matter to the Patel. He used to try his best to arrive at an amicable settlement, failing this, he would refer the case to the *Panchayat*. This was a cosmopolitan body consisting of the *Patel*, the *Kulkarni* and all the village servants including *Mahars* and *Mangs*. Thus, the judgment of the village *Panchayat* in Babaji Javaji vs. Babaji Baji delivered in A.D. 1673 is signed by twenty-three *Patels*, ten *Chougdlas*, four goldsmiths, one carpenter, one potter, two shoemakers, six *Mahars* and one *Mang*. Such is the case also of other Panchayat decisions, both earlier and later, which are usually signed by the paid accountant and *balutedars*. It therefore follows that the Panchayats which used to decide village disputes consisted of various castes and professions residing in the village community.
>
> It was thus the exact prototype of *puga* of the days of *Yajnavalkya* and *Narada*; and the fact that it should have survived the shock of Mahomedan invasions and consequent anarchy in Western India clearly proves that it must have existed as a very popular institution in the preceding age in our presidency.[8]

EPILOGUE

The word 'servant' used in the above description continues to rankle. It was obviously not a word that was used in the original document but in this English translation and, in my opinion, when we look at the lives of independent-minded "scheduled communities", it becomes obvious that the word 'servant' does not literally translate as 'one who serves' but rather as 'one who enables'. See the burgeoning 'service sector' of the modern economy for an analogy. Our so-called SC communities were highly autonomous. They had control over their economic and spiritual destinies and provided essential services, including craft, construction, ritual, medical and security services, that enabled rural life to function smoothly. Some of these professions did attract taboos (that today must be cast aside because they are no longer relevant) but the idea of taboos themselves must be examined in the context of a largely tribal world where the separation of tribes into their own physical and metaphorical spaces was a common phenomenon that enabled work monopolies, spiritual freedoms and firewalled the spread of local conflicts.

Descriptions of life, past and present, in Natarasmpattu and Siruvanjur by J.K. Bajaj and T.M. Mukundan of the Centre for Policy Studies, throws more oblique light onto the lives of scheduled caste communities and their place in the harmonic matrix of traditional Bharatiya life:

> Nattarsampattu survives today only on the strength of its *Harijan* population. They are the ones who look after the lands and thus carry out most of the productive work of the village. In the eighteenth century, the **10 Harijan households inhabited 2.5 acres of land** on the banks of the main *ery*, south-east of the *Reddy* street, near the *Amman* temple and the *mandaiveli*. Today, however, they seem to have been pushed over the banks of the *ery*, out of their original habitation, **which was next to the *Oor* and the temple.**
>
> This new colony has two north-south streets, with almost a hundred households. It is the most vibrant part of the village today. All around the colony can be seen men and women busily involved in various activities connected with cultivation and harvesting. Given the poor state of the *erys*, and lack of any other sources of irrigation, the lands of Nattarsampattu these days could not be producing much of anything. But, in spite of this scarcity of produce and resources, the **colony looks neat and alive, untouched by the sense of decay that pervades the rest of the village.**

EPILOGUE

> Streets in the colony are clean and wide, and most of the houses, made of mud and thatch, are laid out on a fairly grand scale. A typical house consists of two to three rooms, with a thatched roof, which slopes down to almost 3 feet above the ground. This low roof would make the interior comfortable in the hot and dusty summers. Outside the rooms, there is invariably a narrow verandah, covered by the low roof, running all along the length of the house. **The wide courtyard often has another small thatch for the cattle**, and occasionally one more for the implements.
>
> – J. K. Bajaj and T. M. Mukundan (Centre for Policy Studies), *Nattarsampattu: The Wilderness Returns*, The Hindu, 1991 [9]

> These days as you cross the bank of the *ery* and enter the village the first house you come across is that of the *Valluvan*. This isolated house, lying outside both the *Oor* and the Colony, has such a thick cover of vegetation around it, that at a cursory glance, the house is likely to be missed. In the eighteenth century the *Valluvan* house commanded the **largest area in the village. Built on 160 square yards of land, it had a backyard extending to about 7,000 square yards**. On this vast site today there stand three small houses, all belonging to the *Valluvans*. The courtyard between these houses is neatly swept, and the common backyard is covered with a variety of trees.
>
> The ***Valluvans*** **used to be the priests of the Colony and also dealt in herbs and other forest produce**. *Valluvan* women, engaged in **cooking on their separate *chulhas*** in the courtyard, tell us that they used to provide *marundu* and *mantram*, herbal medication and invocatory prayers, for the villagers. Nowadays their men go out of the village probably to ply their paltry trade in dried herbs on the streets of Madras city. But when these traditional physicians and priests return to their garden-like abode in Siruvanjur, they must be once again experiencing to some extent the **dignity and prestige that the profession of their forefathers once enjoyed**.
>
> – J. K. Bajaj and T. M. Mukundan (Centre for Policy Studies), *Siruvanjur: A village of pools and woods*, The Hindu, 1991 [10]

That the communities who were classified as "depressed classes" by the British did not in fact see themselves as depressed at all, is clear when we read accounts of what they had to say about themselves:

> In a note on the *Paraiyans* of the Trichinopoly district, Mr. F. R. Hemingway writes as follows. "They have a very exalted account of their lineage, saying

that they are descended from the *Brahman* priest Sala Sambavan, who was employed in a Siva temple to worship the god with offerings of beef, but who incurred the anger of the god by one day concealing a portion of the meat, to give it to his pregnant wife, and was therefore turned into a *Paraiyan*. The god appointed his brother to do duty instead of him, and the *Paraiyans* say that *Brahman* priests are their cousins. For this reason they wear a sacred thread at their marriages and funerals.[11]

Hemingway continues:

At the festival of the village goddesses, they repeat an extravagant praise of their caste, which runs as follows. 'The *Paraiyans* were the first creation, the first who wore the sacred thread, the uppermost in the social scale, the differentiators of castes, the winners of laurels. They have been seated on the white elephant, the Vira *Sambavans* who beat the victorious drum.' It is a curious fact that, at the feast of the village goddess, a *Paraiyan* is honoured by being invested with a sacred thread for the occasion by the *pujari* of the temple, by having a turmeric thread tied to his wrists, and being allowed to head the procession. This, the *Paraiyans* say, is owing to their exalted origin.[12]

The modern trope that some communities were oppressed for thousands of years seems to come undone when we look at accounts of their interactions with other tribes a mere two hundred years ago. Reality, it appears, was much more nuanced, and descriptions point to a complex society attempting to contain inter-tribal rivalry through a series of ceremonial posturings, thus helping to stave off actual physical violence. Thurston writes:

And, when the ceremonial antipathy between *Brahman* and *Paraiyan* is examined, it points in the same direction. It is well known that a *Brahman* considers himself polluted by the touch, presence, or shadow of a *Paraiyan*, and will not allow him to enter his house, or even the street in which he lives, if it is an *agrahara*. But it is not so well known that the *Paraiyans* will not allow a *Brahman* to enter the *cheri*. Should a *Brahman* venture into the *Paraiyan's* quarter, water with which cow-dung has been mixed is thrown on his head, and he is driven out. It is stated by Captain J. S. F. Mackenzie that "*Brahmans* in Mysore consider that great luck will await them if they can manage to pass through the *Holeya* quarter of a village unmolested, and that, should a *Brahman* attempt to enter their quarters, they turn out in a body and slipper him, in former times it is said to death.[13]

EPILOGUE

Copper plate inscriptions from even as recently as the 19th Century allude to a world where integration and devotion were the norm for all communities.

> According to archaeologist Narayana Moorthy, the Tamil inscription on the copper plate speaks about the 12 sects of Paraiyars giving offerings to Lord Dhandayuthapani in Palani.[14]

We do ourselves a disservice when we are constantly using a modern individualist morality to judge and invariably deride our traditional and community-centric pasts. What was achieved in ancient Bharat was nothing short of a pre-industrial welfare State that guaranteed:

1. Inter-ethnic peace.
2. Self-definition for communities within the larger parliament of communities.
3. A reasonable liberty for individuals within their *Kulas*.
4. A stability built on economic monopolies for all communities.
5. The fostering of a spirit of sacrifice and excellence in both work and spirit.
6. The establishment of a complex economic engine *without* the need for slavery or genocide.

In other words, a *Dharmic Purushaarth* at the societal level.

Sonalee Hardikar, Ashish Dhar and Shivam Mishra, in their 2021 essay "The Real Cost of Leather: Chamars, Cow, and Colonialism", quote Grant Duff and Henry Orenstein to draw us a comprehensive portrait of a different world—one that we no longer experience, but that continues to live deep in our collective consciousness:

> *Mahars* were one of the twelve *Balutas* or *Balutedars*, a group of service providing communities that also included *Sutar* (carpenter), *Lohar* (blacksmith), *Chambhar* (cobbler), *Parit* (washerman), *Kumbhar* (potter), *Navi* (barber), *Mang* (rope-maker), *Kulkarni* (village-accountant), *Joshi* (astrologer), *Gurav* (non-*brahmin* Shrine keeper) and *Potdar* (money-assayer). Grant Duff, an early British soldier and historian, documents the main duties of the *Mahar* as portering, carrying letters from one village to another, keeping vigil, attending to travellers, acting as a guide, and occasionally scouting and spying. *Mahars* also played a key role in the resolution of inter-village land disputes as they knew the area better than everyone else. In return for these services, the *Mahars* were entitled to a grant

of rent-free land by the government. This was called *Chakri-watan*. They were also given land grants by villages directly, called *Hadki-Handola*, in exchange for services like skinning the dead cattle within the village boundaries.

... Suffice it to say here that contrary to their depiction as landless labourers exploited by upper caste landowners under the influence of '*Brahmanism*', *Mahars* were an integral part of the Maharashtrian village who were respected and whose opinions were given great value in legal disputes. In fact, any violence against them was treated as a criminal act and a heavy fine of Rs. 50 was charged from the transgressor. In his fieldwork carried out as late as the 1950s, Henry Orenstein noted that *Mahars* were among the highest-paid groups in the *Balutedari* scheme, with their earnings exceeding those of the higher *Balutedar* castes like *Sonar* and *Gurav*.

It must be pointed out here that *Balutedari* was not an exceptional arrangement peculiar to Maharashtrian society but rather a norm all over India.

Orenstein defends the functionalist character of *Balutedari* and asserts that it cannot be construed as an exploitative system. He adds that the village is a cohesive unit in such an arrangement and takes precedence over caste. He observes, "As I have observed, *balutedars* divide the work among themselves by allocating time or the land of the village, not households of landowners. This gives reasons to believe that the *balutedar* sees his tie as one between his group and village as a whole, rather than as a person-to-person relationship. In this region, a number of people live outside the main settlements of their village, many on distant farms. Some of these are closer to the main settlement of other villages than to their own, yet I found no one who attended religious ceremonies of other villages. Everyone who is able, both *Balutedar* and landowners, make financial contributions to village affairs. Caste conflicts are strongly discouraged at ceremonies. People even disparaged their own caste fellow in order to placate the other and thus maintain harmony. In wrestling contests, people cheer athletes from their own village, irrespective of caste.

It is also this relatively "free" system of organisation that takes care of each artisan by providing for cultivable land, food, occupation, and social participation in festivities that allows for a flourishing of individual innovation not just in terms of technology but in terms of products made.[15]

I think nothing more needs to be said on this matter. We can all be fairly certain that our recent debased inter-community relations and self-hateful self-perception are not reflections of our true selves.

If Turkic colonization was bad for us, then Anglo colonization was terrible. The Anglos did three things that the Turkics never did, or couldn't do:

1. They shut down native education institutions and replaced them with their own.
2. They "nationalized" the Commons (rivers, forests, hills, tanks...everything), all of which became property of the Crown.
3. They brought the rear-end of industrialization to Bharat. Indigenous industry was disincentivized and/or forcibly erased and, for the first time in the history of human civilization, Bharat became a supplier of raw material for the manufacturing centres of Europe.

All communities were hit hard by this upheaval. Some made the transition to a form of quasi-Modernity, others slipped further into relative poverty. The communities hit hardest were those whose skillset lay in the use of hand and land. Their skills were rendered irrelevant by the Industrial Revolution and their traditional resource base of rivers, forests and tanks, was forcibly taken from their control. They were now interlopers in their own ancestral lands, competing with their erstwhile brothers for scarce resources (a.k.a. the 'caste system' as recorded and frozen in time by the British censuses).

It is this history of alienation that is the context for the loss of Mutual Respect and Harmony between our communities that we are witness to today. The blame for our current situation is conveniently laid at the feet of Tradition by the spin-masters of Western civilization and their brainwashed lackeys, but Hindus who are interested in a rejuvenation of a true Hindu Civilization have some basic tasks to accomplish.

We need to:

1. Disseminate a useful understanding of the past that will give people pride and the means to forge connections with their brothers and sisters.
2. Build a Grand Bharatiya Narrative of Hindu history told from the point of view of the followers and resisters, not the apostates and traitors.
3. Encourage an intellectual and cultural fervent that will help Hindu families, communities, and ultimately the nation, rebuild *Swayambodh* and *Shatrubodh*.

4. Work to build an intellectual corpus that is in the best *Sanatana* tradition, one that rejects

   a. the far-Left assertion that Hinduism is merely its parts but not its whole, and
   b. the far-Right assertion that we must divest ourselves of our parts in order to forge a whole.

5. Work towards Hindu *political* unity without committing self-ethnocide of Hindu *cultural* diversity. The reconfiguration of our *jaatis* when people enter the modern industrial economy is inevitable, but this reconfiguration should be allowed to proceed organically without the State constantly seeking to control or hasten the process. This kind of simplistic manipulation of complex social inter-linkages is Soviet in nature and will have Soviet consequences.

6. Build localized institutions for bridge-building and conflict resolution between communities. These can be instituted by a *Dharma*-minded government along with respected spiritual leaders.

7. Press the understanding that decentralization and community autonomy are some of the most characteristic features of *Sanatana* social organization without which even a Hindu *Rashtra* would be in danger of succumbing to centralized, universalist Western-style immorality (like we have seen emerge in Germany, Russia, China and America).

8. For the sake of forging a Hinduized Modernity (that most Indians will inevitably end up living in), work on designing a Hindu religious/cultural body (a Hinduism Lite) that will have centres at the block level (similar to the Christian concept of a diocese). These centres should hold *kirtans*, *pravachans*, book readings etc. along with festival celebrations. New umbrella cultural traditions can be innovated to *explicitly* bring all our communities together (modelled on Tilak's *Ganesh Chaturthi* celebrations in Mumbai or the *Thrissur Pooram*). Ideally, such an organization would spearhead the freeing of Hindu places of worship from government control as well as the institutionalization of a ritual entry mechanism for non-Hindus into our religion.

9. Work on the revival, incentivization and institutionalization of indigenous knowledge systems and practices especially in our schools, colleges and media narratives (news, movies, books, art).

10. Work on the creation of *Dharmic* standards for all walks of modern life and industrial activity—education, manufacture, service, architecture, agriculture etc.—and start certification bodies of our own.

In any new national configuration that may emerge, a minority of true traditionalists from all *jaatis* and *sampradaayas* should continue to practice our time-honoured rituals in the Old Way, with full state protection and support.

Many of the communities whose traditional skill-sets, and therefore rituals, lay in the domain of 'hand and land' find themselves at a crossroads today. Constantly bombarded by colonial tropes that have turned them against the very systems that gifted their ancestors with life and identity, they are today confronted with a future of despiritualized irreverence. Though the Old Way is often projected as *Brahmanism*, it is, ironically, for the communities of 'hand and land' that it holds the most significance and Meaning. It is not the *Brahmana* communities that will face loss of Meaning in Modernity, they will simply carry their texts and their *nityakarma* wherever they go. And even post-deracination, their journey back to their ancestral fold is clear. But for us, the rooted people, the people of the Earth, Modernity poses the greatest of spiritual challenges. When industrialization tears us from our contexts (as it is doing now), it also severs us from the well-springs of our spirituality—our communities, our *Kula Devatas* and our cyclic festivals. Our ancestors may have built many a physical bridge—of brick, mortar, stone and bamboo, but it is *this* bridge, the one our generation will have to build between the old and the new, that will stand out as our most definitive work.

It is therefore that for the majority of Hindus freshly moving into the modern world, the creation of a self-conscious definition of a Hinduized Modernity becomes an inevitable necessity. What would be the underlying values of such a Hinduized Modernity? What would be its uncompromisable principles, its cultural red lines? What would be the fundamental design principles of a nation that represents it? How would that nation relate to the communities that comprise it? What would make our society different from Western Modernity? **What, more than just polytheism, would make our Hinduism Lite different in essence from a globalized Christianity Lite?** The answers to these questions can only be gleaned from a compassionate understanding of our ancestral past and the vision that the *rishis* had for our society. It cannot come from a place of self-hate and blind love of the White Man's model of a world built on his Heaven-centric Progressivism. It's important, therefore, that modern Indians are familiarized with a positive anthropological view of *Sanatana* principles and society.

Sanatana Principles: An Anthropological Understanding

The Western mind sees the world in black and white. In its conception, the world is divided into a series of dichotomies—good and evil, tribal and individual, pagan and civilized, Left and Right, Oppressor and Oppressed. It is this insane way of looking at the world that has led them and, by default, all of us as well, to the unspeakable violence of the past millennium and our modern failure to secure human well-being. But things don't have to be that way. *Sanatana* history shows that we can break free from the pathology of dichotomies and choose a third, humane way of being.

Bharat is the only place on Earth where the full spectrum of human lifestyles existed simultaneously and harmonically with each other and with nature—Forest Tribes, Nomadic Tribes, Agricultural Tribes and Urban Tribes. This is *the* touchstone for judging whether a civilizational system is ethical or not. True diversity is diversity of tradition and not merely diversity of race or even opinion (which is the Western high-water mark). And true ethicality lies in a societal design that exhibits mechanisms of tolerance and conflict resolution that can hold that depth of diversity of tradition without imploding or exploding.

In such a system, diversity is not seen as the enemy that has to be erased to establish an order of uniformity. Simultaneously, diversity is not the aim, but a consequence, of the fundamental health of underlying principles. In the modern West, on the other hand, where a faux diversity is feverishly pursued as a *goal*, we see that society is sickly and the underlying principles rotten. To put it plainly, *the West seeks diversity because it has none*. The analogy of a modern body seeking gymnasiums and supplements because daily life no longer has space for good work and good food comes to mind.

Unlike the Abrahamisms which emerged from the desert with their scarcity mentality and Commandments, *Sanatana* ethics are derived from a forest-paradigm with a vision of abundance, harmony and *Rta*-based principles. These include the familiar ideas of Unity in Diversity, Polytheism, Live-and-Let-Live, Mutual Respect, Cyclic Consciousness, Economy, Sustainability and Balance.

All of these *Rta*-based principles have come to us as a collective *Purusha*-Consciousness. *Purusha*-Consciousness consists in two powerful ideas running in parallel:

1. Seeing the Many in the One
   The idea that the world may take on infinite forms but is rooted in a divine whole. This leads to Mutual Respect and Sacralization of Life.

2. Seeing the One in the Many
   The idea that we are all parts of a greater whole and our reason for being here on *Bhu Devi* is the earthly recreation of that whole. This leads to Collaboration and Sacralization of Work.

The primary goal, then, of Law is to enable this Gods-given diversity to weave itself together into a fine tapestry that will be worthy of offering back to the Gods as a token of our gratitude for their abundance. That law is *Dharma*.

Purusha-Consciousness, we see now, is diametrically opposed to the Pyramid Consciousness (*matsya nyaya*) of Abrahamism and Western Modernity, which believes that the strong (or chosen ones) are destined to lord it over the weak (or ignorant) and *Bhu Devi* Herself.

If and when *Sanatanis* have fallen into a debased pyramid consciousness, it has been because of human failing and not because our ideals ever demanded it of us.

Sanatana Society: An Anthropological Understanding

What I am going to propose below is *not* an insider's view. This is *not* how true Hindus see themselves *at all*. BUT for modernists, who seek answers in history rather than poetry, this explanation could bring some appreciation of our reality.

Here's an idea. Hinduism, as we know it today, is a confluence of Bottom-Up *Bharatiya* Cultures and Top-Down *Sanatana* Civilization. It is not one *or* the other, it's both... a double helix with one strand moving upwards and inward, and another moving downwards and outward. Remember, the word civilization here does *not* refer to either behavioural or material sophistication. Rather, it refers to the universalizing impulse represented by the evolution of a set of uber, umbrella principles capable of bringing disparate cultures together.

Now, imagine a time long past... The ideals and archetypes of *Sanatana* Civilization are spreading through the entire landmass of Bharat, dilating outwards from the *Sindhu-Saraswati* heartland. The dispersed *Bharatiya* tribes are proud and self-conscious peoples, stewards of their own unique cultures and Gods... and yet they recognize the coming wave for what it is, a non-coercive ethical umbrella framework for building unity in diversity while offering the means for cultural embellishment and economic opportunity (*Purusha* and *Purushaarth*).

Many tribes choose to belong, to stake their claim in this new paradigm, settling into roles suited to their personalities, geographies and needs. Some tribes chose to retain their sense of liberty and satisfy themselves with life on the periphery of this growing civilizational wave. Over the millennia, stories are stitched together (*jaati-purana*), creating metaphoric pathways that allow tribes to create their own sense of belonging in the grand narrative. These stories help them express the terms of their engagement with the civilizational Gods and with other tribes. A continent-sized miracle comes into being, not at the point of the sword, but on the wisp-like strands of mere poetry. Through the marriages of Gods was this Sanatani civilization forged. What amazement!

As Hindu moderns, we must recognize that even though this carpet weave of Bottom-Up cultural diversity is the most visible characteristic of this land, it is actually the unseen and yet undefinable Top-Down civilizational force that distinguished this land as unique even among the cultures of the classical world. It was this force that ensured that Bharat continued to exist as Bharat, the homeland of Hindus, rather than succumb to the fates of Egypt, Rome, Persia and Cuzco. It is for this reason, therefore, that the Top-Down *Sanatana* Civilizational impulse deserves to be set apart and held in special regard. Ordinary Hindus do this as a matter of course, but newly modernized Hindus have been taught to be blind to this reality and, in many cases, even oppose it as an unmitigated evil.

With this basic anthropological explanation in our grasp, we can now make the claim that the *more* pan-*Bharatiya* a community's imagination was, the *more* civilizational the responsibilities it assumed, and consequently the more ritual honour it was accorded by society as a whole. Modern readers can now see that any civilizational ritual hierarchy that developed in *Bharatam* was not a measure of 'worth' but a measure of how civilizationally-intentioned a community was. Ultimately, civilizational ideals were fractalized within local spiritual landscapes and *every Sanatani* community honoured itself by carrying a part of that civilizational flame, but it remained commonly accepted that those communities responsible for cultivating the uber vision that all of those tiny, dispersed fractal flames were actually part of one great collective *yaagashaala*, would be ritually exalted as long as their actions stood for the good of all while holding themselves to a high degree of self-denial and dispassion.

That this formula held for so long before it became debased shows that it was understood and accepted by all communities as just. The Local did not begrudge the Civilizational its ritual position, just as surely as the Civilizational did not encroach upon the political and cultural autonomy of the Local. It is apparent that the Local saw the coming of the Civilizational as a force for the good of all, something that brought harmony and prosperity. This is evidenced by the fact (alluded to earlier) that civilizational ritual mores found renewed fractal expression within the local ritual field, thus creating the telescopic layers of Hindu cultural depth—*kutumba*, *jaati*, *kula*, *graama*, *sampradaya* and *rashtra*.

It is also apparent that those local communities that did *not* accept the terms of the civilizational imperative, were free to continue to live their hyper-local lives. This is in fact evidence of non-coercion and not "exclusion". Modern-day descendants of local communities who claim that the coming of the Civilizational was oppressive (and therefore that the more civilizationally-intended communities were oppressors), themselves have no alternate unifying vision that they can offer the nation. They have developed no theory of society or work. If we are interested in being a nation, rather than merely a loose collection of tribes, we need a commonly accepted theory of self that would define both the terms of our liberty and our communion. Sure, we can continue to ride on the coat-tails of European state-craft, no problem, but if we have any self-respect, we would show genuine interest in working on evolving our own theory of state based on our own theory of society (much of which has already been developed for us by our *rishis*)—it is just that we have now been schooled to see those ideas as oppressive. Groups who say that the *Veda* is part of *Brahmanism* and that Hinduism is more than mere *Brahmanism*, need to articulate what alternate indigenous image of society they can offer all of us. Why are we a *nation* and not merely a collection of tribes? There is no indigenous answer to this question outside of the *Veda* and the *puranic* lore.

From a civilizational perspective, it was only with the coming of the *Veda* that the until-then splintered tribes in their localized sacred spaces were presented with the poetic means to embellish those existing sacred nodes, to sanctify new pathways to connect with other nodes *and* to engage with a metaphysics capable of stewarding and harmonizing all that diversity. It follows that the *Brahmana* communities, as *keepers* of the *Veda*, and as the ones who took its unifying language, standardized rituals and integrative vision to the entire landmass, came to be acknowledged as the *agents* of *Sanatana* Civilization. That is why the Left continues to use the term *Brahmanism* when it speaks of Hinduism although they don't understand that, to all true Hindus, *Brahmanism* is not a pejorative. Similarly, *Kshatriya* communities who could imagine this land as a *punyabhoomi* and work towards its complete integration on the physical plane were also acknowledged as guardians of the flame. The wider the horizon of a clan's sacred ambition, the greater its civilizational impact, the greater its claim to ascendancy on the ritual scale. The *Vaishya* communities that contributed to the manifestation of this integrative vision, via the funding of kingdoms, *paatashaalas* and temples were similarly seen as ascendant. The *Shudra* communities that desired to rise above the particularities of place, easily ascended the ritual ladder by outgrowing their local concerns and adopting a civilizational vision. They sharpened their pursuit of excellence to unearthly levels and offered that excellence to the divine (*Vishwakarmas*); they funded the establishment of civilizational temples (*Chozhas*); they carved out kingdoms (*Nayakas*) and eventually empires (*Marathas*) for themselves and for the welfare of *all* Hindus.

Take for example the great Reddi king Prolaya Vema Reddy (1335-1353 CE) who is said to have built 108 Shiva temples and whose Mallavaram record mentions him as "The Agastya to the Ocean of *Mlechhas*"[16] and as having restored the *agrahaaras* to their *Brahmanas*. His successor Anavema Reddi's (1364-1386 CE) inscriptions read "I the valiant member of the fourth (*shudra*) *varna* destroyed the throngs of *mlechhas* and gathered learned *Brahmanas* at this court"[17]. It's clear that mutual respect and an ambition for nobility were the markers of a healthy classical Hindu society all the way till at least the end of the 14th Century and very likely extending well into the Vijayanagara and the Maratha periods.

Bharat is the only nation where the entire spectrum of material cultures continues to live harmoniously cheek by jowl with each other—forest tribes, nomadic tribes, agriculture-dependent tribes, agricultural tribes and agriculture-enabled tribes, to the extent that we had the unique situation where dolmen-building megalithic people were spatial and temporal compatriots of the *vimanam*-building, sea-faring *Pallava* emperors. The continued existence of literally thousands of peripheral and outlier communities (shamanic tribes, forest tribes, nomadic tribes, *sramanic* tribes, atheist tribes, 'heretic' tribes, Abrahamic tribes) demonstrates irrefutably that unlike all other civilizations, *Sanatana* civilization was non-coercive. This simple understanding of our civilizational imperative and its synergistic interaction with local cultures, provides us with a satisfactory explanation for the shape of civilizational ritual hierarchy in *Bharatiya* society.

From this intellectual vantage point, we can approach afresh the phenomena of Exclusion and Mobility that plague the modern Hindu mind:

1. The claim that some communities were 'excluded' is to be understood differently. Ritual exclusion is in fact evidence of the *non-coercive* nature of Sanatana Civilization. Local communities that may have had theological differences with the Civilizational paradigm were left alone to pursue their own truth. What is seen as "exclusion" in our Marx-inspired present was in reality the very face of Liberty in the classical past (live and let live). Thus, we see that ritual exclusion (always accompanied by cultural and economic inclusion as Dharampal ji has shown) was not a function of 'racism' or 'supremacy', but a function of the civilizational horizon that a community occupied. The more civilizationally-intended a community, the more civilizational responsibilities it was expected to assume. The more civilizational responsibilities a community took on, the more ritual respect was accorded it. This makes sense. This is the same reason why, in a modern analogy, a CEO is paid more than a manager—he has a wider field of vision. In classical Hindu society though, the currency of

choice was not money or power but ritual honour (always accompanied by a greater expectation of self-denial). This ritual potential difference was *not* intended as a means to stigmatize communities, as is popularly assumed today, but rather to galvanize them into taking on higher levels of civilizational responsibility (this is, after all, the true reason why all societal potential difference exists, even today). Take, for example, the case of the *Shanars*, by all accounts a peripheral tribe in the 1800s. When Caldwell classified them as a non-Aryan tribe, they were incensed, and broke out into violent protests.[18] Why? *That* impulse to *own* one's identity and expand one's influence into nobility was the hallmark of community self-perception throughout *Bharatiya* history. It is only in the last 170 years, under the baleful influence of Abrahamic victimhood memes, that the race to the bottom has been embraced by so many.

2. Millions today lament the fact that they were 'excluded' and denied ritual fitness by the 'caste system'. If that lament is indeed authentic and not just a ploy to earn political brownie points in the modern electoral landscape, then the solution is as simple today as it has always been. By inverting the modern lens, we can see the matter as our ancestors saw it. We will see that to rise in ritual status is not a matter of gaining privileges, but of taking on civilizational responsibilities. And so, the desire of any community (not individual) to rise up the ritual ladder can be fulfilled immediately simply by demonstrating that civilizational commitment... by caring for, and helping carry, the *purusha*-rooted vision of the whole, rather than merely focusing on gaining local advantages. Goes without saying that we can expect local resistance as a community chooses to expand its horizons beyond those of its neighbours, but that should not come in the way of any community's endeavour to represent a vision higher than merely their parochial interests...

...to carry the mantle of the Gods,

    ...to secure unity under the *Veda* and

        ...to establish *Dharma* in the *punyabhoomi* of our *tirtha-kshetras*.

EPILOGUE

References and Links

1. S.S. Bhandarkar, *A Review of Education in Bombay State (1855-1955)*, 1956 (Quoting G.L. Prendergast, 1820)
https://archive.org/details/AReviewOfEducationInBombayState1855-1955/page/n3/mode/2up

2. Dharampal, *The Beautiful Tree*, 1983 (Quoting from William Adams' reports on Education in the 1830s)
https://archive.org/details/TheBeautifulTree-Dharampal

3. Ibid.

4. Megasthenes, *Indika*, 3rd Century BCE
https://archive.org/details/AncientIndiaAsDescribedByMegasthenesAndArrianByMccrindleJ.W

5. Ibid.

6. Pliny the Elder, *Natural History*, 77CE
https://archive.org/details/naturalhistory01plinuoft

7. Baron de Montesquieu, *The Spirit of Laws*, 1748
https://archive.org/details/spiritoflaws01montuoft

8. A.S. Altekar's, *A History of Village Communities in Western India*, 1927
https://archive.org/details/in.ernet.dli.2015.203016

9. J. K. Bajaj and T. M. Mukundan (Centre for Policy Studies), *Nattarsampattu: The Wilderness Returns*, The Hindu, 1991

10. Ibid.

11. Edgar Thurston, *Castes And Tribes Of Southern India Vol.6*, 1909

12. Ibid.

13. Ibid.

EPILOGUE

14. Express News Service, *19th-century Tamil copper plate spotted in New York museum,* The New Indian Express, 2025
    https://www.newindianexpress.com/states/tamil-nadu/2024/Oct/27/19th-century-tamil-copper-plate-spotted-in-new-york-museum

15. Sonalee Hardikar, Ashish Dhar and Shivam Mishra, *The Real Cost of Leather: Chamars, Cow, and Colonialism,* 2021
    https://pragyata.com/the-real-cost-of-leather-chamars-cow-and-colonialism/

16. Mallapuram Inscription,
    https://www.mcrhrdi.gov.in/images/epigraphia/Vol-III.pdf

17. Srisailam Inscription,
    https://www.scribd.com/doc/50370214/Reddy-Dynasty

18. Nicholas Dirks, *Castes of Mind*, Princeton University Press, 2001

On this auspicious day of *Thai Poosam*,
Year 5125 of the *Kali Yuga*,
When the star *Pushyam* rises in the East,
and the *Poornima* Moon sets in the West...
when the people of *Tamilagam* celebrate
my *kula devata*'s victory over the *asura Surapadman*,
I lay down this pen that I picked up four and a half years ago.

"பழனிமலை முருகனுக்கு அரோகரா"

Appendix

I offer you a *Purushaartha* timetable to structure your kids' activities. Modify this to suit your needs and your kids' interests. It will be of special interest to parents of homeschooled kids but partially useful for parents of kids who attend conventional school. Restructure the way you think about life activities. Hindus must take back power from the industrial framework. Work with this *Dharmic* framework to help your children think about all the inputs they are receiving. Controlling inputs is a losing battle, but being able to *arrange* these inputs is a powerful way to gain control over the Liberal religion's ubiquitous propaganda. Note that the entries are mine. Feel free to fit in whatever subjects or activities you want to.

APPENDIX

WORK	Fill in Number of Hours for each activity							Artha								Weekly Hrs
Kama	M	T	W	Th	F	Sa	Su	Weekly Hrs	M	T	W	Th	F	Sa	Su	
Farming								0	Math								0
Gardening								0	Science								0
Painting								0	Reading English								0
Music								0	Writing English								0
Cooking								0	Speaking English								0
Nature/Photography								0	Computer Programming								0
Travelling in Bharat								0	Spoken Hindi								0
Computer Modelling								0	Join Appa at work								0
Carpentry								0	Join Amma at work								0
Sports								0	Apprenticeships								0
Swimming								0									
Running								0									
Craft								0									
Household Work								0									
Daily Totals	0	0	0	0	0	0	0		Daily Totals	0	0	0	0	0	0	0	0

Dharma	M	T	W	Th	F	Sa	Su	Weekly Hrs	**Moksha**	M	T	W	Th	F	Sa	Su	Weekly Hrs
Carnatic Music								0	Dhyanam								0
Shloka Chanting								0	Puja								0
Kalaripayattu								0									
Tamil								0									
Sanskrit								0									
Study of Puranas								0									
History								0									
Geography								0									
Dharmic Movies								0									
								0									
								0									
								0									
Daily Totals	0	0	0	0	0	0	0		Daily Totals	0	0	0	0	0	0	0	0

PLAY	M	T	W	Th	F	Sa	Su	Weekly Hrs
Rajasic								
Outdoor Games								0
Indoor Games								0
Fooling Around								0
Daily Totals	0	0	0	0	0	0	0	0
								<25
Tamasic								
Pop Movies								0
Comics								0
Pop Fiction								0
Pop Music								0
Video Games								0
Daily Totals	0	0	0	0	0	0	0	0
								<10

TOTAL Weekly Waking Hours – 12x7=84 Hrs

WORK Activities divided into Kama, Artha, Dharma and Moksha.
Kama – Physical, Sensorial, Material Activities > 15 Hrs per Week
Artha – Activities geared towards making a livelihood > 15 Hrs per Week
Dharma – Activites geared towards preservation and protection of our civilizational values > 15 Hrs per Week
Moksha – Activities geared towards working on oneself > 4 Hrs per Week

PLAY Activites divided into Rajasic and Tamasic
Rajasic activites are important for creativity, socialization, learning teamwork, victory, defeat, power etc < 25 Hrs per Week
Tamasic activities are ideally to be avoided but in most cases unavoidable especially becasue these activities are passing for culture these days and it becomes important to for kids to stay in touch with whats happening in the liberal world. These activities lead to addiction and laziness and should be limited to < 10 Hrs per Week

www.ingramcontent.com/pod-product-compliance
Lightning Source LLC
Chambersburg PA
CBHW020217170426
43201CB00007B/237